2022
青岛统计年鉴

QINGDAO STATISTICAL YEARBOOK

（总第43期　　VOL.43）

青　岛　市　统　计　局
国家统计局青岛调查队　编
QINGDAO MUNICIPAL BUREAU OF STATISTICS
NBS SURVEY OFFICE IN QINGDAO

中国统计出版社
China Statistics Press

图书在版编目（CIP）数据

青岛统计年鉴.2022 = Qingdao Statistical Yearbook 2022：汉、英对照 / 青岛市统计局，国家统计局青岛调查队编 .-- 北京：中国统计出版社，2022.7
ISBN 978-7-5037-9822-1

Ⅰ.①青… Ⅱ.①青…②国… Ⅲ.①统计资料－青岛－2022－年鉴－汉、英Ⅳ.①C832.523-54

中国版本图书馆 CIP 数据核字（2022）第 106406 号

青岛统计年鉴 2022

作　　者 / 青岛市统计局　国家统计局青岛调查队
责任编辑 / 钟钰
装帧设计 / 中闻集团青岛印务有限公司
出版发行 / 中国统计出版社有限公司
地　　址 / 北京市丰台区西三环南路甲 6 号
邮政编码 /100073
电　　话 / 邮购（010）63376909　书店（010）68783171
网　　址 / http://www.zgtjcbs.com
印　　刷 / 中闻集团青岛印务有限公司
经　　销 / 新华书店
开　　本 / 890mm × 1240mm　1/16
字　　数 / 864 千字
印　　张 / 27　彩页 1.25
版　　别 / 2022 年 7 月第 1 版
版　　次 / 2022 年 7 第 1 次印刷
定　　价 / 280.00 元　Price:280.00yuan(RMB)

如有印装差错，由本社发行部调换。

编辑委员会

EDITORIAL BOARD

编者说明

一、《青岛统计年鉴 2022》是一部全面反映青岛市国民经济和社会发展情况、信息高度密集的资料工具书。

二、本年鉴共包括发展成果图、统计公报、统计表、附录四大部分。

统计表部分收录了 2021 年青岛市经济和社会等各方面的统计数据，以及中华人民共和国成立以来重要年份和改革开放以来的主要统计数据，包括：综合，人口，从业人员及职工工资，固定资产投资，对外经济贸易，城市建设、环境保护，能源消耗，财政金融和保险业，价格指数，人民生活，农业，工业，服务业，建筑业，运输、邮电，批发和零售业，住宿、餐饮业和旅游，教育、科技和文化，体育、卫生和民政、司法。

为方便读者正确地使用年鉴资料，各篇章前设有《简要说明》，概括介绍各篇主要内容和资料来源；篇末还附有《主要统计指标解释》。

三、本年鉴部分历史数据已根据经济普查、农业普查、人口普查数据进行了修订调整，在此之前公布的数据凡与本年鉴数字不符的一律以本年鉴为准。

四、部门分区市数据按照所属职能部门提供的区市名称范围划分。

五、本年鉴中的符号说明：年鉴各表中的“空格”表示该项统计指标数据不足本表最小单位数、数据不详或无该项数据；“#”表示其中的主要项。

六、《青岛统计年鉴》自公开出版以来，受到社会各界的关心和支持，对于年鉴的内容和编辑工作提出了许多宝贵的意见，对此我们深表谢意。限于我们的水平，欢迎读者继续对年鉴的不足之处给予批评和指正，帮助我们进一步改进年鉴编辑工作，以期更好地为广大读者服务。

《青岛统计年鉴》编委会

2022 年 7 月

Editor's Note

Ⅰ. *Qingdao Statistical Yearbook 2022* is a very important reference book, which reflects various aspects of Qingdao's social and economic development and contains High-density information.

Ⅱ.The yearbook contains the following four parts: achievement graphs, statistic gazette, statistics and appendixes.

Statistics contains all kinds of data on Qingdao's social and economic development in 2021, and data in significant year or data since the beginning of reform and opening up, including: General Survey; Population; Employment and Wages; Investment in Fixed Assets; Foreign Trade; City Construction and Environment Protection ; Consumption of Energy; Government Finance ,Financial Intermediation and Insurance; Price; People's Living Conditions; Agriculture ; Industry ; Service Enterprices ; Construction ; Transport, Postal and Telecommunication Services ; Wholesale and Retail Trades ; Hotels, Catering Services and Tourism ; Education, Science and Culture; Sports, Public Health and Civil Affairs, Judicial Affairs; Enterprises Survey.

In brief introduction at the beginning of each chapter, main coverage, data sources and statistical coverage are concerned. Meanwhile explanatory notes on major statistical indicators have been attached for readers to use the data correctly.

Ⅲ. All of the data in the book are in accordance with new administrative division.

Some of the data have been adjusted on the basis of statistics of economic census. In any case the data of this book shall be deemed as the authentic ones.

Ⅳ. Departmental district city data is divided according to the range of district and city names provided by the functional department to which it belongs.

Ⅴ.Explanation of symbols in this yearbook : "blanks" in the tables in the yearbook indicate that the statistical indicator data is insufficient to the minimum unit number in this table, the data is unknown or there is no such data; "#" indicates the main item.

Ⅵ. Since the publication of the "*Qingdao Statistical Yearbook*" , it has received care and support from all walks of life, and has put forward many valuable opinions on the content and editing of the yearbook, for which we are deeply grateful. Limited to our level, readers are welcome to continue to criticize and correct the deficiencies of the yearbook, and to help us further improve the editing of the yearbook in order to better serve the readers.

Editorial Board

July, 2022

全市生产总值构成（%）

Composition Of Gross Domestic Product（%）

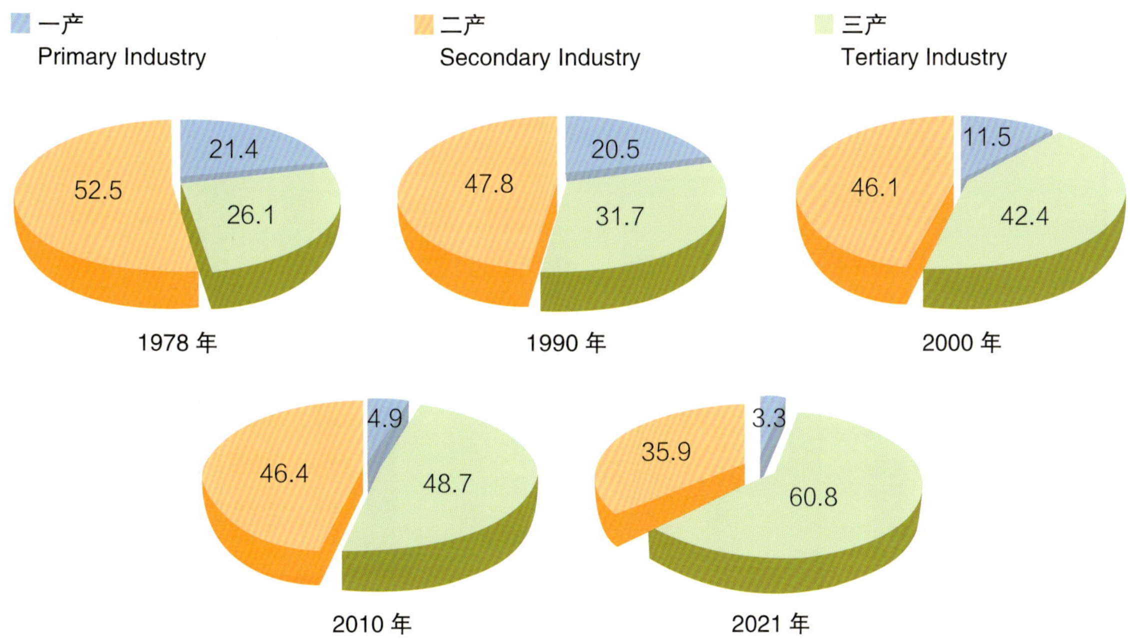

全市生产总值（亿元）

Gross Domestic Product（100 million yuan）

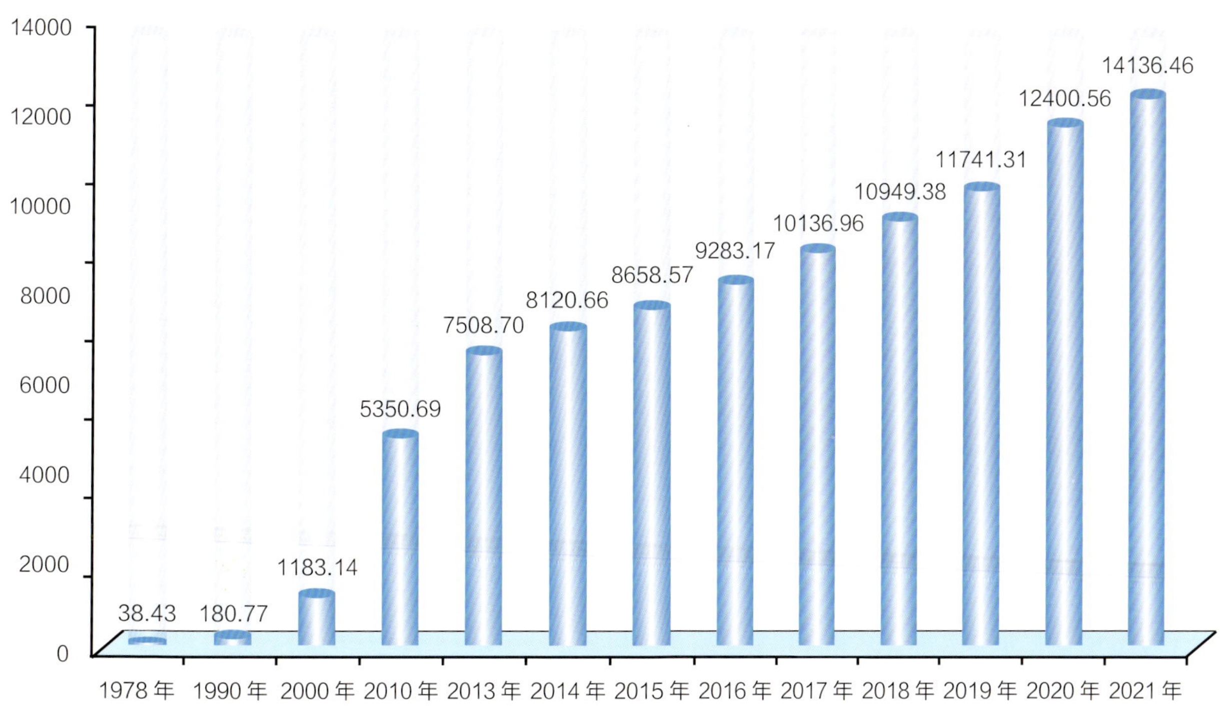

房地产开发投资（亿元）

Investment In Real Estate Development (100 million yuan)

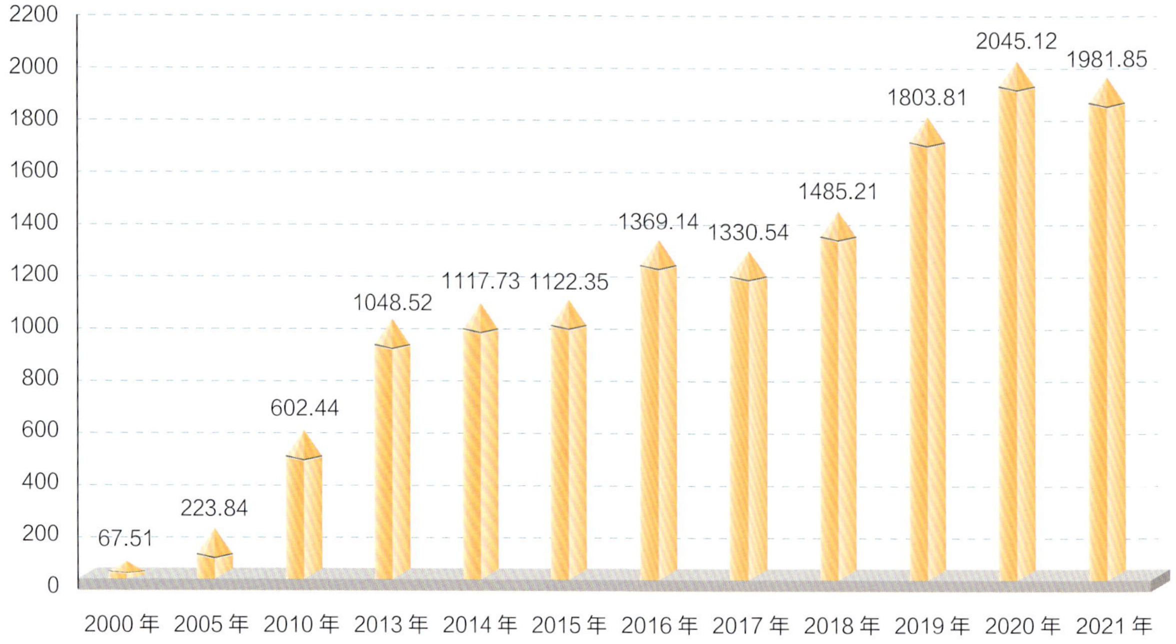

房屋销售面积（万平方米）

Floor Space Of Commercial Buildings Sold (10 000 sq.m)

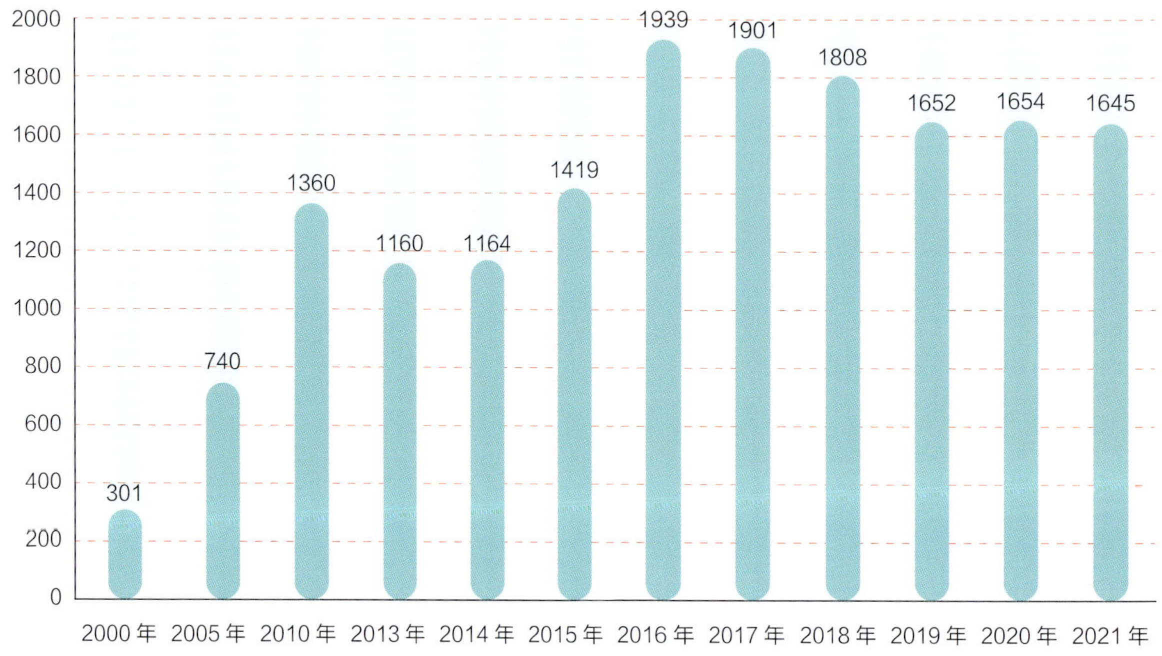

消费构成（%）（2021年）

2021 Composition Of Consumption（%）

社会消费品零售总额（亿元）

Total Retail Sales Of Consumer Goods（100 million yuan）

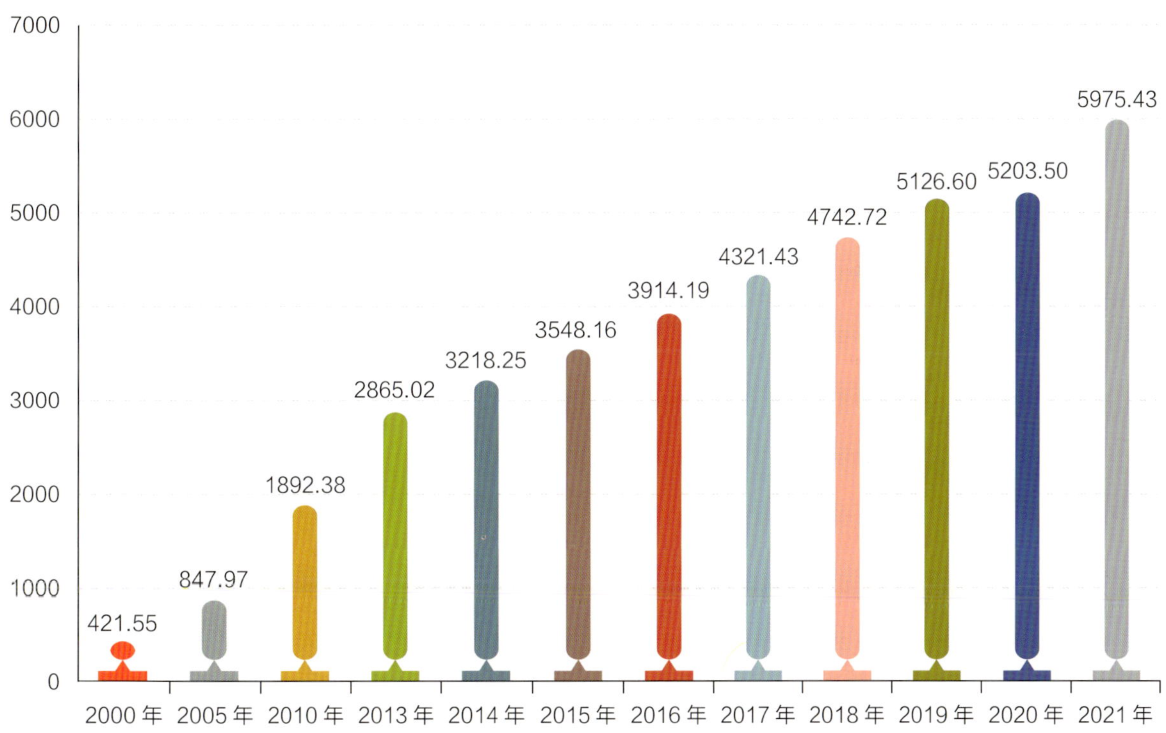

旅游总人数（万人次）

Number Of Tourists（10 000 person-times）

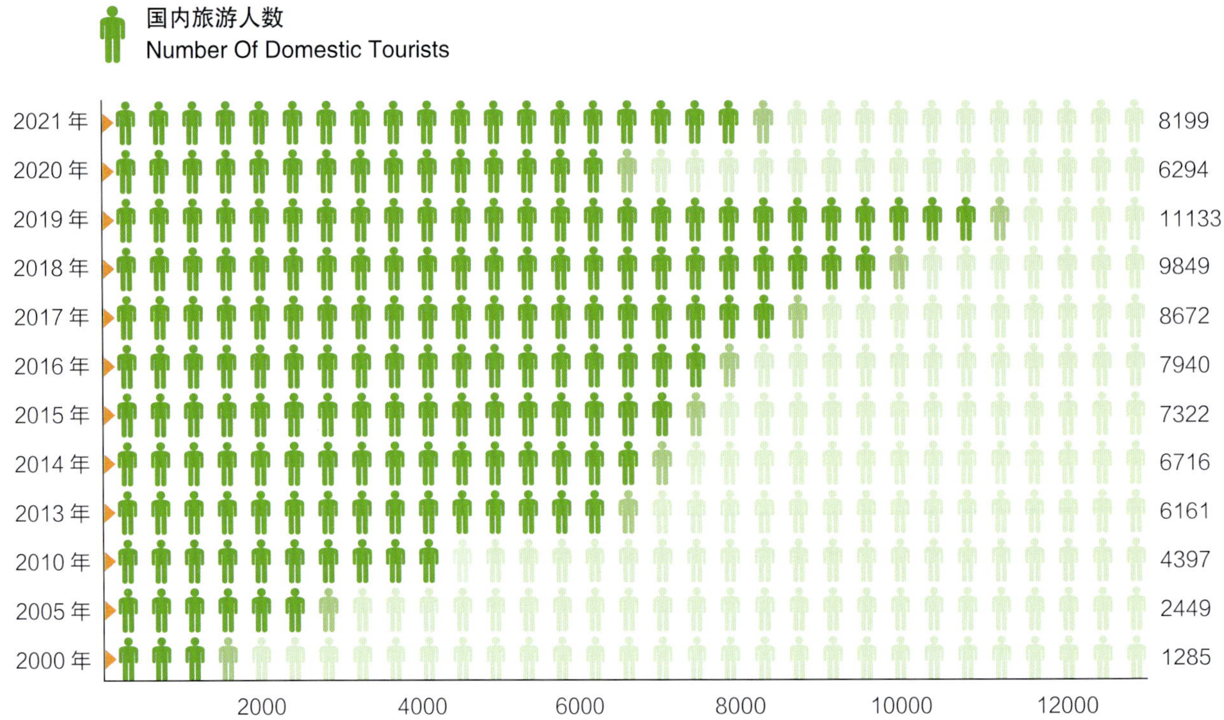

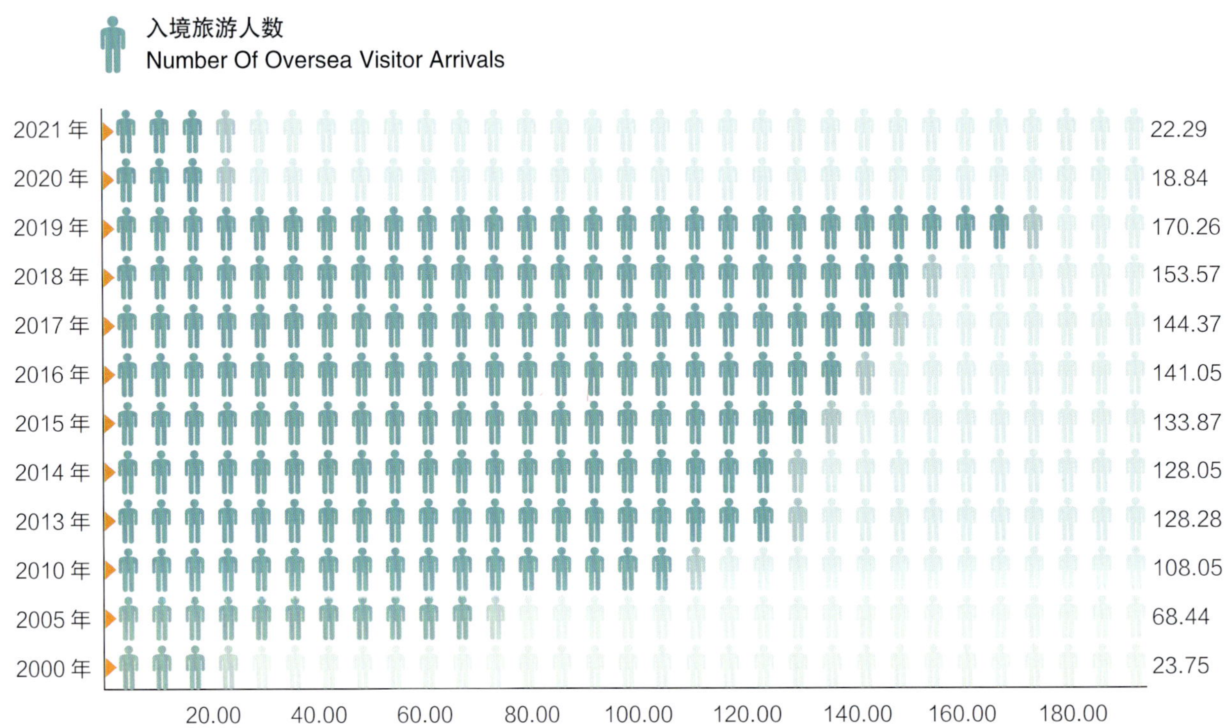

地方财政收入（亿元）

Revenue Of Local Government Finance（100 million yuan）

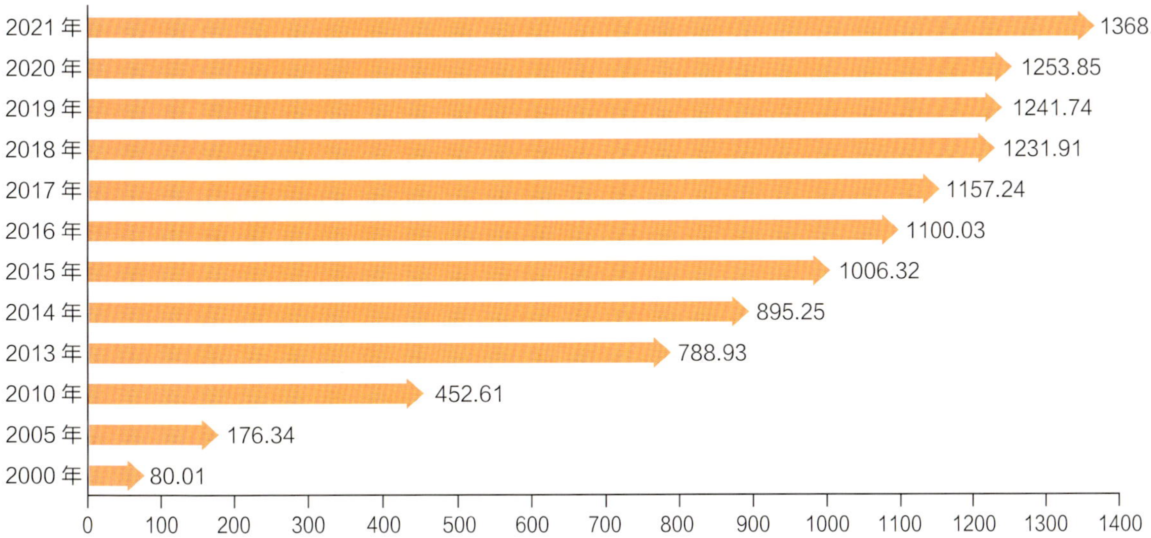

注：2002 年以后财政收入为一般预算收入数。

Note：Since 2002，revenue of government finance refers to general budgetary revenue.

金融机构年末人民币存贷款余额（亿元）

Year-end Savings Deposits And Loans Of Financial Institution（RMB）（100 million yuan）

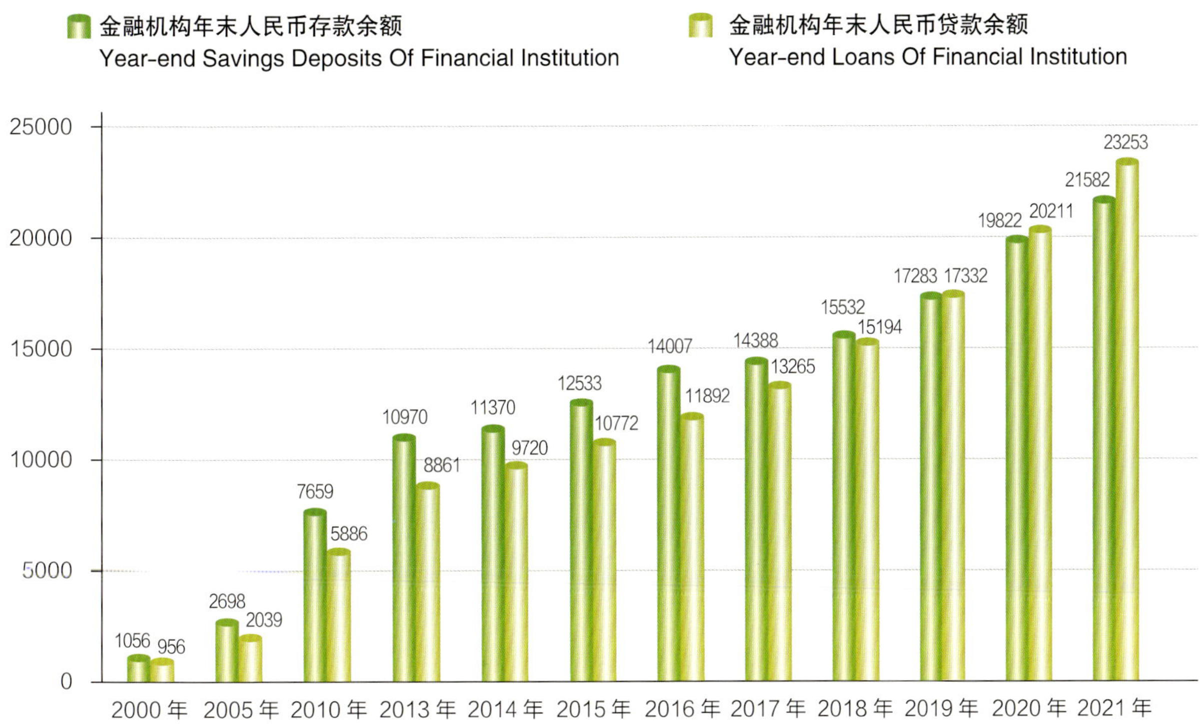

社会从业人数（万人）

Social Employment（10 000 persons）

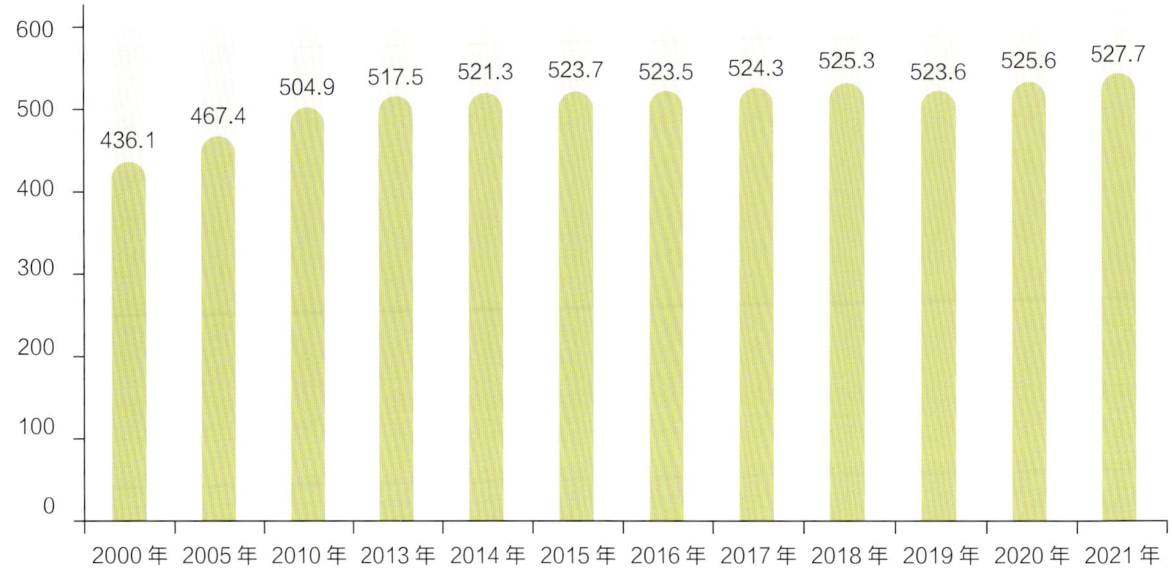

城镇非私营单位平均工资（元）

Average Salary Of Urban Non-Private Units（yuan）

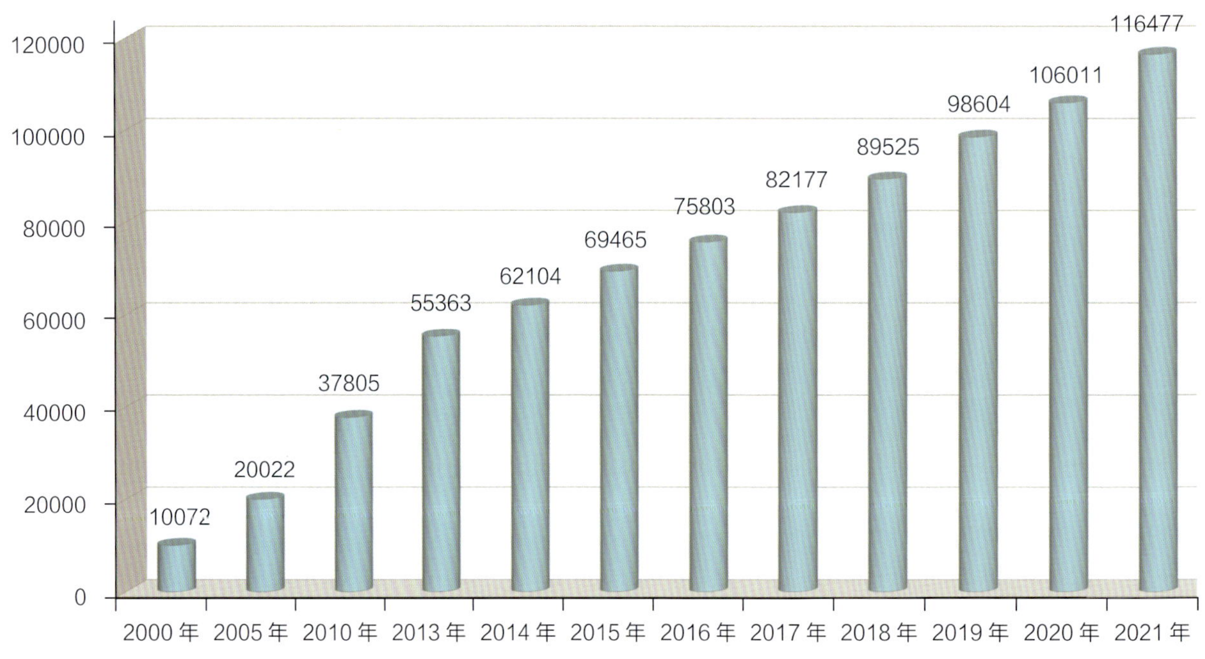

居民消费价格指数（上年= 100）

Consumer Price Indices（preceding year = 100）

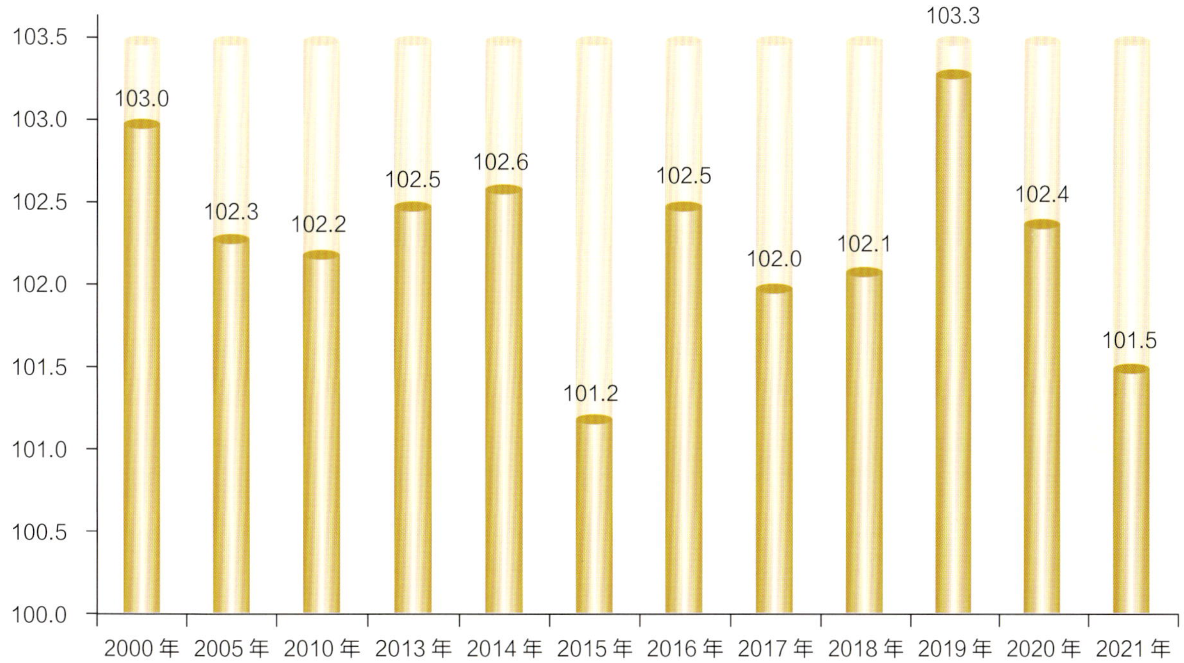

商品零售价格指数（上年= 100）

Retail Price Indices（preceding year = 100）

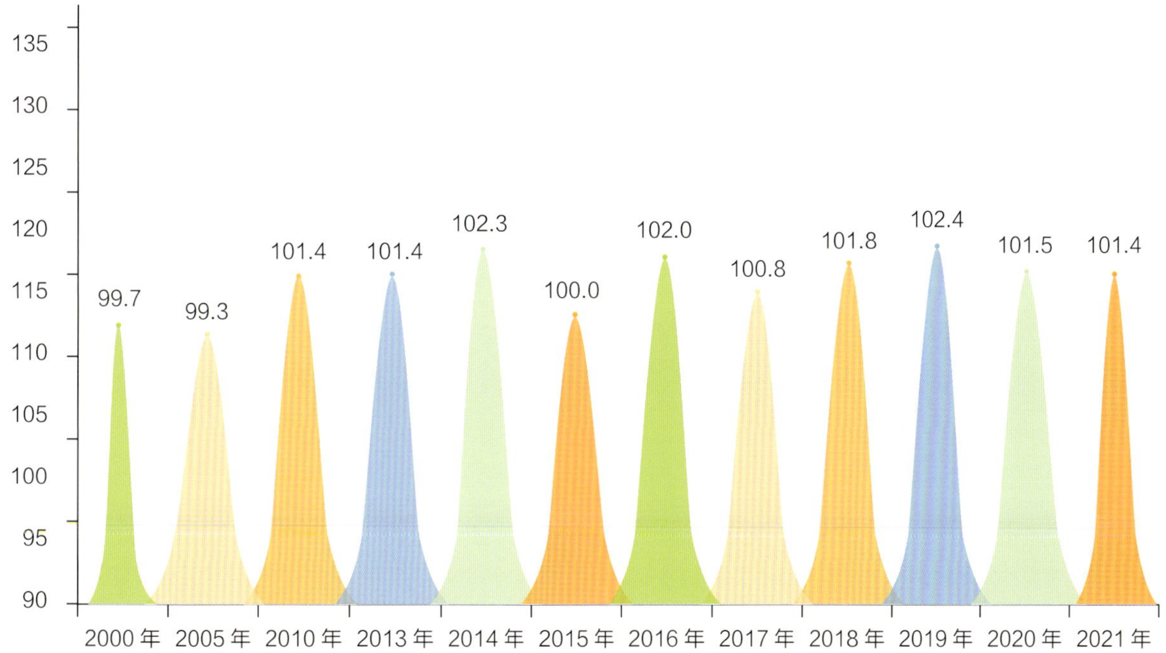

城市建成区面积（平方公里）

Developed Area Of the City（sq.km）

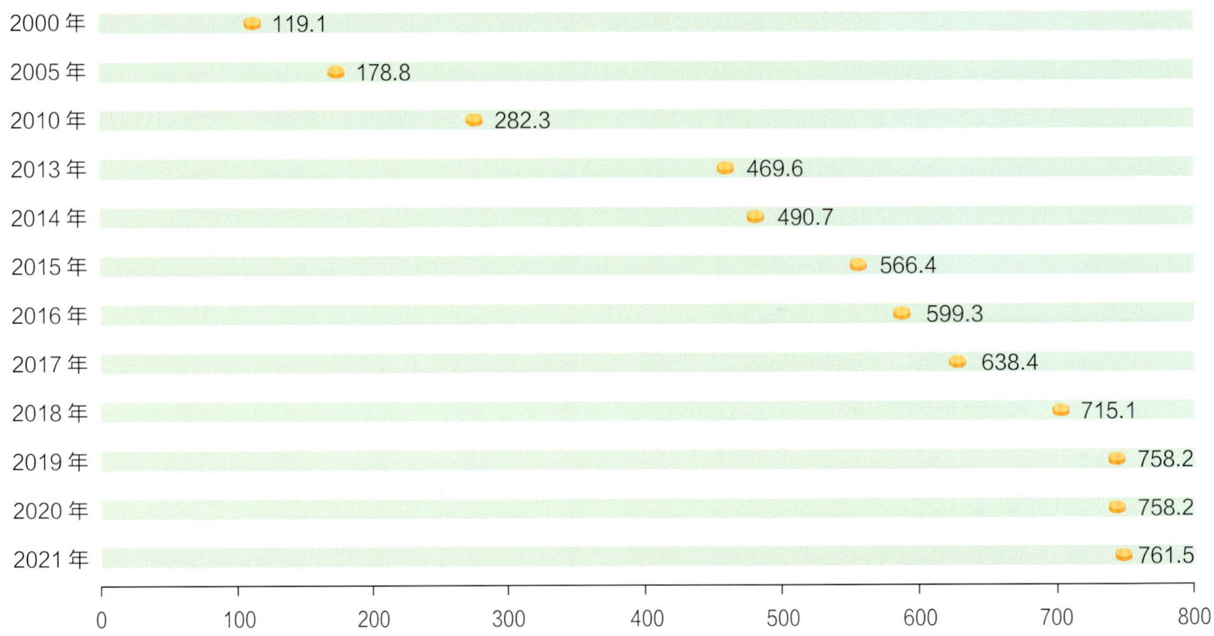

铺装道路面积（万平方米）

Area Of Roads（10 000 sq.m）

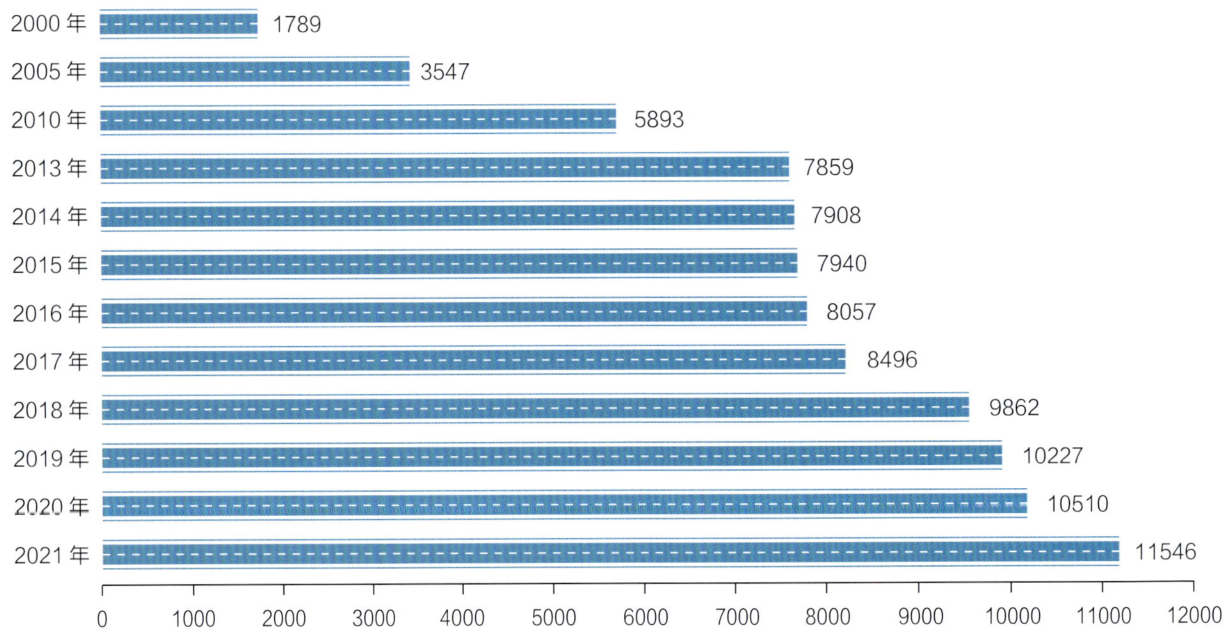

医疗卫生机构（个）

Health Care Institutions (unit)

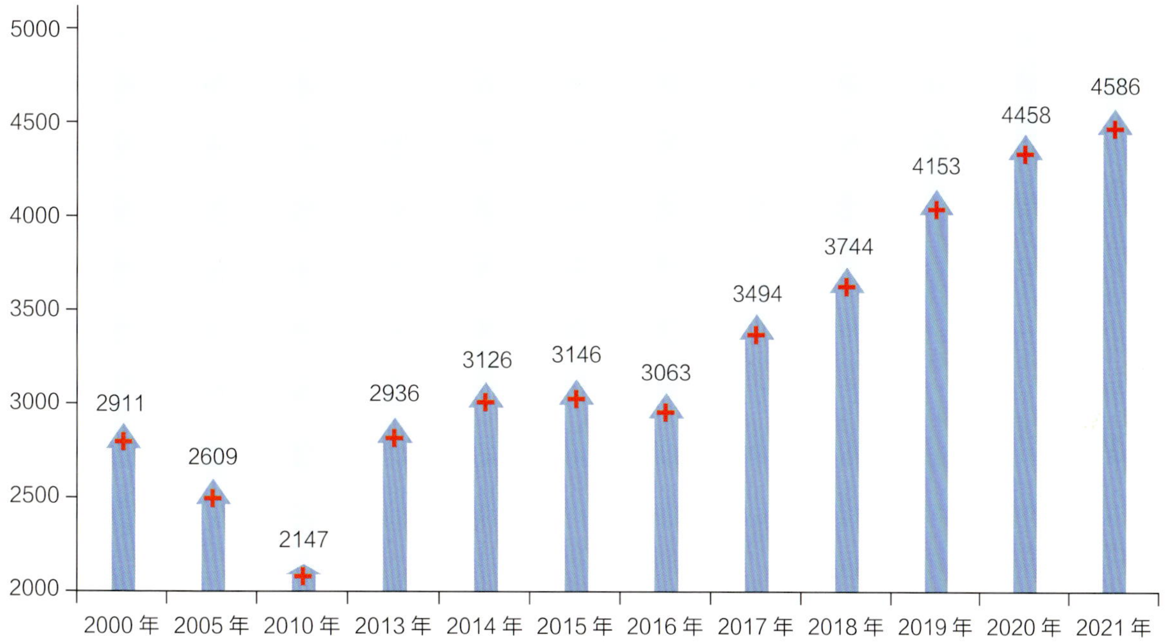

普通高校在校人数（万人）

Students Enrollment Of Regular Institutions Of Higher Education (10 000 persons)

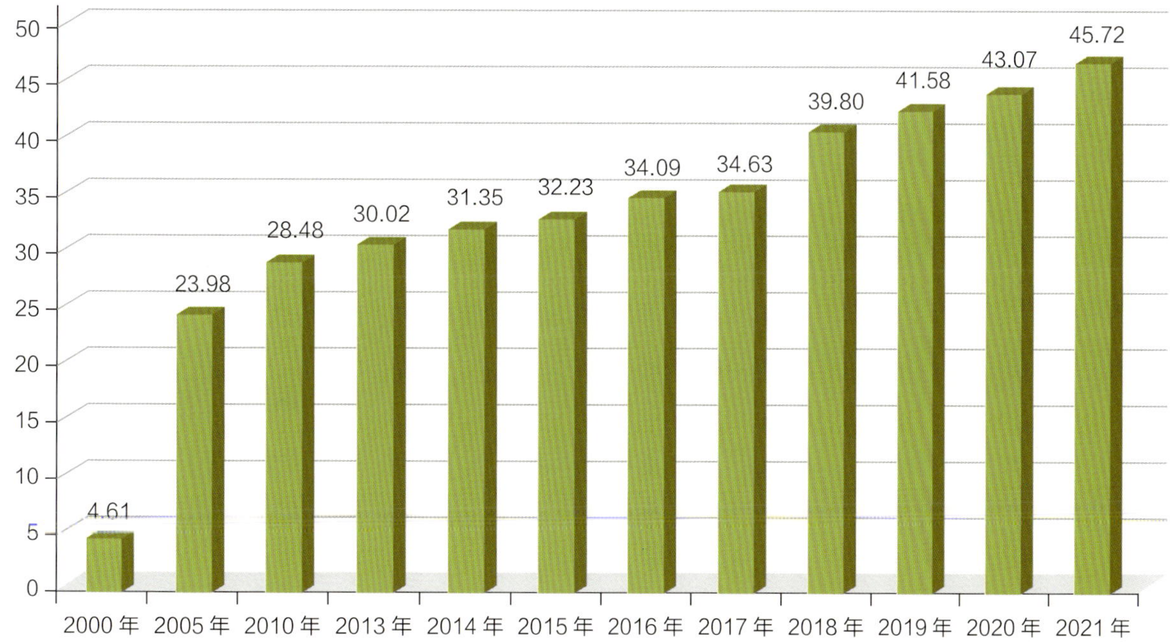

目　　录
CONTENTS

一、综　　合
Chapter 1.　GENERAL SURVEY

二、人　口
Chapter 2.　POPULATION

三、从业人员及职工工资
Chapter 3.　EMPLOYMENT AND WAGES

四、固定资产投资
Chapter 4.　INVESTMENT IN FIXED ASSETS

五、对外经济贸易
Chapter 5.　FOREIGN TRADE

六、城市建设、环境保护
Chapter 6. COTY CONSTRUCTION AND ENVIRONMENT PROTECTION

七、能源消耗
Chapter 7.　CONSUMPTION OF ENERGY

八、财政、金融和保险业
Chapter 8.　GOVERNMENT FINANCE, FINANCIAL AND INSURANCE

九、价格指数
Chapter 9.　PRICE INDICES

十、人民生活
Chapter 10.　PEOPLE'S LIVELI HOODS

十一、农　业
Chapter 11.　AGRICULTURE

十二、工　业
Chapter 12.　INDUSTRY

十三、服务业
Chapter 13.　SERVICE ENTERPRISES

十四、建筑业
Chapter 14.　CONSTRUCTION

十五、运输、邮电
Chapter 15.　TRANSPORT，POSTAL AND TELECOMMUNICATION SERVICES

十六、批发和零售业
Chapter 16.　WHOLESALE AND RETAIL TRADES

十七、住宿、餐饮业和旅游
Chapter 17.　HOTELS，CATERING SERVICES AND TOURISM

十八、教育、科技和文化
Chapter 18.　EDUCATION SCIENCE & TECHNOLOY AND CULTURE

十九、体育、卫生和民政、司法

Chapter 19.　SPORTS，PUBLIC HEALTH AND CIVIL AFFAIRS，JUDICIAL AFFAIRS

附　录
APPENDIX

2021 年
青岛市国民经济和社会发展
统 计 公 报[1]

青岛市统计局

国家统计局青岛调查队

（2022 年 3 月 17 日）

2021 年，是中国共产党成立 100 周年，是全面迈入社会主义现代化新征程起步之年和“十四五”开局之年。全市上下坚持以习近平新时代中国特色社会主义思想为指导，全面贯彻党的十九大和十九届历次全会精神，深入贯彻落实习近平总书记对山东、对青岛工作的重要指示要求，在中央和省、市委的坚强领导下，完整、准确、全面贯彻新发展理念，主动服务和融入新发展格局，统筹疫情防控和经济社会发展，全市经济运行稳中向好、进中提质，经济社会发展韧性和活力持续彰显，高质量发展取得新成效，“十四五”实现良好开局。

一、综　合

经济总量再上新台阶。初步核算，全市实现生产总值[2]14136.46 亿元，按可比价格计算，比上年增长 8.3%，两年平均增长[3]6.0%。其中，第一产业增加值 470.06 亿元，增长 6.7%；第二产业增加值 5070.33 亿元，增长 6.9%；第三产业增加值 8596.07 亿元，增长 9.2%。三次产业比例由 2020 年的 3.4∶35.3∶61.3 调整为 3.3∶35.9∶60.8。

图 1：2016-2021 年地区生产总值及增速

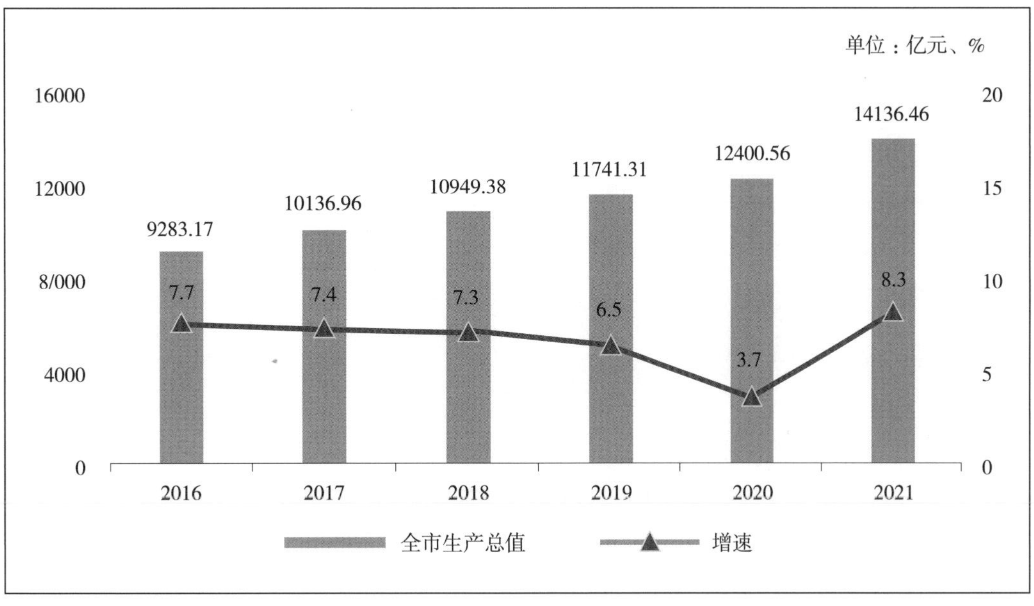

市场价格温和上涨。全年居民消费价格指数 (CPI) 为 101.5, 涨幅比上年缩小 0.9 个百分点。其中，食品烟酒类价格指数为 100.8，居住类价格指数为 101.1，医疗保健类价格指数为 100.5，服务价格指数为 102.0。

表 1：2021 年居民消费价格指数

指标名称	全年（上年同期 =100）
居民消费价格总指数	101.5
非食品价格指数	101.9
服务价格指数	102.0
消费品价格指数	101.2
一、食品烟酒	100.8
食品	99.7
#粮食	101.4
鲜菜	106.1
猪肉	68.8
鸡蛋	116.3
二、衣着	100.6
三、居住	101.1
四、生活用品及服务	98.9
五、交通和通信	106.1
六、教育文化和娱乐	102.7
七、医疗保健	100.5
八、其他用品和服务	98.2

人口总量平稳增长。年末，全市常住人口 1025.67 万人，比上年末增长 1.49%。其中，城镇常住人口 791.51 万人，常住人口城镇化率达 77.17%，比上年末提高 0.83 个百分点。

就业形势总体稳定。城镇新增就业 38.13 万人。其中，失业人员再就业 6.8 万人，困难群体再就业 5.35 万人。城镇登记失业率为 2.74%，比上年降低 0.29 个百分点。

市场活力稳步增强。全年新登记市场主体 30.1 万户。其中，企业 12.6 万户，个体工商户 17.5 万户，农民专业合作社 906 户。年末，全市实有各类市场主体 195.4 万户，比上年末增长 8.2%。其中，企业 72.9 万户，增长 10.0%；个体工商户 120.7 万户，增长 7.3%; 农民专业合作社 1.8 万户。实有民营经济市场主体 191.9 万户，增长 8.4%，占全部市场主体比重达到 98.2%。

新旧动能转换加速提效。智能家电和轨道交通装备产业集群成功入选国家先进制造业集群。全年“新经济”投资比上年增长 7.1%，占全部投资比重达 50.4%。规模以上工业[4]中，高技术制造业增加值比上年增长 17.1%；装备制造业增加值增长 4.2%；战略性新兴产业增加值占规模以上工业比重达 24.5%。生产性服务业增加值 4826.7 亿元，比上年增长 11.4%，占全市生产总值比重为 34.1%。规模以上软件和信息技术服务业营业收入 291.7 亿元，比上年增长 22.2%。限额以上单位网上零售额比上年增长 28.1%，占限额以上社会消费品零售额的比重达到 28.1%。全年城市轨道车辆产量 1587 辆，智能电视产量 1881.6 万台，工业机器人产量 1964 套。

二、农　业

农林牧渔业发展稳中有进。全年农林牧渔业增加值 500.50 亿元，比上年增长 6.8%。其中，农林牧渔服务业增加值 30.44 亿元，增长 9.0%。

种植业平稳发展。全年粮食播种面积 48.0 万公顷，蔬菜播种面积 10.9 万公顷，花生播种面积 6.9 万公顷。全年粮食产量 312.8 万吨，比上年增长 2.7%；蔬菜及食用菌产量 661.8 万吨，增长 0.9%；花生产量 33.9 万吨，下降 5.7%；水果（含果用瓜）产量 119.8 万吨，增长 2.8%。

图 2：2016-2021 年粮食产量

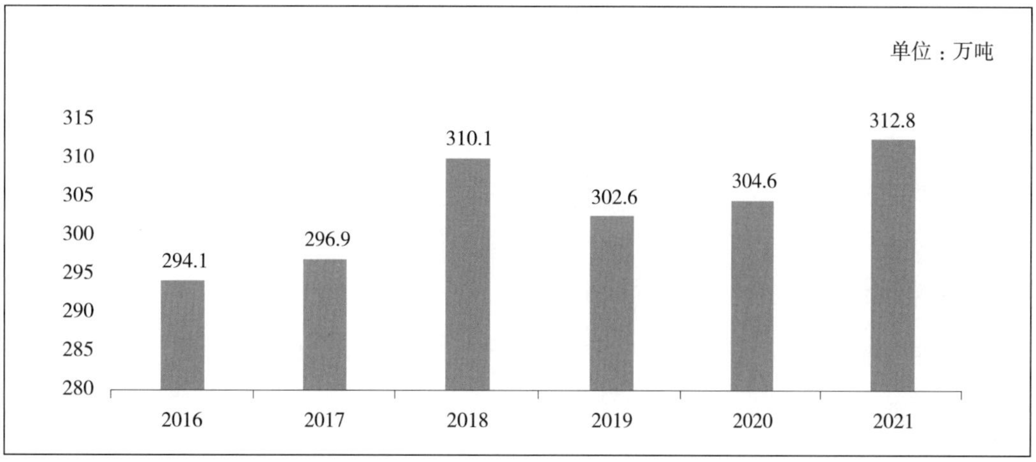

林牧渔业稳固增效。全年完成荒山造林面积 1.03 万公顷。全年肉类产量 50.4 万吨，禽蛋产量 28.9 万吨，牛奶产量 33.3 万吨。全年水产品产量（不包括远洋捕捞）101.3 万吨，比上年增长 0.2%；海、淡水养殖面积 3.7 万公顷，增长 5.8%；远洋渔业产量 14.8 万吨，增长 0.7%。

现代高效农业加快建设。全年现代高效农业增加值 100.3 亿元，比上年增长 15.1%。截至年末，创建市级以上现代农业产业园 10 个，产业强镇 15 个。全年已建成市级以上田园综合体 5 个、农业绿色园艺标准园 40 个、标准化示范场 31 家；“三品一标”（无公害农产品、绿色食品、有机农产品和农产品地理标志）1005 个，其中国家地理标志保护产品 54 个。农机总动力 757 万千瓦，比上年增加 2.5 万千瓦。农作物生产综合机械化水平达到 90.2%。

表 2：2021 年主要种植业产品产量及增速

指标	单位	产量	增长（%）
粮食	万吨	312.8	2.7
夏粮	万吨	143.0	7.2
秋粮	万吨	169.8	-0.8
油料	万吨	33.9	-5.7
蔬菜及食用菌	万吨	661.8	0.9
水果	万吨	119.8	2.8
园林水果	万吨	80.5	7.4

三、工业与建筑业

工业生产稳中加固。全年工业增加值 3884.07 亿元，比上年增长 8.8%。规模以上工业增加值增长 8.1%。分门类看，采矿业增长 6.6%，制造业增长 8.0%，电力、热力、燃气及水生产和供应业增长 11.0%。分重点行业看，汽车制造业下降 12.2%，电气机械和器材制造业增长 16.4%，石油、煤炭及其他燃料加工业增长 18.5%，化学原料和化学制品制造业增长 18.8%，通用设备制造业增长 19.2%。全年规模以上工业企业产销率达到 100.1%。

表 3：2021 年规模以上工业主要产品产量及增速

产品名称	单位	产量	增长（%）
彩色电视机	万台	1986.7	11.9
智能电视	万台	1881.6	11.9
家用电冰箱	万台	888.8	8.1
家用洗衣机	万台	730.8	27.0
房间空气调节器	万台	1150.4	24.9
智能手机	万台	449.6	-10.5
啤酒	万千升	197.2	12.0
橡胶轮胎外胎	万条	5033.8	2.1
平板玻璃	万重量箱	998.2	-0.4
粗钢	万吨	325.0	-3.0
汽车	万辆	21.2	-26.8
动车组	辆	503	-49.5
城市轨道车辆	辆	1587	-13.6
金属集装箱	万立方米	2141.0	54.7

发展质效稳步提高。全年规模以上工业实现利润 576.1 亿元，比上年增长 2.8%。其中，国有控股企业实现利润 204.3 亿元，增长 27.8%，股份制企业实现利润 379.8 亿元，增长 15.7%，外商及港澳台商投资企业实现利润 194.0 亿元，下降 15.9%。

表 4：2021 年规模以上工业利润增速

指标	增长 (%)
规模以上工业利润	2.8
国有控股	27.8
股份制企业	15.7
外商及港澳台商投资企业	-15.9

建筑业持续壮大。全年资质内总承包、专业承包建筑业企业 889 家，实现增加值 1214.7 亿元，比上年增长 2.0%。完成建筑业总产值 3297.3 亿元，增长 9.9%；签订合同额 7405.5 亿元，增长 23.5%。

图 3：2016-2021 年建筑业总产值及增速

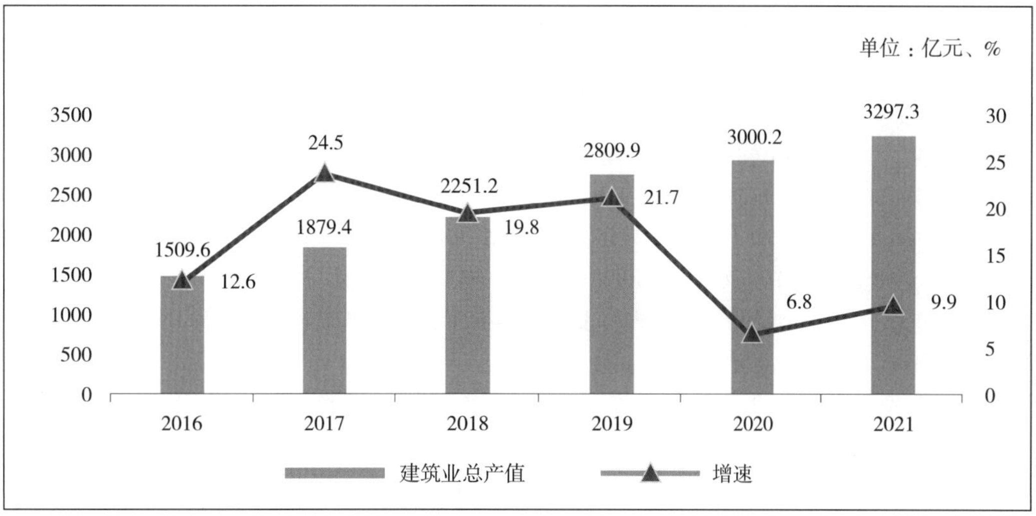

四、交通、邮电和旅游

交通运输稳步复苏。全年铁路、公路、水路共完成货运量 4.0 亿吨，比上年增长 11.8%；完成客运量 5144 万人次，增长 63.3%。全年港口吞吐量 6.3 亿吨，比上年增长 4.3%；外贸吞吐量 4.6 亿吨，增长 3.2%；集装箱吞吐量 2371 万标准箱，增长 7.8%。年末，拥有空中国内航线 185 条，国际航线 19 条，港澳台地区航线 2 条，全年新开航线 25 条；全年航空旅客吞吐量 1603 万人次，比上年增长 10.1%；航空货邮吞吐量 24 万吨，增长 14.9%。

表 5：2021 年主要运输方式完成的运输量及增速

运输方式	单位	运输量	增长 (%)
旅客发送量	万人	5144	63.3
铁路	万人	1912	54.3
公路	万人	3113	68.8
水运	万人	119	80.1
货运运输量	万吨	39969	11.8
铁路	万吨	8494	0.9
公路	万吨	28407	10.4
水运	万吨	3068	29.8

年末，全市轨道交通运营线路 6 条，长度达到 284 公里，运营车站 128 个，开行列车 67 万列次，总运营里程 2177 万列公里，年客运量 24659 万人次，日均客运量 68 万人次。地面公交运营车辆达 10595 辆，公交运营线路 925 条，线网长度 9377 公里，年客运量 82765 万人次，日均客运量 227 万人次。运营巡游出租车 11638 辆，年客运量 18435 万人次，日均客运量 51 万人次。

年末，全市机动车保有量 354 万辆，比上年增长 7.3%；其中，私人汽车 293 万辆，增长 7.1%。

邮政电信快速发展。全年完成邮电业务总量 224.3 亿元，比上年增长 27.8%。其中，邮政业务总量 88.0 亿元，增长 28.2%；电信业务总量 136.3 亿元，增长 27.5%。快递业务量 7.7 亿件，增长 31.6%。固定宽带互联网用户 498 万户，增长 7.3%。全市移动电话 1295 万户，增长 3.0%。获批建设国家级互联网骨干直联点，入选全国首批“千兆城市”。新建 5G 基站 1 万余个，累计建成并开通 5G 基站超过 2 万个。

旅游市场快速复苏。全年接待游客 8221.2 万人次，比上年增长 30.2%，实现旅游总收入 1411 亿元，增长 37.4%。年末，拥有 A 级旅游景区 109 处。其中，5A 级旅游景区 1 处，4A 级旅游景区 25 处，3A 级旅游景区 7 处。拥有星级酒店 85 个。其中，5 星级酒店 11 个，4 星级酒店 22 个，3 星级酒店 39 个。拥有旅行社 605 个。其中，经营出境旅游业务旅行社 56 个。

五、固定资产投资和房地产

投资保持稳定增长。全年固定资产投资比上年增长 4.1%。分产业看，第一产业投资增长 20.7%，第二产业投资增长 25.4%，第三产业投资下降 1.8%。

投资结构不断优化。全年制造业投资比上年增长 24.8%，对全部投资增长贡献率为 115.6%。工业战略新兴产业和高技术制造业投资分别增长 22.2% 和 60.5%，工业技改投资增长 29.6%。民间投资增长 8.3%，占固定资产投资比重达 59.8%。

图 4：2021 年三次产业投资占固定资产投资比重

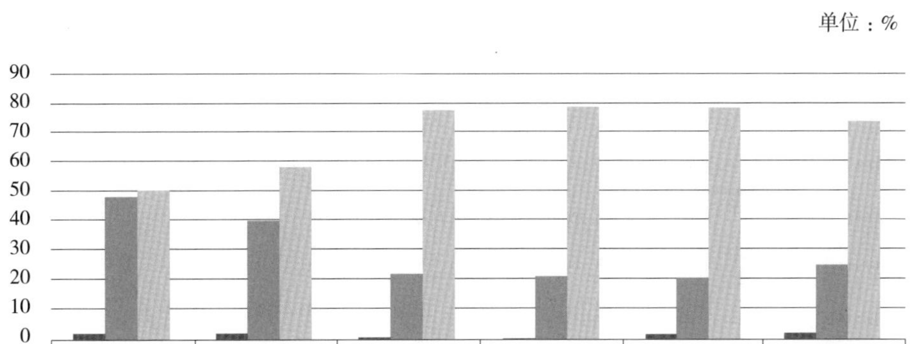

	2016 年	2017 年	2018 年	2019 年	2020 年	2021 年
第一产业	1.5	1.7	0.9	0.6	1.3	1.5
第二产业	48.1	39.9	21.5	20.9	20.6	24.9
第三产业	50.4	58.4	77.6	78.5	78.1	73.6

第一产业　第二产业　第三产业

房地产市场平稳运行。全年房地产开发完成投资 1981.8 亿元，比上年下降 3.1%。其中，住宅投资 1481 亿元，增长 0.1%。商品房销售面积 1644.5 万平方米，比上年下降 0.5%。其中，住宅销售面积 1419.6 万平方米，下降 0.8%。

表 6：2021 年房地产开发投资、商品房销售面积及增速

分 类	房地产开发投资（亿元）	增长（%）	商品房销售面积（万平方米）	增长（%）
总计	1981.8	-3.1	1644.5	-0.5
住宅	1481.0	0.1	1419.6	-0.8
办公楼	123.7	-8.5	75.5	17.3
商业营业用房	114.7	-24.6	61.0	27.2
其他	262.4	-5.9	88.4	-20.3

全年开工建设公共租赁住房 1062 套，基本建成公共租赁住房 1418 套。建设筹集人才住房 60101 套。截至年末，全市正在享受租赁补贴家庭共 13822 户，全年发放租赁补贴 10721.7 万元。

六、国内贸易

消费市场持续回暖。全年实现社会消费品零售额 5975.4 亿元，比上年增长 14.8%。其中，批发和零售业实现零售额 5343.4 亿元，增长 14.1%；住宿和餐饮业实现零售额 632.0 亿元，增长 21.6%。按经营地统计，城镇消费品零售额 4933.7 亿元，增长 14.9%；乡村消费品零售额 1041.8 亿元，增长 14.6%。

图 5：2016-2021 年社会消费品零售总额及增速

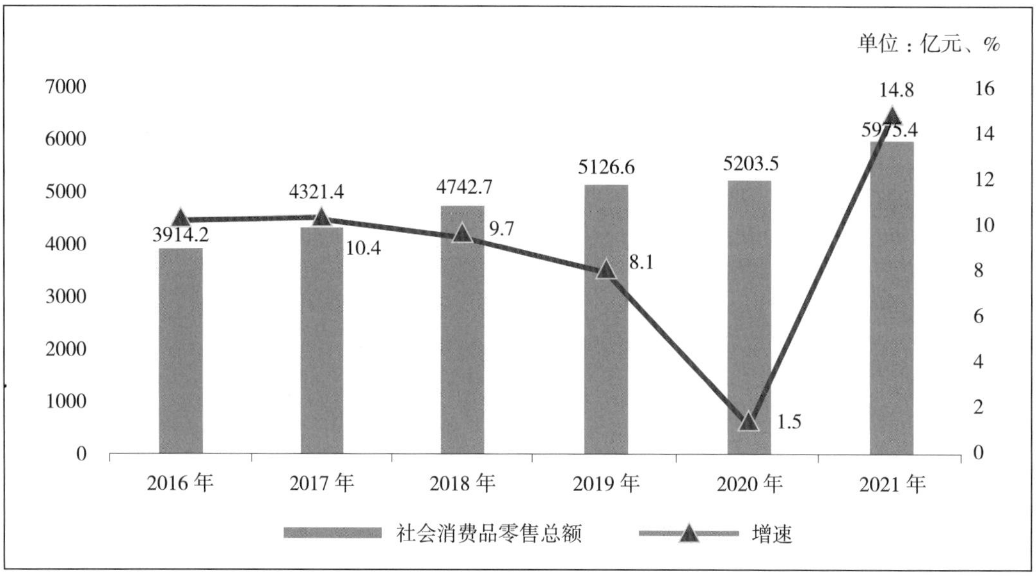

升级类消费需求持续释放。全年限额以上单位商品零售额中，新能源汽车零售额比上年增长 74.5%，化妆品类增长 24.5%，金银珠宝类增长 62.4%，智能家用电器和音像器材类增长 32.5%，通讯器材类增长 159.7%，智能手机类增长 152.1%，体育娱乐用品类增长 128.5%。

线上市场快速拓展。全年电子商务交易平台[5]实现交易额 1.5 万亿元，比上年增长 26.1%；限额以上批发和零售业企业网络销售额 742.7 亿元，增长 26.9%。

七、对外经济

更高水平开放不断扩大。全年实现货物进出口总额 8498.4 亿元，比上年增长 32.4%。其中，出口额 4921.3 亿元，增长 27.0%；进口额 3577.2 亿元，增长 40.7%。分经济类型看，私营企业实现进出口 5613.8 亿元，增长 35.6%，占进出口总额的比重达 66.1%；三资企业[6]实现进出口 1735.3 亿元，增长 18.0%；国有企业实现进出口 1039.7 亿元，增长 49.7%。从产品结构看，机电产品出口 2345.1 亿元，增长 29.8%，占全市出口总值的 47.7%。其中，机械设备、电器及电子产品、运输工具出口分别增长 35.2%、31.1%、60.0%。从贸易市场看，对前三大贸易市场东盟、美国和欧盟进出口分别为 1353.7、998.0 和 988.7 亿元，分别增长 43.1%、28.4% 和 19.1%，分别占全市进出口总值的 15.9%、11.7% 和 11.6%；对“一带一路”沿线国家进出口 2640.0 亿元，增长 44.8%，占全市进出口总值的 31.1%；对 RCEP 其他成员国进出口 3196.5 亿元，增长 35.4%，占全市进出口总值的 37.6%；对上合组织成员国进出口 499.9 亿元，增长 34.3%，占全市进出口总值的 5.9%。

图 6：2016-2021 年外贸货物进出口总额及增速

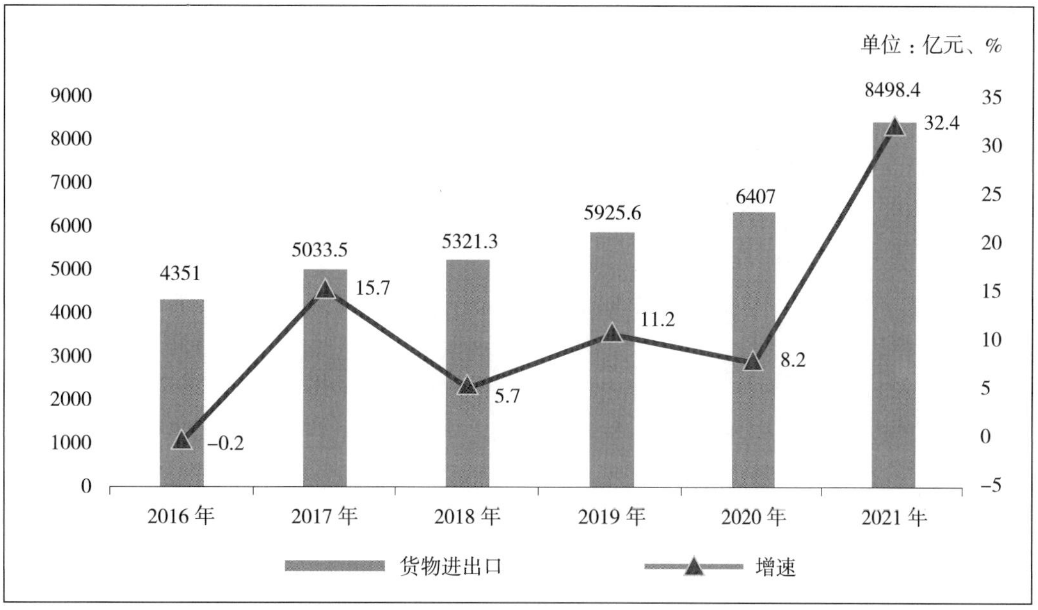

表 7：2021 年全市主要商品进出口情况

项 目	进出口		出 口		进 口	
	金 额（亿元）	增 长（%）	金 额（亿元）	增 长（%）	金 额（亿元）	增 长（%）
纺织服装	593.1	10.4	571.3	10.8	21.8	1.5
农产品	1056.4	9.2	370.8	−5.8	685.6	19.5
机电产品	2967.0	31.5	2345.1	29.8	621.9	38.5
高新技术产品	759.2	39.4	393.7	24.9	365.4	59.4

表 8：2021 年对主要国家和地区货物进出口额及增速

国别（地区）	出口额（亿美元）	增 长（%）	进口额（亿美元）	增 长（%）
亚洲	358.2	36.4	263.7	69.1
中国香港	36.0	75.7	0.6	−17.7
中国台湾	7.3	31.7	20.3	74.5
日本	71.0	19.4	24.2	25.7
韩国	67.3	46.1	44.6	41.6
东盟	98.2	30.1	111.4	80.3
南亚	32.2	48.8	10.5	32.8

国别（地区）	出口额（亿美元）	增长（%）	进口额（亿美元）	增长（%）
中东	39.4	33.6	45.2	145.9
非洲	36.6	51.6	29.3	42.2
南非	6.6	54.0	3.5	18.0
欧洲	155.1	36.3	73.1	20.9
欧盟	105.9	28.0	47.2	26.4
德国	23.3	29.5	12.6	0.2
法国	9.6	16.6	4.4	20.4
意大利	10.1	35.4	3.9	44.0
独联体及东欧	40.1	82.9	18.0	6.2
俄罗斯	22.5	119.7	13.7	−2.7
南美洲	25.0	45.4	83.5	25.2
巴西	8.8	42.0	64.8	27.9
北美洲	135.6	30.3	41.3	46.1
美国	119.9	32.6	34.5	55.8
加拿大	15.6	15.1	6.3	12.1
大洋洲	21.5	28.2	58.9	79.0
澳大利亚	16.6	18.6	51.3	82.9

注：本表非全口径。

利用外资量稳质升。全年新设外商投资企业 908 家，比上年增长 4.4%；合同外资 214.3 亿美元，增长 20.1%。全市实际使用外资 61.7 亿美元，比上年增长 5.4%。

对外合作稳步推进。全年青岛口岸对外贸易进出口总额 15167.4 亿元，比上年增长 29.6%。其中，出口额 8550.6 亿元，增长 29.3%；进口额 6616.8 亿元，增长 30.0%。全市对外承包工程业务新承揽项目 43 个，新签合同额 31.2 亿美元，比上年减少 10.3%；完成营业额 30.2 亿美元，增长 4.8%。对外劳务合作业务派出各类劳务人员 11806 人。新增中欧班列线路 11 条，开行中欧班列 621 列，增长 54.9%。

“一带一路”融合发展。全年全市企业对“一带一路”沿线国家和地区投资项目 15 个，中方协议投资额 12.2 亿美元，比上年增长 213.0%；中方实际投资额 3.3 亿美元，增长 174.6%。

八、财政金融

财政运行保障稳固。全年财政总收入 4298.4 亿元，一般公共预算收入 1368.3 亿元，比上年增长 9.1%。其中，税收收入 1016.9 亿元，增长 13.1%，占一般公共预算收入比重为 74.3%，比上年提高 2.6 个百分点。全年一般公共预算支出

1705.7 亿元，比上年增长 7.6%。其中，一般公共服务支出 199.2 亿元，下降 0.1%；教育支出 308.8 亿元，增长 7.0%；科学技术支出 51.3 亿元，增长 9.5%；社会保障和就业支出 243.1 亿元，增长 9.0%；城乡社区事务支出 243.8 亿元，增长 3.0%。全年税务系统组织税收收入（含海关代征）2636.5 亿元，比上年增长 18.8%。其中，国内税收 1994.4 亿元，增长 16.7%。

金融市场健康发展。山东港信期货开业运营。截至年末，金融机构本外币存款余额 22374.9 亿元，比年初增加 1867.7 亿元，其中人民币存款余额 21582.3 亿元，比年初增加 1760.5 亿元。本外币贷款余额 24089.1 亿元，比年初增加 3024.3 亿元，其中人民币贷款余额 23253.5 亿元，比年初增加 3042.5 亿元。全年保险业累计实现保费收入[7]461.9 亿元，比上年增长 6.2%。其中，人身险公司保费收入 305.5 亿元，增长 5.8%；财产险公司保费收入 156.4 亿元，增长 7.0%。全年证券分支机构证券交易额 70901.8 亿元，比上年增长 20.7%；法人机构证券交易额 65946.0 亿元，增长 50.9%。全年新增境内上市公司 14 家，境内上市公司达到 58 家。在中国证券投资基金业协会登记的私募基金管理人 441 家，管理基金规模 1639.4 亿元，比上年增长 57.7%。全市不良贷款率降至 1.08%，较年初下降 0.2 个百分点。

九、科学技术和教育

创新动力显著增强。国家高端智能化家用电器创新中心获批建设。中科院海洋大科学研究中心、中国海洋工程研究院（青岛）投入运营。海洋试点国家实验室超算升级项目投入运行。中车四方世界首套时速 600 公里高速磁浮交通系统下线。新建省级以上技术创新中心 8 家，总数达 24 家。高新技术企业总数达到 5554 家，比上年增加 1158 家，入库国家科技型中小企业 6306 家。新培育国家专精特新“小巨人”企业 50 家，总数达 97 家。累计有 13 家企业入选全球独角兽企业 500 强榜单。现有国家知识产权示范企业 12 家，国家知识产权优势企业 107 家，国家重点实验室 9 家，国家级工程技术研究中心 10 家，省级工程技术研究中心 82 家。新引进集聚人才 26.1 万人，人才总量突破 251.1 万人。

创新成果持续涌现。初步统计，全市共取得重要科技成果 409 项，获得省级科技奖励 102 项。其中，自然科学奖 12 项，技术发明奖 4 项，科技进步奖 85 项，最高奖项 1 项。技术合同交易额 320.1 亿元，比上年增长 11.7%。涉海技术合同成交额 31.8 亿元，增长 12.2%。有效发明专利[8]46609 件，比上年增长 22.6%。每万人有效发明专利拥有量 46.28 件，比上年增加 5.28 件。PCT 国际专利申请 1616 件。

图 7：2016-2021 年高新技术企业数量及增速

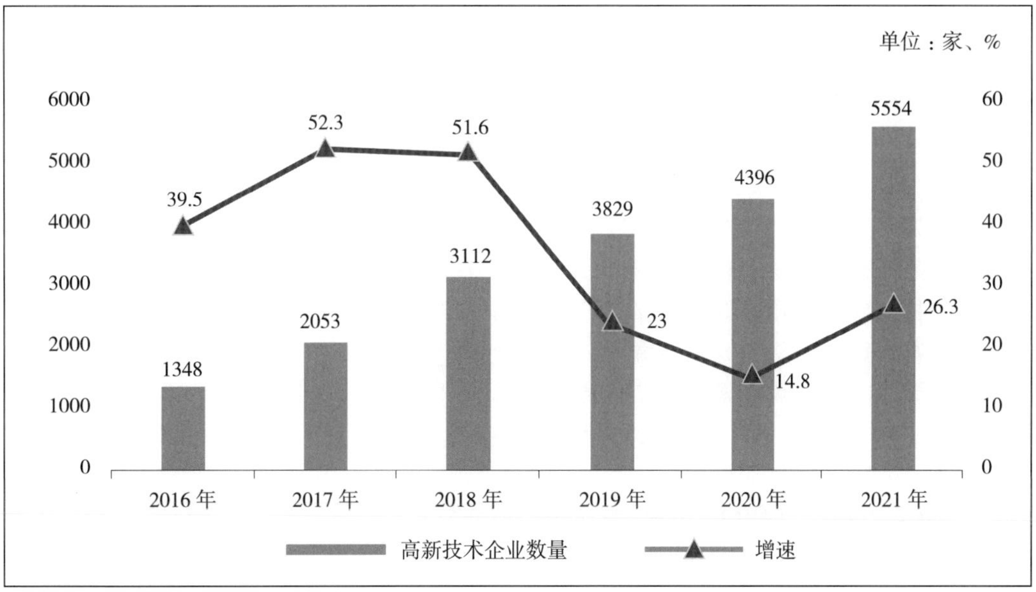

教育事业不断进步。全年新建改扩建中小学和幼儿园 104 所。义务教育学校课后服务惠及学生 63.5 万人。截至年末，全市共有各类大专院校（含民办高校）29 所。其中，普通高校 14 所。全年研究生招生 2.1 万人，在校研究生 6.2 万人，毕业生 1.4 万人（不含驻青科研院所研究生）。普通本专科招生 11.5 万人，在校生 39.5 万人，毕业生 10.0 万人；中等职业教育招生 2.7 万人，在校生 9.0 万人，毕业生 2.5 万人；普通高中招生 5.3 万人，在校生 15.2 万人，毕业生 3.8 万人；初中招生 9.3 万人，在校生 29.4 万人，毕业生 8.5 万人；普通小学招生 11.8 万人，在校生 63.1 万人，毕业生 9.3 万人；特殊教育招生 0.05 万人，在校生 0.25 万人，毕业生 0.03 万人；幼儿园在园幼儿 36.8 万人。

图 8：2016-2021 年各类学校招生人数

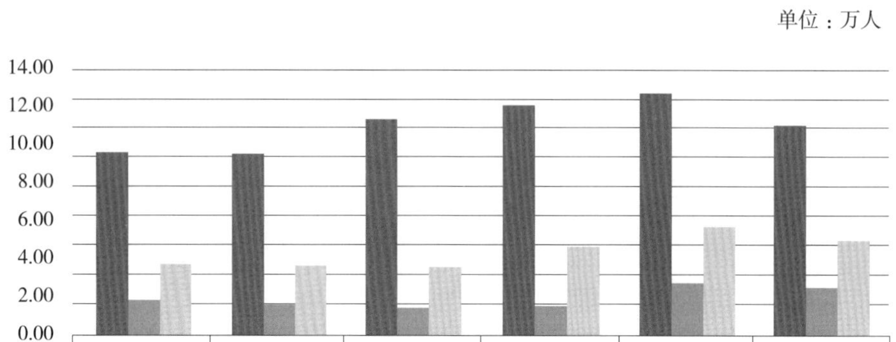

	2016 年	2017 年	2018 年	2019 年	2020 年	2021 年
普通高等学校	10.05	9.90	11.82	12.64	13.22	11.53
中等职业学校	1.99	1.80	1.59	1.70	2.97	2.72
普通高中	3.97	3.96	3.83	4.94	6.03	5.28

■普通高等学校　■中等职业学校　■普通高中

十、文化、卫生和体育

文化事业繁荣发展。成功举办中国歌剧节、青岛国际影视博览会等文化活动。海军博物馆开馆，国家海洋考古博物馆（青岛）获批建设。年末，全市共有影剧院 118 处，文化馆（站）150 处，博物馆 108 处，公共图书馆 14 处，国有文艺院团 8 个，广播电台 6 座、11 套节目，电视台 6 座、17 套节目。全市共有档案馆 12 处。

医疗卫生服务能力持续增强。北京大学人民医院青岛医院、市公共卫生应急备用医院投入使用。年末，全市共有卫生机构（不含村卫生室）4587 处。其中，医院、卫生院 449 处，疾病预防控制中心 41 处，妇幼保健机构 12 处，门诊部（所）、诊所、卫生所、医务室 3704 处。各类卫生技术人员 9.67 万人。其中，医生 3.98 万人。全市拥有医疗床位 6.79 万张。其中，医院、卫生院床位 6.52 万张。大幅提升常态化疫情防控能力，建立系统协作、部门协同、跨区域联动的流调溯源工作机制，疾控流调队伍 491 支共 4838 人；建成 2 个国家公共检测实验室和 3 个城市检测基地；核酸检测机构 83 家，日检测能力 50.8 万人份；设置普通发热门诊 43 个、入境专用发热门诊 5 个、发热哨点诊室 184 个。

体育事业蓬勃发展。全年新建体育公园、笼式多功能运动场、社区健身健康中心 40 处，更新、新建健身设施 220 处。成功承办第十四届全国学生运动会。我市 11 名运动员代表国家参赛东京奥运会，陈梦勇夺 2 枚金牌，实现青岛运动员连续四届奥运会摘金壮举；190 名运动员代表山东参赛第 14 届全运会，取得了 15 金 18 银 15 铜优异成绩。年末，全市共有重点体校 1 所，学员 1150 人；业余体校 10 所，学员 1810 人。

十一、城市建设

城乡环境品质不断提升。地铁三期获批建设，1 号线全线贯通运营。新机场高速连接线建成通车，明村至董家口高速开工建设。官路水库工程全面启动。深化全国文明典范城市创建，城市更加宜居宜业。中山路、台东步行街、邮轮母港区等历史城区保护更新加快推进。年末，全市建成区面积 964.39 平方公里。全年实施老旧小区改造 216 个，启动棚户区改造 1.4 万套（户）。着力优化市区交通环境，环湾路—长沙路立交、太原路东延段建成通车，整治提升 53 条市政道路，打通 30 余条未贯通道路。新增公共停车泊位 1.7 万余个，向社会开放机关事业单位停车场 360 个。乡村建设行动扎实推进。创建 10 个市级美丽乡村示范村、10 个示范片。改造农村危房 604 户。

十二、能源、环境和安全生产

能源消费结构逐步优化。全社会用电量 552.7 亿千瓦时，比上年增长 16.0%。其中，工业用电量 298.0 亿千瓦时，增长 15.1%；服务业用电量 143.8 亿千瓦时，增长 21.5%；城乡居民生活用电量 91.3 亿千瓦时，增长 12.2%。全市规模以上工业综合能源消费量 1591.9 万吨标准煤，增长 12.2%。其中，煤炭消费量增长 2.0%；石油消费量增长 13.2%；天然气消费量增长 26.6%。

图 9：2016-2021 年全社会用电量及增速

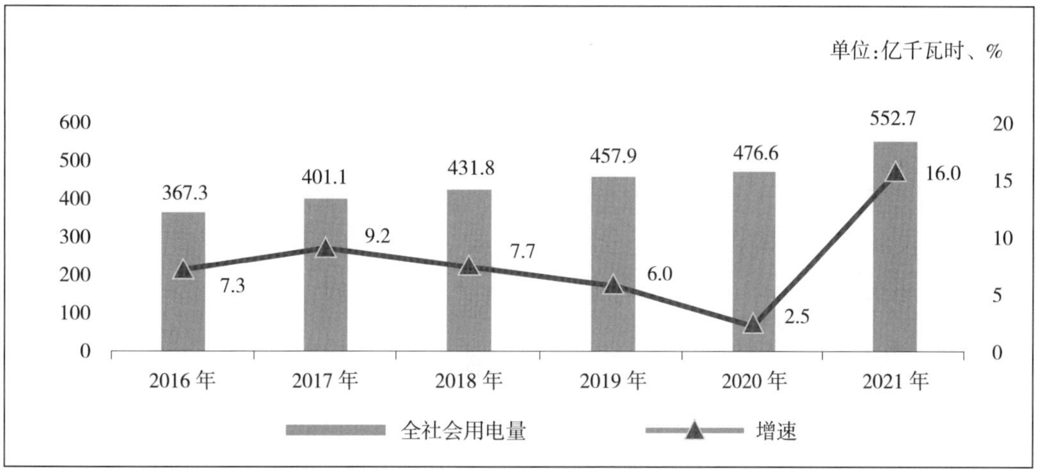

能源生产更加低碳清洁。全年能源生产量 2885.7 万吨标准煤，比上年增长 11.5%。其中，原油加工量 1473.5 万吨，增长 10.0%；汽油生产量 435.8 万吨，增长 17.5%；柴油生产量 355.3 万吨，增长 7.1%。发电量 187.9 亿千瓦时，增长 4.9%。新能源发电量 33.3 亿千瓦时，增长 22.1%，占全市发电总量比重为 17.7%。其中，风力发电量增长 47.1%，垃圾焚烧发电量增长 12.7%。

生态环境保护持续加强。成功应对最大规模浒苔侵袭。全市年平均气温 13.9℃，平均年降水量为 826.3 毫米。市区空气质量优良天数达 310 天，占全年的 84.9%。市区区域环境噪声平均值 57.0 分贝，市区交通干线噪声平均值 68.6 分贝。全市主要污染物细颗粒物（PM2.5）、二氧化硫、氮氧化物年均值分别为 28、8、30 微克 / 立方米，与上年相比，PM2.5 改善 12.5%，二氧化硫持平，氮氧化物改善 3.2%，空气质量全面达到国家二级标准。20 个国省控地表水考核断面水质全部达标，近岸海域水质优良比例面积达到 99%。

安全生产形势稳定。全市共发生各类生产安全事故 215 起[9]，死亡 129 人，分别比上年下降 1.4% 和 3.7%。亿元 GDP 生产安全事故死亡率 0.0091，十万工矿商贸企业就业人员生产安全事故死亡率 0.63。

十三、人民生活和社会保障

居民生活质量稳步提升。全年全市居民人均可支配收入[10]51223 元，比上年增长 8.6%。按常住地分，城镇居民人均可支配收入 60239 元，增长 7.8%；农村居民人均可支配收入 26125 元，增长 10.4%。全市居民人均消费支出 32878 元，比上年增长 8.5%，恩格尔系数为 28.0%。按常住地分，城镇居民人均消费支出 38574 元，增长 7.3%；农村居民人均消费支出 17021 元，增长 12.4%。据抽样调查，年末城镇居民人均现住房建筑面积 32.1 平方米，农村居民人均现住房建筑面积 37.4 平方米。

表 9：2021 年城乡居民人均可支配收入构成情况

指标名称	全体居民		城镇居民		农村居民	
	绝对值（元）	增长（%）	绝对值（元）	增长（%）	绝对值（元）	增长（%）
可支配收入	51223	8.6	60239	7.8	26125	10.4
工资性收入	30491	8.6	36222	7.7	14536	10.5
经营净收入	9701	10.0	9416	11.1	10495	8.0
财产净收入	4319	7.8	5706	6.4	458	25.6
转移净收入	6712	7.4	8895	5.6	636	51.1

表 10：2021 年城乡居民人均消费支出情况

指标名称	全体居民		城镇居民		农村居民	
	绝对值（元）	增长（%）	绝对值（元）	增长（%）	绝对值（元）	增长（%）
消费支出	32878	8.5	38574	7.3	17021	12.4
食品烟酒	9204	8.0	10727	7.0	4965	10.9
衣着	2973	9.9	3596	8.8	1237	12.8
居住	7707	7.5	9152	6.1	3685	12.7
生活用品及服务	2192	9.7	2571	8.7	1138	12.5
交通和通信	4873	8.8	5556	7.8	2972	11.8
教育文化娱乐	3363	11.7	3972	10.1	1668	18.1
医疗保健	1789	6.5	2079	5.2	980	11.4
其他用品和服务	777	6.5	920	5.0	377	12.2

表 11：2021 年每百户居民家庭主要耐用消费品拥有量

指标名称	单位	数量		
		全体居民	城镇居民	农村居民
家用汽车	辆	64	67	55
摩托车	辆	20	10	46
电冰箱（柜）	台	108	108	109
洗衣机	台	100	103	92
热水器	台	98	99	95
空调	台	122	129	101
彩色电视机	台	103	104	101
计算机	台	66	72	49
移动电话	部	245	245	244

社会保障更加完善。截至年末，全市城乡居民最低生活保障人数 8.3 万人，城乡居民最低生活保障资金支出 7 亿元；城乡特困供养人数 1.2 万人，城乡特困人员救助供养金支出 2.4 亿元。全市城镇职工基本养老保险参保缴费人数为 326.0 万人，全市养老、医疗、失业和工伤保险参保人数分别达到 782.9 万、911.9 万、271.3 万和 315.0 万人。新增养老床位 3.1 万张，基本实现城乡居家社区养老服务全覆盖。为 9.5 万名困难群众发放救助金 9.4 亿元，为 7.49 万名大病群众报销医疗费 46.12 亿元。

图 10：2016-2021 年城镇职工基本养老保险参保缴费人数

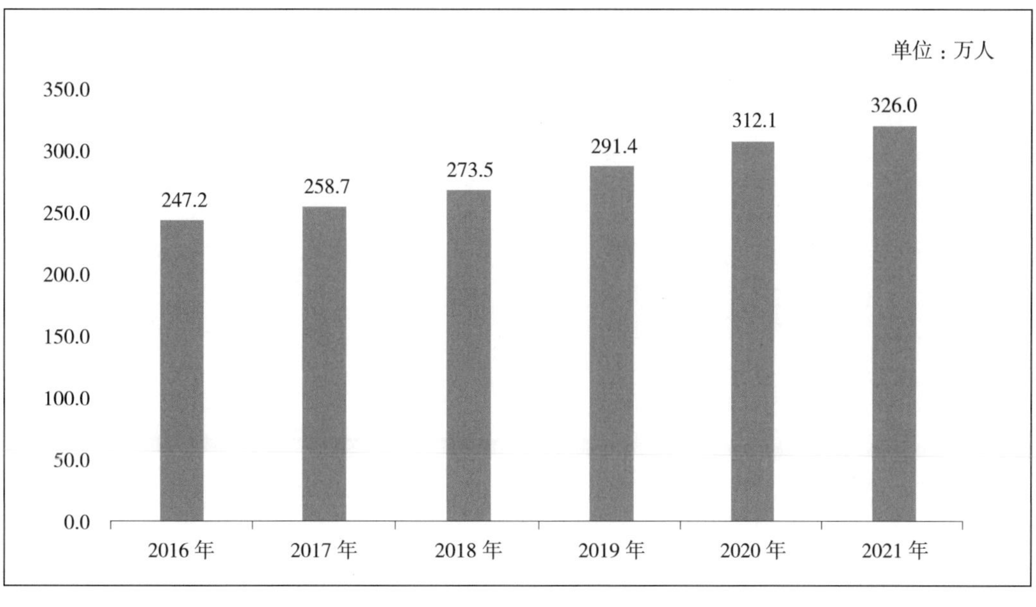

注释：

[1] 本公报中数据均为初步统计数，部分数据因四舍五入的原因，存在总计与分项合计不等的情况。

[2] 全市生产总值及各产业增加值绝对数按现价计算，增长速度按可比价格计算。

[3] 两年平均增速是指以 2019 年同期数为基数，采用几何平均的方法计算的增速。

[4] 规模以上工业企业为年主营业务收入 2000 万元及以上企业。

[5] 电子商务交易平台统计范围包括辖区内规模以上工业、有资质的建筑业、限额以上批发和零售业、限额以上住宿和餐饮业、有开发经营活动的全部房地产开发经营业、规模以上服务业法人单位拥有的电子商务交易平台，以及年交易额 1000 万元及以上的其他电子商务交易平台。

[6] 三资企业是指在中国境内设立的中外合资经营企业、中外合作经营企业、外商独资经营企业三类外商投资企业。

[7] 因部分保险机构正在进行风险处置，保险业相关数据暂不包括这部分机构。

[8] 有效发明专利、PCT 国际专利相关数据均为 1-11 月份数据。PCT（Patent Cooperation Treaty）即专利合作条约，是专利领域的一项国际合作条约。

[9] 各类生产安全事故起数、死亡人数统计范围包括农林牧渔业、采矿业、商贸制造业、建筑业、交通运输业和其他行业发生的事故。

[10] 居民人均可支配收入比上年增长指名义增速，计算方法是：(当年居民人均可支配收入/上年居民人均可支配收入 –1)×100%；居民人均可支配收入实际增速 =(当年居民人均可支配收入 / 上年居民人均可支配收入 / 同期居民消费价格指数 –1)×100%。

资料来源：本公报中财政数据来自青岛市财政局；税务数据来自青岛市税务局；人才、登记失业率、社会保障等数据来自青岛市人力资源和社会保障局；银行数据来自中国人民银行青岛市中心支行；证券保险数据来自中国证券监督管理委员会青岛监管局、中国银行保险监督管理委员会青岛监管局；水产品数据来自青岛市海洋发展局；林业数据来自青岛市园林和林业局；“三品一标”、农机等数据来自青岛市农业农村局；交通运输数据来自青岛市交通运输局；邮政数据来自青岛市邮政管理局；固定电话、宽带、移动电话等数据来自青岛市通信管理局；进出口、外资、对外承包工程、对外劳务合作等数据来自青岛市商务局；旅游数据来自青岛市文化和旅游局；教育数据来自青岛市教育局；科技数据来自青岛市科学技术局；市场主体、专利等数据来自青岛市市场监督管理局；低保数据来自青岛市民政局；体育数据来自青岛市体育局；卫生数据来自青岛市卫生健康委员会；环境数据来自青岛市生态环境局；用电量数据来自青岛供电公司；气象数据来自青岛市气象局；安全生产数据来自青岛市应急管理局；城市建设数据来自青岛市住房和城乡建设局；汽车保有量数据来自青岛市公安局；粮食数据、畜牧数据、居民生活数据、价格数据来自国家统计局青岛调查队；其他数据来自青岛市统计局。

STATISTICS COMMUNIQUE QINGDAO'S ECONOMIC AND SOCIAL DEVELOPMENT IN THE YEAR OF 2021[1]

Qingdao Municipal Statistics Bureau

NBS Survey Office In Qingdao

(March 17, 2022)

The year 2021 marked the centenary of the Communist Party of China CPC. It has embarked on a new journey toward building China into a modern socialist country and marked the launch of the 14th Five-Year Plan. All of us throughout the whole city followed the guidance of Xi Jinping Thought on Socialism with Chinese Characteristics for a New Era, comprehensively implemented the guiding principles of the Party's 19th National Congress and all plenary sessions of the 19th Party Central Committee, and fully implemented the important instructions and requirements of Xi Jinping, general secretary of the CPC Central Committee on the work of Shandong and Qingdao. Under the strong leadership of Communist Party of China (CPC) Central Committee, the provincial and municipal party committees, we applied the new development philosophy in full, in the right way, and in all fields, and actively served and integrated into the new development paradigm. Efforts have been made to coordinate COVID-19 response with economic and social development. The city's economy has registered stable performance with good momentum for growth and improved performance with development. The resilience and dynamism of socioeconomic development was given full expression and the economy has made new progress in high-quality development. We got the 14th Five-Year Plan off to a good start.

I. General

The total economic output has been brought to a new level. Preliminary accounting shows that the city's GDP [2] is 1,413.646 billion yuan, increasing 8.3% year on year and an average growth rate of 6.0% in the two years[3] based on comparable prices. The added value of the primary industry was worth 47.006 billion yuan, up 6.7% from 2020; the added value of the secondary industry was worth 507.033 billion yuan, up 6.9% from 2020; the added value of the tertiary industry was 859.607 billion yuan, up 9.2% year on year. The ratio of the three industries was adjusted from 3.4 : 35.3 : 61.3 in 2020 to 3.3 : 35.9 : 60.8 in 2021.

Market prices rose moderately. The annual consumer price index (CPI) was 101.5, 0.9 percentage points lower than that of the previous year. In particular, the price index of food, tobacco and alcohol was 100.8, that of housing 101.1, of medical care 100.5, and of services 102.0.

Figure 1: GDP and Growth rate from 2016 to 2021

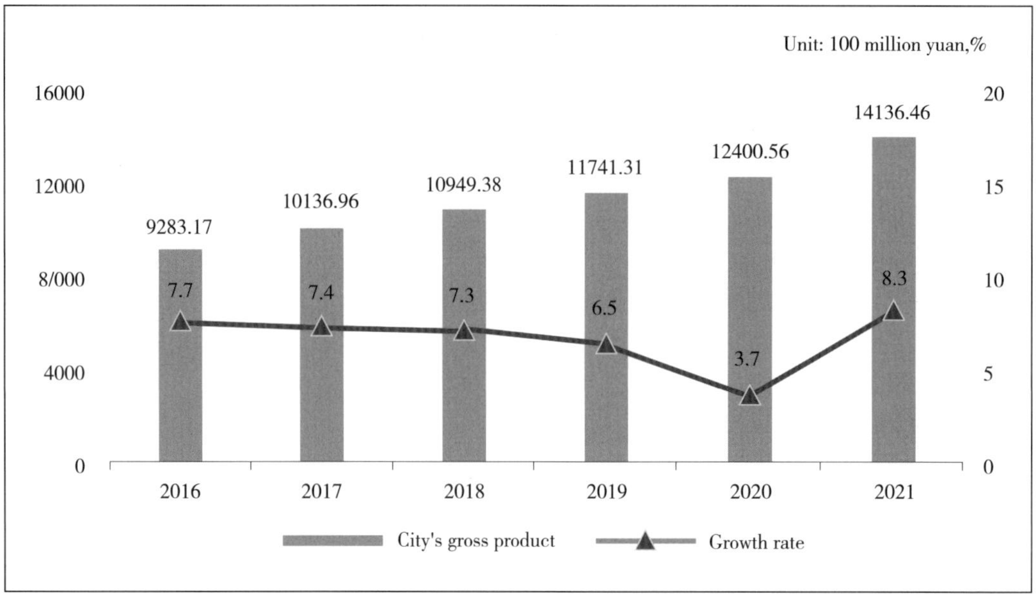

Table 1: Consumer Price Index of the City in 2021

Indicator name	The whole year（the same period last year=100)
General Consumer Price Index	101.5
Non–Food Price Index	101.9
Service Price Index	102.0
Consumer Goods Price Index	101.2
1. Food, Tobacco and Liquor	100.8
Food	99.7
#Grain	101.4
Vegetables	106.1
Pork	68.8
Egg	116.3
2. Clothing	100.6
3. Residence	101.1
4. Supplies and Services	98.9
5. Transportation and Communication	106.1
6. Education, Culture and Recreation	102.7
7. Medical Care	100.5
8. Other supplies and services	98.2

The total population grew steadily. By the end of the year, the city's resident population was 10.2567 million, up 1.49% over the same period last year. The urban permanent population was 7.9151 million, and the urbanization rate of the permanent population reached 77.17%, 0.83 percentage points higher over the end of the previous year.

The overall employment situation remained stable. Among the 381,300 new jobs created in urban areas, 68,000 unemployed people found new jobs, and 53,500 people from disadvantaged groups found new jobs. The registered urban unemployment rate was 2.74%, 0.29 percentage points lower than the previous year.

The market vitality increased steadily. There were 301,000 newly registered market entities in the year, among which 126,000 were enterprises, 175,000 were self-employed households, and 906 were specialized farm cooperatives. By the end of the year, there were 1.954 million market entities of all kinds in the city, up 8.2% year on year, among which 729,000 were enterprises, up 10.0%; 1.207 million self-employed households, up 7.3%;18,000 specialized farmer cooperatives. There were 1.919 million private economic market entities, up 8.4%, accounting for 98.2 % of the total market entities.

The replacement of old growth drivers with new ones speeded up with greater intensity and enhanced performance. The smart home appliance and rail transit equipment industry clusters were successfully selected as the national advanced manufacturing clusters. The annual "New Economy" investment increased by 7.1% over the previous year, accounting for 50.4% of the total investment. Among the industrial firms of designated size[4], output of the high-tech manufacturing industry went up 17.1 % year on year, and equipment manufacturing increased 4.2%; the added value of strategic emerging industries accounted for 24.5% of the industry above designated size. The added value of producer services was 482.67 billion yuan, surging 11.4% from a year earlier, accounting for 34.1% of the city's GDP. The operating income of software and information technology services above designated size was 29.17 billion yuan, an increase of 22.2% over the previous year. The online retail sales of businesses above designated size grew by 28.1% over the previous year, accounting for 28.1% of the retail sales of consumer goods above designated size. The annual output was 1,587 urban rail vehicles, 18.816 million smart televisions and 1,964 sets of industrial robots.

Ⅱ . Agriculture

Steady progress was made in agriculture, forestry, animal husbandry and fishery. The added value of agriculture, forestry, animal husbandry and fishery reached 50.05 billion yuan with an increase of 6.8% over the previous year. The added value of agriculture, forestry, animal husbandry and fishery services reached 3.044 billion yuan, surging 9.0% the previous year.

The planting industry developed steadily. The total grain acreage was 480 thousand hectares, vegetables acreage 109,000 hectares and peanut acreage 69,000 hectares. The total grain output reached 3.128 million tons, up 2.7% year on year. The output of vegetables and edible fungi was 6.618 million tons, growing by 0.9% from 2020; peanut output was 339,000 tons, down 5.7% from last year; the output of fruits (including melons) was 1.198 million tons, increasing by 2.8% year on year.

Figure 2 : 2016–2021 Grain Production

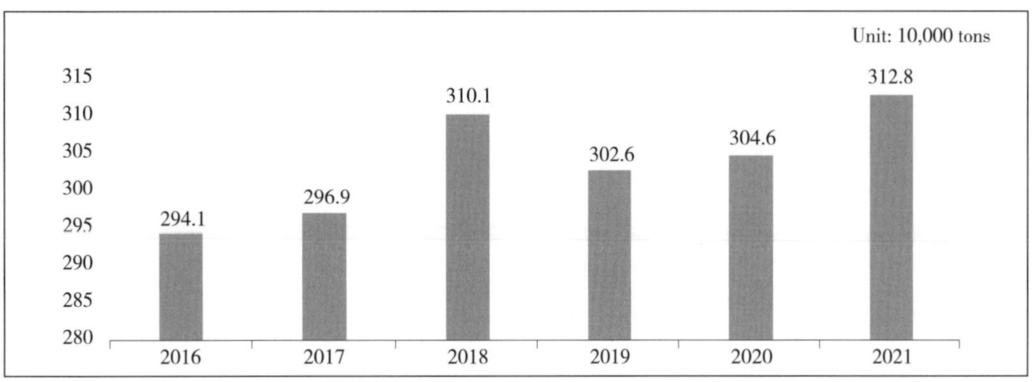

The forestry, animal husbandry and fishery industries became more solid and the quality and performance was enhanced. Afforested areas on barren hills were 10,300 hectares. The annual output of meat was 504,000 tons, eggs 289,000 tons, and milk 333,000 tons. The annual output of aquatic products (excluding deep-sea fishing) was 1.013 million tons, surging 0.2% last year. The area of marine freshwater aquaculture was 37,000 hectares, increasing by 5.8% year on year; the output of far-ocean fisheries was 148,000 tons, rising by 0.7% year on year.

Development of modern and efficient agriculture was accelerated. The annual added value of modern efficient agriculture was 10.03 billion yuan, rising by 15.1% year on year. By the end of the year, 10 modern agricultural industrial parks at or above the municipal level had been established, and 15 strong industrial towns have been established. Throughout the year, 5 rural complexes, 40 agricultural green horticulture standard gardens, and 31 standardized demonstration fields have been established at municipality level and above. There were 1,005 San Pin Yi Biao agricultural products (healthy food, organic produces, and agricultural products with geographical indications), among which were 54 agricultural products with National geographical indications. The total power of agricultural machinery was 7.57 million kW with an increase of 25,000 kW over the previous year. The comprehensive mechanization rate for growing crops has reached 90.2%.

Table 2: Output and Growth Rate of Main Planting Products in 2021

Indicators	Unit	Yield	Growth（%）
Grain	10 000 tons	312.8	2.7
Summer grain	10 000 tons	143.0	7.2
Autumn grain	10 000 tons	169.8	−0.8
Oilseed	10 000 tons	33.9	−5.7
Vegetable and edible fungi	10 000 tons	661.8	0.9
Fruit	10 000 tons	119.8	2.8
Garden fruit	10 000 tons	80.5	7.4

Ⅲ. Industry and Construction

The industrial production maintained steady growth. The annual industrial added value was 388.407 billion yuan with an increase of 8.8% from the previous year. The added value of industries above designated size increased by 8.1%. By category, mining firms grew by 6.6 %, manufacturing by 8.0% and electricity, heat, gas and water production and supply by 11.0%. By key industries, the automobile manufacturing industry fell by 12.2%; the electrical machinery and equipment manufacturing industry increased by 16.4%; the petroleum, coal and other fuel processing industry increased by 18.5%; the chemical raw materials and chemical products manufacturing industry increased by 18.8%, and the general equipment manufacturing industry rose by 19.2%. The annual production and marketing rate of industrial enterprises above designated size reached 100.1%.

Table 3 : Output and Growth Rate of Main Products of Industries Above Designated Size in 2021

Description	Unit	Output	Growth (%)
Color TV sets	10 000 sets	1986.7	11.9
Of which: Smart TV	10 000 sets	1881.6	11.9
Household refrigerators	10 000 sets	888.8	8.1
Household washing machine	10 000 sets	730.8	27.0
Room air conditioners	10 000 sets	1150.4	24.9
Smart phone	10 000 sets	449.6	-10.5
Beer	10 000 KL	197.2	12.0
Rubber tire casing	10 000 tires	5033.8	2.1
Plate glass	10 000 weight cases	998.2	-0.4
Crude steel	10 000 tons	325.0	-3.0
Automobile	10 000 vehicle	21.2	-26.8
Motor train units	vehicle	503	-49.5
Urban rail vehicle	vehicle	1587	-13.6
Metal shipping containers	10 000 cu.m	2141.0	54.7

The quality and efficiency of development have been steadily improved. Profits of industries above designated size reached 57.61 billion yuan with an increase of 2.8% over the previous year. Profits of state-owned holding enterprises reached 20.43 billion yuan, soaring 27.8% from last year; profits of joint-stock enterprises reached 37.98 billion yuan, surging 15.7%, and profits of enterprises invested by foreign investors, Hong Kong, Macao, and Taiwan enterprises reached 19.40 billion yuan, down 15.9 % year on year.

Table 4 : The profit Growth Rate of Industrial Enterprises Above Designated Size in 2021

Indicators	Growth(%)
Industrial profits above designated size	2.8
State-owned holding	27.8
Shareholder businesses	15.7
Businesses invested by foreigner or by compatriots from Hong Kong , Macao and Taiwan	-15.9

Continuous progress has been made in the construction industry. There were 889 construction enterprises qualified for general contracting, realizing an added value of 121.47 billion yuan, rising by 2.0% year on year. The total output value of the construction industry was 329.73 billion yuan, up 9.9% year on year. The value of signed contracts reached 740.55 billion yuan, up 23.5% year on year.

Figure 3 : 2016–2021 Total Output Value and Growth Rate of Construction Industry

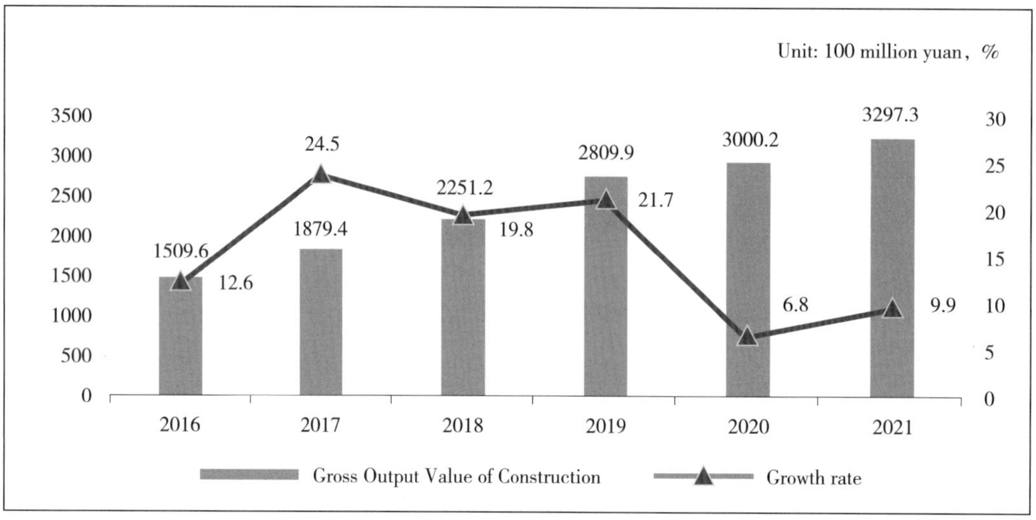

Ⅳ. Transport, Postal Service, Travel

Transportation has been recovering steadily. An annual total of 400 million tons of freight was transported by railways, highways, and waterways with an increase of 11.8% from last year. Passenger trips totaled 51.44 million, soaring 63.3% from 2020. The annual port throughput the year reached 630 million tons, up 4.3% year on year. Foreign trade throughput was 460 million tons, increasing by 3.2%. By the end of the year, there were 185 domestic routes, 19 international routes, 2 routes between Hong Kong, Macao, and Taiwan, and 25 new routes were opened in the year. The annual air passenger throughput was 16.03 million, surging 10.1% over the previous year. Air cargo throughput was 240,000 tons, soaring by 14.9 percent year on year.

Table 5. Transportation volume and growth rate completed by major transportation modes in 2021

Mode of transport	Units	Volume	Growth(%)
Passenger Volume	10, 000persons	5144	63.3
Railway	10, 000persons	1912	54.3
Highway	10, 000persons	3113	68.8
Waterway	10, 000persons	119	80.1
Freight volume	10, 000tons	39969	11.8
Railway	10, 000tons	8494	0.9
Highway	10, 000tons	28407	10.4
Waterway	10, 000tons	3068	29.8

By the end of the year, the city's rail transit operated 6 lines with a length of 284 kilometers, 128 stations, 670,000 trains, a total mileage of 21.77 million kilometers, handling 246.59 million passenger trips a year, and an average daily 680,000 passenger trips. There were 10,595 operating buses, 925 bus routes with a total length of 9,377 kilometers. The annual passenger trips were 827.65 million, and average 2.27 million daily passenger trips. There were 11,638 operating cruise taxis, with an annual 184.35 million passenger trips and an average daily passenger volume of 510,000.

By the end of the year, the number of motor vehicles in the city reached 3.54 million, an increase of 7.3% over the previous year. There were 2.93 million private cars, up 7.1 % year on year.

The postal and telecommunications developed quickly. The total amount of postal and telecommunications services was 22.43 billion yuan, a year– on–year increase of 27.8%. The total postal business was 8.80 billion yuan, soaring 28.2% from last year. The total number of telecommunication services reached 13.63 billion yuan, soaring 27.5%. 770 million express services surged 31.6% last year. There were 4.98 million fixed broadband Internet users with an increase of 7.3 percent over last year. 12.95 million mobile phone users demonstrated an increase of 3.0%. It was approved to build a national Internet backbone direct connection point and Qingdao was selected as one of the first "Gigabit cities" in China. More than 10,000 5G base stations have been built, and a total of more than 20,000 5G base stations have been established or put into operation.

The tourism market made a rapid recovery. 82.212 million visits were paid for the whole year with an increase of 30.2% over the previous year, and the total revenue of tourism was 141.1 billion yuan, soaring 37.4% year on year. There were 109 A–level tourist attractions, including one 5A– level scenic spot, twenty–five 4A–level ones, seven 3A– level ones. There were 85 starred hotels, among which were 11 five–star hotels, 22 four–star hotels and 39 three–star hotels. There were 605 travel agencies, among which 56 were engaged in overseas tourism business.

V . Fixed–asset Investment and Real Estate

Investment maintained steady growth. Investment in fixed–assets grew by 4.1 percent over the previous year. From the industry's perspective, investment in the primary industry increased by 20.7% and 25.4 % in the secondary industry, while fell by 1.8 pecent in the tertiary industry.

The investment structure was constantly optimized. Investment in the manufacturing industry grew by 24.8% year on year, contributing 115.6% to the growth in total. Investment in strategic industrial emerging industries and high–tech manufacturing increased by 22.2% and 60.5%, respectively. Investment in industrial technological upgrading increased by 29.6% and private investment by 8.3%, accounting for 59.8% of fixed asset investment.

Figure 4 : The Proportion of Investment in Three Industries in Fixed Asset Investment in 2021

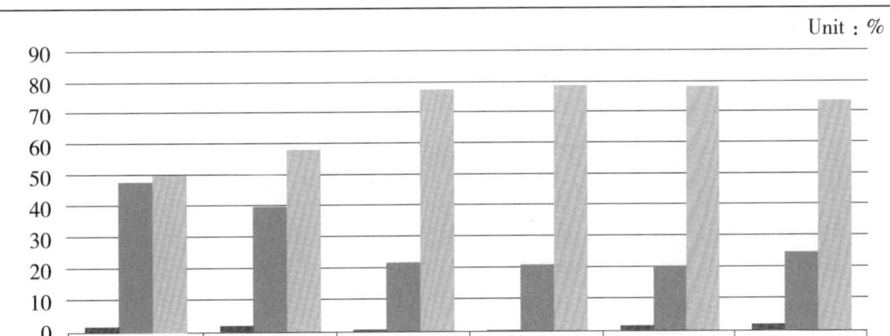

	2016	2017	2018	2019	2020	2021
Primary Industry	1.5	1.7	0.9	0.6	1.3	1.5
Secondary Industry	48.1	39.9	21.5	20.9	20.6	24.9
Tertiary Industry	50.4	58.4	77.6	78.5	78.1	73.6

Primary Industry　Secondary Industry　Tertiary Industry

The real estate market operated smoothly. The investment in real estate development was 198.18 billion yuan, down 3.1% from last year. The residential investment was 148.1 billion yuan, up 0.1%, and the sales area of commercial housing was 16.445 million square meters, with a drop of 0.5% year on year. Housing sales was 14.196 million square meters, down 0.8% from last year.

Table 6 : The City's Real Estate Development Investment, Commercial Housing Sales Area and Growth Rate in 2021

Classification	Real Estate Development Investment (100 million yuan)	Growth (%)	Commercial Housing Sales Area (ten thousand square meters)	Increase (%)
Total	1981.8	-3.1	1644.5	-0.5
Residential	1481.0	0.1	1419.6	-0.8
Office Building	123.7	-8.5	75.5	17.3
Commercial Premises	114.7	-24.6	61.0	27.2
Other	262.4	-5.9	88.4	-20.3

Construction began on 1,062 units of public rental housing, and 1,418 units have been basically completed and funds were collected to build 60,101 units for talents. By the end of the year, there were13,822 families in the city enjoying rental subsidies, and 107.217 million yuan of rental subsidies were granted in the whole year.

Ⅵ. Domestic Trade

The consumer market continued to pick up. The annual retail sales of consumer goods reached 597.54 billion yuan, rising 14.8% year on year. The retail sales of wholesale and retail reached 534.34 billion yuan with an increase of 14.1%. The retail sales of the accommodation and catering industries reached 63.20 billion yuan, up 21.6% year on year. In terms of statistics by place of operation, retail sales of urban consumer goods totaled 493.37 billion yuan, up 14.9%, while that of rural consumer goods reached 104.18 billion yuan, up 14.6% year on year.

Figure 5 : 2016-2020 Total Retail Sales of Consumer Goods and Growth Rate

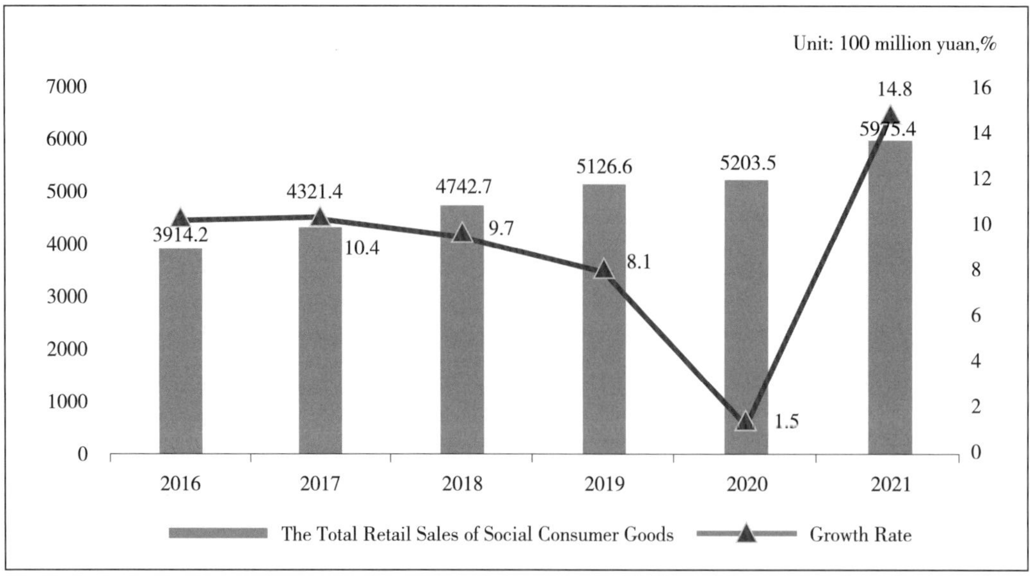

Upgrading consumer demand continued to release. Among the annual retail sales of units above the quota, the retail sales of new energy vehicles, cosmetics, gold, silver and jewelry, smart home appliances and audio and video equipment, communication equipment, smart phones , and sports and recreation items increased by 74.5%, 24.5% 62.4%, 32.5%, 159.7%, 152.1%, and 128.5 % respectively.

The e-commerce trading platform[5] achieved rapid expansion, with retail sales having amounted to a stunning $1.5 trillion, up 26.1% year on year. Online sales of wholesale and retail enterprises above designated size reached 74.27 billion yuan, up 26.9%..

Ⅶ. Foreign Economy

Opening-up at a higher level continued to expand. The city's volume of trade in goods totaled 849.84 billion yuan for the year, soaring 32.4% from 2020. Exports were worth 492.13 billion yuan, which was 27% more than that in 2020; and imports were worth 357.72 billion yuan, up 40.7% year on year. By types of economy, the import and export volume of private enterprises reached 561.38 billion yuan, up 35.6%, accounting for 66.1% of the total import and export volume. Foreign-funded enterprises[6] achieved 173.53 billion yuan of import and export, up 18.0%. Imports and exports of state-owned enterprises reached 103.97 billion yuan, up 49.7%. In terms of product structure, the export of mechanical and electrical products reached 234.51 billion yuan, up 29.8%, accounting for 47.7% of the total export value of the city. The export of mechanical equipment, electrical appliances and electronic products and conveyance increased 35.2%, 31.1% and 60.0% respectively. In terms of trade market, the import and export to the top three trade markets, ASEAN, the United States, and the European Union, were 135.37, 99.80 and 98.87 billion yuan respectively, up 43.1%, 28.4% and 19.1% respectively, accounting for 15.9%, 11.7% and 11.6% of the total import and export value of the city respectively. Imports and exports to countries along the Belt and Road reached 264.0 billion yuan, up 44.8%, accounting for 31.1% of the city's total import and export value. Imports and exports to other RCEP members reached 319.65 billion yuan, up 35.4%, accounting for 37.6% of the city's total import and export value. Imports and exports to SCO member states reached 49.99 billion yuan, up 34.3% and accounting for 5.9% of the city´s total import and export value.

Figure 6 : 2016–2020 total import and Export Volume and Growth R ate of Foreign Trade Goods

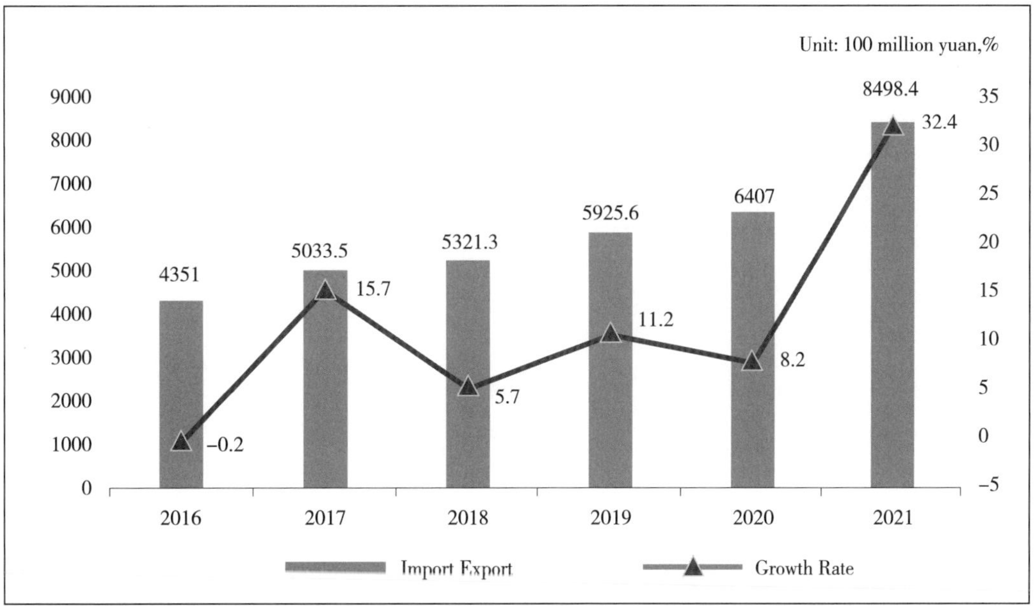

Table 7: Imports and Exports of Major Commodities in the City i n 2020

Project	Import & Export		Export		Import	
	Amount (100 million yuan)	Growth (%)	Amount (100 million yuan)	Growth (%)	Amount (100 million yuan)	Growth (%)
Textile and Apparel	593.1	10.4	571.3	10.8	21.8	1.5
Agricultural products	1056.4	9.2	370.8	-5.8	685.6	19.5
Electronics	2967.0	31.5	2345.1	29.8	621.9	38.5
High-tech products	759.2	39.4	393.7	24.9	365.4	59.4

Table 8 : Import and Export Volume and Growth Rate of Goods to Major Countries and Regions in 2021

Country (Region)	Export Amount (100 million USD)	Growth (%)	Import Amount (100 million USD)	Growth (%)
Asia	358.2	36.4	263.7	69.1
Hong Kong, China	36.0	75.7	0.6	-17.7
Taiwan, China	7.3	31.7	20.3	74.5
Japan	71.0	19.4	24.2	25.7
Korea	67.3	46.1	44.6	41.6
ASEAN	98.2	30.1	111.4	80.3
South Asia	32.2	48.8	10.5	32.8
Middle East	39.4	33.6	45.2	145.9
Africa	36.6	51.6	29.3	42.2
South Africa	6.6	54.0	3.5	18.0
Europe	155.1	36.3	73.1	20.9
EU	105.9	28.0	47.2	26.4
Germany	23.3	29.5	12.6	0.2
France	9.6	16.6	4.4	20.4
Italy	10.1	35.4	3.9	44.0
CIS and Eastern Europe	40.1	82.9	18.0	6.2
Russia	22.5	119.7	13.7	-2.7
South America	25.0	45.4	83.5	25.2
Brazil	8.8	42.0	64.8	27.9
North America	135.6	30.3	41.3	46.1
USA	119.9	32.6	34.5	55.8
Canada	15.6	15.1	6.3	12.1
Oceania	21.5	28.2	58.9	79.0
Australia	16.6	18.6	51.3	82.9

Note : This table is not full caliber.

The amount of foreign investment utilized rose steadily and qualitatively. There were 908 new foreign–invested enterprises, up 4.4% year on year. The contracted foreign investment was US$21.43 billion, up 20.1%. The city saw foreign capital in actual use growing by 5.4 percent year–on–year, to US $6.17 billion.

International cooperation progressed smoothly. The annual total volume of foreign trade of Qingdao port was 1516.74 billion yuan, up 29.6% year on year. The exports were worth 855.06 billion yuan, up 29.3%; the imports were 661.68 billion yuan, rising by 30.0%. There were 43 new projects of the city's foreign contracted engineering business, and the newly signed contracts were worth US $ 3.12 billion, 10.3% less than the previous year. And the turnover reached US $3.02 billion, an increase of 4.8% over the previous year. In the business of overseas labor service cooperation, 11,806 labor personnel of various types were dispatched. Eleven new China–Europe freight train lines were added, and 621 China–Europe Railway Express were put into operation, soaring 54.9% from last year.

The Belt and Road initiative has enjoyed integrated development. For the year, the city of Qingdao saw 15 projects invested by enterprises in countries and regions along the Belt and Road. The agreed investment from China was 1.22 billion US dollars with an increase of 213.0% over the previous year. China's actual investment amounted to US $330 million, up 174.6% year on year.

Ⅷ. Finance

Solid fiscal operations were ensured. The total fiscal revenue for the year was 429.84 billion yuan, and the revenue in the general public budget was 136.83 billion yuan, rising by 9.1% over the previous year. Tax revenue totaled 101.69 billion yuan, up 13.1% and accounting for 74.3% of the total revenue in the general public budget, up 2.6% year on year. Expenditures in the general public budget for the year was 170.57 billion yuan, rising by 7.6% than 2020. Expenditure on general public services was 19.92 billion yuan, down 0.1%; 30.88 billion yuan for education, up 7.0%; 5.13 billion yuan for science and technology, up 9.5%; 24.31 billion yuan for social security and employment, up 9.0%. The expenditure on community affairs in urban and rural areas was 24.38 billion yuan, up 3.0% year on year. The annual tax revenue of the taxation system (including collection by customs) was 263.65 billion yuan, an increase of 18.8% over the previous year, including 199.44 billion yuan of domestic tax revenue, up 16.7% year on year.

The financial market developed healthily. Shandong Gangxin Futures opened for business. By the end of the year, the balance of domestic and foreign currency deposits in financial institutions was 2.23749 trillion yuan, an increase of 186.77 billion yuan from the beginning of the year, of which the balance of RMB deposits was 2.15823 trillion yuan, an increase of 176.05 billion yuan from the beginning of the year. The balance of domestic and foreign currency loans was 2.40891 trillion yuan, an increase of 302.43 billion yuan from the beginning of the year, of which the balance of RMB loans was 2.32535 trillion yuan, an increase of 304.25 billion yuan from the beginning of the year. The insurance industry achieved a total of 46.19 billion yuan in premium income[7], rising by 6.2% from the previous year. The premium income of life insurance companies was 30.55 billion yuan, up 5.8%; the premium income of property insurance companies was 15.64 billion yuan, up 7.0% year on year. For the year, the turnover of securities branches was 7.09018 trillion yuan, an increase of 20.7% over the previous year; the turnover of corporate securities reached 6.5946 trillion yuan, soaring by 50.9%. The year 2021 saw 14 domestic listed companies newly added, bringing the number of domestic listed companies to 58. There were 441 private fund managers registered with the Asset Management Association of China, with a fund scale of 163.94 billion yuan, up 57.7% from a year earlier. The city's non–performing loan ratio fell to 1.08%, down 0.2 percentage points from the beginning of the year.

Ⅸ. Science and Technology and Education

The drive for innovation has increased significantly. The National High–end Intelligent Home Appliance Innovation Center was approved for construction. The Marine Research Center of Chinese Academy of Sciences, China Academy of Ocean Engineering (Qingdao) were put into operation. The supercomputing upgrading project of the Ocean Pilot National Laboratory was put into operation. The first high–speed maglev transportation system of CRRC Sifang in the world, with a speed of 600 kilometers per hour, rolled off the assembly line. Eight new technology innovation centers above the provincial level have been built, bringing the total number to 24. The total number of high-tech enterprises reached 5,554, an increase of 1,158 from the last year, and 6,306 national technology-based small and medium-sized enterprises entered the database. 50 national outstanding "little giant" enterprises were newly cultivated, bringing the total to 97. A total of 13 companies have been selected as the top 500 global unicorn companies. There are 12 national intellectual property demonstration enterprises, 107 national intellectual property advantageous enterprises, 9 national key laboratories, 10 national engineering technology research centers, and 82 provincial engineering technology research centers. A total of 261 thousand talents were newly introduced, and the total number of talents exceeded 2.511 million.

Innovations continued to emerge. According to preliminary statistics, 409 important scientific and technological achievements have been made in the city, and won 102 provincial-level scientific and technological awards for Qingdao. There were 12 Natural Science Awards, 4 Technological Invention Awards, 85 Science and Technology Advancement Award), and one top award. The turnover of technology contracts was 32.01 billion yuan, up 11.7% from last year. The turnover of marine technology contracts was 3.18 billion yuan, up 12.2% year on year. There were 46,609 valid invention patents[8], an increase of 22.6% over the previous year. The number of effective invention patents per 10 thousand people was 46.28, increasing 5.28 ones over the previous year. We have applied for 1,616 PCT international patents.

Figure 7: Number and Growth rate of high-tech enterprises from 2016-2021

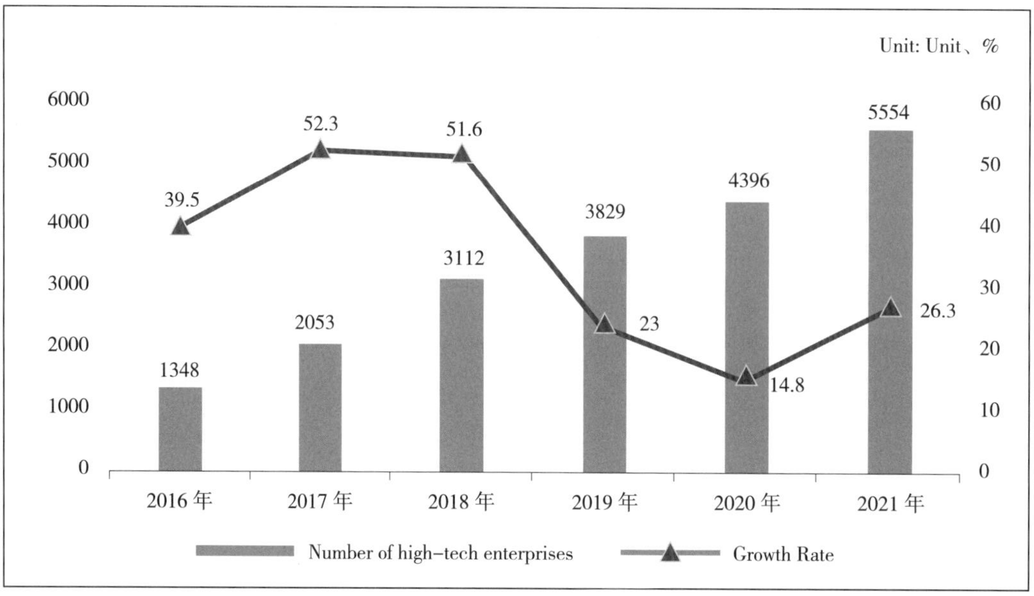

Continuous progress was made in education. Over the year, 104 primary and secondary schools and kindergartens in total were newly built, renovated or expanded. After-school services in compulsory education schools benefited 635,000 students. By the end of the year, there were 29 colleges and universities (including private colleges) of various types in Qingdao. There were 14 general colleges and universities. Throughout the year, 21,000 graduate students were enrolled, 62,000 graduate students were in school, and 14,000 students graduated (excluding postgraduates in the Research Institutes in Qingdao). In 2021, 115,000 undergraduate students enrolled in colleges and universities, with a total of 395,000 students in schools and 100,000 graduates; 27,000 students enrolled in secondary vocational education, with a total of 90,000 students in schools and 25,000 graduates; 53,000 students enrolled in regular high schools with a total of 152,000 students in schools, 38,000graduates; 93,000 students enrolled in junior high schools, with a total of 294,000 students in schools, and 85,000 graduates; 118,000 students enrolled in ordinary primary schools, with a total of 631,000 students in schools and 93,000 graduates; 500 enrolled in special education, with a total of 2,500 students in schools and 3,000 graduates; and 368,000 kids were in kindergartens.

Figure 8 : The Number of Students Enrolled by Various Schools in 2016–2021

Unit: Ten Thousand people

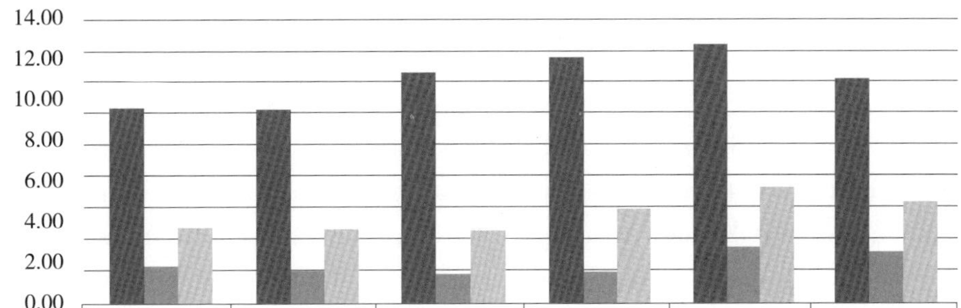

	2016	2017	2018	2019	2020	2021
Colleges and Universities	10.05	9.90	11.82	12.64	13.22	11.53
Secondary Vocational Schools	1.99	1.80	1.59	1.70	2.97	2.72
Normal High School	3.97	3.96	3.83	4.94	6.03	5.28

Colleges and Universities　Secondary Vocational Schools　Normal High School

X . Culture, Health and Sports

The cultural sector flourished. Cultural activities, such as China Opera Festival and Qingdao International Film and Television Expo have been successfully held. The Naval Museum opened, and the National Maritime Archaeology Museum (Qingdao) was approved for construction. By the end of the year, there have been 118 theaters, 150 cultural centers (stations), 108 museums, 14 public libraries, 8 state–owned art troupes, 6 radio stations with 11 programs, and 6 TV stations with 17 programs. There were 12 archives in the city.

The city's capability of medical care and health services was continuously enhanced. Peking University People's Hospital (Qingdao), and the municipal public health emergency hospital were put into use. By the end of the year, the city′s total of health institutions (including village clinics) was 4,587 with 449 hospital institutes, 41 centers for disease control and prevention, 12 maternal and child health care institutions, and 3,704 outpatient departments (institutes), clinics, health clinics, infirmaries. There were 96,700 health technicians of all kinds, among whom were 39.8 thousand doctors. The city had 67,900 medical beds, including 65,200 ones in hospitals. The capacity of normal epidemic prevention and control has been greatly improved and the systematic cooperation between departments, the cross–regional linkage working mechanism of epidemic control and tracing have been established with a total of 4,838 people in 491 epidemic control teams; two national public testing laboratories and three urban testing bases have been built. There are 83 nucleic acid testing institutions, with a daily testing capacity of 508,000 people. 43 general fever clinics and 5 fever clinics specially for all people entering China, and 184 sentinel fever clinics were set up.

Sports boomed vigorously. Throughout the year, 40 new sports parks, cage–style multi–purpose sports fields, and community fitness and health centers were built, and 220 fitness facilities were renovated or newly built. The 14th National Student Games was successfully hosted. 11 athletes from Qingdao participated in the Tokyo Olympic Games on behalf of the country. Chen Mengyong won 2 gold medals, and achieved the feat of Qingdao athletes winning gold in four consecutive Olympic Games; 190 athletes represented Shandong and participated in the 14th National Games and won 15 gold, 18 silver and 15 bronze medals. By the end of the year, Qingdao had one key sports school with 1,150 students and 10 amateur sports schools with 1,810 students.

Ⅺ. Urban Construction

Urban and rural environmental quality continued to improve. The third phase of the planning for metro construction was approved, and metro line 1 has been completed and put into operation. The new airport high-speed connections opened, and the highway connecting Ming village with Dong Jia Kou has been under construction. The Guanlu reservoir project was launched. The efforts to build national civilized demonstration city deepened, and the city became more livable and appropriate for business and industry. The project of protecting and renewal of historical city sites, such as Zhongshan road, Taidong pedestrian street, the Cruise Home port, was accelerated. By the end of the year, the city's built-up area was 964.39 square kilometers. In 2021, 216 old residential areas and 14,000 housing in rundown areas were renovated. Efforts were made to optimize the urban traffic environment; the section between Huanwan Road and Changsha Road interchange and the east extension section of Taiyuan Road were completed and opened to traffic; 53 municipal roads were renovated and upgraded, and more than 30 unconnected roads were opened. More than 17,000 public parking spaces were added, and 360 parking lots of government and public institutions were opened to the public. Solid progress was made in rural development. 10 municipal-level models for beautiful villages, 10 demonstration sites have been completed. 604 dilapidated houses in rural areas were renovated.

Ⅻ. Energy, Environment and Safety Production

The energy consumption structure was gradually improved. The electricity consumption in Qingdao totaled 55.27 billion kWh, up 16.0% year on year, of which 29.80 billion kWh was consumed by industry, up 15.1%; 14.38 billion kWh by the service sector, up 21.5%; 9.13 billion kWh by urban and rural residents, up 12.2%. The comprehensive energy consumption of industrial enterprises above designated size was 15.919 million tons of standard coal, up 12.2% year on year. Coal consumption increased by 2.0%, oil consumption by 13.2% and natural gas consumption by 26.6% from last year.

Figure 9 : The Electricity Consumption and Growth Rate of the Whole Society from 2016 to 2021

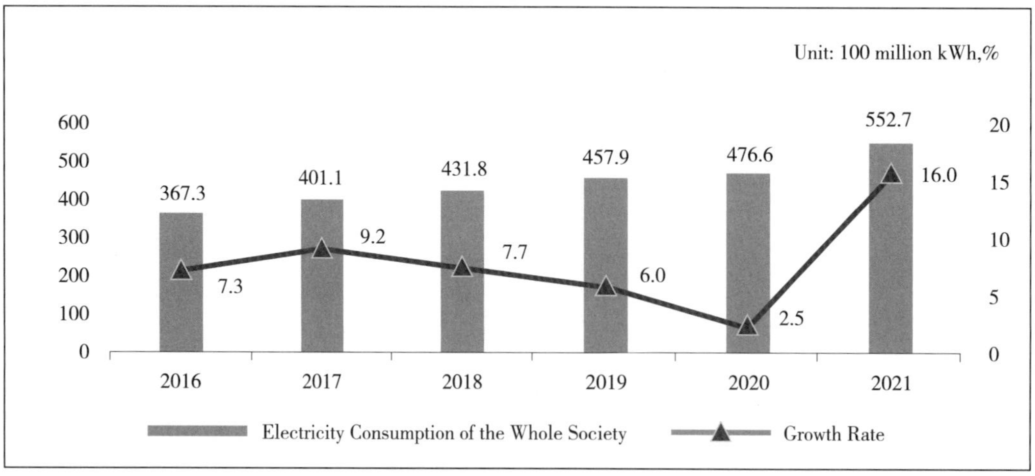

Energy production became more low-carbon and cleaner. The annual energy output was 28.857 million tons of standard coal, an increase of 11.5% over the previous year. The crude oil processing volume was 14.735 million tons, an increase of 10.0%. Gasoline production reached 4.358 million tons, up 17.5%. The production of diesel oil was 3.553 million tons, up 7.1% year on year. The power generation reached 18.79 billion kWh, up 4.9% year on year. New energy generated 3.33 billion kWh in total, up 22.1% year on year, accounting for 17.7% of the city's total power generation. Among them, the wind power generation increased by 47.1%, and the waste incineration power generation increased by 12.7%.

Ecological and environmental protection continued to be strengthened. The largest invasion of Enteromorpha prolifera was successfully handled. The average annual temperature was 13.9℃ , and the average annual precipitation was 826.3 mm. The number of days with good air quality reached 310, accounting for 84.9%. The annual environmental noise average was 57.0 dB in the urban area, and the noise average was 68.6 dB in the urban traffic trunk line. The annual average values of the main pollutant in fine particulate matter (PM2.5), sulfur dioxide and nitrogen oxide were 28, 8 and 30 micrograms cubic meters, respectively. Compared with the previous year, the index of PM2.5 was improved by 12.5%, sulfur dioxide remained the same, and nitrogen oxide improved by 3.2%. The air quality fully met the second-class national standards. The water quality of all 20 national-level and provincial-level surface water examination sections reached the standard, and the proportion of coastal areas with good water quality reached 99%.

The situation of workplace safety was stable. A total of 215 workplace accidents[9] occurred in the city, resulting in 129 deaths, with a decrease of 1.4% and 3.7% respectively. Workplace accident mortality rate of 100-million-yuan GDP was 0.0091. and the mortality rate of workplace accidents was 0.63 for 100,000 employees of industrial, mining, and commercial enterprises.

XIII. People's Livelihood and Social Security

People's quality of life has been steadily improved. The annual per capita disposable income of the city's residents[10] was 51,223 yuan, an increase of 8.6% over the previous year. In terms of habitual residence, the per capita disposable income of urban residents was 60,239 yuan, up 7.8% year on year. The per capita disposable income of rural residents was 26,125 yuan, up 10.4%. The per capita consumption expenditure of urban residents was 32,878 yuan, an increase of 8.5% over the previous year, and the Engel coefficient was 28.0%. In terms of habitual residence, the per capita consumption expenditure of rural residents was 17,021 yuan, up 12.4%. According to a sample survey, by the end of the year, the per capita housing floor space of urban residents was 32.1 square meters, and that of rural residents was 37.4 square meters.

Table 9 : The Composition of Per Capita Disposable Income of Urban and Rural Residents in 2021

Description of indicators	Residents		Urban Residents		Rural Residents	
	Absolute Value (yuan)	Growth (%)	Absolute Value (yuan)	Growth (%)	Absolute Value (yuan)	Growth (%)
Disposable income	51223	8.6	60239	7.8	26125	10.4
Salary income	30491	8.6	36222	7.7	14536	10.5
Operating net income	9701	10.0	9416	11.1	10495	8.0
Property net income	4319	7.8	5706	6.4	458	25.6
Transfer net income	6712	7.4	8895	5.6	636	51.1

Table 10 : Per Capita Consumption Expenditure of Urban and Rural Residents in 2021

Description of indicators	Residents		Urban Residents		Rural Residents	
	Absolute Value (yuan)	Growth (%)	Absolute Value (yuan)	Growth (%)	Absolute Value (yuan)	Growth (%)
Expenditures	32878	8.5	38574	7.3	17021	12.4
Food, Tobacco and Liquor	9204	8.0	10727	7.0	4965	10.9
Clothing	2973	9.9	3596	8.8	1237	12.8
Residence	7707	7.5	9152	6.1	3685	12.7
Supplies and Services	2192	9.7	2571	8.7	1138	12.5
Transportation and Communication	4873	8.8	5556	7.8	2972	11.8
Education, Culture and Recreation	3363	11.7	3972	10.1	1668	18.1
Medical Care	1789	6.5	2079	5.2	980	11.4
Other supplies and services	777	6.5	920	5.0	377	12.2

Table 11 : Ownership of Main Durable Consumer Goods Per 100 Households in 2021

Description of indicators	Unit	Quantity		
		Residents	Urban Residents	Rural Residents
Household automobiles	vehicle	64	67	55
Motorcycles	vehicle	20	10	46
Refrigerators	set	108	108	109
Washing machines	set	100	103	92
Water heaters	set	98	99	95
Air-conditioners	set	122	129	101
Color TV	set	103	104	101
Computers	set	66	72	49
Mobile telephones	set	245	245	244

Social security has been better improved. By the end of the year, the number of people with minimum living allowance in urban and rural area was 83 thousand, and the minimum living allowance for urban and rural residents was 700 million yuan. A total of 240 million yuan was spent to support 12,000 people in extreme poverty in both urban and rural areas. The number of urban and rural workers participating in basic old-age insurance reached 3.260 million. The number of urban workers participating in old-age, medical, unemployment insurance and work-related injury insurance reached 7.829, 9.19, 2.713 and 3.150 million respectively. We provided

31,000 beds for the elderly care, and basically realized full coverage of home-based community elderly care services in both urban and rural areas. 940 million yuan was provided to 95 thousand people in need, and medical expenses of 4.612 billion yuan were reimbursed to 74,900 seriously sick people.

Figure 10 : 2016–2020 Urban Employee Basic Pension Insurance Participation and Payment

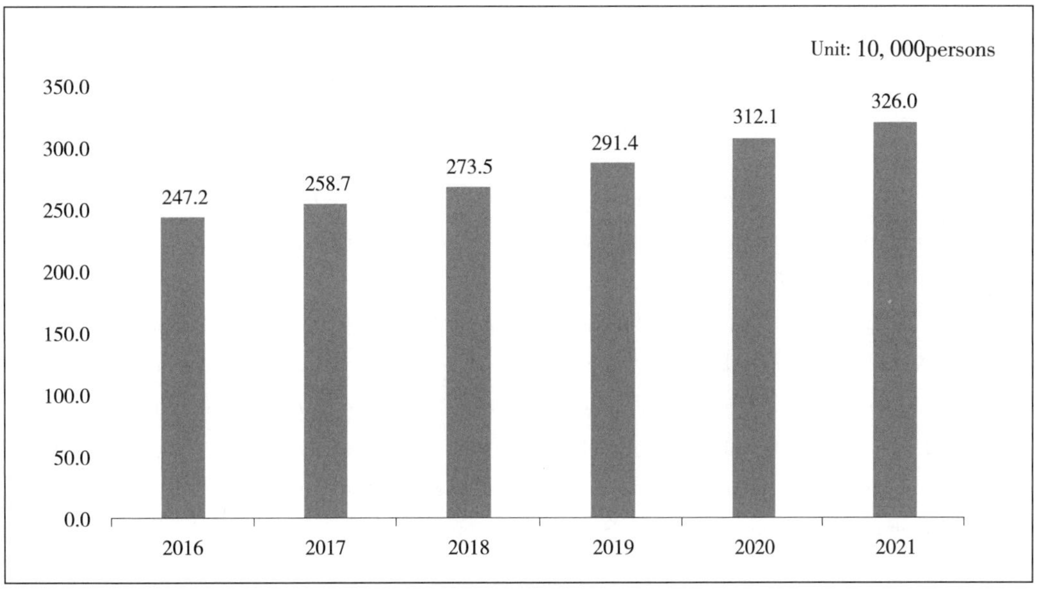

Notes :

[1] The data in this bulletin are all preliminary statistics, and some data may not be equal to the total and sub-total due to rounding.

[2] The city's gross domestic product and the absolute number of added value of various industries are calculated at current prices, and the growth rate is calculated at comparable prices.

[3] The two-year average growth rate refers to the growth rate calculated using the geometric mean method based on the same period in 2019.

[4] Industrial enterprises above designated size are enterprises with annual main business income of 20 million yuan and above.

[5] The statistical scope of e-commerce trading platforms includes industries above designated size, qualified construction industries, wholesale and retail industries above designated size, accommodation and catering industries above designated size, all real estate development and operation industries with development and operation activities, and. E-commerce transaction platforms owned by services industrial legal entities above designated size, and other e-commerce transaction platforms with an annual transaction volume of 10 million yuan or more.

[6] Three kinds of foreign-funded enterprises refer to three types of foreign-invested enterprises established in China: Sino-foreign joint ventures, Sino-foreign cooperative ventures, and exclusively foreign-owned enterprises.

[7] Because some insurance institutions are in the process of risk disposal, the insurance industry-related data do not include those of these institutions for the time being.

[8] The data related to valid invention patents and PCT international patents are from January to November. PCT refers to the

Patent Cooperation Treaty, which is an international cooperation treaty in the field of patents.

[9] The statistical scope of the number of various workplace accidents and the number of fatalities includes accidents in agriculture, forestry, husbandry and fishery, mining, commerce and manufacturing, construction, transportation and other industries.

[10] The growth of per capita disposable income of residents over the previous year refers to the nominal growth rate, and the calculation method is: (per capita disposable income of residents in the current year/per capita disposable income of residents in the previous year−1) ×100%; the actual growth rate of per capita disposable income of residents = (per capita disposable income of residents in the current year/per capita disposable income of residents in the previous year/consumer price index for the same period −1) ×100%.

Source: The fiscal data in this bulletin comes from Qingdao Municipal Finance Bureau; the tax data come from the Qingdao Tax Service, State Taxation Bureau; the data on talents, registered unemployment rate, and social security are from the Qingdao Municipal Human Resources and Social Security Bureau; the bank data come from the People's Bank of China, Qingdao Central sub-branch; securities insurance data come from Qingdao Supervision Bureau of China Securities Regulatory Commission and Qingdao Supervision Bureau of China Banking and Insurance Regulatory Commission; aquatic product data come from Qingdao Municipal Ocean Development Bureau; forestry data come from Qingdao Municipal Gardening and Forestry Bureau; agricultural machinery and other data come from Qingdao Municipal Bureau of Agriculture and Rural Affairs; transportation data come from Qingdao Municipal Transportation Bureau; postal data come from Qingdao Municipal Postal Administration; fixed telephone, broadband, mobile phone and other data come from Qingdao Municipal Communications Administration; data on import and export , foreign investment, foreign contracted projects, and foreign labor service cooperation come from Qingdao Municipal Bureau of Commerce; tourism data come from Qingdao Municipal Culture and Tourism Bureau; educational data come from Qingdao Municipal Education Bureau; scientific and technological data come from Qingdao Municipal Science and Technology Bureau; market entities, patents and other data come From Qingdao Municipal Market Regulation Bureau; data on subsistence allowances come from Qingdao Civil Affairs Bureau; sports data from Qingdao Sports Bureau; health data come from Qingdao Municipal Health Commission; environmental data from Qingdao Municipal Bureau of Ecology and Environment; electricity consumption data come from Qingdao Power Supply Company; meteorological data come from Qingdao Meteorological Bureau; safety production data come from Qingdao Emergency Management Bureau; urban construction data come from Qingdao Housing and Urban-Rural Development Bureau; car ownership data from Qingdao Public Security Bureau; food data, animal husbandry data, residents' life data Data and price data are from the National Bureau of Statistics Qingdao Survey Team; other data are from the Qingdao Municipal Bureau of Statistics.

综 合 1

GENERAL SURVEY

简要说明

一、本篇资料的主要内容

本篇资料是对我市行政区划、气象情况、分行业法人单位数、各部门机构数和国民经济、社会发展的综合反映，主要包括行政区划、气象情况、分行业法人单位数、各部门机构数、国民经济主要比例关系、国民经济和社会发展主要指标占全国全省比重、国民经济和社会发展主要指标及其增长速度等资料。

二、本篇资料的来源

1.“行政区划”主要包括2021年底各区（市）街道办事处（乡镇）、社区居委会（村民委员会）区划资料，数据来源于市民政局。

2.“气象情况”包括分区市、市区分月气象资料，数据来源于市气象局。

3.“全市生产总值”来源于国民经济核算统计报表，由市统计局国民经济核算处整理提供。

4. 国民经济和社会发展综合部分来源于本年鉴各篇章中的资料，由市统计局国民经济综合统计处加工整理。

Brief Introduction

Ⅰ. Main Content

The information in this article is a comprehensive reflection of Qingdao's administrative divisions, meteorological conditions, the number of legal entities by industry, the number of various departments and institutions, and the national economic and social development, including administrative divisions, meteorological conditions, the number of legal entities by industry, the number of agencies, the main proportions of the national economy, the proportion of the main indicators of national economic and social development in the province, the main indicators of national economic and social development and their increase speed and other information.

Ⅱ. Source of Data

1. "Administrative divisions" mainly include the division data of district (city) sub-district offices (townships) and community neighborhood committees (village committees) at the end of 2021. The data comes from Qingdao Civil Affairs Bureau.

2. "Meteorological conditions" includes monthly meteorological data of district cities and cities, and the data comes from Qingdao Meteorological Bureau.

3. The "Gross Product of the City" comes from the national economic accounting statistical report, which is compiled and provided by the National Economic Accounting Office of Qingdao Statistics Bureau.

4. The comprehensive part of the national economy and social development is derived from the data in each chapter of this yearbook, processed and compiled by the National Economic Comprehensive Statistics Division of Qingdao Bureau of Statistics.

1-1 行政区划(2021年底)
ADMINISTRATIVE DIVISION (END OF 2021)

单位：个（unit）

市区名称	Region	街道办事处 Subdistrict Offices	社区居委会 Community Residents' Committees	镇 Town	村民委员会 Villagers' Committees
全　市	**Whole Municipality**	**108**	**1175**	**36**	**896**
市南区	Shinan District	14	50		
市北区	Shibei District	29	137		
李沧区	Licang District	11	123		
崂山区	Laoshan District	5	98		69
黄岛区	Huangdao District	14	231	8	145
城阳区	Chengyang District	8	264		17
即墨区	Jimo District	11	60	4	136
胶州市	Jiaozhou	8	85	4	120
平度市	Pingdu	5	59	12	298
莱西市	Laixi	3	68	8	111

1-2 气象情况(2021 年)
METEOROLOGY (2021)

市区名称	Region	平均气温（摄氏度）Average Temperature（℃）	极端气温 Extreme Temperature (centigrade)		降水量（毫米/年）Precipitation (millimeter/year)	日照时数（小时/年）Sunshine Hours (hour/year)	平均气压（百帕）Average Atmospheric Pressure（100 pa）
			最高（摄氏度）Maximum（℃）	最低（摄氏度）Minimum（℃）			
市　区	Urban Area	14.3	34.3	−15.9	847.0	2212.9	1007.6
崂山区	Laoshan District	14.1	33.1	−16.9	939.1	2245.6	1010.2
黄岛区	Huangdao District	13.9	34.2	−17.3	929.1	2139.4	1016.1
即墨区	Jimo District	14.0	35.4	−18.0	776.1	2159.4	1011.1
胶州市	Jiaozhou	14.1	34.8	−18.1	698.1	2296.3	1006.6
平度市	Pingdu	13.7	35.5	−18.1	794.3	2099.4	1009.1
莱西市	Laixi	13.1	34.7	−14.4	800.5	2222.4	1007.5

注：以上为 7 个国家基准站或基本站。
Note：These are 7 national reference or base stations.

1-3 市区分月气象情况(2021 年)
MONTHLY METEOROLOGY OF URBAN AREA (2021)

月　份	Month	平均气温（摄氏度）Average Temperature（℃）	降水量（毫米）Precipitation (millimeter)	日照时数（小时）Sunshine Hours (hour)
一月	Jan.	0.6	2.3	156.5
二月	Feb.	4.9	24.9	166.2
三月	Mar.	8.3	35.4	212.9
四月	Apr.	12.4	62.2	199.0
五月	May.	16.9	55.2	241.0
六月	Jun.	21.8	28.5	163.6
七月	Jul.	25.3	203.1	175.1
八月	Aug.	25.7	168.7	186.9
九月	Sep.	23.3	159.3	169.7
十月	Oct.	16.7	50.6	164.3
十一月	Nov.	11.2	55.8	186.3
十二月	Dec.	4.7	1.0	191.4
全　年	Annual Total	14.3	847.0	2212.9

1-4 各部门机构数 (2021 年底)
GRASS-ROOTS UNITS IN VARIOUS SECTORS (END OF 2021)

项目	Item	单位	Unit	机构数 Grass-roots Units
农村基层单位	**Rural Grass-roots Units**			
镇政府	Town Governments	个	unit	36
乡村户数	Number of Rural Households	万户	10 000 households	122.8
规模以上工业企业单位	**Industrial enterprises above designated size**	**个**	**unit**	**4280**
#国有企业	State-owned Enterprises	个	unit	226
集体企业	Collective-owned Enterprises	个	unit	4
外商及港澳台商投资企业	Enterprises with Funds from Hong Kong, Macao, Taiwan and Foreign Countries	个	unit	817
交通运输业	**Transportation**			
铁路	Railway	个	unit	2
公路	Highway	个	unit	319
水运	Waterway	个	unit	21
邮电业	**Rostal and Telecommunication Services**			
邮电局所	Post Offices	处	unit	267
电信营业网点（自有）	Telecom business outlets	个	unit	397
建筑业企业	**Construction Enterprises**	**个**	**unit**	**889**
国有企业	State-owned Enterprises	个	unit	19
集体企业	Collective-owned Enterprises	个	unit	7
其他	Others	个	unit	863
规模以上服务业企业单位	**Service industry enterprises above designated size**	**个**	**unit**	**2513**
内资企业	Domestic Funded Enterprises	个	unit	2384
港、澳、台商投资企业	Enterprises with Funds from Hong Kong, Macao and Taiwan	个	unit	48
外商投资企业	Foreign Funded Enterprises	个	unit	81
批发和零售业、住宿和餐饮业	**Wholesale & Retail Trades, Hotels and Catering Services**			
限额以上批发业	Wholesale Trade above Designated Size	个	unit	2994
限额以上零售业	Retail Trade above Designated Size	个	unit	830
限额以上住宿业	Hotel above Designated Size	个	unit	332
限额以上餐饮业	Catering Service above Designated Size	个	unit	433

注：该表邮政局（所）为中国邮政集团公司青岛市分公司提供；电信营业网点（自有）由三大电信运营商提供数据汇总。

Note: In the tables, the post offices are provided by Qingdao Branch of China Post Group Corporation; and the Telecom business outlets (self-owned) are from the data summary provided by the three major telecom operators.

1-4 续表
Continued

项目	Item	单位	Unit	机构数 Grass-roots Units
教育事业	**Education**			
普通高等学校	Regular Institutions of Higher Education	所	unit	27
普通中等职业学校	Regular Secondary Vocational School	所	unit	52
普通中学	Regular Secondary Schools	所	unit	345
普通小学	Regular Primary Schools	所	unit	676
幼儿园	Kindergartens	所	unit	2518
文化及相关产业	**Culture and Related Industry**			
公共图书馆	Public Libraries	个	unit	11
卫生事业	**Public Health**			
# 医院	Hospitals	个	unit	449
民政行政单位	**Civil Affairs Departments**			
# 提供住宿的社会服务机构	Social service agencies that provide accommodation	个	unit	301

1-5 按行业分法人单位数
NUMBER OF CORPORATE UNITS BY SECTOR

单位：个（unit）

行 业	Sector	2021 年
总 计	**Total**	**528232**
农、林、牧、渔业	Agriculture, Forestry, Animal Husbandry and Fishery	9520
采矿业	Mining	193
制造业	Manufacturing	72608
电力、热力、燃气及水生产和供应业	Electricity, heat, gas, water production and supply industry	760
建筑业	Construction	43316
批发和零售业	Wholesale and Retail Trades	173629
交通运输、仓储和邮政业	Transport, Storage and Post	21642
住宿和餐饮业	Hotels and Catering Services	8915
信息传输、软件和信息技术服务业	Information Transmission, Computer Services and Software	26048
金融业	Financial Industry	3775
房地产业	Real Estate	13613
租赁和商务服务业	Leasing and Business Services	75618
科学研究和技术服务业	Scientific Research and Technical Services	34478
水利、环境和公共设施管理业	Management of Water, Conservancy Environment and Public Facilities	3799
居民服务、修理和其他服务业	Resident Services, Repairs and Other Services	10684
教育	Education	7716
卫生和社会工作	Health Social Security and Social Welfare	2852
文化、体育和娱乐业	Culture, Sports and Entertainment Industry	9920
公共管理、社会保障和社会组织	Public Administration, Social Security and Social Organization	9146

1-6 国民经济主要平均指标
AVERAGE INDICATORS ON NATIONAL ECONOMY

指　标	Indicator	单位	Unit	2000年	2005年
人口密度	Density of Population	人/平方公里	person/sq.km	664	695
每户年平均人口	Average Household Size	人	person	3.14	3.12
城镇非私营单位在岗职工年平均工资	The Average Annual Wage of Staff and Workers in the Post in Non-Private Units in Towns and Cities	元	yuan	10 072	19086
城市居民人均年可支配收入	Annual Per Capita Net Income of urban Households	元	yuan	7971	12725
农民人均年纯收入	Annual Per Capita Net Income of Rural Households	元	yuan	3534	5384
每一播亩平均粮食产量	Output of Grain Per Mu of Sowing Area	千克	kg	411	421
每亩蔬菜平均产量	Average Output of Vegetables Per Mu	千克	kg	2 735	2985
每亩茶叶平均产量	Average Output of tea Per Mu	千克	kg	8.1	16.5
每亩花生平均产量	Average Output of Peanut Per Mu	千克	kg	298	327
每亩棉花平均产量	Average Output of Cotton Per Mu	千克	kg	83	74
每台拖拉机负担耕地面积	Cultivated Area Ploughed by Per Tractor	亩/台	mu/unit	56	39
每亩耕地施用化肥量（折纯）	Chemical Fertilizer Consumption Per Mu (convert to pure amount)	千克	kg	45	52
每人平均消费品零售额	Per Capita Retail Sales of Consumer Goods	元	yuan	5965	11445
城市每天平均生活用水量	Daily Residential Consumption of Water	万吨	10 000 tons	33.33	34.35
城市每人平均公园绿地面积	Per Capita Public Green Areas	平方米	sq.m	8.50	11.82
每万人拥有医疗床位	Number of Hospital Beds Per 10000 Population	张	bed	34.5	41.3
每万人拥有医生数	Number of Doctors per 10000 Population	人	person	21.0	20.3
每万人中高等学校学生数	Students Enrollment of Institutions of Higher Education per 10000 Population	人	person	65	324
每万人中中等学校学生数	Students Enrollment of Secondary Schools per 10000 Population	人	person	704	768
每万人中小学学生数	Students Enrollment of primary Schools per 10000 Population	人	person	757	648

注：1. 自2015年开始，全市城乡住户调查统一使用一体化改革后的数据，与原数据相比，城乡居民收支指标的调查范围和口径均存较大变化。原“城市居民人均可支配收入”调整为“城镇居民人均可支配收入”；原“农民人均纯收入”调整为“农村居民人均可支配收入”。
2. 2008—2017年农作物数据为根据第三次农业普查结果核定修正后数据。

Notes：1. Since 2015, the urban and rural households investigation unified the data after the integrated reform, compared with the original data, the investigation scope and the caliber of urban and rural residents' income and expenditure indicators have changed greatly. The original “per capita disposable income of urban residents” is adjusted to be a “per capita disposable income of urban residents”. The original “per capita net income of farmers” is adjusted to “per capita disposable income of rural residents”.
2. Crop data from 2008 to 2017 are revised based on hte results of the third agricultural census.

	2010年	2011年	2012年	2013年	2014年	2015年	2016年	2017年	2018年	2019年	2020年	2021年
	677	679	682									
	3.10	3.09	3.09									
	37501	43077	49052	55363	62104	69465	76616	83539	90840	103108	116115	127228
	24380	28567	31349	34356	37346	40370	43598	47176	50817	54484	55905	60239
	9326	12370	12366	13905	15434	16730	17969	19364	20820	22573	23656	26125
	399	407	411	407	396	400	404	414	430	425	432	434
	3689	3867	3887	3957	3963	3889	3760	3931	3796	3883	3992	4046
	44	47	51	49	52	57	74	75	80	75	78	79
	306	316	326	314	305	287	294	319	321	305	321	326
	62	74	81	81	89	86	82	85	110	105	97	93
	32	31			38	38	37	36	36	36	36	31
	47	47			37	36	36	36	35	34	34	38
	24781	28932	32917	37032	41226	45309	49360	53722	57991	61862	62180	70615
	34.31	27.53	33.21	32.50	40.60	42.10	67.60	50.3	50.6	54.3	58.0	60.0
	14.58	14.58	14.60	14.60	14.60	14.60	18.60	17.4	16.3	16.9	19.0	18.0
	47.2	52.2	61.4	58.0	60.3	62.0	63.9	69.4	68.2	72.8	77.0	80.1
	23.2	23.9	28.1	31.2	32.0	33.5	34.9	38.4	42.3	45.5	47.4	47.2
	373	380	386	388	402	411.0	430.0	431.0	486.6	500.3	514.6	540.3
	701	659	635	626	614	596.0	593.0	611.0	612.5	627.8	653.3	675.5
	606	626	630	642	662	685.0	690.0	685.3	696.9	702.4	721.5	745.1

1-7　主要年份社会经济主要指标
MAJOR YEAR'S INDICATORS ON SOCIETY AND ECONOMY

指标	Indicator	单位	Unit	2000 年	2005 年
人口	**Population**				
总人口（年末）	Population at Year-end	万人	10 000 persons	706.65	740.91
男性人口	Male	万人	10 000 persons	357.74	374.03
女性人口	Female	万人	10 000 persons	348.91	366.87
市区人口	Urban Area	万人	10 000 persons	234.60	265.43
就业	**Employment**				
社会从业人员	Employment	万人	10 000 persons	436.1	467.4
#单位从业人员	Employed Persons in Units	万人	10 000 persons	118.3	224.3
经济总量	**Gross Economic Amount**				
全市生产总值（当年价）	GDP（at current price）	亿元	100 million yuan	1183.14	2576.95
第一产业增加值	Primary Industry	亿元	100 million yuan	135.81	168.06
第二产业增加值	Secondary Industry	亿元	100 million yuan	546.12	1292.49
第三产业增加值	Tertiary Industry	亿元	100 million yuan	501.21	1116.4
人均生产总值	Per Capita GDP	元	yuan	15900	31725
农林牧渔业总产值（当年价）	Gross Output Value of Farming, Forestry, Animal Husbandry and Fishery（at current price）	亿元	100 million yuan	248.33	320.51
工业总产值（当年价）	Gross Industrial Output Value（at current price）	亿元	100 million yuan	1940.83	5001.78

注：1. 单位从业人员 2004 年以前为职工人数（不含私营企业）。
2. 规模以上固定资产投资数据 2003 年以前为城镇以上统计范围。
3. 2002 年以前地方财政一般预算收支数据为地方财政收支口径。
4. 2008—2017 年农林牧渔业总产值为根据第三次农业普查结果核定修正后数据。
5. 全国第四次经济普查后，对 2000 年至 2018 年历年 GDP 数据进行了修订（以下相关表同）。

Notes：1.Before 2004, the data of employed persons in units refers to the number of staff and workers（excluding private enterprises）.
2.Before 2003, the data of investment in fixed assets above designated size refers to urban investment.
3.Before 2002, the data of general budgetary revenue and expenditure of local government finance refers to revenue and expenditure of local government finance.
4.Gross output value of farming, forestry, animal husbandry and fishery from 2008 to 2017 is revised according to the results of the third agricultural census.
5.After the fourth national economic census, the GDP data from 2000 to 2018 was revised（the following related tables are the same）.

2010年	2011年	2012年	2013年	2014年	2015年	2016年	2017年	2018年	2019年	2020年	2021年
763.64	766.36	769.56									
381.92	382.69	383.82									
381.72	383.67	385.74									
275.50	277.09	279.57									
504.9	510.8	515.5	517.5	521.3	523.7	523.5	524.3	525.3	523.6	525.6	527.71
269.4	275.9	283.2	293.7	303	309.2	315.6	321.4	330.4	146.6	147.7	147.7
5350.69	6248.48	6869.61	7508.7	8120.66	8658.57	9283.17	10136.96	10949.38	11741.31	12400.56	14136.46
261.03	288.73	305.72	332.1	341.68	356.19	357.4	367.71	386.91	409.98	425.41	470.06
2482.6	2823.7	3010.6	3225.9	3389.1	3503.4	3592.80	3849.18	4033.33	4182.76	4381.44	5070.33
2607.08	3136.06	3553.33	3950.68	4389.87	4798.98	5332.96	5920.06	6529.14	7148.57	7593.71	8596.07
62148	70945	76636	82463	87677	92157	97430	104905	112129	118978	123828	138849
480.2	534.6	567.3	610.6	627.9	612.4	669.1	697.9	737	778.1	807.1	897.1
11614.83	13277.96	15306.32	16897.18	17444.21	18019.43	17415.71	13019.73	11389.78			

1-7 续表 1
Continued

指　标	Indicator	单位	Unit	2000 年	2005 年
财政	**Government Finance**				
公共财政预算收入	Public Budget Revenue	亿元	100 million yuan	80.01	176.34
公共财政预算支出	Public Budget Expenditure	亿元	100 million yuan	87.87	203.06
规模以上固定资产投资额	**Investment in Fixed Assets above Designated Size**	亿元	**100 million yuan**	**242.68**	**1403.30**
社会消费品零售额	**Total Retail Sales of Consumer Goods**	亿元	**100 million yuan**	**421.55**	**847.97**
港口吞吐量	**Volume of Freight Handled in Ports**	万吨	**10 000 tons**	**8661**	**18727**
集装箱吞吐量	**Volume of Containers Handled**	万标箱	**Ten Thousand TEUs**	**212.0**	**630.7**
民航货邮吞吐量	**Civil Aviation Cargo and Mail Throughput**	万吨	**10 000 tons**	**3.44**	**8.91**
对外贸易	**Foreign Trade**				
外贸进出口总额	Imports and Exports（excluding central and provincial companies）	亿美元	100 million USD	108.31	304.55
#出口总额	Exports	亿美元	100 million USD	61.14	175.88
教育、卫生、文化	**Education，Public Health and Culture**				
小学在校学生数	Students Enrollment in Primary Schools	万人	10 000 persons	53.49	47.98
普通中学在校学生	Students Enrollment in Regular Secondary Schools	万人	10 000 persons	39.85	39.11

2010 年	2011 年	2012 年	2013 年	2014 年	2015 年	2016 年	2017 年	2018 年	2019 年	2020 年	2021 年
452.61	566.14	670.18	788.93	895.25	1006.32	1100.03	1157.24	1231.91	1241.74	1253.85	1368.30
532.39	658.06	765.98	1014.23	1074.71	1222.87	1352.85	1403.03	1561.23	1575.97	1584.65	1706.76
3022.48	**3502.54**	**4153.91**	**5027.86**	**5766.03**	**6555.70**	**7454.70**	**7777.09**				
1892.38	**2217.26**	**2533.16**	**2865.02**	**3218.25**	**3548.16**	**3914.19**	**4321.43**	**4742.72**	**5126.6**	**5203.5**	**5975.4**
35012	**37971**	**41465**	**45782**	**47701**	**49749**	**51463**	**51314**	**54250**	**57736**	**60459**	**63029**
1201	**1302**	**1450**	**1552**	**1658**	**1743**	**1805**	**1831**	**1932**	**2101**	**2201**	**2371**
16.37	**16.65**	**17.19**	**18.62**	**20.44**	**20.81**	**23.69**	**23.21**	**22.45**	**25.63**	**20.7**	**23.8**
561.49	712.63	732.08	779.12	798.88	702.22	4350.67（亿元）	5033.50（亿元）	5321.26（亿元）	5925.58（亿元）	6407.01（亿元）	8498.43（亿元）
333.51	400.56	408.20	419.86	457.77	453.50	2821.91（亿元）	3031.81（亿元）	3172.22（亿元）	3411.90（亿元）	3876.76（亿元）	4921.28（亿元）
46.27	47.95	49.50	49.63	51.65	53.65	54.72	55.05	56.99	58.38	60.4	63.1
38.00	37.32	36.96	36.51	36.26	35.54	35.61	37.22	38.54	40.9	43.0	44.6

1-7 续表 2
Continued

指　标	Indicator	单位	Unit	2000 年	2005 年
高等学校在校学生	Students Enrollment in Institutions of Higher Education	万人	10 000 persons	4.61	23.98
小学专任教师	Full-time Teachers in Primary Schools	万人	10 000 persons	3.17	3.17
普通中学专任教师	Full-time Teachers in Regular Secondary Schools	万人	10 000 persons	2.63	2.97
医生总数	Doctors	万人	10 000 persons	1.49	1.50
医院床位数	Hospital Beds	万张	10 000 beds	2.01	2.86
人民生活	**People's Living Conditions**				
就业人员工资总额	Total wages of Employed Persons	亿元	100 million yuan	120.4	359.5
城乡人民币储蓄存款余额	Savings Deposit of Urban and Rural Households	亿元	100 million yuan	535.32	1343.10
物价指数	**Price Indexes**				
商品零售价格指数（以 1950 年价格为 100）	Retail Price Index（1950=100）	%	%	520.5	495.0
居民消费价格指数（以 1950 年价格为 100）	Consumer Price Index（1950=100）	%	%	711.9	753.1
#食品价格指数（以 1950 年价格为 100）	Food Price Index（1950=100）	%	%	800.1	871.8

注：1. 就业人员工资总额 2005 年前统计范围为全部职工不含私营企业，2015 年及以前为在岗职工工资总额。
2. 2015 年"城乡人民币储蓄存款余额"改为"住户存款"。

Notes：1. The total wages of employees before 2005 included all employees excluding private enterprises, and the total wages of employees in 2015 and before were the total wages of employees on the job.
2. In 2015,"balance of RMB deposits in urban and rural areas" changed to "household deposits."

2010年	2011年	2012年	2013年	2014年	2015年	2016年	2017年	2018年	2019年	2020年	2021年
28.49	29.15	29.66	30.02	31.35	32.23	34.09	34.62	39.8	41.58	43.1	45.7
3.20	3.16	3.17	3.28	3.22	3.45	3.42	3.47	3.69	3.53	3.52	3.92
3.08	3.14	3.20	3.18	3.20	3.29	3.39	3.47	3.60	3.98	3.83	3.95
1.77	1.83	2.16	2.41	2.50	2.63	2.76	3.09	3.46	3.78	3.97	4.0
3.34	3.56	4.12	3.97	4.30	4.51	4.73	4.63	5.08	5.85	6.23	6.50
738.0	877.5	1044.3	1251.7	1456.0	1644.4	1852.7	2034.7	2251.7			
2912.33	3198.51	3757.60	4141	4436	5024	5326	5394	5914	6755	8031	9028
526.5	550.2	559.6	567.4	580.5	580.5	592.1	596.8	607.6	622.2	631.5	640.3
854.0	896.7	920.9	943.9	968.4	980.0	1004.5	1024.6	1046.1	1080.6	1106.5	1123.1
1194.9	1327.5	1384.6	1458.0	1522.2	1548.1	1625.5	1619.0	1669.2	1862.8	2045.4	2039.3

1-8 国民经济主要结构指标
COMPOSITION INDICATORS ON NATIONAL ECONOMY

指　标	Indicator	2000 年	2005 年	2010 年	2011 年
社会从业人员	**Employment**				
产业结构	Industrial Composition				
第一产业	Primary Industry	36.4	22.2	19.5	19.2
第二产业	Secondary Industry	33.9	41.8	41.4	41.2
第三产业	Tertiary Industry	29.7	36.0	39.1	39.6
全市生产总值	**GDP**				
产业结构	Industrial Composition				
第一产业	Primary Industry	11.5	6.5	4.9	4.6
第二产业	Secondary Industry	46.1	50.2	46.4	45.2
第三产业	Tertiary Industry	42.4	43.3	48.7	50.2
农业	**Agriculture**				
农林牧渔业产值结构	Composition of Farming, Forestry, Animal Husbandry and Fishery				
#农业	Farming	45.0	39.5	45.8	40.9
林业	Forestry	0.8	0.8	0.4	0.4
牧业	Animal Husbandry	27.9	33.4	25.5	28.1
渔业	Fishery	26.4	26.3	24.6	26.7
工业	**Industry**				
轻重工业产值结构	Composition of Output Value of Light and Heavy Industry				
轻工业	Light Industry	64.1	49.4	38.7	38.3
重工业	Heavy Industry	35.9	50.6	61.3	61.7
固定资产投资	**Investment in Fixed Assets**				
投资结构	Composition of Investment				
生产性	Productive	54.0	65.4	53.6	53.2
非生产性	Non-productive	46.0	34.6	46.4	46.8

注：2008—2017 年农业数据为根据第三次农业普查结果核定修正后数据。
Note: Agricultural data from 2008 to 2017 are revised according to the results of the third agricultural census.

2012 年	2013 年	2014 年	2015 年	2016 年	2017 年	2018 年	2019 年	2020 年	2021 年
18.8	18.8	18.4	18.1	17.8	16.9	16.2	15.7	15.6	15.6
41.0	40.6	39.0	38.6	38.0	37.8	36.4	38.3	31.9	31.9
40.2	40.6	42.6	43.3	44.2	45.3	47.4	46.0	52.5	52.5
4.5	4.4	4.2	4.1	3.9	3.6	3.5	3.5	3.4	3.3
43.8	43.0	41.7	40.5	38.7	38.0	36.9	35.6	35.3	35.9
51.7	52.6	54.1	55.4	57.4	58.4	59.6	60.9	61.3	60.8
40.0	41.7	42.1	40.3	42.5	43.0	44.7	46.3	46.2	47.1
0.4	0.4	0.4	0.4	0.4	0.4	0.5	0.6	0.6	0.5
26.6	25.5	24.8	25.0	24.2	23.8	22.1	21.5	22.3	20.5
28.8	28.0	27.7	29.6	26.6	26.2	26.1	24.9	24	25.1
39.5	39.5	38.8	39.5	39.4	37.6	34.3			
60.5	60.5	61.2	60.5	60.6	62.4	65.7			
58.4	61.65	57.08	63.16	59.81	53.64				
41.6	38.35	42.92	36.84	40.19	46.36				

1-9　平均每天主要社会经济活动

SELECTED INDICATORS ON AVERAGE DAILY SOCLAL AND ECONOMIC ACTIVITIES

指　标	Indicator	单位	Unit	2000 年	2005 年
全市生产总值	GDP	万元	10 000 yuan	32415	70601
工业总产值	Gross Industrial Output Value	万元	10 000 yuan	53174	137035
农林牧渔业总产值	Gross Output Value of Farming，Forestry，Animal Husbandry and Fishery	万元	10 000 yuan	6803	8781
主要工业产品产量	Output of Major Industrial Products				
发电量	Electricity	万千瓦时	10 000 kW・h	2489	2701
钢材	Rolled-steel	吨	ton	2558	9049
纱	Yarn	吨	ton	191	198
布	Cloth	万米	10 000 m	114	141
家用电冰箱	Refrigerator	台	unit	8523	24899
彩色电视机	Color TV set	台	unit	10395	36282
社会消费品零售总额	Total Retail Sales of Consumer Goods	万元	10 000 yuan	11549	23232
固定资产投资	Investment in Fixed Assets above Designated Size	万元	10 000 yuan	6649	38446
外贸进出口总额	Imports and Exports	万美元	10 000 USB	3707	9047
港口吞吐量	Volume of Freight Handled in Ports	万吨	10 000 tons	23.73	51.31

注：1. 固定资产投资包括城镇、农村 500 万元以上投资项目。
2. 一年按照 365 天计算。
3.2008—2017 年农林牧渔业总产值为根据第三次农业普查结果核定修正后数据。

Notes：1. Investment in fixed assets includes construction projects involving an urban or rural investment of 5 million yuan an d over.
2. A year is computed according to 365 days.
3. Gross output value of farming, forestry, animal husbandry and fishery from 2008 to 2017 is revised according to the results of the third agricultural census.

2010年	2011年	2012年	2013年	2014年	2015年	2016年	2017年	2018年	2019年	2020年	2021年
146594	171191	188208	205718	222484	237221	254333	277725	299983	321680	339741	387300
318215	363780	419351	462936	477924	493683	477143	356705	312048			
13157	14646	15541	16728	17203	16777	18331	19120	20192	21318	22112	24576
4984	4759	4787	4935	4885	4754	4805	4981	5271	4947	4725	5148
9136	9101	7525	6312	5830	3853	5243	7996	8764	9211	10663	14927
97	53	53	92	89	76	92	73	79	111	83	167
48	120	134	141	122	77	68	65	127	31	44	63
21951	19686	15754	14366	16714	23893	24170	22429	24290	20050	22521	24351
30444	31622	39452	41426	46984	37704	57855	46658	46443	43299	48626	54431
51846	60747	69402	78494	88171	97210	107238	118395	129938	140455	142562	163700
82808	95960	113806	137751	157973	179608	204238	213071				
15633	19768	20057	21346	21887	19239	119196（万元）	137904（万元）	145787（万元）	162345（万元）	175534（万元）	232834（万元）
96	104	114	125	131	136	141	141	149	158	166	173

1-10　主要指标占全国全省比重（2021 年）

PERCENTAGE OF MAIN INDICATORS TO CHINA AND SHANDONG（2021）

指　标	Indicator	单位	Unit
一、生产总值	**GDP**	**亿元**	**100 million yuan**
第一产业	Primary Industry	亿元	100 million yuan
第二产业	Secondary Industry	亿元	100 million yuan
第三产业	Tertiary Industry	亿元	100 million yuan
二、年末总人口（常住人口）	**Total Year-end Population（Resident population）**	**万人**	**10 000 persons**
三、主要工业产品产量	**Output of Major Industrial Products**		
发电量	Electricity	亿千瓦小时	100 million kW·h
房间空气调节器	Air Conditioner	万台	10 000 units
家用电冰箱	Refrigerator	万台	10 000 units
彩色电视机	Color TV Set	万台	10 000 units
钢材	Rolled-steel	万吨	10 000 tons
水泥	Cement	万吨	10 000 tons
四、主要农产品产量	**Output of Major Farm Products**		
粮食	Grain	万吨	10 000 tons
油料	Oil Plants	万吨	10 000 tons
猪牛羊禽肉类产量	Output of Pork, Beef, Mutton And Poultry	万吨	10 000 tons
水产品	Aquatic Products	万吨	10 000 tons
五、房地产开发投资	**Investment In Real Estate Development**	**亿元**	**100 million yuan**
六、货物进出口总额	**Imports and Exports**	**亿元**	**100 million yuan**
其中：出口	Export	亿元	100 million yuan
进口	Import	亿元	100 million yuan

注：1. 本表全国、全省均为公报数。
　　2. 青岛市主要工业产品产量数据为本地口径。

Notes：1. The number of the country and province in the table are obtained from the statistical report.
　　2. The output of main industrial products of qingdao are at local calibre.

全国 China	全省 Shandong	青岛市 Qingdao	青岛市占全国比重（%） Qingdao/China	青岛市占全省比重（%） Qingdao/Shandong
1143670	**83095.9**	**14136.46**	**1.24**	**17.01**
83086	6029.03	470.06	0.57	7.80
450904	33187.16	5070.33	1.12	15.28
609680	43879.71	8596.07	1.41	19.59
141260	**10170**	**1025.67**	**0.73**	**10.09**
85342.5	5808.0	187.9	0.22	3.24
21835.7	1207.8	1150.4	5.30	95.25
8992.1	888.8	888.8	9.88	100.00
18496.5	1986.7	1986.7	10.74	100.00
133666.8	10667.6	544.8	0.41	5.11
238000	16444.7	522.4	0.22	3.18
68285	5500.75	312.77	0.46	5.69
3613	286	34	0.94	11.89
8887	815.1	50.4	0.57	6.18
6693	821	101	1.51	12.30
147602	**9819.7**	**1981.8**	**1.34**	**20.18**
391009	**29304**	**8498.4**	**2.17**	**29.00**
217348	17583	4921.3	2.26	27.99
173661	11721	3577.2	2.06	30.52

1-11 主要年份全市生产总值（按当年价格计算）
MAJOR YEAR'S GROSS DOMESTIC PRODUCT (AT CURRENT PRICE)

单位：亿元（100 million yuan）

年 份 Year	全市生产总值 GDP	第一产业 Primary Industry	第二产业 Secondary Industry	#工 业 Industry	第三产业 Tertiary Industry	人均生产总值（元） Per Capita GDP (yuan)
1949	2.87	1.19	1.10		0.58	71
1952	6.74	1.76	3.25	2.95	1.73	163
1957	10.82	2.00	5.76	5.39	3.06	239
1962	9.69	1.11	4.68	4.27	3.90	205
1965	15.50	1.80	8.96	8.48	4.74	325
1970	23.23	3.15	14.46	13.86	5.62	451
1975	29.07	6.93	15.39	14.67	6.75	522
1978	38.43	8.23	20.16	19.15	10.04	663
1980	48.65	9.61	26.15	24.28	12.90	819
1985	82.28	20.06	37.37	34.03	24.84	1311
1988	142.87	30.84	69.99	63.42	42.04	2199
1990	180.77	37.00	86.36	78.94	57.41	2714
1991	205.65	40.56	98.48	89.64	66.61	3053
1992	261.35	41.39	129.67	117.61	90.29	3856
1993	371.90	58.62	182.50	164.35	130.79	5455
1994	510.81	80.21	243.17	218.87	187.43	7436
1995	631.45	106.04	293.07	263.98	232.34	9089
1996	713.60	125.59	320.84	289.87	267.17	10130
1997	802.59	110.71	376.50	342.80	315.39	11235
1998	901.19	132.56	407.70	369.89	360.93	12443
1999	1018.97	133.27	466.50	424.15	419.20	13884
2000	1183.14	135.81	546.12	497.34	501.21	15900
2001	1349.98	139.14	625.59	566.71	585.24	17882
2002	1551.42	141.89	728.77	658.00	680.76	20236
2003	1819.03	143.51	877.95	786.49	797.58	23340

1-11　续表 1
Continued

单位：亿元（100 million yuan）

年　份 Year	全市生产总值 GDP	第一产业 Primary Industry	第二产业 Secondary Industry	#工业 Industry	第三产业 Tertiary Industry	人均生产总值（元） Per Capita GDP（yuan）
2004	2193.60	157.52	1080.95	961.94	955.13	27577
2005	2576.95	168.06	1292.49	1156.53	1116.40	31725
2006	3029.40	173.35	1528.60	1374.12	1327.45	36743
2007	3545.48	191.86	1752.63	1577.15	1600.99	42509
2008	4141.91	210.53	2007.89	1795.88	1923.49	49183
2009	4534.22	216.99	2146.53	1887.38	2170.70	53481
2010	5350.69	261.03	2482.57	2155.73	2607.08	62148
2011	6248.48	288.73	2823.69	2430.66	3136.06	70945
2012	6869.61	305.72	3010.56	2608.44	3553.33	76636
2013	7508.70	332.10	3225.92	2752.90	3950.68	82463
2014	8120.66	341.68	3389.11	2878.71	4389.87	87677
2015	8658.57	356.19	3503.40	2944.80	4798.98	92157
2016	9283.17	357.40	3592.80	2989.24	5332.96	97430
2017	10136.96	367.71	3849.18	3133.78	5920.06	104905
2018	10949.38	386.91	4033.33	3161.34	6529.14	112129
2019	11741.31	409.98	4182.76	3159.86	7148.57	118978
2020	12400.56	425.41	4381.44	3296.87	7593.71	123828
2021	14136.46	470.06	5070.33	3884.07	8596.07	138849

注：1. 人均生产总值按常住人口计算，2011—2020 年人均生产总值根据第七次人口普查人口修订结果进行了修订（以下相关表同）。
2. 三次产业分类采用《国民经济行业分类》（GB/T 4754—2017）和《三次产业划分规定》（国统字［2012］108 号），将农林牧渔业中的农、林、牧、渔专业及辅助性活动以及工业中的开采专业及辅助性活动和金属制品、机械和设备修理业归入第三产业。
3. 全国第四次经济普查后，对 2000 年至 2018 年历年 GDP 数据进行了修订（以下相关表同）。
4. 2021 年 GDP 数据为初步核算数，2020 年 GDP 数据为最终核实数（以下相关表同）。

Notes：1. The per capita GDP is calculated based on the permanent population, and the 2011—2020 per capita GDP has been revised according to the population revision results of the seventh census（the following related tables are the same）.
2. The classification of the three industries adopts the "Classification of National Economic Industries"（GB/T 4754–2017）and the "Regulations on the Classification of the Three Industries"（Guo Tong Zi［2012］No. 108）, which classifies the agricultural, forestry, animal husbandry and fishery Professional and ancillary activities, mining professional and ancillary activities in industry, and metal products, machinery and equipment repair businesses are included in the tertiary industry.
3. After the fourth national economic census, the GDP data from 2000 to 2018 was revised（the following related tables are the same）.
4. GDP data for 2020 are preliminary accounting figures and the GDP data for 2020 are the final verified figures（The same applies to tables following）.

1-12 主要年份全市生产总值构成(以全市生产总值为 100)

COMPOSITION OF MAJOR YRAR'S GROSS DOMESTIC PRODUCT (GROSS DOMESTIC PRODUCT=100)

单位:%

年 份 Year	全市生产总值 GDP	第一产业 Primary Industry	第二产业 Secondary Industry	#工 业 Industry	第三产业 Tertiary Industry
1952	100	26.1	48.2	43.8	25.7
1957	100	18.5	53.3	49.8	28.2
1962	100	11.4	48.3	44.1	40.3
1965	100	11.6	57.8	54.7	30.6
1970	100	13.6	62.2	59.7	24.2
1975	100	23.9	52.9	50.5	23.2
1978	100	21.4	52.5	49.8	26.1
1980	100	19.8	53.7	49.9	26.5
1985	100	24.4	45.4	41.4	30.2
1988	100	21.6	49.0	44.4	29.4
1990	100	20.5	47.8	43.7	31.7
1991	100	19.7	47.9	43.6	32.4
1992	100	15.8	49.6	45.0	34.6
1993	100	15.7	49.1	44.2	35.2
1994	100	15.7	47.6	42.8	36.7
1995	100	16.8	46.4	41.8	36.8
1996	100	17.6	45.0	40.6	37.4
1997	100	13.8	46.9	42.7	39.3
1998	100	14.7	45.2	41.0	40.1
1999	100	13.1	45.8	41.6	41.1
2000	100	11.5	46.1	42.0	42.4
2001	100	10.3	46.3	42.0	43.4
2002	100	9.1	47.0	42.4	43.9
2003	100	7.9	48.3	43.2	43.8
2004	100	7.2	49.3	43.9	43.5
2005	100	6.5	50.2	44.9	43.3
2006	100	5.7	50.5	45.4	43.8
2007	100	5.4	49.4	44.5	45.2
2008	100	5.1	48.5	43.4	46.4
2009	100	4.8	47.3	41.6	47.9
2010	100	4.9	46.4	40.3	48.7
2011	100	4.6	45.2	38.9	50.2
2012	100	4.5	43.8	38.0	51.7
2013	100	4.4	43.0	36.7	52.6
2014	100	4.2	41.7	35.4	54.1
2015	100	4.1	40.5	34.0	55.4
2016	100	3.9	38.7	32.2	57.4
2017	100	3.6	38.0	30.9	58.4
2018	100	3.5	36.9	28.9	59.6
2019	100	3.5	35.6	26.9	60.9
2020	100	3.4	35.3	26.6	61.3
2021	100	3.3	35.9	27.5	60.8

1-13 主要年份全市生产总值增长速度（以上年为100）
GROWTH RATE OF MAJOR YEAR'S GROSS DOMESTIC PRODUCT (PRECEDING YEAR=100)

单位：%

年份 Year	全市生产总值 GDP	第一产业 Primary Industry	第二产业 Secondary Industry	第三产业 Tertiary Industry	人均生产总值 Per Capita GDP
1979	12.0	10.6	12.9	11.4	10.4
1980	10.4	4.3	13.1	10.3	9.4
1981	−2.0	−3.6	−1.9	−1.0	−3.2
1982	4.1	5.5	−0.2	11.9	2.6
1983	16.9	42.8	9.3	12.7	15.3
1984	13.0	18.9	11.5	10.3	12.0
1985	9.9	5.4	5.8	21.3	9.3
1986	9.2	2.6	12.1	10.0	8.3
1987	12.0	3.6	16.0	12.0	10.6
1988	13.8	−0.3	21.5	11.2	12.1
1990	9.3	9.8	7.3	12.2	8.0
1991	10.6	16.6	11.6	5.4	9.4
1992	18.2	−1.6	22.9	24.7	17.4
1993	22.4	20.4	21.1	25.5	21.7
1994	14.4	3.7	14.7	19.7	13.5
1995	12.0	10.9	12.1	12.3	10.8
1996	7.2	7.6	7.6	6.5	5.7
1997	11.5	−10.7	16.8	14.1	9.9
1998	12.9	17.6	11.3	13.4	11.3
1999	13.9	4.0	15.5	15.2	12.4
2000	14.3	6.4	14.9	16.0	12.7
2001	13.0	1.8	14.9	13.9	11.3
2002	13.7	3.1	15.5	14.2	11.9
2003	15.4	2.4	18.8	14.5	13.5
2004	15.8	2.7	18.8	14.9	13.5
2005	15.6	0.4	18.1	15.3	13.2

1-13 续表 1
Continued

单位：%

年 份 Year	全市生产总值 GDP	第一产业 Primary Industry	第二产业 Secondary Industry	第三产业 Tertiary Industry	人均生产总值 Per Capita GDP
2006	14.5	0.5	15.3	15.6	12.8
2007	14.6	-2.6	13.8	17.8	13.3
2008	12.5	1.4	10.0	16.6	11.4
2009	11.3	3.0	11.3	12.0	10.5
2010	12.1	1.4	11.2	14.0	10.4
2011	11.0	4.5	11.0	11.8	8.5
2012	9.9	3.2	10.0	10.4	8.0
2013	9.4	2.1	8.5	10.9	7.7
2014	7.8	3.9	7.2	8.6	6.0
2015	7.9	3.6	7.0	9.0	6.3
2016	7.7	2.9	5.7	9.4	6.2
2017	7.4	3.1	5.8	8.7	5.9
2018	7.3	3.4	6.8	7.8	6.1
2019	6.5	1.6	4.7	8.0	5.3
2020	3.7	2.6	3.0	4.1	2.1
2021	8.3	6.7	6.9	9.2	6.6
1978—2010 平均每年增长 1978—2010 Average Increase Rate	12.1	5.5	12.6	13.4	10.7
1991—2010 平均每年增长 1991—2010 Average Increase Rate	13.7	4.2	14.8	15.0	12.3
1996—2010 平均每年增长 1996—2010 Average Increase Rate	13.2	2.4	14.2	14.2	11.6
2001—2010 平均每年增长 2001—2010 Average Increase Rate	13.8	1.4	14.7	14.9	12.2
2006—2010 平均每年增长 2006—2010 Average Increase Rate	13.0	0.7	12.3	15.2	11.7
2011　2020 平均每年增长 2011—2020 Average Increase Rate	7.8	3.1	7.0	8.8	6.2
2016—2020 平均每年增长 2016—2020 Average Increase Rate	6.5	2.7	5.2	7.6	5.1

1-14　分市、区生产总值(2021 年)
GROSS DOMESTIC PRODUCT BY REGION (2021)

单位：亿元（100 million yuan）

市、区名称	Region	地区生产总值 GDP	第一产业 Primary Industry	第二产业 Secondary Industry	第三产业 Tertiary Industry
市南区	Shinan District	1400.58		135.02	1265.56
市北区	Shibei District	1063.56		208.27	855.29
李沧区	Licang District	601.21		173.46	427.75
崂山区	Laoshan District	1011.08	6.92	309.06	695.10
黄岛区（西海岸新区）	Huangdao District (West Coast New Area)	4368.53	92.15	1638.33	2638.05
城阳区（含高新区）	Chengyang District (Including High tech District)	1334.20	20.15	650.13	663.92
即墨区	Jimo District	1452.52	85.07	737.60	629.85
胶州市	Jiaozhou	1456.27	63.94	707.90	684.43
平度市	Pingdu	821.14	124.17	312.06	384.91
莱西市	Laixi	625.50	74.38	237.18	313.94

1-15 全市生产总值构成(2021 年)
COMPOSITION OF GROSS DOMESTIC PRODUCT (2021)

指　标	Indicator	增加值(亿元) Added Value (100 million yuan)	2021 年为 2020 年 % 2021/2020 (%)
地区生产总值	**GDP**	**14136.46**	**108.3**
农林牧渔业	Farming, Forestry, Animal Husbandry and Fishery	500.50	106.8
# 农林牧渔服务业	Agriculture, Forestry, Animal Husbandry and Fishery Service Industry	30.44	109.0
工业	Industry	3884.07	108.8
# 开采辅助活动	#Mining Auxiliary Activities	0.97	99.1
# 金属制品、机械和设备修理业	#Metal Products, Machinery and Equipment Repair Industries	27.50	146.0
建筑业	Construction	1214.73	102.0
批发和零售业	Wholesale and Retail Trade	2390.50	114.7
批发业	Wholesale	1532.01	116.2
零售业	Retail Trade	858.49	112.4
交通运输、仓储和邮政业	Transport, Storage and Post	1045.34	113.2
住宿和餐饮业	Hotels and Catering Services	247.57	111.3
住宿业	Hotels	26.23	103.0
餐饮业	Catering Services	221.34	112.3
金融业	Financial Industry	937.35	106.2
房地产业	Real Estate	875.23	102.7
房地产业(K 门类)	Real Estate (K category)	649.63	101.9
自有房地产经营活动	Self-Owned Real Estate Business Activities	225.60	105.0
其他服务业	Other Services	3041.17	106.6
营利性服务业	For-Profit Services	1624.40	108.4
非营利性服务业	Non-Profit Services	1416.77	104.7
第一产业	Primary Industry	470.06	106.7
第二产业	Secondary Industry	5070.33	106.9
第三产业	Tertiary Industry	8596.07	109.2

主要统计指标解释

国内生产总值（GDP） 指按市场价格计算的一个国家（或地区）所有常住单位在一定时期内生产活动的最终成果。国内生产总值有三种表现形态，即价值形态、收入形态和产品形态。从价值形态看，它是所有常住单位在一定时期内生产的全部货物和服务价值超过同期中间投入的全部非固定资产货物和服务价值的差额，即所有常住单位的增加值之和；从收入形态看，它是所有常住单位在一定时期内创造并分配给常住单位和非常住单位的初次收入分配之和；从产品形态看，它是所有常住单位在一定时期内最终使用的货物和服务价值与货物和服务净出口价值之和。在实际核算中，国内生产总值有三种计算方法，即生产法、收入法和支出法。三种方法分别从不同的方面反映国内生产总值及其构成。对于一个地区来说，称为地区生产总值或地区 GDP。

人均 GDP 人均 GDP 是一定时期内 GDP 与同期人口平均数的比值。按照国际标准，人口平均数应该是同期平均常住人口。我国在核算制度中也规定，无论是国家还是地区，人口数都采用常住人口。国家统计局规定从 2004 年开始，过去采用户籍人口计算人均 GDP 的地区，作为过渡性措施，可在两年内同时计算两种口径的人均 GDP（数据后面必须注明是什么口径），两年后取消按户籍人口计算的人均 GDP。我市采用常住人口计算人均 GDP。

三次产业 是根据社会生产活动历史发展的顺序对产业结构的划分，产品直接取自自然界的部门称为第一产业，对初级产品进行再加工的部门称为第二产业，为生产和消费提供各种服务的部门称为第三产业。它是世界上通用的产业结构分类，但各国的划分不尽一致。我国的三次产业划分是：

第一产业是指农、林、牧、渔业（不含农、林、牧、渔服务业）。

第二产业是指采矿业（不含开采辅助活动），制造业（不含金属制品、机械和设备修理业），电力、热力、燃气及水生产和供应业，建筑业。

第三产业即服务业，是指除第一产业、第二产业以外的其他行业。第三产业包括：批发和零售业，交通运输、仓储和邮政业，住宿和餐饮业，信息传输、软件和信息技术服务业，金融业，房地产业，租赁和商务服务业，科学研究和技术服务业，水利、环境和公共设施管理业，居民服务、修理和其他服务业，教育，卫生和社会工作，文化、体育和娱乐业，公共管理、社会保障和社会组织，国际组织，以及农、林、牧、渔业中的农、林、牧、渔服务业，采矿业中的开采辅助活动，制造业中的金属制品、机械和设备修理业。

气候 指地球与大气之间长期能量交换与质量交换所形成的一种自然环境状态，它是多种因素综合作用的结果。气候既是人类生活和生产的环境要素之一，又是供给人类生活和生产的重要资源。气温、降水、湿度等气象要素的多年平均值是用来描述一个地区气候状况的主要参数，而各种气象要素某年、某月的平均值（或总量）则可以反映出该时期天气气候状况的重要特征。

气温 指空气的温度，我国一般以摄氏度（℃）为单位表示。气象观测的温度表是放在离地面约 1.5 米处通风良好的百叶箱里测量的，因此，通常说的气温指的是离地面 1.5 米处百叶箱中的温度。其统计计算方法为：月平均气温是将全月各日的平均气温相加，除以该月的天数而得。

年平均气温 是将 12 个月的月平均气温累加后除以 12 而得。

降水量 指从天空降落到地面的液态或固态（经融化后）水，未经蒸发、渗透、流失而在地面上积聚的深度。其统计计算方法为：月降水量是将全月各日的降水量累加而得。年降水量是将 12 个月的月降水量累加而得。

Explanatory Notes on Main Statistical Indicators

Gross Domestic Product（GDP） refers to the final products at market prices produced by all resident units in a country（or a region）during a certain period of time.Gross domestic product is expressed in three different perspectives, namely value, income, and products respectively. GDP in its value perspective refers to the total value of all goods and services produced by all resident units during a certain period of time, minus the total value of input of goods and services of the nature of non–fixed assets, in other words, it is the sum of the value–added of all resident units. GDP from the perspective of products refers to the value of all goods and services for final consumption by all resident units minus the net exports of goods and services during a given period of time. In the practice of national accounting, gross domestic product is calculated from three approaches,namely production approach, income approach and expenditure approach, which reflect gross domestic product and its composition from different angles. For a certain region, it refers region gross product or region GDP.

Per Capita GDP refers to the ratio of GDP in a certain term and average population in the same term. According to the international standard, average population should be average permanent population in the same term. In the account regulation, population of both the country and the region should be permanent population. In the after two years since 2004, per capita GDP can be calculated at two coverage.i.e. at permanent population and household registered population（the note of coverage should follow the data）. The per capita GDP calculated with household registered population will be abolished after two years. Per capita GDP of Qingdao is calculated at permanent population.

Three Strata of Industries has been classified according to the historical sequence of development. Primary industry refers to extraction of natural resources, secondary industry involves processing of primary products, and tertiary industry provides services of various kinds for production and consumption. The above classification is universal although it varies to some extent from country to country. In China economic activities are categorized into the following three strata of industry：

Primary industry refers to agriculture, forestry, animal husbandry, and fishery（excluding agriculture, forestry, animal husbandry,and fishery service industries）.

The secondary industry refers to mining industry（excluding mining auxiliary activities）, manufacturing industry（excluding metal products, machinery and equipment repair industry）, electricity, heat, gas and water production and supply industry, and construction industry.

The tertiary industry is the service industry, which refers to industries other than the primary industry and the secondary industry. The tertiary industry includes: wholesale and retail industry, transportation, storage and postal industry, accommodation and catering industry, information transmission, software and information technology service industry, financial industry, real estate industry,leasing and business service industry, scientific research and technical service Industry, water conservancy, environment and public facilities management industry, resident service, repair and other service industry, education, health and social work, culture, sports and entertainment industry, public management, social security and social organization, international organization, and agriculture, forestry Agriculture, forestry, animal husbandry, and fishery services in agriculture, animal husbandry and fishery, mining auxiliary activities in mining, and metal products, machinery and equipment repair in manufacturing.

Climate refers to the natural environmental status formed by the long–term exchange of energy and mass between the earth and the air, and is the results of interaction of many factors. Climate is both one of the environment factors and the important resources for the living and production activities of the human being. The average values across several years of meteorological factors such as temperature, rainfall and humidity are used as important parameters to describe the climate of a region, while the average values（or total values）of a given year or month of meteorological factors reflect the key characteristics of climate for that period of time.

Temperature refers to the air temperature. China uses centigrade as the unit. The thermometry used for weather observation is put in a breezy shutter, which is 1.5 meters high from the ground. Therefore, the commonly used temperature refers to the temperature in the breezy shutter 1.5 meters away from the ground. The calculation method is as follows: Monthly average temperature is the summation of average daily temperature of one month divided by the actual days of that particular month.

Annual average temperature is the summation of monthly average of a year divided by 12 months.

Volume of Precipitation refers to the deepness of liquid state or solid state (thawed) water falling from the sky to the ground that has not been evaporated, infiltrated or run off. The calculation method is as follows: Monthly precipitation is the summation of daily precipitation of a month. Annual precipitation is the summation of 12 months precipitation of a year.

人 口 2

POPULATION

简要说明

一、本篇资料的主要内容

本篇资料主要反映了全市人口方面的基本情况，包括全市主要年份和区（市）的户数、人口数、人口密度、常住人口、城镇化率、土地面积数据、计划生育等数据。另外还对中华人民共和国成立以来开展的七次人口普查主要数据进行了比较。

二、本篇资料的来源

本篇资料分别来源于国家开展的人口普查、人口抽样调查和市公安局的户籍登记资料，由市统计局人口就业和社会科技文化统计处整理提供。

Brief Introduction

Ⅰ. Main Content

The information in this chapter mainly reflects the basic demographic situation of the city, including the number of households, population, population density, permanent population, urbanization rate, land area data, family planning, etc. in main years and districts (cities) of the city data. Furthermore, relevant figures obtained from seven national population censuses have been compared.

Ⅱ. Source of Data

The data in this article are derived from the national population census, population sample survey and household registration data of Qingdao Public Security Bureau, compiled and provided by the Population Employment and Social Science, Technology and Culture Statistics Department of Qingdao Statistics Bureau.

2-1 主要年份全市户籍人口数
MAJOR YEAR'S TOTAL REGISTERED POPULATION

单位：人（person）

年 份 Year	总人口 Total Population	按性别分 Grouped by Gender 男 Male	按性别分 Grouped by Gender 女 Female	平均人口 Average Population
1949	4056550	1997293	2059257	4054431
1952	4233586	2125392	2108194	4203428
1957	4822756	2424729	2398027	4773862
1962	4627432	2319658	2307774	4578313
1965	4901670	2461629	2440041	4859712
1970	5391852	2720633	2671219	5337282
1975	5742206	2904347	2837859	5717456
1978	5853321	2959800	2893521	5841638
1980	5961129	3015357	2945772	5937187
1985	6267223	3185409	3081814	6253157
1988	6516920	3319534	3197386	6474541
1989	6571597	3348454	3223143	6544259
1990	6666482	3392253	3274229	6619040
1991	6709277	3411776	3297501	6687880
1992	6731072	3420886	3310186	6720175
1993	6753497	3431149	3322348	6742285
1994	6785291	3446019	3339272	6769394
1995	6846346	3476300	3370046	6815819
1996	6902677	3502600	3400077	6874512
1997	6954391	3527588	3426803	6928534
1998	6995666	3545403	3450263	6975029
1999	7029707	3561061	3468646	7012687
2000	7066481	3577367	3489114	7048094
2001	7104875	3595652	3509223	7085678
2002	7156537	3619778	3536759	7130706
2003	7206806	3644032	3562774	7181672
2004	7311228	3692991	3618237	7259017
2005	7409052	3740309	3668743	7360140
2006	7493812	3779891	3713921	7451432
2007	7579910	3816620	3763290	7536861
2008	7615647	3824665	3790982	7597779
2009	7629161	3823534	3805627	7622404
2010	7636392	3819240	3817152	7632777
2011	7663612	3826931	3836681	7650002
2012	7695585	3838205	3857380	7679599

注：截至出书前，未获得公安部门青岛市 2013—2021 年户籍人口信息。
Note：Data come from the Qingdao Municipal Public Security Bureau，and the Data of 2013—2021 are absent.

2-2　主要年份全市户数、人口数、人口密度（户籍）

MAJOR YEAR'S HOUSEHOLDS, POPULATION AND DENSITY OF POPULATION（WITH PERMANENT RESIDENCE）

年　份 Year	总户数（万户） Total Households （10000 households）		总人口（万人） Total Population （10000 persons）		平均每户人口（人） Average Persons Per Household（person）		人口密度（人/平方公里） Density of Population （person/sq.km）	
	全市 Whole Municipality	市区 Urban Area	全市 Whole Municepality	市区 Urban Area	全市 Whole Municepality	市区 Urban Area	全市 Whole Municepality	市区 Urban Area
1949	90.64	21.68	405.66	103.69	4.48	4.78	381	941
1952	93.96	22.70	423.36	107.62	4.51	4.74	397	977
1957	102.56	27.41	482.28	134.76	4.70	4.92	453	1223
1962	106.11	29.29	462.74	137.86	4.36	4.71	434	1251
1965	105.31	29.64	490.17	146.74	4.65	4.95	460	1332
1970	113.07	32.14	539.19	150.81	4.77	4.69	506	1369
1975	123.18	36.56	574.22	161.13	4.66	4.41	539	1462
1978	131.27	40.08	585.33	168.00	4.46	4.19	549	1525
1980	138.44	43.03	596.11	175.27	4.31	4.07	560	1591
1985	157.06	53.43	626.72	190.87	3.99	3.57	588	1732
1988	169.72	58.95	651.69	201.38	3.84	3.42	612	1827
1989	177.47	61.57	657.16	203.63	3.70	3.31	617	1848
1990	186.79	63.94	666.65	205.78	3.57	3.22	626	1867
1991	192.46	67.15	670.93	207.22	3.49	3.09	630	1880
1992	199.08	68.94	673.11	209.28	3.38	3.04	632	1899
1993	201.36	70.13	675.35	212.06	3.35	3.02	634	1924
1994	204.05	71.24	678.53	214.97	3.33	3.02	637	1951
1995	208.13	72.53	684.63	218.38	3.29	3.01	643	1982
1996	212.40	75.11	690.27	223.86	3.25	2.98	648	2032
1997	215.12	76.39	695.44	227.22	3.23	2.97	653	2062
1998	218.59	77.90	699.57	229.58	3.20	2.95	657	2084
1999	222.61	79.27	702.97	231.94	3.16	2.93	660	2105
2000	224.73	80.46	706.65	234.60	3.14	2.92	664	2129
2001	227.43	81.41	710.49	237.60	3.12	2.92	667	2156
2002	229.67	82.85	715.65	241.74	3.12	2.92	672	2194
2003	232.26	84.15	720.68	246.77	3.10	2.93	677	2240
2004	235.29	86.93	731.12	258.40	3.11	2.97	686	2229
2005	237.35	87.99	740.91	265.43	3.12	3.02	695	2290
2006	239.33	89.12	749.38	271	3.13	3.04	703	2338
2007	241.55	90.21	757.99	275.55	3.14	3.05	711	2377
2008	243.18	91.22	761.56	276.25	3.13	3.03	715	2384
2009	244.74	92.15	762.92	275.47	3.12	2.99	676	1873
2010	246.11	93.30	763.64	275.50	3.10	2.95	677	1873
2011	247.94	94.69	766.36	277.09	3.09	2.93	679	1884
2012	249.27	95.87	769.56	279.57	3.09	2.92	682	1901

注：截至出书前，未获得公安部门青岛市 2013—2021 年户籍人口信息。

Note：Data come from the Qingdao Municipal Public Security Bureau，and the Data of 2013—2021 are absent.

2-3 主要年份全市常住人口数
MAJOR YEAR' S TOTAL RESIDENT POPULATION

单位：万人（10 000 persons）

年　份 Year	总人口 Total Population
2005	819.55
2006	829.42
2007	838.67
2008	845.61
2009	850.03
2010	871.51
2011	889.60
2012	903.20
2013	917.90
2014	934.50
2015	944.60
2016	961.00
2017	971.60
2018	981.40
2019	992.30
2020	1010.57
2021	1025.67

注：2011—2019 年为山东省统计局根据第七次人口普查结果修订数据。
Note：From 2011 to 2019, the Shandong Provincial Statistics Bureau revised the feedback data based on the results of the seventh census.

2-4 青岛市常住人口
TOTAL RESIDENT POPULATION

单位：万人（10 000 persons）

市、区名称	Region	2021 年	2020 年	2021 年比 2020 年 ±% 2021/2020（±%）
全市	**Whole Municipality**	**1025.67**	**1010.57**	**1.49**
市南区	Shinan District	48.85	48.60	0.51
市北区	Shibei District	110.23	110.08	0.14
李沧区	Licang District	75.25	74.09	1.57
崂山区	Laoshan District	51.08	50.29	1.57
黄岛区（西海岸新区）	Huangdao District（West Coast New Area）	196.42	191.37	2.64
城阳区（含高新区）	Chengyang District（Including High tech District）	114.78	111.59	2.86
即墨区	Jimo District	136.18	134.26	1.43
胶州市	Jiaozhou	102.19	99.25	2.96
平度市	Pingdu	118.78	119.07	−0.24
莱西市	Laixi	71.91	71.97	−0.08

注：2021 年数据为根据 2021 年 1% 人口抽样调查结果推算数据。
Note：The figures for 2021 is estimated based on the sample survey of the 1% population.

2-5 主要年份常住人口城镇化率
THE URBANIZATION RATE OF THE MAIN YEAR PERMANENT RESIDENTS

单位：%

年 份 Year	城镇化率 Urbanization rate
2005	63.20
2006	63.59
2007	63.90
2008	64.31
2009	64.68
2010	65.81
2011	66.04
2012	66.09
2013	66.23
2014	66.31
2015	68.04
2016	70.54
2017	71.87
2018	74.20
2019	74.85
2020	76.34
2021	77.17

注：1. 2011-2019 年为山东省统计局根据第七次人口普查结果修订数据。
　　2. 2021 年数据为根据 2021 年 1% 人口抽样调查结果推算数据。
Notes：1. From 2011 to 2019, the Shandong Provincial Statistics Bureau revised the feedback data based on the results of the seventh census.
　　3. The figures for 2021 is estimated based on the sample survey of the 1% population.

2-6 分市、区土地面积（2021 年底）
LAND AREA（END OF 2021）

市、区名称	Region	土地面积（平方公里） Land Area（aq.km）
全　市	**Whole Municipality**	**11293.36**
市南区	Shinan District	32.21
市北区	Shibei District	65.85
李沧区	Licang District	99.10
崂山区	Laoshan District	395.79
黄岛区	Huangdao District	2128.31
城阳区	Chengyang District	583.68
即墨区	Jimo District	1920.90
胶州市	Jiaozhou	1323.65
平度市	Pingdu	3175.65
莱西市	Laixi	1568.22

注：2018 年度土地变更调查结果。
Note：Survey results of land quality change in 2018.

2-7　第一、二、三、四、五、六、七次人口普查主要数据
MAIN DATA OF THE FIRST, SECOND, THIRD, FOURTH, FIFTH, SIXTH AND SEVENTH CENSUSES

项　目	Item	第一次人口普查 1st National Population Census	第二次人口普查 2nd National Population Census	第三次人口普查 3rd National Population Census	第四次人口普查 4th National Population Census	第五次人口普查 5th National Population Census	第六次人口普查 6th National Population Census	第七次人口普查 7th National Population Census
一、总人口（万人）	**Total Population (10000 persons)**	**91.68**	**138.34**	**422.76**	**666.40**	**749.42**	**871.51**	**1007.17**
按性别分	By Gender							
男（万人）	Male (10000 persons)	48.44	69.64	214.09	338.86	375.74	439.18	513.22
女（万人）	Female (10000 persons)	43.24	68.71	208.67	327.54	373.68	432.33	493.95
二、总户数（万户）	**Total Household (10000 households)**	**19.27**	**28.01**	**101.41**	**186.61**	**241.62**	**296.64**	**385.70**
家庭户（万户）	Family Household (10000 households)			101.09	185.56	232.70	282.43	362.32
平均家庭户规模（人）	Average Family Household Size (person)			4.07	3.49	2.97	2.79	2.55
三、民　族	**Ethnicity**							
民族个数（个）	Number of Ethnic groups (unit)	14	16	25	41	51	53	56
汉族人口（万人）	Population of Han (10000 persons)	91.33	137.76	422.09	665.58	746.12	863.84	995.39
少数民族人口（万人）	Populaiton of Ethnic Minorities (10000 persons)	0.36	0.58	0.67	0.82	3.30	7.67	11.78
四、各种文化程度人口	**Population with Various Education Attainments**							
大　学（万人）	College (10000 persons)		1.51	3.62	12.39	41.64	129.54	227.12
高　中（万人）	Senior Secondary School (10000 persons)		4.86	34.82	68.42	111.40	150.82	176.69
初　中（万人）	Junior Secondary School (10000 persons)		13.72	102.28	195.10	281.91	334.22	323.79
小　学（万人）	Primary School (10000 persons)		51.25	144.52	236.34	206.91	170.77	187.26

2-8 计划生育情况（1978—2020年）
FAMILY PLANNING SITUATION（1978 — 2020）

年 份 Year	已婚有生育能力的人数（人） Married and Fertile Persons（person）	节育人数（人） Persons under Birth Control（person）	节育率（%） Contraceptive Prevalence Rate（%）	四项手术人数（人） Persons Performed Four-operation（person）	#放环人数 Persons Set Rings
1978	694292	571077	82.25	125913	68475
1980	763226	673069	88.19	180979	70927
1985	1017649	929284	91.32	146742	67234
1990	1258232	1165216	92.61	149327	70964
1991	1319722	1219795	92.43	153970	77406
1992	1348503	1256271	93.16	90107	56226
1993	1380717	1271884	92.12	76783	45492
1994	1400425	1268378	90.57	73169	41482
1995	1427442	1285264	90.04	84099	52716
1996	1459465	1316516	90.21	84370	57648
1997	1482204	1340399	90.43	76579	55285
1998	1505499	1367648	90.84	74199	50526
1999	1523471	1378131	90.46	73663	44976
2000	1521331	1371447	90.15	74285	45999
2001	1514274	1360543	89.85	70205	43601
2002	1541855	1400145	90.81	50575	45453
2003	1518448	1354917	89.23	57458	47953
2004	1540706	1357703	88.04	52934	42859
2005	1590476	1417755	89.14	58097	49716
2006	1604665	1427785	88.98	51864	42457
2007	1595390	1426787	89.43	50074	41198
2008	1587344	1410426	88.85	120539	93291
2009	1623969	1418178	87.33	111084	100193
2010	1591103	1377726	86.59	78721	51794
2011	1581231	1355808	85.74	70823	48210
2012	1575996	1349572	85.63	62880	43021
2013	1527731	1293810	84.69	53252	30851
2014	1506274	1275142	84.66	34008	12827
2015	1475887	1226439	83.10	34879	9108
2016	1456953	1183221	81.21	36449	4474
2017	1439008	1188307	82.58	20905	4669
2018	1406047	1159775	82.48	17786	5097
2019	1375598	1141584	82.92	12582	3959
2020	1310212	1109885	84.71	342553	339219

注：2021年起，卫健部门的省报表已不再统计以上指标。
Note：From 2021, the provincial report of the health department would have no longer counted the above indicators.

2-9　分市、区计划生育情况（2021年）
FAMILY PLANNING SITUATION BY REGION（2021）

市、区名称	Region	计划生育率（%）Fertility Rate（%）	计划内出生（人）Birth within the Plan（person）		计划外出生（人）Birth without the Plan（person）		多胎（人）Third Birth and Above（person）
			一胎 First Birth	二胎 Second Birth	一胎 First Birth	二胎 Second Birth	
全市	**Whole Municipality**	**98.54**	**28267**	**25371**	**90**	**45**	**3002**
市南区	Shinan District	99.46	1910	986		4	70
市北区	Shibei District	99.81	3166	1875	1		109
李沧区	Licang District	99.54	2029	1787	3	1	76
崂山区	Laoshan District	99.50	1241	886		1	69
黄岛区（西海岸新区）	Huangdao District（West Coast New Area）	98.45	5093	5101	14	10	627
城阳区（含高新区）	Chengyang District（Including High tech District）	99.17	3027	2648	5	8	195
即墨区	Jimo District	98.55	3693	3544	6	1	473
胶州市	Jiaozhou	97.43	2656	2723	11	1	489
平度市	Pingdu	97.63	3536	3835	20	10	604
莱西市	Laixi	97.59	1916	1986	30	9	290

主要统计指标解释

常住人口　指经常居住在某一地区的人口，主要包括居住在本乡镇街道且户口在本乡镇街道或户口待定的人，居住在本乡镇街道且离开户口登记地所在的乡镇街道半年以上的人，户口在本乡镇街道且外出不满半年或在境外工作学习的人。

户籍人口　指公民依照《中华人民共和国户口登记条例》已在其经常居住地的公安户籍管理机关登记了常住户口的人。

城镇化率　指一个国家（地区）城镇的常住人口占该国家（地区）常住总人口的比例。计算公式为：

$$\text{城镇化率}=\frac{\text{城镇常住人口}}{\text{常住总人口}}\times 100‰$$

Explanatory Notes on Main Statistical Indicators

Permanent Population　refers to the population that often resides in a certain place, mainly consisting of the people who live in the streets of the township and have registered in the streets or whose residence-registration is to be determined, the people who reside in the streets of the town and have been away from their registration areas for more than half a year, and the people who registered in the streets of the township and have gone out for less than half a year or have worked and studied abroad.

Registered Population　refers to those who have registered their permanent residence with the public security household registration management authority in the place of their habitual residence in accordance with the Regulations of the People's Republic of China on Household Registration.

Urbanization rate　refers to the proportion of the resident population of cities and towns in a country (region) to the total resident population of the country (region). The calculation formula is.

$$\text{Urbanization rate}=\frac{\text{Permanent population of a town}}{\text{Resident Population}}\times 100‰$$

从业人员及职工工资 3

EMPLOYMENT AND WAGES

简 要 说 明

一、本篇资料的主要内容

本篇资料主要反映了全市单位从业人员、工资总额和平均工资等方面的资料。

二、本篇资料的来源

全市单位从业人员、工资总额和平均工资来源于劳动工资统计年报，由市统计局人口就业和社会科技文化统计处整理提供。

Brief Introduction

Ⅰ. Main Content

The data in this chapter mainly reflects the data on the employees, total wages and average wages of the city' s units.

Ⅱ. Source of Data

The employees, total wages and average wages of the city' s units are derived from the annual labor wage statistics report, which is compiled and provided by the Population Employment and Social Science, Technology and Culture Statistics Department of Qingdao Statistics Bureau.

3-1 社会就业人数（1978—2021年）
SOCIAL EMPLOYMENT（1978—2021）

单位：万人（10 000 persons）

年份 Year	合计 Total	第一产业 Primary Industry	第二产业 Secondary Industry	第三产业 Tertiary Industry
1978	256.7	157.4	65.6	33.7
1979	265.6	156.1	72.2	37.3
1980	270.1	153.0	77.3	39.8
1981	278.9	153.6	82.1	43.2
1982	282.7	151.1	86.2	45.4
1983	289.6	156.4	85.0	48.1
1984	304.2	149.2	97.7	57.4
1985	315.3	149.2	104.5	61.7
1986	326.4	149.6	112.1	64.6
1987	334.8	149.9	120.2	64.7
1988	336.5	147.6	123.2	65.7
1989	344.2	152.5	122.1	69.6
1990	352.8	156.5	123.3	73.1
1991	361.2	161.9	124.3	74.9
1992	370.3	161.7	127.8	80.8
1993	365.7	160.5	128.8	76.4
1994	367.6	157.1	129.4	81.2
1995	374.2	155.4	132.4	86.4
1996	381.5	152.2	137.1	92.2
1997	388.7	155.2	138.1	95.3
1998	393.1	154.8	138.6	99.7
1999	396.1	150.3	142.0	103.8
2000	436.1	158.7	148.0	129.4

3-1 续表
Continued

年份 Year	合计 Total	第一产业 Primary Industry	第二产业 Secondary Industry	第三产业 Tertiary Industry
2001	439.5	146.9	156.2	136.4
2002	447.8	131.5	166.7	149.6
2003	450.8	123.1	168.4	159.3
2004	459.6	114.2	180.9	164.5
2005	467.4	103.7	195.3	168.4
2006	475.2	99.8	203.5	171.9
2007	481.5	97.4	207.3	176.8
2008	484.8	96.6	208.3	179.9
2009	489.3	98.3	205.1	185.9
2010	504.9	98.3	209.2	197.4
2011	510.8	98.2	210.4	202.2
2012	515.5	96.6	211.6	207.3
2013	517.5	97.4	210.3	209.8
2014	521.3	96.0	203.5	221.8
2015	523.7	94.9	201.8	227.0
2016	523.5	93.4	198.8	231.3
2017	524.3	88.4	198.1	237.8
2018	525.3	85.1	191.2	249.0
2019	523.6	82.2	200.5	240.9
2020	525.6	82.0	167.7	275.9
2021	527.7	82.3	168.3	277.1

注：第七次全国人口普查后，对 2000 年至 2020 年历年社会就业人数进行修订。
Note: After the seventh national census, the number of social employment in the calendar years from 2000 to 2020 will be revised.

3-2 分市、区社会就业人数（2021 年）
NUMBER OF EMPLOYED PERSONS BY CITY AND REGION（2021）

单位：万人（10 000 persons）

市、区名称	Region	2021 年
全市	**Whole Municipality**	**527.7**
市南区	Shinan District	25.5
市北区	Shibei District	57.5
李沧区	Licang District	38.6
崂山区	Laoshan District	26.3
黄岛区（西海岸新区）	Huangdao District（West Coast New Area）	99.7
城阳区（含高新区）	Chengyang District（Including High tech District）	58.2
即墨区	Jimo District	70.0
胶州市	Jiaozhou	51.8
平度市	Pingdu	62.4
莱西市	Laixi	37.7

3-3 主要年份全市单位就业人员人数
MAJOR YEAR'S NUMBER OF EMPLOYEES IN THE CITY

单位：万人（10 000 persons）

年份 Year	合计 Total	#市区 Urban Area	#国有单位 State-owned Units	#集体单位 Collective-owned Units	其他所有制单位 Other Ownership Units
1949	14.8	13.4	9.3	5.5	
1952	23.4	20.1	18.3	5.1	
1957	29.7	24.5	24.1	5.6	
1962	32.3	26.8	24.5	7.8	
1965	36.7	30.6	26.8	9.9	
1970	45.6	37.4	32.2	13.4	
1975	53.4	43.5	38.0	15.4	
1978	70.7	54.5	49.2	21.5	
1980	79.2	61.5	55.0	24.2	
1985	88.8	66.7	59.8	28.9	0.1
1988	98.2	70.0	66.7	31.2	0.3
1990	103.2	70.6	69.5	32.9	0.8
1991	105.4	78.4	71.5	32.5	1.4
1992	108.2	80.4	73.6	32.8	1.8
1993	109.4	80.8	75.3	29.5	4.6
1994	110.1	80.2	72.4	28.3	9.4
1995	111.6	80.2	72.4	27.5	11.7
1996	118.4	81.1	71.6	26.0	20.8
1997	117.1	78.1	69.0	22.6	25.5
1998	116.2	75.6	64.2	19.0	33.0
1999	119.0	78.3	60.4	16.6	42.0
2000	118.3	76.6	57.6	14.2	46.5
2001	117.5	75.1	53.2	12.2	52.1

3-3 续表
Continued

年份 Year	合计 Total	#市区 Urban Area	#国有单位 State-owned Units	#集体单位 Collective-owned Units	其他所有制单位 Other Ownership Units
2002	119.1	75.2	49.5	10.3	59.3
2003	118.0	74.3	47.2	8.9	61.9
2004	207.1	111.1	43.7	18.0	145.4
2005	224.3	122.3	43.9	18.2	162.2
2006	243.2	133.7	41.7	16.2	185.3
2007	249.8	137.3	45.1	17.9	186.8
2008	254.1	140.9	44.4	15.4	194.3
2009	260.5	145.6	44.4	14.6	201.5
2010	269.4	151.1	44.6	15.1	209.7
2011	275.9	156.5	44.3	14.7	216.9
2012	283.2	162.1	44.0	13.8	225.4
2013	293.7	184.1	37.8	5.4	250.5
2014	303.0	191.4	36.7	4.9	261.4
2015	309.2	192.4	35.8	4.6	268.8
2016	315.6	196.4	35.5	4.7	275.4
2017	321.4	249.1	35.1	4.6	281.7
2018	330.4	258.3	34.7	2.0	293.7
2019	146.6	118.5	34.1	1.1	111.4
2020	147.7				
2021	147.7				

注：1. 2004 年以前为城镇单位职工人数。
2. 2013 年统计口径变化，国有单位、集体单位数据与上年不可比。
3.2019 年统计口径变化，全市单位就业人员人数为全市城镇非私营口径。
4.2020 年劳动工资改革，单位就业人数不再分登记注册类型。

Notes：1. Before 2004，the data refer to number of staff and workers in urban units.
2. Because of the adjustment about the statistics system，the data of State-owned Units and Collective-owned Units since 2013 are not fully comparable with historical statistics.
3. The statistical caliber changes in 2019, the number of employees in the city's units is the city's urban non-private caliber.
4. In 2020, the labor and wage reform will no longer divide the number of employees into registration types.

3-4 全市城镇非私营单位国民经济各行业就业人员人数（2021 年）

NUMBER OF EMPLOYED PERSONS IN NON-PRIVATE UNITS OF THE CITY BY SECTOR（2021）

单位：万人（10 000 persons）

		2021 年		2020 年	
		合计 Total	女性 Female	合计 Total	女性 Female
总计	**Total**	**147.7**	**61.2**	**147.7**	**60.2**
1. 农、林、牧、渔业	Farming，Forestry，Animal Husbandry and Fishery	0.1	0.0	0.0	0.0
2. 采矿业	Mining	0.0	0.0	0.0	0.0
3. 制造业	Manufacturing	45.0	15.6	44.5	15.7
4. 电力、热力、燃气及水生产和供应业	Electricity，Heat，Gas and Water Production and Supply Industry	2.2	0.6	2.1	0.5
5. 建筑业	Construction	12.2	2.0	15.8	2.1
6. 批发和零售业	Wholesale and Retail Trade	8.6	4.7	8.3	4.7
7. 交通运输、仓储和邮政业	Transport，Storage and Post	9.0	2.7	9.3	2.6
8. 住宿和餐饮业	Hotels and Catering Services	3.0	1.6	2.7	1.5
9. 信息传输、软件和信息技术服务业	Information Transmission Computer Services and Software	2.8	1.2	2.4	1.0
10. 金融业	Financial Industry	11.3	7.3	11.4	7.5
11. 房地产业	Real Estate	5.1	2.1	5.0	2.0
12. 租赁和商务服务业	Leasing and Business Services	3.4	1.4	3.5	1.4
13. 科学研究和技术服务业	Scientific Research and Technical Services	5.5	1.8	4.3	1.5
14. 水利、环境和公共设施管理业	Management of Water Conservancy，Environment and Public Facilities	2.2	0.8	2.4	0.8
15. 居民服务、修理和其他服务业	Residents Service，RePair and Other Services	0.5	0.2	0.5	0.2
16. 教育	Education	14.2	9.0	13.9	8.6
17. 卫生和社会工作	Health and Social Welfare	8.6	6.1	7.7	5.6
18. 文化、体育和娱乐业	Culture，Sports and Entertainment	1.3	0.6	1.2	0.5
19. 公共管理、社会保障和社会组织	Public Management，Social Security and Social Organization	12.6	3.5	12.6	3.7

3-5 全市就业人员工资总额、平均工资（1978—2021 年）
TOTAL WAGES AND AVERAGE WAGE OF CITYWIDE FULL-TIME EMPLOYEES（1978—2021）

年份 Year	工资总额（亿元） Total Wage Bill（100 million yuan）		平均工资（元） Average Wage（yuan）	
	全社会单位 All Units	其中：非私营单位 of which：Non-private Units	全社会单位 All Units	其中：非私营单位 of which：Non-private Units
1978		4.0		584
1979		4.8		662
1980		6.0		782
1981		6.3		778
1982		6.6		785
1983		6.9		809
1984		9.0		1041
1985		9.6		1103
1986		11.8		1311
1987		14.2		1519
1988		18.0		1862
1989		20.7		2120
1990		24.4		2400
1991		26.4		2553
1992		31.8		2970
1993		40.4		3694
1994		59.5		5455
1995		68.3		6164
1996		78.2		6640
1997		82.5		7030
1998		87.2		7518
1999		100.1		8405
2000		120.4		10072
2001		135.8		11426
2002		153.8		12839
2003	225.6	160.3	12597	15335
2004	280.5	193.4	13932	17190
2005	359.5	242.8	16015	20022
2006	445.6	292.0	18574	23457
2007	518.1	338.6	21419	27083
2008	578.7	371.9	23296	30233
2009	638.1	393.2	25396	33258
2010	738.0	446.8	28549	37805
2011	877.5	522.0	32763	43077
2012	1044.3	613.1	37399	49052
2013	1251.7	785.7	42688	55363
2014	1456.0	890.5	48453	62104
2015	1644.4	993.0	53715	69465
2016	1852.7	1088.5	58551	75803
2017	2034.7	1193.6	63047	82177
2018	2251.7	1290.8	68197	89525
2019		1438.3		98604
2020		1560.4		106011
2021		1700.4		116477

注：1. 2003 年以前为职工工资总额、平均工资。
2. 2015 年以前为在岗职工工资总额、平均工资。
3. 自 2019 年统计口径变化，无全部单位工资数据。

Notes：1. The data before 2003 refer to the total wage bill and average wage of stall and workers.
2. It was the total salary and average salary of the on-spot staff before 2015.
3. Since the statistical caliber change in 2019, there is no wage data for all units.

3-6　全市就业人员工资总额、平均工资指数（1978-2021年）
INDEXES OF TOTAL WAGES AND AVERAGE WAGE OF CITYWIDE FULL-TIME EMPLOYEES（1978-2021）

年份 Year	工资总额指数 Total Wage Bill Indexed		平均工资指数 Average Wage Indexes	
	全社会单位 All Units	其中：非私营单位 of which：Non-private Units	全社会单位 All Units	其中：非私营单位 of which：Non-private Units
1978		120.80		104.66
1979		119.53		113.36
1980		123.95		118.13
1981		106.71		99.49
1982		103.80		100.90
1983		104.14		103.06
1984		130.64		128.68
1985		107.11		105.96
1986		123.22		118.86
1987		120.10		115.87
1988		126.48		122.58
1989		115.29		113.86
1990		117.66		113.21
1991		108.28		106.38
1992		120.26		116.33
1993		127.09		124.38
1994		147.46		147.67
1995		114.76		113.00
1996		114.54		107.72
1997		105.50		105.87
1998		105.64		106.94
1999		114.81		111.80
2000		120.29		119.83
2001		112.77		113.44
2002		113.31		112.37
2003		108.84		110.30
2004	124.34	120.65	110.60	112.10
2005	128.16	125.54	114.95	116.47
2006	123.95	120.26	115.98	117.16
2007	116.27	115.96	115.32	115.46
2008	111.70	109.83	108.76	111.63
2009	110.26	105.73	109.01	110.01
2010	115.66	113.63	112.42	113.67
2011	118.90	116.83	114.76	113.95
2012	119.01	117.45	114.15	113.87
2013	119.86	128.15	114.14	112.87
2014	116.32	113.34	113.50	112.18
2015	112.94	111.51	110.86	111.85
2016	110.25	106.49	109.71	110.33
2017	109.82	109.66	107.68	108.41
2018	110.66	108.14	108.17	108.94
2019		111.43		110.14
2020		108.49		107.51
2021		108.97		109.87

注：1. 2004年以前为职工工资总额、平均工资指数。
2. 2015年以前为在岗职工工资总额、平均工资。
3. 自2019年统计口径变化，无全部单位工资数据。

Notes：1. The data before 2004 refer to the indexes of total wage of stall and workers.
2. It was the total salary and average salary of the on-spot staff before 2015.
3. Since the statistical caliber change in 2019, there is no wage data for all units.

3-7 城镇非私营和城镇私营单位分行业就业人员平均工资（2021 年）
AVERAGE WAGES OF EMPLOYED PERSONS IN URBAN NON-PRIVATE AND URBAN PRIVATE UNITS BY SECTOR（2021）

行业	Sector	非私营单位（元）Non-private Units (yuan)	私营单位（元）Private Units (yuan)
总计	**Total**	**116477**	**63631**
（一）农、林、牧、渔业	Farming, Forestry, Animal Husbandry	69573	52279
（二）采矿业	Mining	54373	62075
（三）制造业	Manufacturing	94413	60761
（四）电力、热力、燃气及水生产和供应业	Electricity, Heat, Gas and Water Production and Supply Industry	113909	66192
（五）建筑业	Construction	93571	73974
（六）批发和零售业	Wholesale and Retail Trade	92353	61193
（七）交通运输、仓储和邮政业	Transport, Storage and Post	114457	63157
（八）住宿和餐饮业	Hotels and Catering Services	62953	46026
（九）信息传输、软件和信息技术服务业	Information Transmission Computer Services and Software	149555	90503
（十）金融业	Financial Industry	121891	89323
（十一）房地产业	Real Estate	121628	65914
（十二）租赁和商务服务业	Leasing and Business Services	92586	61975
（十三）科学研究和技术服务业	Scientific Research and Technical Services	145469	72462
（十四）水利、环境和公共设施管理业	Management of Water Conservancy, Environment and Public Facilities	63178	44518
（十五）居民服务、修理和其他服务业	Residents Service, RePair and Other Services	81068	48408
（十六）教育	Education	154351	59516
（十七）卫生和社会工作	Health and Social Welfare	165553	69715
（十八）文化、体育和娱乐业	Culture, Sports and Entertainment	130475	64287
（十九）公共管理、社会保障和社会组织	Public Management, Social Security and Social Organization	161618	—

3-8 城镇非私营和城镇私营单位分市区就业人员平均工资（2021年）
AVERAGE WAGES OF EMPLOYED PERSONS IN URBAN NON-PRIVATE AND URBAN PRIVATE UNITS BY DISTRICTS (2021)

市、区名称	Region	非私营单位（元）Non-private Units (yuan)	私营单位（元）Private Units (yuan)
全市	**Whole Municipality**	**116477**	**63631**
市南区	Shinan District	120379	71329
市北区	Shibei District	127369	66893
李沧区	Licang District	104201	62654
崂山区	Laoshan District	148391	72321
黄岛区（西海岸新区）	Huangdao District (West Coast New Area)	115696	62979
城阳区（含高新区）	Chengyang District (Including High tech District)	116584	69047
即墨区	Jimo District	95374	58971
胶州市	Jiaozhou	99599	59457
平度市	Pingdu	92121	50790
莱西市	Laixi	87329	59774

主要统计指标解释

单位从业人员 指报告期末最后一日24时在本单位中工作，并取得工资或其他形式劳动报酬的人员数。该指标为时点指标，不包括最后一日当天及以前已经与单位解除劳动合同关系的人员，是在岗职工、劳务派遣人员及其他就业人员之和。就业人员不包括：

（1）离开本单位仍保留劳动关系，并定期领取生活费的人员；

（2）在本单位实习的各类在校学生；

（3）本单位因劳务外包而使用的人员。

在岗职工 指在本单位工作且与本单位签订劳动合同，并由单位支付各项工资和社会保险、住房公积金的人员，以及上述人员中由于学习、病伤、产假等原因暂未工作仍由单位支付工资的人员。在岗职工还包括：

（1）应订立劳动合同而未订立劳动合同人员（如使用的农村户籍人员）；

（2）处于试用期人员；

（3）编制外招用的人员；

（4）派往外单位工作，但工资仍由本单位发放的人员（如挂职锻炼、外派工作等情况）。

工资总额 指根据《关于工资总额组成的规定》(1990年1月1日国家统计局发布的一号令)进行修订,在报告期内(季度或年度)直接支付给本单位全部就业人员的劳动报酬总额。包括计时工资、计件工资、奖金、津贴和补贴、加班加点工资、特殊情况下支付的工资，是在岗职工工资总额、劳务派遣人员工资总额和其他就业人员工资总额之和。

工资总额是税前工资，包括单位从个人工资中直接为其代扣或代缴的房费、水费、电费、住房公积金和社会保险基金个人缴纳部分等。

工资总额不论是计入成本的还是不计入成本的，不论是以货币形式支付的还是以实物形式支付的，均应列入工资总额的计算范围。

平均工资 指单位就业人员在一定时期内平均每人所得的工资额。它表明一定时期工资收入的高低程度，是反映就业人员工资水平的主要指标。

Explanatory Notes on Main Statistical Indicators

Jobholders refers to the number of employees who works in the institution or company and gets salary or other form of labor reward at 24:00 of the last day of the report period. This is a time-point indicator which is the total of on-spot staff, labor dispatched personnel and other employees, excluding persons that have released the employment contract with the institution or company on the last day or before. The following are not deemed as Jobholders：

(1) Persons that keep the employment relations and get regular living expenses after leaving the institution or company.

(2) All kinds of students who intern in our company.

(3) Personnel that uses by the institution or company in labour outsourcing.

On-spot staff refers to the employees that works for and signs the employment contract with the institution or company, and relevant salary, social insurance and house funding are paid by the institution or company, and the persons of the previous employees that are not working but still gets salary from the institution or company due to the reason of learning, injury, maternity leave, etc. It also includes the following:

(1) Employees who shall sign the employment contract with institution or company but not signed (for example, employees of rural household registration).

(2) Employees that are still in probation period.

(3) Employees that are recruited outside the authorized size.

(4) Employees that are sent to other institution or company but the salaries are still paid by the institution or company (such as onsite training and labour dispatching).

Total salary refers to total payment for labour made directly to all jobholders of the institution or company within the report period (quarterly or annually) revised according to Regulations on Constitution of Total Salary, Order No. 1 released by National Bureau of Statistics on January 1, 1990, including hourly wage, piece wage, bonus, allowance and subsidy, overtime wage, and wages paid under special situations. It is also the total volume of on–spot staff, labour dispatching staff and other employment.

Total salary is the pre–tax salary, including the expenses of housing, water, power and the personal part of house funding and social insurance funds, which has been withheld and paid by the institution or company from personal salaries.

No matter it is credited into cost or not, no matter it is paid in currency or in kind, all total salary shall be categorized as total salary.

Average salary refers to the total salary per capita of employees of the institution or company within the certain period, which is the major indicator of the salary level of employees and the level of salary income of the certain salary.

固定资产投资 4

INVESTMENT IN FIXED ASSETS

简 要 说 明

一、本篇资料的主要内容

本篇资料主要反映了全市固定资产投资及房地产开发方面的情况，主要包括固定资产投资的规模、结构、资金来源和房地产开发投资、施竣工及销售情况等方面的资料

二、本篇资料的来源

本篇资料来源于固定资产投资及房地产开发投资统计年报，由市统计局固定资产投资统计处整理提供。

Brief Introduction

Ⅰ. Main Content

Data in this chapter show the basic conditions of investment in fixed assets and real estate development of the whole city, mainly including the total investment in fixed assets, the structure of investment, the resources of investment and investment in real estate development, construction, completion and sales, etc.

Ⅱ. Source of Data

Data in this chapter are based on the annual report on investment in fixed assets and real estate development, and provided by the Division of Investment and Construction Statistics of Qingdao Municipal Bureau of Statistics.

4-1 主要年份固定资产投资
MAJOP YEAP' S INVESTMENT IN FIXED ASSETS

单位：万元（10 000 yuan）

年份 Year	规模以上固定资产投资总额 Investment in Fixed Assets above Designated Size	按用途分 Grouped by Use		
		生产性投资 Productive Investment	非生产性投资 Non-Productive Investment	#住宅投资 Investment in Residential Buildings
1949	16	12	4	3
1952	3097	1368	1729	1007
1957	5923	3947	1976	1151
1962	2747	2049	698	192
1965	5481	4155	1326	375
1970	6100	5813	287	154
1975	15839	13548	2381	1064
1978	29660	23499	6161	3203
1980	47499	33865	13634	9335
1985	107421	60643	73424	19058
1990	284576	210453	74123	38898
1991	349031	256633	92398	51898
1992	583068	420748	162320	83844
1993	953274	511684	441590	162419
1994	1329716	728532	601184	324094
1995	1648281	925194	723087	390206
1996	1610562	972398	638164	285412
1997	1611902	932207	679695	278951
1998	1909711	1125821	783890	316999

4-1 续表 1
Continued

单位：万元（10 000 yuan）

年 份 Year	规模以上固定资产投资总额 Investment in Fixed Assets above Designated Size	按用途分 Grouped by Use		
		生产性投资 Productive Investment	非生产性投资 Non-Productive Investment	# 住宅投资 Investment in Residential Buildings
1999	2205891	1246328	959563	421151
2000	2426820	1311538	1115282	470963
2001	2934728	1487762	1446966	729181
2002	3683623	1962588	1721035	765030
2003	5475526	3023930	2451596	1038304
2004	9845646	6336279	3509367	1608738
2005	14032960	9172206	4860754	1841644
2006	14856894	9214578	5642316	2222733
2007	16353636	10231673	6121963	2720970
2008	20190098	12443179	7746919	3315538
2009	24588889	13852653	10736236	3831976
2010	30224785	16207885	14016900	5609189
2011	35025382	18622819	16402563	5707625
2012	41539146	24246803	17292343	6689114
2013	50278649	30996768	19281881	7220432
2014	57660308	32913906	24746402	7311090
2015	65556685	41402714	24153971	7569123
2016	74547006	44588200	29958806	9561782
2017	77770902	41719893	36051009	9255095

注：1. 规模以上固定资产投资数据 2003 年以前为城镇以上统计范围。
　　2. 因 2004 年以来数据有调整，故表中数据不可比。

Notes：1. The data of investment above designated size refer to investment above city and town level before 2003.
　　2. The data since 2004 are not comparable with other data because of the adjustment.

4-1 续表 2
Continued

单位：万元（10 000 yuan）

年份 Year	按构成分 Grouped by Composition of Funds			按资金来源分 Grouped by Sources of Funds			
	建筑安装工程 Construction and Installation	设备工器具购置 Purchase of Equipment and Instruments	其他费用 Others	国家投资 State Investment	国内贷款 Domestic Loans	利用外资 Foreign Investment	自筹及其他 Self-raising Fund and Others
1949	11	3	2	16			
1952	2146	870	81	1512			1585
1957	2853	2773	297	3816			2107
1962	1631	984	132	2205			542
1965	3346	1859	276	4451			1030
1970	3136	2835	129	2721			3379
1975	7489	8133	217	9378	1362		5099
1978	19968	9124	568	16828	1601		11231
1980	30993	15541	965	10371	12925	1420	22783
1985	64665	35100	7656	17377	35888	1136	53020
1990	167731	91305	25540	24687	91895	23688	144306
1991	196212	108929	43890	22615	131676	38325	156415
1992	304060	208384	70624	22660	213217	89130	258061
1993	600011	225555	127708	23736	208672	94469	626397
1994	842809	272126	214781	26062	318334	221265	764055
1995	1020484	385934	241863	25683	379198	328124	915276
1996	929735	458284	222543	35639	444443	310722	819758
1997	875057	485122	251723	27928	297089	363789	923096
1998	1034500	574852	300359	67762	491812	170709	1179428

4-1 续表 3
Continued

单位：万元（10 000 yuan）

年 份 Year	按构成分 Grouped by Composition of Funds			按资金来源分 Grouped by Sources of Funds			
	建筑安装工程 Construction and Installation	设备工器具购置 Purchase of Equipment and Instruments	其他费用 Others	国家投资 State Investment	国内贷款 Domestic Loans	利用外资 Foreign Investment	自筹及其他 Self-raising Fund and Others
1999	1456473	459596	289822	128603	584120	145589	1347579
2000	1476397	652640	297783	75978	489697	164175	1806238
2001	1781235	744549	408944	93491	620562	217526	2157787
2002	2328492	796685	558446	78775	719677	411704	2831288
2003	3544790	1133333	797403	127861	989178	722644	4237643
2004	6413046	2312139	1120461	85549	1100297	1016145	8245272
2005	8949231	3141732	1941997	136632	1250343	1850921	11540604
2006	8818614	3668191	2370089	391315	2126523	1662897	11856506
2007	9981666	4171878	2200092	215649	2427031	1788056	13109824
2008	11795435	5907195	2487468	322484	3309471	1951468	15855082
2009	14911874	5869214	3807801	778090	4217265	1593287	21555685
2010	18725922	6362880	5135983	1305737	5881886	2135736	27898294
2011	22865421	7521441	4638520	1640702	5871709	1766278	33579182
2012	26080239	8601282	6857625	1324159	5484459	1561597	37356847
2013	33237368	9969777	7071504	1959340	8154829	1528585	49552883
2014	39006113	11640126	7014069	1404667	7452983	1181541	55024776
2015	42893643	15972153	6690889	2067396	7249574	1098178	62458544
2016	45915827	16425993	8789790	1788103	14203650	903773	66069945
2017	55647641	10977494	11145767	2257927	14569701	641216	65055089

4-2 主要年份固定资产投资构成（以投资总额为100）
COMPOSITION OF MAJOR YEAR'S INVESTMENT IN FIXED ASSETS（TOTAL INVESTMENT=100）

年份 Year	按用途分 Grouped by Use		
	生产性投资 Productive Investment	非生产性投资 Non-Productive Investment	#住宅投资占非生产性比重 Percentage of Investment in Residential Buildings to Non-Productive Investment
1949	75.00	25.00	75.00
1952	44.17	55.83	58.24
1957	66.64	33.36	58.25
1962	74.59	25.41	27.51
1965	75.81	24.19	28.28
1970	95.30	4.70	53.66
1975	84.97	15.03	44.69
1978	79.23	20.77	51.99
1980	71.30	28.70	68.47
1985	56.45	43.55	40.74
1990	73.95	26.05	52.50
1991	73.53	26.47	56.17
1992	72.16	27.84	51.65
1993	53.68	46.32	36.78
1994	54.79	45.21	53.91
1995	56.10	43.90	54.00
1996	60.40	39.60	44.70
1997	57.80	42.20	41.00
1998	59.00	41.00	16.60

4-2 续表 1
Continued

年 份 Year	按用途分 Grouped by Use 生产性投资 Productive Investment	非生产性投资 Non-Productive Investment	#住宅投资占非生产性比重 Percentage of Investment in Residential Buildings to Non-Productive Investment
1999	56.50	43.50	19.10
2000	54.00	46.00	19.40
2001	50.70	49.30	50.40
2002	53.30	46.70	44.50
2003	55.20	44.80	42.40
2004	64.40	35.60	45.80
2005	65.40	34.60	37.90
2006	62.00	38.00	39.40
2007	62.60	37.40	44.40
2008	61.60	38.40	42.80
2009	56.30	43.70	35.70
2010	53.62	46.38	40.02
2011	53.17	46.83	34.80
2012	58.37	41.63	38.68
2013	61.65	38.35	37.45
2014	57.08	42.92	29.54
2015	63.16	36.84	31.34
2016	59.81	40.19	31.92
2017	53.64	46.36	25.67

4-2 续表 2
Continued

年 份 Year	按构成分 Grouped by Composition of Funds			按资金来源分 Grouped by Sources of Funds			
	建筑安装工程 Construction and Installation	设备工器具购置 Purchase of Equipment and Instruction	其他费用 Others	国家投资 State Investment	国内贷款 Domestic Loans	利用外资 Foreign Investment	自筹及其他 Self-raising Fund and Others
1949	68.75	18.75	12.5	100			
1952	69.29	28.09	2.62	48.82			51.18
1957	48.17	46.82	5.01	64.43			35.57
1962	59.37	35.82	4.81	80.27			19.73
1965	61.05	33.92	5.03	81.21			18.79
1970	51.41	46.48	2.11	44.61			55.39
1975	47.28	51.35	1.37	59.21	8.60		32.19
1978	67.32	30.76	1.92	56.74	5.40		37.86
1980	65.25	32.72	2.03	21.83	27.21	2.99	47.97
1985	60.2	32.68	7.12	16.18	33.41	1.06	49.35
1990	58.94	32.08	8.98	8.68	32.29	8.32	50.71
1991	56.22	31.21	12.57	6.48	37.73	10.98	44.81
1992	52.15	35.74	12.11	3.89	36.56	15.29	44.26
1993	62.94	23.66	13.4	2.49	21.89	9.91	65.71
1994	63.38	20.46	16.16	1.96	23.94	16.64	57.46
1995	61.9	23.4	14.7	1.6	23.0	19.9	55.5
1996	57.7	28.5	13.8	2.2	27.6	19.3	50.9
1997	54.3	30.1	15.6	1.7	18.4	22.6	57.3
1998	54.2	20.8	15.7	3.5	25.8	8.9	61.8
1999	66.0	20.8	13.2	5.8	26.5	6.6	61.1
2000	60.8	26.9	12.3	3.1	20.2	6.8	74.4

4-2 续表 3
Continued

年 份 Year	按构成分 Grouped by Composition of Funds			按资金来源分 Grouped by Sources of Funds			
	建筑安装工程 Construction and Installation	设备工器具购置 Purchase of Equipment and Instruction	其他费用 Others	国家投资 State Investment	国内贷款 Domestic Loans	利用外资 Foreign Investment	自筹及其他 Self-raising Fund and Others
2001	60.7	25.4	13.9	3.0	20.1	7.0	69.9
2002	63.2	21.6	15.2	1.9	17.8	10.2	70.1
2003	64.7	20.7	14.6	2.1	16.3	11.9	69.7
2004	65.1	23.5	11.4	0.8	10.6	9.7	78.9
2005	63.8	22.4	13.8	0.9	8.5	12.5	78.1
2006	59.4	24.7	15.9	2.4	13.3	10.4	73.9
2007	61.0	25.5	13.5	1.2	13.8	10.2	74.8
2008	58.4	29.3	12.3	1.5	15.4	9.1	74.0
2009	60.6	23.9	15.5	2.8	15.0	5.6	76.6
2010	62.0	21.0	17.0	3.5	15.8	5.7	75.0
2011	65.3	21.5	13.3	3.8	13.7	4.1	78.4
2012	62.8	20.7	16.5	2.9	12.0	3.4	81.7
2013	66.1	19.8	14.1	3.2	13.3	2.5	81.0
2014	67.6	20.2	12.2	2.2	11.5	1.8	84.6
2015	65.4	24.4	10.2	2.8	10.0	1.5	85.7
2016	61.6	22.0	11.8	2.2	17.1	1.1	79.6
2017	71.6	14.1	14.3	2.7	17.7	0.8	78.8
2018	68.8	7.8	23.4	2.9	15.2	0.4	81.5
2019	65.3	7.0	27.7	1.8	16.2	1.3	80.7
2020	63.8	5.9	30.3	3.8	14.9	0.8	80.5
2021	71.5	6.2	22.3	4.0	11.2	0.2	84.6

4-3 按三次产业分规模以上固定资产投资增速（2021 年）
GROWTH RATE OF INVESTMENT IN FIXED ASSETS ABOVE DESIGNATED SIZE BY THREE STRATA OF INDUSTRY (2021)

单位：%

指　标	Indicator	2021 年
总　计	**Total**	**4.1**
第一产业	Primary Industry	20.7
第二产业	Secondary Industry	25.4
#工业	Industry	25.5
第三产业	Tertiary Industry	-1.8

4-4 分市、区规模以上固定资产投资增速(2021 年)
GROWTH RATE OF FIXED ASSET INVESTMENT ABOVE DESIGNATED SIZE BY CITY AND DISTRICT (2021)

单位：%

市、区名称	Region	规模以上固定资产投资增速 Growth Rate Of Investment In Fixed Assets Above Designated Size	#房地产开发投资增速 Real Estate Development Investment Growth Rate
全　市	**Whole Municipality**	**4.1**	**-3.1**
市南区	Shinan District	0.7	-44.4
市北区	Shibei District	10.6	13.4
李沧区	Licang District	-29.1	-41.0
崂山区	Laoshan District	12.1	0.8
黄岛区（西海岸新区）	Huangdao District (West Coast New Area)	4.6	20.2
城阳区	Chengyang District	6.2	-19.3
城阳区（不含高新区）	Chengyang District (Excluding High tech District)	5.0	-17.6
高新区	High tech District	12.1	-25.0
即墨区	Jimo District	5.8	23.3
胶州市	Jiaozhou	8.0	-31.1
平度市	Pingdu	12.2	12.2
莱西市	Laixi	13.5	-19.0

4-5 规模以上固定资产投资(2021 年)
INVESTMENT IN FIXED ASSETS ABOVE DESIGNATED SIZE (2021)

单位：%

项 目	Item	合计 Total	#房地产开发 Investment in Real Estate Development
一、本年施工项目(个)	**Projects Under Construction This Year (unit)**	**7038**	**1436**
#本年新开工(个)	of which: Newly Started (unit)	3159	189
二、本年建成投产项目(个)	**Projects Completed and Put into Use This Year (unit)**	**2440**	
三、本年完成投资增速(%)	**Complete Investment Growth Rate This Year (%)**	**4.1**	**-3.1**
1. 按构成分	Grouped by Composition		
#建筑安装工程	Construction installation project	10.6	0.4
设备工器具购置	Purchase of Equipment and Instruments	9.4	-27.6
2. 按建设性质分	Grouped by Type of Construction		
#新建	New Construction	6.2	
扩建	Expansion	24.6	
改建和技术改造	Reconstruction	8.9	
3. 按国民经济行业分	Grouped by Economic Sector		
(1)农、林、牧、渔业	Farming, Forestry, Animal Husbandry and Fishery	22.7	
农业	Farming	2.4	
林业	Forestry	37.6	
畜牧业	Animal Husbandry	31.6	
渔业	Fishery	220.8	
农、林、牧、渔服务业	Farming, Forestry, Animal Husbandry and Fishery Services	32.7	
(2)采矿业	Mining	633.5	
煤炭开采和洗选业	Mining and Washing of Coal		
石油和天然气开采业	Extraction of Petroleum and Natural Gas		
黑色金属矿采选业	Mining of Ferrous Metal Ores	640.7	
有色金属矿采选业	Mining of Non-ferrous Metal Ores	619.8	
非金属矿采选业	Mining and Processing of Non-metal Ores	237.5	
开采辅助活动	Auxiliary Activities of Mining		
其他采矿业	Mining of Other Ores		

4-5 续表 1
Continued

单位：%

项　目	Item	合计 Total	#房地产开发 Investment in Real Estate Development
（3）制造业	Manufacturing	24.8	
农副食品加工业	Processing of Food from Agricultural Products	86.2	
食品制造业	Manufacture of Foods	11.0	
酒、饮料和精制茶制造业	Manufacture of Liquor，Beverages and Refined Tea	34.1	
烟草制品业	Manufacture of Tobacco	261.5	
纺织业	Manufacture of Textile	4.7	
纺织服装、服饰业	Manufacture of Textile Wearing Apparel	31.9	
皮革、毛皮、羽毛及其制品和制鞋业	Manufacture of Leather，Fur，Feather & Its Products Footwear	-61.0	
木材加工和木、竹、藤、棕、草制品业	Processing of Timber, Manufacture of Wood, Bamboo, Rattan, Palm and Straw Products	105.9	
家具制造业	Manufacture of Furniture	86.3	
造纸和纸制品业	Manufacture of Paper and Paper Products	19.5	
印刷和记录媒介复制业	Printing，Reproduction of Recording Media	58.1	
文教、工美、体育和娱乐用品制造业	Manufacture of Articles for Culture，Arts & Crafts，Sports and Entertainment	178.8	
石油、煤炭及其他燃料加工业	Processing of petroleum, coal and other fuels	-68.5	
化学原料和化学制品制造业	Manufacture of Chemical Raw Material and Chemical Products	-9.1	
医药制造业	Manufacture of Medicines	37.8	
化学纤维制造业	Manufacture of Chemical Fibres	118.8	
橡胶和塑料制品业	Manufacture of Rubber and Plastic	40.2	
非金属矿物制品业	Manufacture of metallic Mineral Products	2.2	
黑色金属冶炼和压延加工业	Smelting and Pressing of Ferrous Metals	-33.9	
有色金属冶炼和压延加工业	Smelting and Pressing of Non-ferrous Metals	112.0	
金属制品业	Manufacture of Metal Products	-10.7	
通用设备制造业	Manufacture of General Purpose Machinery	-14.0	
专用设备制造业	Manufacture of Special Purpose Machinery	3.9	
汽车制造业	Manufacture of Vehicle	136.6	
铁路、船舶、航空航天和其他运输设备制造业	Manufacture of Transport Equipment for Railway，Shipping，Aerospace and other uses	37.3	
电气机械和器材制造业	Manufacture of Electrical Machinery and Equipment	5.7	
计算机、通信和其他电子设备制造业	Manufacture of Computer，Communication Equipment and Other Electronic Equipment	96.5	
仪器仪表制造业	Manufacture of Measuring Instrument	76.5	
其他制造业	Manufacture of Other Products	-6.9	
废弃资源综合利用业	Recycling and Disposal of Waste Resources	19.7	
金属制品、机械和设备修理业	Maintenance of Metal Products，Machinery and Equipment		

4-5 续表 2
Continued

单位：%

项　　目	Item	合计 Total	# 房地产开发 Investment in Real Estate Development
（4）电力、热力、燃气及水生产和供应业	Electricity, heat, gas, water production and supply industry	24.9	
电力、热力生产和供应业	Electricity and Heat Production and Supply Industry	15.2	
燃气生产和供应业	Gas Production and Supply Industry	101.9	
水的生产和供应业	Water Production and Supply Industry	23.9	
（5）建筑业	Construction	-40.2	
房屋建筑业	Housing Building Industry	15.2	
土木工程建筑业	Civil Engineering Construction Industry	-68.4	
建筑安装业	Construction and Installation Industry		
建筑装饰装、装修和其他建筑业	Building Decoration and Other Construction Industries	-100.0	
（6）批发和零售业	Wholesale and Retail Trade	-57.4	
批发业	Wholesale Trade	-36.7	
零售业	Retails Trade	-63.9	
（7）交通运输、仓储和邮政业	Transport Storage and Post	-6.2	
铁路运输业	Railway Transport	-80.3	
道路运输业	Road Transport	31.2	
水上运输业	Water Transport	-53.1	
航空运输业	Air Transport	-53.1	
管道运输业	Pipeline Transport	-17.4	
多式联运和运输代理业	Multi-dimensional Transportation & Transportation Forwarding Industry	140.6	
装卸搬运和仓储业	Handing，Carrying and Ware houses and Storage	-25.8	
邮政业	Post	409.8	
（8）住宿和餐饮业	Hotels and Catering Services	3.6	
住宿业	Hotels Services	-9.2	
餐饮业	Catering Services	209.1	
（9）信息传输、软件和信息技术服务业	Information Transmission, Software and Information Technology Service Industry	-26.7	
电信、广播电视和卫星传输服务	Telecommunications, Radio, Television and Satellite Transmission Services	-45.3	
互联网和相关服务	Internet and Related Services	6.5	
软件和信息技术服务业	Software and Information Technology Services	-36.7	
（10）金融业	Financial Industry	-25.8	
货币金融服务	Monetary and Financial Services	86.3	
资本市场服务	Capital Markets Services	-87.7	
保险业	Insurance Industry		
其他金融业	Other Financial Industries	-4.4	

4-5 续表 3
Continued

单位：%

项　　目	Item	合计 Total	#房地产开发 Investment in Real Estate Development
（11）房地产业	Real Estate Industry	7.8	-3.1
（12）租赁和商务服务业	Leasing and Business Services	19.7	
租赁业	Leasing Services	-66.7	
商务服务业	Business Services	23.7	
（13）科学研究和技术服务业	Scientific Research，Technical Service and Geologic Prospecting	-27.4	
研究和实验进展	Research and Experimental Development	-36.5	
专业技术服务业	Professional Technical Service Industry	11.2	
科技推广和应用服务业	Technology Promotion and Application Service Industry	6.0	
（14）水利、环境和公共设施管理业	Management of Water Conservancy，Environment and Pubic Facilities	-6.3	
水利管理业	Management of Water Conservancy	-48.3	
生态保护和环境治理业	Ecological protection and environmental governance	6.8	
公共设施管理业	Management of Public Facilities	-1.4	
土地管理业	Land Management	-86.0	
（15）居民服务、修理和其他服务业	Residents Service, Repair and Other Services	13.4	
居民服务业	Serviced to Households	31.6	
机动车、电子产品和日用产品修理业	Maintenance of Vehicle，Electronic Products and Daily Articles	-24.8	
其他服务业	Other Services	-45.1	
（16）教育	Education	-3.7	
（17）卫生和社会工作	Health and Social Work	2.3	
卫生	Health	17.1	
社会工作	Social Work	-46.1	
（18）文化、体育和娱乐业	Culture，Sports and Entertainment	-42.9	
新闻和出版业	Journalism and Publishing Activities		
广播、电视、电影和录音制作业	Broadcasting, Televisions, Movies and Audio Production Industry	-30.8	
文化艺术业	Cultural and Art Activities	-79.2	
体育	Sports Activities	6.8	
娱乐业	Entertainment	-44.9	
（19）公共管理、社会保障和社会组织	Public Management，Social Security and Social Organzation	-17.3	
中国共产党机关	Communist Party of China		
国家机构	Government Agencies	-25.6	
人民政协、民主党派	People's Political Consultative Conference，Democratic Party		
社会保障	Social Security	-100.0	
群众团体、社会团体和其他成员组织	Non-Governmental Institutions，Social Organizations and Other Organizations	80.3	
基层群众自治组织	Local People Self-government Organization	2178.2	
（20）国际组织	International Organization		

4-5 续表 4
Continued

单位：%

项　　目	Item	合计 Total	#房地产开发 Investment in Real Estate Development
四、本年资金来源合计	**Total Funds This Year**	**-1.8**	**-5.7**
上年末结余资金	Balance of Last Year	-1.8	-7.7
本年资金来源小计	Sub-total Funds This Year	-1.8	-4.7
国家预算内资金	State Budget	3.1	
国内贷款	Domestic Loans	-28.4	-34.9
债券	State Treasury Bond	2095.8	—
利用外资	Foreign Investment	-77.2	-89.8
自筹资金	Self-raising Funds	-0.5	-12.6
其他资金来源	Others	11.7	12.6

4-6 主要年份房地产开发投资
MAJOR YEAR'S INVESTMENT IN REAL ESTATE DEVELOPMENT

单位：万元、万平方米（10 000 yuan，10 000 sq.m）

年 份 Year	房地产开发投资额 Investment in Real Estate Development	房屋施工面积 Floor Space Under Construction	房屋竣工面积 Floor Space Completed	房屋实际销售面积 Floor Space of Buildings Sold	房屋实际销售额 Sale of Buildings
1995	562861	1008	240	103	185384
1996	455765	748	203	80	125150
1997	426570	675	237	113	216311
1998	438059	742	259	178	351805
1999	629717	900	474	240	430123
2000	675142	1047	352	301	550401
2001	925153	1374	532	406	802364
2002	1036476	1417	537	427	933031
2003	1277969	1765	552	469	1121885
2004	1626965	2101	635	516	1530964
2005	2238370	2363	811	740	2666738
2006	2683631	2751	654	719	3054907
2007	3223547	3224	641	833	4333566
2008	3805652	3773	672	770	3924175
2009	4594829	4310	814	1262	7036744
2010	6024387	5058	1020	1360	8952942
2011	7827193	5693	925	1026	7702379
2012	9301099	6474	1212	951	7660684
2013	10485229	7073	957	1160	9786176
2014	11177297	8171	1136	1164	9708984
2015	11223458	8971	1523	1419	12628568
2016	13691425	9101	1426	1939	17899532
2017	13305432	9533	1487	1901	19992012
2018	14852089	10390	1625	1808	22824618
2019	18038081	11580	1602	1652	22469992
2020	20451153	12528	1154	1654	22168506
2021	19818480	13012	1657	1645	22672959

4-7 房地产开发投资情况(2021年)
INVESTMENT IN REAL ESTATE DEVELOPMENT（2021）

单位：万元(10 000 yuan)

指标名称	Indicator	合计 Total	按经济类型分 Grouped by Economic Types		
			国有经济 State-owned	集体经济 Collective-owned	其他经济 Others
本年完成投资额	**Investment Completed This Year**	**19818480**	**821667**	**339122**	**18657691**
1. 住宅	Residential Buildings	14810338	593394	201260	14015684
2. 办公楼	Office Buildings	1236892	67521	15504	1153867
3. 商业营业用房	Houses for Business Use	1147261	57599	3490	1086172
4. 其他	Others	2623989	103153	118868	2401968

4-7 续表
Continued

单位：万元(10 000 yuan)

指标名称	Indicator	按资质等级分 Grouped by Qualification Criteria					
		一级 First Grade	二级 Second Grade	三级 Third Grade	四级 Fourth Grade	暂定 Provisional	其他 Others
本年完成投资额	**Investment Completed This Year**	**253697**	**805420**	**527148**	**91898**	**15120262**	**3020055**
1. 住宅	Residential Buildings	198517	635821	370704	74302	11245884	2285110
2. 办公楼	Office Buildings	5808	39331	30625	112	973877	187139
3. 商业营业用房	Houses for Business Use	18594	38416	62373	12755	893193	121930
4. 其他	Others	30778	91852	63446	4729	2007308	425876

4-8 房地产施工、竣工面积及竣工价值(2021 年)
FLOOR SPACE UNDER CONSTRUCTION AND COMPLETED AND COMPLETED VALUE OF REAL ESTATE (2021)

单位：万平方米 (10 000 sq.m)

施工、竣工房屋面积及竣工价值	Construction and Completed Housing Area and Completed Value	施工面积 Floor Space Under Construction	#新开工 Newly Started	竣工房屋 Floor Space Completed	竣工房屋价值 (万元) Completed Value (10 000 yuan)
房屋建筑面积总计	**Floor Space of Buildings**	**13012**	**2180**	**1657**	**6787620**
住宅	Residential Buildings	8555	1413	1111	4841834
办公楼	Office Buildings	856	129	81	424698
商业营业用房	Houses for Business Use	910	148	100	419961
其他	Others	2691	490	365	1101127

4-9 商品房屋销售情况(2021 年)
BASIC STATISTICS ON SALES OF COMMERCIALIZED BUILBINGS (2021)

商品房屋销售情况	Sales and Rental of Commercialized Buildings	实际销售 (万平方米) Actual Sales (10 000sq.m)	实际销售额 (万元) Actual Sales Volume (10 000 yuan)	待售面积 (万平方米) Area for Sale (10 000sq.m)
房屋面积总计	**Floor Space of Buildings**	**1645**	**22672959**	**577**
住宅	Residential Buildings	1420	20392399	264
办公楼	Office Buildings	76	1010440	93
商业营业用房	Houses for Business Use	61	864768	152
其他	Others	88	405352	68

主要统计指标解释

固定资产投资 是以货币形式表现的在一定时期内建造和购置固定资产的工作量以及与此有关的费用的总称。

房地产开发投资 指各种登记注册类型的房地产开发法人单位统一开发的住宅、厂房、仓库、饭店、宾馆、度假村、写字楼、办公楼等房屋建筑物，配套的服务设施，土地开发工程（如道路、给水、排水、供电、供热、通讯、平整场地等基础设施工程）和土地购置的投资；不包括单纯的土地开发和交易活动。

固定资产投资的资金来源 根据固定资产投资的资金来源不同，分为国家预算资金、国内贷款、利用外资、自筹资金和其他资金。

固定资产投资 按建设性质分建设项目的性质一般分为新建、扩建、改建和技术改造、单纯建造生活设施、迁建、恢复、单纯购置。

固定资产投资 按构成分固定资产投资活动按其工作内容和实现方式分为建筑安装工程，设备、工具、器具购置，其他费用三个部分。

新增生产能力（或工程效益） 指建成投产项目或工程新增生产能力（或工程效益）的名称。

房屋施工面积 是指报告期内施工的全部房屋建筑面积。包括本期新开工的面积和上期开工跨入本期继续施工的房屋面积，以及上期已停缓建在本期恢复施工的房屋面积。本期竣工和本期施工后又停缓建的房屋，其建筑面积仍计入本期房屋施工面积中。

房屋竣工面积 是指在报告期内房屋建筑按照设计要求全部完工，达到住人和使用条件，经验收鉴定合格（或达到竣工验收标准），正式移交使用单位的各栋房屋建筑面积的总和。

本年新增固定资产 指在报告期已经完成建造和购置过程，并已交付生产或使用单位的固定资产的价值，包括已经建成投入生产或交付使用的工程投资和达到固定资产标准的设备、工具、器具的投资及有关应摊入的费用。

Explanatory Notes on Main Statistical Indicators

Fixed investment is a generic term of quantity of work from building and acquiring of fixed assets over a period of time and any relevant expenses incurred thereby in the form of currency.

Real estate development investment means investments in all kinds of registered housing & building, including residences, plants, warehouses, restaurants, hotels, resorts, office buildings and administrative buildings which are developed uniformly by real estate development corporation, supporting service facilities and land development projects (such as road, water supply & drainage, power supply, heat supply, telecommunication and ground leveling and other infrastructure projects) and land acquisition, excludes simple land development and transaction activities.

Source of funds for fixed-asset investment can be divided into national budget funds, domestic loans, utilization of foreign capital, self-raised funds and other funds in accordance with the different sources.

Construction items of fixed-asset investment can be divided into new construction, extension, reconstruction, technical reform, simply-constructed living facilities, relocation, restoration and simple acquisition by property of construction.

Fixed-asset investment activities can be divided into three parts, namely construction and installation project, acquisition of equipment, tools and appliances and other expenses by working content and method of achieving.

New productive capacity (or project benefit) means the completed projects or new productive capacity (or project benefit) of project.

Construction area means total areas of all buildings which are under construction in the report period, including the area which is newly constructed in this period and the areas of buildings which commence in the last period and carry forward to this period for continuing construction. and the areas of buildings which stop constructing in the last period and resume to be constructed in this period. The areas of the buildings which are completed in this period and stop constructing after this period' s construction are still reckoned in floor space under construction in this period.

Completed area means the sum total of areas of housings & buildings which are completed according to design requirements in the report period, reach conditions of living and using and are transferred to building users formally after checked and accepted (or reach the standards of completion and acceptance).

New fixed assets in this year means the value of fixed assets which are completed and acquired in the report period and delivered for production or use, including investment in constructions which are put into production or service, investment in equipment, tools and appliances which reach the standards of fixed asset, and the expenses which should be added into fixed assets.

对外经济贸易 5

FOREIGN TRADE

简要说明

一、本篇资料的主要内容

本篇资料主要反映了全市外经外贸和外资企业的基本情况，主要包括外贸进出口、利用外资、对外投资与经济合作等方面的资料。

二、本篇资料的来源

1. 口岸进出口数据来源于青岛海关。

2. 进出口、利用外资等资料、对外投资与经济合作来源于市商务局。

本篇资料由市统计局外经贸易统计处整理提供。

Brief Introduction

Ⅰ. Main Content

Data in this chapter show the basic conditions of foreign trade and foreign-funded enterprises, mainly including imports and exports, utilization of foreign capitals, production and operation condition of foreign-funded enterprises, etc.

Ⅱ. Source of Data

1. Port import and export data comes from Qingdao Customs.

2. Data on imports & exports and utilization of foreign capitals are provided by Qingdao Municipal Commerce Bureau.

Data in this chapter are prepared and compiled by the Division of Trade and External Economic Relations Statistics of Qingdao Municipal Bureau of Statistics.

5-1 青岛口岸进出口总额(1985—2021 年)

TOTAL VALUE OF IMPORTS AND EXPORTS OF QINGDAO PORT（1985—2021）

单位：万美元（10 000 USD）、万元（10 000 yuan）

年 份 Year	青岛口岸进出口总额 Total Value of Imports and Exports Qingdao Port	出口 Exports	进口 Imports
1985	414448	234652	179796
1986	382840	191926	190914
1987	445090	259458	185632
1988	474516	259176	215340
1989	506152	268397	237755
1990	477117	304011	173106
1991	519273	332949	186324
1992	581495	350163	231332
1993	678013	360297	317716
1994	888574	510760	377814
1995	1307508	705245	602263
1996	1391323	760566	629757
1997	1542284	936142	609142
1998	1463718	933392	530326
1999	1696514	1063768	632746
2000	2520420	1423266	1097154
2001	2797085	1636888	1160197
2002	3128048	1889612	1238436
2003	4088096	2366046	1722050
2004	5677570	3197697	2479873
2005	6932944	3959947	2972997
2006	8019198	4495731	3523467
2007	9257099	5263539	3993560
2008	11558079	5953501	5604578
2009	9049699	4694832	4354867
2010	11912702	5988254	5924448
2011	15095088	7294226	7800862
2012	14888716	7120813	7767903
2013	15662732	7696141	7966591
2014	16489966	8736358	7753608
2015	14448349	8776286	5672063
2016	94927180	56513317	38413863
2017	111024375	63298062	47726314
2018	121968146	67385279	54582867
2019	127239314	69443761	57795553
2020	116719854	66149587	50570266
2021	151615242	85492319	66122923

注：2016 年起，统计单位为人民币万元。
Note：Statistic unit is RMB ten thousand Yuan as from 2016.

5-2 进出口总额(1988—2021年)
TOTAL VALUE OF IMPORTS AND EXPORTS（1988—2021）

单位：万美元（10 000 USD）、万元（10 000 yuan）

年份 Year	进出口总额（含中央、省驻青公司）Total Value of Imports and Exports（including central and provincial companies）	出口 Exports	进口 Imports	进出口总额（不含中央、省驻青公司）Total Value of Imports and Exports（including central and provincial companies）	出口 Exports	进口 Imports
1988				28097	21731	6366
1989				39327	27797	11530
1990				41649	33529	8120
1991				54624	44746	9878
1992				88600	66291	22309
1993	517643	346288	171355	139048	100201	38847
1994	633213	434102	199111	234978	164135	70843
1995	858560	536386	322174	376372	245072	131300
1996	863521	516317	347204	461950	287123	174827
1997	916269	579261	377008	521967	338535	183432
1998	882042	573020	309022	595826	382657	213169
1999	1009885	631072	378813	775565	446260	329305
2000	1353222	826891	526331	1083133	611426	471707
2001	1541564	950160	591404	1235781	712024	523757
2002	1692567	1057141	635426	1409598	850420	559178
2003	2065912	1239199	826713	1784556	1035528	749028
2004	2698781	1578167	1120614	2433188	1391171	1042017
2005	3302230	1942242	1359988	3045542	1758834	1286708
2006	3911543	2346552	1564991	3655737	2164541	1491196
2007	4572534	2831004	1741530	4360499	2677596	1682903
2008	5363659	3262476	2101183	5215886	3146246	2069640
2009	4485115	2729865	1755250	4398639	2692197	1706442
2010	5705963	3391560	2314403	5614928	3335141	2279787
2011	7215217	4061309	3153908	7126310	4005572	3120738
2012				7320781	4081968	3238813
2013				7791217	4198605	3592612
2014				7988833	4577696	3411137
2015				7022243	4535015	2487228
2016				43506659	28219059	15287600
2017				50334973	30318103	20016870
2018				53212551	31722209	21490342
2019				59255880	34119000	25136880
2020				64070068	38767641	25302427
2021				84984331	49212763	35771568

注：1. 2012年起，中央、省驻青公司外贸统计划归青岛，取消含中央、省驻青公司统计口径。
2. 2016年起，统计单位为人民币万元。

Notes：1. Since 2012，the statistical calibre including central and provincial companies has been canclled.
2. Statistic unit is RMB ten thousand Yuan as from 2016.

5-3 分国别外贸出口总额
TOTAL VALUE OF EXPORTS BY COUNTRIES OR REGIONS

单位：万美元（10 000 USD）

国别（地区）	Country（Region）	2021 年	2021 年比 2020 年 ±% 2021/2020（±%）	占比 % Ratio（%）
亚洲	Asia	3581590	36.4	47.0
中国香港	Hong Kong, China	360326	75.7	4.7
日本	Japan	710439	19.4	9.3
韩国	Korea	673048	46.1	8.8
东盟	ASEAN	982412	30.1	12.9
非洲	Africa	366165	51.6	4.8
南非	South Africa	66035	54.0	0.9
欧洲	Europe	1550966	36.3	20.4
欧盟	EU	1058522	28.0	13.9
南美洲	South America	249903	45.4	3.3
北美洲	North America	1355801	30.3	17.8
美国	USA	1199450	32.6	15.7
大洋洲	Oceanica	215128	28.2	2.8
澳大利亚	Australia	166497	18.6	2.2

5-4 外贸出口商品分类
EXPORT COMMODITIES BY CATEGORY

单位：万元（10 000 yuan）

项目	Item	2021 年	2021 年比 2020 年 ±% 2021/2020（±%）	占比 % Ratio（%）
合 计	**Total**	**49212763**	**27.0**	**100.0**
按企业性质划分	By Enterprises Nature			
国有企业	State-owned Enterprises	3472747	19.0	7.1
三资企业	Foreign-funded Enterprise	10709647	21.5	21.8
其他企业	Other Enterprises	35030369	29.6	71.2
#集体企业	#Collective-owned Enterprises	847940	3.7	1.7
私营企业	Private Enterprises	34139972	30.6	69.4
按贸易方式划分	By Customs Regime			
一般贸易	Ordinary Trade	36053571	24.6	73.3
加工贸易	Processing Trade	8986753	6.7	18.3
其他贸易	Others	4172438	200.3	8.5
按大类商品划分	By Category of Commodities			
纺织服装	Textile Garments	5712924	10.8	11.6
农产品	Agricultural Products	3708404	-5.8	7.5
机电产品	Mechanical and Electrical Products	23451346	29.8	47.7
高新技术产品	High-tech Products	3937160	24.9	8.0

5-5 外贸进口商品分类
IMPORT COMMODITIES BY CATEGORY

单位：万元（10 000 yuan）

项　目	Item	2021年	2021年比2020年 ±% 2021/2020（±%）	占比 % Ratio（%）
合　计	**Total**	**35771568**	**40.7**	**100.0**
按企业性质划分	By Enterprises Nature			
国有企业	State-owned Enterprises	6923840	71.9	19.4
三资企业	Foreign-funded Enterprise	6643108	12.7	18.6
其他企业	Other Enterprises	22204620	43.2	62.1
#集体企业	#Collective-owned Enterprises	88007	19.9	0.2
私营企业	Private Enterprises	21998333	44.1	61.5
按贸易方式划分	By Customs Regime			
一般贸易	Ordinary Trade	21638294	38.9	60.5
加工贸易	Processing Trade	3102520	11.4	8.7
其他贸易	Others	11030755	56.2	30.8
按大类商品划分	By Category of Commodities			
纺织服装	Textile Garments	218110	1.5	0.6
农产品	Agricultural Products	6855907	19.5	19.2
机电产品	Mechanical and Electrical Products	6218752	38.5	17.4
高新技术产品	High-tech Products	3654431	59.4	10.2

5-6 二十大出口商品出口情况
INFORMATION ON THE EXPORTATION OF TOP 20 PRODUCTS

单位：万美元（10 000 USD）

商品名称	Name	2021 年	2021 年比 2020 年 ±% 2021/2020（±%）	占比 % Ratio（%）
合 计	**Total**	**6381049**	**33.3**	**83.7**
机械设备	Machinery and Equipment	1193643	35.2	15.7
电器及电子产品	Electric Appliance and Electronic Products	787703	31.1	10.3
运输工具	Garments	724663	60.0	9.5
服装及衣着附件	Clothing and Clothing Accessories	543461	40.1	7.1
金属制品	Metal Products	472180	40.2	6.2
化工产品	Chemical Products	453672	43.7	6
纺织纱线、织物及制品	Textile Yarns, Fabric and Textile Products	341191	-4.2	4.5
汽车零配件	Automobile Parts	286589	31.5	3.8
塑料制品	Plastic Articles	264011	32.6	3.5
钢材	Rolled Steel	260727	103.5	3.4
轮胎	Tyre	190945	26.9	2.5
家具及其零件	Furniture	176948	23.7	2.3
水海产品	Aquatic and Seawater Products	122756	-3.0	1.6
鞋类	Shoes	118870	34.1	1.6
仪器仪表	Instrumentation	89463	41.2	1.2
蔬菜	Vegetables	88537	-6.4	1.2
箱包及类似容器	Bags and Similar Containers	88436	50.4	1.2
陶瓷产品	Ceramic Products	78874	4.7	1
床垫、寝具及类似品	Mattresses，Bedding and Similar Products	63837	23.1	0.8
鲜、干水果及坚果	Fresh and Dried Fruits and Nuts	34543	-39.5	0.5

5-7 二十大进口商品进口情况
INFORMATION ON THE IMPORTATION OF TOP 20 PRODUCTS

单位：万美元（10 000 USD）

商品名称	Name	2021 年	2021 年比 2020 年 ±% 2021/2020（±%）	占比 % Ratio（%）
合　计	**Total**	**4639652**	**55.2**	**83.8**
原油	Crude Oil	818056	101.1	14.8
铁矿砂及其精矿	Iron Ore and Concentrate	798411	58.0	14.4
以天然沥青等为基本成分的沥青混合物	Bituminous mixtures based on natural bitumen, etc	423890	259.8	7.7
机械设备	Machinery and Equipment	399358	95.3	7.2
肉类	Meat	374210	22.5	6.8
电器及电子产品	Electric Appliance and Electronic Products	307067	18.1	5.5
粮食	Grain	225671	53.4	4.1
仪器仪表	Instruments and Meters	202846	50.5	3.7
集成电路	Integrated Circuits	144856	24.3	2.6
成品油	Refined Petroleum Products	143676	174.1	2.6
水海产品	Aquatic and Seawater Products	141941	9.3	2.6
初级形状的塑料	Plastic in primary form	134376	16.3	2.4
铜矿砂及其精矿	Copper Ore and Concentrate	116910	53.5	2.1
合成橡胶（包括胶乳）	Synthetic Rubber (including latex)	91358	-27.3	1.7
铝矿砂及其精矿	Aluminum Ore and Concentrate	71523	17.3	1.3
天然橡胶（包括胶乳）	Natural Rubber(including latex)	63148	9.2	1.1
棉花	Cotton	62606	40.9	1.1
纸浆	Pulp	49162	-17.8	0.9
钢材	Rolled Steel	39891	3.4	0.7
纺织纱线、织物及制品	Textile Yarns, Fabric and Textile Products	30696	5.9	0.6

5-8 利用外资情况（2000—2021年）
UTILIZATION OF FOREIGN CAPITAL（2000 — 2021）

项　目	Item	单位	Unit	2000年	2005年
批准企业（项目）个数	**Number of Enterprises（Projects）Approved**	**个**	**unit**	**1132**	**2530**
一、外商直接投资	Foreign Direct Investments	个	unit	1128	2530
中外合资企业	Sino-foreign Joint Ventures	个	unit	303	274
中外合作企业	Sino-foreign Cooperative Enterprises	个	unit	57	18
外商独资企业	Foreign-owned Enterprises	个	unit	76	2236
外商投资股份制	Foreign-invested joint-stock system	个	unit	1	2
合伙企业	Partnership	个	unit		
二、外商其他投资	Other Foreign Investments	个	unit	4	
合同外资金额	**Total Amount of Contracted Foreign Investment**	**万美元**	**10000 USD**	**269081**	**954486**
一、外商直接投资	Foreign Direct Investments	万美元	10000 USD	266221	954486
中外合资企业	Sino-foreign Joint Ventures	万美元	10000 USD	69889	112777
中外合作企业	Sino-foreign Cooperative Enterprises	万美元	10000 USD	26835	17588
外商独资企业	Foreign-owned Enterprises	万美元	10000 USD	169370	813485
外商投资股份制	Foreign-invested joint-stock system	万美元	10000 USD	127	10636
合伙企业	Partnership	万美元	10000 USD		
二、外商其他投资	Other Foreign Investments	万美元	10000 USD	2860	
实际利用外资金额	**Total Amount of Foreign Investment Actually Utilized**	**万美元**	**10000 USD**	**128171**	**365625**
一、外商直接投资	Foreign Direct Investments	万美元	10000 USD	126132	365625
中外合资企业	Sino-foreign Joint Ventures	万美元	10000 USD	39224	77636
中外合作企业	Sino-foreign Cooperative Enterprises	万美元	10000 USD	3886	5654
外商独资企业	Foreign-owned Enterprises	万美元	10000 USD	82992	280130
外商投资股份制	Foreign-invested joint-stock system	万美元	10000 USD	30	2205
合伙企业	Partnership	万美元	10000 USD		
二、外商其他投资	Other Foreign Investments	万美元	10000 USD	2039	

单位：万美元（10 000 USD）

2010年	2011年	2012年	2013年	2014年	2015年	2016年	2017年	2018年	2019年	2020年	2021年
731	**707**	**553**	**645**	**619**	**763**	**680**	**650**	**956**	**954**	**882**	**908**
731	707	553	645	619	763	680	650	956	954	882	908
153	158	113	165	140	162	154	188	294	358	190	327
4	4	2	2	1	2		1	8	1		
574	544	438	478	475	597	523	457	653	586	661	531
	1			3	2	3	4	1	2	3	3
									7	25	47
475723	**528501**	**600231**	**758063**	**638637**	**827357**	**769101**	**909629**	**980231**	**1335551**	**1785353**	**2143457**
475723	528501	600231	758063	638637	827357	769101	909629	980231	1335551	1785353	2143457
124148	142535	102252	191172	126878	116013	207933	246280	195336	415708	431250	703368
9179	15173	122	4765	-849	1731	28	327	34333	1010		4567
341977	369425	490764	562208	506271	706172	554073	655377	756426	794686	1321040	1260406
419	1368	7093	-82	6337	3441	7067	7645	-5864	93315	9547	32843
									30832	23446	142273
284281	**363350**	**460027**	**552227**	**608100**	**669062**	**700273**	**773500**	**869257**	**584193**	**585297**	**616897**
284281	363350	460027	552227	608100	669062	700273	773500	869257	584193	585297	616897
84920	100699	169469	159424	172180	135671	171051	195189	191040	215914	230342	258490
3567	2759	6262	2355	128	1570	251	220	19032	68		3000
194500	255763	275579	390210	435102	531544	520052	569461	658368	299610	352179	340031
1294	4129	8717	238	690	277	8918	8325	817	68585	441	15329
									16	1275	47

5-9 当年外商直接投资项目数和投资额（2021年）
NUMBER OF PROJECTS AND TOTAL AMOUNT OF FOREIGN DIRECT INVESTMENT (2021)

项　　目	Item	批准企业项目数（个）Number of Projects Approved (unit)	实际利用外资金额（万美元）Total Amount of Foreign Investment Actually Utilized (10000 USD)
外商直接投资	**Foreign Direct Investments**		
一、按投资方式分	**Grouped by Investment Form**		
#中外合资企业	Sino-foreign Joint Ventures	327	258490
中外合作企业	Sino-foreign Cooperative Enterprises		3000
外商独资企业	Foreign-owned Enterprises	531	340031
二、按主要行业分	**Grouped by Sector**		
#农、林、牧、渔业	Farming, Foresty, Animal Husbandry and Fishery	2	225
制造业	Manufacturing	125	75929
电力、燃气及水的生产和供应业	Production and Supply of Electricity, Gas and Water	15	6740
建筑业	Construction	11	26618
信息传输、计算机服务和软件业	Information transmission, computer services and software industry	45	66403
批发和零售业	Wholesale and Retail Trades	331	151404
房地产业	Real estate industry	27	88930
租赁和商务服务业	Leasing and Business Services	144	107417
科学研究、技术服务和地质勘查业	Scientific Research, Technical Service and Geological Survey	91	46848
三、按主要国别（地区）分	**Grouped by Countries (Regions)**		
#中国香港	Hong Kong, China	332	518118
韩国	Korea	243	8065
美国	USA	36	4746
日本	Japan	33	25389
德国	Germany	20	1632
澳大利亚	Australia	16	8
新加坡	Singapore	33	35945

5-10 对外投资与经济合作
OUTBOUND INVESTMENT AND INTERNATIONAL ECONOMIC COOPERATION

名称	Name	单位	Unit	2021年	2021年比2020年 ±% 2021/2020（±%）
对外投资项目数	Number of Outbound Investment Projects	个	unit	67	6.4
对外投资中方投资额	The Amount of Investment by Chinese Sides in Outbound Investment	万美元	10000 USD	162138.83	36.4
对外承包工程新签合同额	The Amount of New Contracts for Foreign Contracted Projects	万美元	10000 USD	312244	-10.3
对外承包工程完成营业额	The Completed Turnover of Foreign Contracted Projects	万美元	10000 USD	301613	4.8
对外劳务合作	Number of Persons Sent Overseas for International Labor Service Cooperation	人	Person	11806	29.6

5-11 对外投资分国别（地区）情况表（2021年）
TABLE OF FOREIGN INVESTMENT BY COUNTRY（REGION）（2021）

国别（地区）	Country（Region）	项目数量（个） Number of Projects （unit）	2021年比2020年 ±% 2021/2020 （±%）	中方投资额（万美元） Amount of Investment by Chinese Sides （10000 USD）	2021年比2020年 ±% 2021/2020 （±%）
总计	**Total**	**67**	**6.35**	**162138.83**	**36.4**
亚洲	Asia	37	-2.6	130926.28	280.74
中国香港	Hong Kong，China	16	-30.4	4753.94	329.09
韩国	Korea	5	150	1239.86	-69.33
日本	Japan	4	100	2969.16	1217.75
新加坡	Singapore	4	33.33	1491.26	-78.26
马尔代夫	Maldives	1	—	15.4	—
柬埔寨	Cambodia	1	0	35225	10907.81
阿拉伯联合酋长国	United Arab Emirates	1	—	10	—
巴基斯坦	Pakistan	1	—	1	—
印度尼西亚	Indonesia	1	—	30.98	-99.39
越南	Vietnam	1	0	76218.02	380990.08
斯里兰卡	Sri Lanka	1	—	20	—
泰国	Thailand	1	-50	8951.66	-47.65

5-11 续表
Continued

国别（地区）	Country（Region）	项目数量（个）Number of Projects（unit）	2021年比2020年±% 2021/2020（±%）	中方投资额（万美元）Amount of Investment by Chinese Sides（10000 USD）	2021年比2020年±% 2021/2020（±%）
非洲	Africa	11	450	250.87	95.12
坦桑尼亚	Tanzania	3	—	92.94	—
赞比亚	Zambia	2	—	61.96	—
莫桑比克	Mozambique	2	—	61.96	—
马达加斯加	Madagascar	2	—	2.93	—
南非	South Africa	1	0	30.98	8.43
肯尼亚	Kenya	1	0	0.11	-99.89
欧洲	Europe	8	-27.27	18396.16	42.58
俄罗斯联邦	Russia	2	0	464.65	-91.75
荷兰	Netherlands	1	—	235.5	—
比利时	Belgium	1	0	46.22	-84.96
德国	Germany	1	0	17718	1194965.15
亚美尼亚	Armenia	1	—	0.01	—
意大利	Italy	1	—	58.06	—
英国	UK	1	—	1.36	—
瑞典	Sweden	减资	-100	-127.64	-132.42
拉丁美洲	Latin America	5	-28.57	9007.25	19.82
墨西哥	Mexico	2	0	8646.85	20.77
圭亚那	Guyana	1	—	15.4	—
巴西	Brazil	1	0	10	-75
英属维尔京群岛	British Virgin Islands	1	0	0	-99.98
阿根廷	Argentina	增资	-100	335	11.67
北美洲	North America	5	0	3208.66	-94.97
美国	USA	5	0	3208.66	54.45
大洋洲	Oceania	1	—	349.61	128.07
澳大利亚	Australia	1	—	349.61	128.07

主要统计指标解释

批准企业（项目）个数 是指外商直接投资中批准设立的外商投资企业个数、批准的合作开发项目个数。

合同外资金额 是指批准外商投资企业的合同、章程中规定的外国投资者认缴的出资额和企业投资总额内的应由外方投资者以自己的境外自有资金直接向企业提供的贷款。包括新批准企业合同外资和原有企业的增资减资，增资减资不对企业（项目）个数进行调整。

实际使用外资金额 是指合同外资金额的实际执行金额。

外商直接投资 是指外国企业和经济组织或个人（包括华侨、港澳台胞以及我国在境外注册的企业）按我国有关政策、法规，用现汇、实物、技术等在我国境内开办外商独资企业、与我国境内的企业或经济组织共同举办中外合资经营企业、合作经营企业或合作开发资源的投资（包括外商投资收益的再投资）以及经政府有关部门批准的项目投资总额内，企业从境外借入的资金。

外商其他投资 是指除外商直接投资以外其他方式吸收的外资。

进出口总额 指实际进出我国国境的货物总金额。包括对外贸易实际进出口货物，来料加工装配进出口货物，国家间、联合国及国际组织无偿援助物资和赠送品，华侨、港澳台同胞和外籍华人捐赠品，租赁期满归承租人所有的租赁货物，进料加工进出口货物，边境地方贸易及边境地区小额贸易进出口货物（边民互市贸易除外），中外合资企业、中外合作经营企业、外商独资经营企业进出口货物和公用物品，到、离岸价格在规定限额以上的进出口货样和广告品（无商业价值、无使用价值和免费提供出口的除外），从保税仓库提取在中国境内销售的进口货物，以及其他进出口货物。

Explanatory Notes on Main Statistical Indicators

Enterprises（Projects）Permitted refers to number of foreign invested enterprises and developed projects under cooperation through the permission.

Contracted Foreign Investment refers to expenditure promised by the foreign investor and loan stemmed from broad innate fund of the foreign investor, according to the contract and regulation approved of enterprise invested by foreigner. Including the newly approved enterprise contract foreign investment and the capital increase and decrease of the original enterprise, the capital increase and decrease do not adjust the number of enterprises（projects）.

Actual Utilization of Foreign Investment refers to actual usage of contracted foreign investment, including cash, investment in kind and incorporeal agreed by the both sides as part of the investment, such as services and technology.

Foreign Direct Investment refers to the investments by foreign enterprises and economic organizations or individuals（including overseas Chinese, compatriots from Hong dong, Macao and Taiwan and Chinese enterprises registered abroad）, following the relevant policies and laws of China, for the establishment of ventures and cooperative enterprises or cooperative exploration of resources with enterprises or economic organizations in China, It includes the reinvestment of the foreign entrepreneurs with the profits gained from the investment and the funds that enterprises borrow from aboard in the total investment of projects which are approved by the relevant department of the government.

Other Investment by Foreign Entrepreneurs refers to all forms of utilization of foreign capitals other than foreign direct investment.

Total Imports and Exports refers to the real value of commodities imported into and exported from the boundary of China. They include the actual imports and exports through foreign trade, imported and exported goods under the processing and assembling trades and materials, supplies and gifts as aid given gratis between governments and by the United Nations and other international organizations, and contributions donated by overseas Chinese, compatriots in Hong Kong, Macao and Chinese with foreign citizenship, leasing commodities owned by tenant at the expiration of leasing period, the imported and exported commodities processed with imported materials, commodities trading in border areas (excluding mutual exchange goods), the imported and exported commodities and articles for public use of the Sino-foreign joint ventures, cooperative enterprises and ventures exclusively with foreign own investment. Also included are import or export of samples and advertising goods for whose CIF or FOB value are beyond the permitted ceiling (excluding goods of no trading or use value and free commodities for export), imported goods sold in China from bonded warehouses and other imported or exported goods.

城市建设、环境保护 6

COTY CONSTRUCTION AND ENVIRONMENT PROTECTION

简 要 说 明

一、本篇资料的主要内容

本篇资料主要反映了全市城市基础设施基本情况，包括市政设施、供水、供电、公共交通、园林绿化、燃气供热、城市环卫、环境保护及工业“三废”排放情况等方面的资料。

二、本篇资料的来源

1. 本篇资料中市政设施、供水、公共交通、园林绿化、燃气供热、城市环卫相关资料来源于市住房和城乡建设局、市交通运输局，由市统计局固定资产投资统计处整理提供。

2. 本篇资料中供电资料来源于青岛供电公司，由市统计局能源统计处整理提供。

3. 本篇资料中环境保护、环境质量及工业“三废”排放情况来源于市生态环境局，由市统计局能源统计处整理提供。

Brief Introduction

Ⅰ. Main Content

The data in this chapter mainly reflects the basic conditions of the city's urban infrastructure, including information on municipal facilities, water supply, power supply, public transportation, landscaping, gas heating, urban sanitation, environmental protection, and industrial “three wastes” emissions.

Ⅱ. Source of Data

1. The relevant information on municipal facilities, water supply, public transportation, landscaping, gas heating, and urban environmental sanitation in this article comes from the Municipal Housing and Urban-Rural Construction Bureau and the Municipal Transportation Bureau, and is provided by the Fixed Assets Investment Statistics Department of the Municipal Bureau of Statistics.

2. The power supply data in this data comes from Qingdao Power Supply Company, which is compiled and provided by the Energy Statistics Division of the Municipal Bureau of Statistics.

3. The environmental protection, environmental quality, and industrial “three wastes” emissions in this data come from the Municipal Ecological Environment Bureau and are compiled and provided by the Energy Statistics Division of the Municipal Bureau of Statistics.

6-1 主要年份城市建设和公用事业
MAJOR YEAR'S CITY CONSTRUCTION AND PUBLIC UTILITIES

年 份 Year	建成区面积 （平方公里） Developed Areas （sq.km）	年末道路长度 （公里） Length of Roads at Year-end（km）	年末道路面积 （万平方米） Area of Roads at Year-end（10 000 sq.m）	公共汽车、电车线路网长度 （公里） Network Length of Bus and Trolley Bus（km）
1949	27	243	206	26.4
1952	29	245	213	124.4
1957	36	248	217	232.3
1962	55	266	235	252.8
1965	57	266	235	308.1
1970	59	374	346	358.5
1975	63	392	355	389.3
1978	66	408	368	422.1
1980	72	408	377	474.1
1985	79	462	464	611.3
1990	94.3	667	786	777
1991	94.7	673	826	922
1992	95.4	683	840	988
1993	99.9	764	944	1094
1994	103.9	811	985	1372
1995	106	936	1177	1101
1996	110	991	1339	1211
1997	112	1047	1436	1492
1998	114	1106	1436	1859
1999	116	1171	1698	2339
2000	119.1	1192	1789	2711
2001	123	1248	2169	2521
2002	133	1426	2594	896
2003	145.9	1595	2816	973
2004	154.8	1755	3254	1185
2005	178.8	1862	3547	1159
2006	227.5	3160	5218	1362
2007	250.7	3288	5411	1480
2008	267.1	3318	5596	1470
2009	272.9	3402	5763	1216
2010	282.3	3409	5893	1383
2011	291.5	3705	6605	1719
2012	374.6	4281	7528	1978
2013	469.6	4334	7859	2002
2014	490.7	4393	7908	2023
2015	566.4	4375	7940	2106
2016	599.3	4484	8057	2116
2017	638.4	4865	8496	2220
2018	715.1	5770	9862	2400
2019	758.2	6315	10227	3973
2020	758.2	6374	10510	4044
2021	761.5	6352	11546	9377

6-1 续表 1
Continued

年份 Year	自来水供水管道长度（公里）Length of Tap Water Pipelines (km)	全年供水总量（万立方米）Annual Volume of Tap Water Supply (10 000 cu.m)	#全年售水量（万立方米）Annual Volume of Tap Water Sale (10 000 cu.m)	#居民家庭用水 of which: Consumption for Residential Use	用水普及率（%）Coverage Rate of Population with Access to Tap Water (%)	排水管道长度（公里）Length of Sewage Pipes (km)	全年用电量（亿千瓦时）Annual Volume of Electricity Supply (100 million kW·h)	#居民生活用电 of which: Consumption for Residential Use
1949	308	721	456	331	89	200	0.88	0.14
1952	341	778	612	310	90	227	1.85	0.14
1957	412	1392	1 296	606	93	273	2.61	0.26
1962	483	2700	2 512	937	98	290	3.77	0.57
1965	500	3220	2 979	929	98	295	5.92	0.68
1970	521	4503	4106	1085	99	350	9.83	1.02
1975	564	6726	6302	1950	99	361	12.41	1.43
1978	572	5334	4975	1314	99	382	16.34	1.62
1980	588	8224	7874	2577	99	394	21.48	2.78
1985	685	7557	7038	2628	99.9	505	26.39	2.87
1990	873	11896	10211	4270	96.9	645	41.08	4.32
1991	908	13865	11760	4990	96.6	649	44.51	5.34
1992	1035	16385	13070	5931	96.5	672	51.78	6.84
1993	1123	16137	14027	6124	99.1	734	55.02	7.66
1994	1124	17367	14716	6405	100	811	60.74	8.78
1995	1046	22513	15810	7050	100	990	67.23	10.16
1996	1182	23277	16566	7731	100	1051	72.87	12.23
1997	1266	24130	17215	8787	100	1167	77.82	13.73
1998	1390	23845	17271	9115	100	1210	79.65	14.28
1999	1471	23849	18558	10032	100	1301	88.12	15.31
2000	1524	25414	20642	11405	100	1460	106.80	16
2001	1665	22225	18556	10555	100	1539	116.10	17.62
2002	1781	27662	21684	10129	100	1641	131.44	18.31
2003	2060	27594	21483	10142	100	1884	147.68	19.88
2004	2566	30877	23864	11695	100	2002	167.95	23.63
2005	2876	33265	25874	12536	100	2309	193.81	33.76
2006	3984	30524	25572	10682	100	3994	215.35	34.87
2007	4187	31533	26454	11408	100	4079	236.42	37.40
2008	4642	32675	27396	11301	100	4229	250.07	40.31
2009	4767	33490	28274	12250	100	4555	259.42	43.29
2010	4926	34909	29617	12524	100	4708	292.97	49.50
2011	5121	34109	28837	10049	100	5187	313.44	50.13
2012	5243	38945	33039	12121	100	6814	318.36	51.64
2013	5522	38331	32418	11851	100	6536	339.27	57.52
2014	6177	46649	40612	14834	100	6840	337.82	59.95
2015	6142	46203	40202	15381	100	6993	342.29	64.71
2016	6132	43033	36748	14430	100	7146	367.26	69.52
2017	6498	45991	38963	17439	100	7367	401.06	74.84
2018	7531	53235	43298	18473	100	8854	431.82	77.39
2019	7997	52203	44597	19809	100	9350	457.9	81.95
2020	8207	55352	48408	21166	100	9713	476.59	81.36
2021	8249	55561	48155	21988	100	10213	552.65	91.21

6-1 续表 2
Continued

年 份 Year	公共汽车、电车营运车辆（辆） Number of Bus and Trolley Bus under Operation (unit)	全年客运量（万人次） Annual Passenger Traffic (10 000 person-times)	出租汽车（辆） Number of Taxi (unit)	使用液化气、煤气、天然气人数（万人） Population with Access to Gas (10 000 persons)	液化气 Liquefied Petroleum	煤气 Coal Gas	天然气 Natural Gas	液化气供气量（吨） Volume of Liquefied Petroleum Supply (ton)
1949	32	298						
1952	76	932						
1957	112	4110						
1962	127	4747						
1965	173	6092						
1970	224	13002						
1975	324	14426		2	2			184.9
1978	409	27351		17	17			3246
1980	485	38981	48	24	24			4345
1985	621	48852	219	42.1	42.1			10619
1990	801	63495	832	75.0	57.4	17.6		17512
1991	1372	67552	1070	76.2	57.4	18.8		17963
1992	1470	73529	1828	82.8	62.0	20.8		19565
1993	1875	72427	4874	88.4	64.6	23.8		22224
1994	1850	78231	5806	103.6	77.4	26.2		24684
1995	1891	71867	5887	116.2	82.9	33.3		32443
1996	2012	49077	6660	126.0	88.0	38.0		4065
1997	2148	55642	6861	133.6	92.9	40.7		38717
1998	2184	51042	7469	146.8	97.8	49.0		45381
1999	2470	55414	7839	154.9	98.3	56.6		40537
2000	3141	59879	7933	164.1	93.3	70.8		46951
2001	3453	60167	8110	168.8	87.5	81.3		45295
2002	3681	61713	8376	224.2	133.8	90.4		60123
2003	3648	58792	8109	246.7	138.3	93.1	15.3	67803
2004	3848	66463	8144	258.4	140.6	78.8	39.0	58548
2005	4039	68776	8121	265.0	132.6	45.7	86.7	78000
2006	4167	73726	8146	271.0	112.5	49.5	109.0	97343
2007	4524	78702	8221	275.6	104.1	12.1	159.4	79715
2008	4701	82460	9241	276.3	91.9	10.5	173.9	81987
2009	4288	81768	9316	276.1	59.8	12.3	204.0	96721
2010	4664	85251	9539	276.3	36.7	12.6	227.0	80073
2011	5419	89614	9683	277.1	25.8	12.6	238.7	79812
2012	5640	97922	9693	313.7	36.7	13.1	263.9	54341
2013	6179	101108	9826	318.9	33.0	0.0	285.9	41302
2014	6515	105592	9720	325.4	33.0	0.0	292.4	39255
2015	6748	102402	10033	338.3	28.9	0.0	309.4	35255
2016	7210	99596	10048	441.6	29.0	0.0	412.6	32291
2017	7420	104898	10875	445.8	26.2	0.0	419.6	28309
2018	7795	104782	10867	512.7	29.9	0.0	482.8	30427
2019	8489	108339	10877	529.5	27.0	0.0	502.5	30210
2020	8553	65014	10877	550.1	23.8	0.0	526.3	29029
2021	10592	86073	11992	580.2	23.0	0.0	557.2	31287

注：1990 年以前公共营运车辆不包括系统外及个体。
Note: Vehicles not belonging to system and individual vehicles are not contained in public operating vehicles before 1990.

6-1 续表 3
Continued

年 份 Year	煤气供气量（万立方米）Volume of Coal Gas Supply（10 000 cu.m）	天然气供气量（万立方米）Volume of Natural Gas Supply（10 000 cu.m）	燃气普及率（%）Coverage Rate of Population with Access to Gas（%）	绿地面积（公顷）Area of Green Areas（hectare）	公园绿地面积（公顷）Park Green Areas（hectare）	人均公园绿地面积（平方米）Per Capita Park Green Areas（sq.m）	建成区绿化覆盖率（%）Green Coverage Rate of Developed Areas（%）	公园（个）Number of Parks and Zoos（unit）	公园面积（公顷）Area of Parks and Zoos（hectare）
1949				133	42	0.7	4.9	3	43
1952				134	43	0.7	4.4	4	45
1957				245	132	1.7	6.9	10	122
1962				771	184	2.2	14.0	12	174
1965				777	184	2.1	13.7	12	174
1970				772	184	2.1	13.0	6	117
1975			2.3	465	162	1.8	7.6	5	134
1978			18.6	469	162	1.7	7.6	6	165
1980			24.5	625	206	2.1	10.4	6	152
1985			36.3	1072	255	2.3	17.3	7	153
1990	3073		56.2	2120	492	3.7	22.8	26	404
1991	3439		56.5	2318	500	3.7	24.4	28	443
1992	3824		60.0	2471	515	3.7	25.9	28	417
1993	4215		63.1	2488	543	3.9	26.5	31	453
1994	4116		63.1	2866	572	4.0	27.9	31	463
1995	4734		79.2	4547	771	5.3	30.1	33	675
1996	5447		83.9	4679	836	5.6	30.4	33	675
1997	5920		87.3	4717	924	6.0	31.3	34	730
1998	5959		92.5	6812	1047	6.6	35.0	35	775
1999	7319		96.0	7007	1186	7.4	35.9	36	791
2000	9567		98.0	7439	1423	8.5	37.0	37	790
2001	11814		99.0	7688	1588	9.3	37.5	39	832
2002	13500		99.5	7967	1791	8.1	36.4	43	926
2003	14826	1181	100	8829	2305	9.3	37.5	45	1034
2004	15503	2710	100	10047	2842	11.0	38.0	48	1421
2005	16573	7456	100	11137	3132	11.8	38.8	47	1110
2006	9821	13876	100	11756	3198	11.8	39.2	47	1188
2007	9516	18103	100	15369	3661	13.3	37.8	73	1268
2008	8691	21780	100	15630	4014	14.5	41.5	77	1815
2009	7523	26948	100	16003	4003	14.5	43.4	71	1897
2010	9153	35681	100	16619	4027	14.6	43.4	72	1917
2011	9137	46147	100	18013	4041	14.6	44.7	74	1931
2012	8148	68397	100	21471	4573	14.6	44.7	78	2112
2013	0	70918	100	28007	4649	14.6	44.7	87	2698
2014	0	74823	100	28805	4741	14.6	44.7	91	2988
2015	0	70311	100	29117	4802	14.6	44.7	87	3163
2016	0	70586	100	34851	8194	18.6	38.6	151	4460
2017	0	91572	100	36209	7763	17.4	39.1	175	4727
2018	0	120089	100	39229	8587	16.3	39.2	191	5767
2019	0	131867	100	40844	8922	16.9	40.2	192	5773
2020	0	130745	100	41829	10508	19.0	41.0	212	8426
2021	0	147284	100	42661	10465	18.0	43.1	236	7943

注：1. 自 2002 年起人均公共绿地面积按辖区内全部人口计算。
2. 2005 年以前所用园林绿地面积；公共绿地面积；人均公共绿地面积；公园、动物园个数；公园、动物园面积指标分别改为现在的绿地面积；公共绿地面积；人均公园绿地面积；公园个数；公园面积。
3. 由于城阳区绿化指标进行了调整，部分绿地属性发生变化，导致 2017 年公园绿地面积及人均公园绿地面积的数据小于 2016 年。

Notes：1. Per capita public green areas is calculated at total population in the area under jurisdiction since 2002.
2. Before 2005, the corresponding indicators of greenbelt area, public greenbelt area, public greenbelt area, per capita public greenbelt area, coverage rate of green, number of parks and zoos, area of parks and zoos.
3. As the green index of Chengyang District has been adjusted, some green space properties have changed. As a result, the data of park green area and per capita park green area in 2017 are smaller than 2016.

6-2 全年供电(2021 年)
ANNUAL ELECTRICITY SUPPLY (2021)

全年供电项目	Item	单位	Unit	2021 年
发电设备总容量	Total Capacity of Generation Equipment	万千瓦	10 000 kW	344.70
#青岛电厂	Qingdao Power Plant	万千瓦	10 000 kW	127.00
黄岛电厂	Huangdao Power Plant	万千瓦	10 000 kW	157.50
全年发电量	Annual Electricity Generation	亿千瓦时	100 million kW · h	187.91
#青岛电厂	Qingdao Power Plant	亿千瓦时	100 million kW · h	57.62
黄岛电厂	Huangdao Power Plant	亿千瓦时	100 million kW · h	62.42
全年实际用电量	Annual Electricity Consumption	亿千瓦时	100 million kW · h	552.65
#工业	Industrial Consumption	亿千瓦时	100 million kW · h	297.99
农业	Agricultural Consumption	亿千瓦时	100 million kW · h	9.84
生活	Residential Consumption	亿千瓦时	100 million kW · h	91.21
平均每日用电量	Average Daily Consumption	万千瓦时	10 000 kW · h	15141

6-3 分行业用电(2021 年)
ELECTRICTTY CONSUMPTION BY SECTOR (2021)

单位：万千瓦时(10 000 kW·h)

行 业	Sector	2021 年	2021 年比 2020 年增长(%) Growth Rate in 2021 over 2020(%)
全社会用电总计	**Total Electricity Consumption**	**5526513.14**	**15.96**
一、农、林、牧、渔业	Farming, Forestry, Animal Husbandry and Fishery	98446.30	-0.96
二、工业	Industry	2979899.61	15.14
三、建筑业	Construction	114601.10	12.30
四、交通运输、仓储和邮政业	Transport, Storage and Post	266550.73	20.16
五、信息传输、计算机服务和软件业	Information Transmission, Computer Services and Software	89430.00	15.05
六、商业、住宿和餐饮业	Trade, Hotels and Catering Services	309912.12	23.03
七、金融、房地产、商务及居民服务业	Financial, Real Business and Residential Services	323412.11	21.06
八、公共事业及管理组织	Public Management and Social Organization	427309.91	24.27
九、城乡居民生活用电	Household Consumption	912090.85	12.07
城镇居民	Urban Area	568767.13	10.53
乡村居民	Rural Area	343323.72	14.73

6-4 城市供水
URBAN WATER SUPPLY

项　目	Item	单位	Unit	2021 年
自来水供水管道长度	Length of Tap Water Pipelines	公里	km	8249
综合生产能力	Synthesis Production Capacity	万立方米 / 日	10 000 cu.m/day	235
全年供水总量	Annual Volume of Tap Water Supply	万立方米	10 000 cu.m	55561
# 售水量	Volume of Tap Water Supply	万立方米	10 000 cu.m	48155
# 生产运营用水	Consumption for Production Use	万立方米	10 000 cu.m	17326
公共服务用水	Consumption for Public Services Use	万立方米	10 000 cu.m	8612
居民家庭用水	Consumption for Residential Use	万立方米	10 000 cu.m	21988
其他用水	Consumption for Other Uses	万立方米	10 000 cu.m	228
平均每日供水量	Daily Volume of Tap Water Supply	万立方米	10 000 cu.m	152
# 生产用	Consumption for Production Use	万立方米	10 000 cu.m	48
生活用	Consumption for Residential Use	万立方米	10 000 cu.m	60
用水户数	Households with Access to Water	户	household	2145638
用水人口	Population with Access to water	万人	10 000 persons	580
工业用水量重复利用率	Recycle Rate of water for Industrial Use	%	%	91

6-5 城市公共交通
URBAN PUBLIC TRAFFIC

项 目	Item	单位	Unit	2021 年
公共汽车、电车线路网长度	Network Length of Bus and Trolley Bus	公里	km	9377
轨道交通线路长度	Rail Transit Line Length	公里	km	284
公共汽车、电车营运车辆	Number of Bus and Trolley Bus under Operation	辆	unit	10592
#汽车	Bus	辆	unit	4884
电车	Trolley Bus	辆	unit	5708
公共汽车、电车全年客运量	Annual Passenger Traffic of Bus and Trolley Bus	万人次	10 000 person-times	86073
公共汽车、电车平均每日客运量	Daily Passenger Traffic of Bus and Trolley Bus	万人	10 000 persons	235.8
出租汽车数	Number of Taxi	辆	unit	11992
轮渡运营船数	Number of Ferry Boat under Operation	艘	ship	—
轮渡客运总量	Passenger Traffic of Ferry Boat	万人次	10 000 person-times	—
轮渡平均每日客运量	Daily Passenger Traffic of Ferry Boat	万人	10 000 persons	—
轨道交通客运总量	Total Passenger Traffic Of Rail Transit	万人次	10 000 person-times	24782
轨道交通平均每日客运量	Average Daily Passenger Volume of Rail Transit	万人	10 000 persons	68

6-6 城市供气
URBAN GAS SUPPLY

项　目	Item	单位	Unit	2021 年
煤气供应总量	Volume of Coal Gas Supply	万立方米	10 000 cu.m	0
#家庭用量	Household Consumption	万立方米	10 000 cu.m	0
煤气用气户数	Households with Access to Coal Gas	户	household	0
#家庭用户	Household Users	户	household	0
液化石油气供应总量	Volume of Liquefied Petroleum Supply	吨	ton	31287
#家庭用量	Household Consumption	吨	ton	12404
液化石油气用气户数	Households with Access to Liquefied Petroleum	户	household	113177
#家庭用户	Household Users	户	household	106673
天然气供应总量	Volume of Natural Gas Supply	万立方米	10 000 cu.m	147284
#家庭用量	Household Consumption	万立方米	10 000 cu.m	36993
天然气用气户数	Households with Access to Natural Gas	户	household	2332404
#家庭用户	Household Users	户	household	2309729
燃气普及率	Coverage Rate of Population with Access to Gas	%	%	100

6-7 城市环境卫生
URBAN ENVIRONMENTAL SANITATION

项　目	Item	单位	Unit	2021 年
市容环卫专用车辆总数	Number of Special Vehicles for Environmental Sanitation	辆	unit	4451
生活垃圾清运量	Volume of Garbage Disposal	万吨	10 000 ton	304
生活垃圾无害化处理厂（场）数	Number of Bio-safety Disposal Plant of Garbage	座	unit	9
生活垃圾无害化处理能力	Bio-safety Disposal Capacity of Garbage	吨 / 日	ton/dan	8700
生活垃圾无害化处理量	Bio-safety Disposal Volume of Garbage	万吨	10 000 ton	304
道路清扫保洁面积	Area under Cleaning Program	万平方米	10 000 sq.m	7561
#机械化	of which：Mechanization	万平方米	10 000 sq.m	6539
公共厕所	Public Toilets	个	unit	1015

6-8 城市道路、下水道及绿化
URBAN ROAD, SEWAGE AND GREEN

项　目	Item	单位	Unit	2021 年
道路	**Road**			
年末道路长度	Length of Roads at Year-end	公里	km	6352
年末道路面积	Area of Roads at Year-end	万平方米	10 000 sq.m	11546
# 人行道面积	Area of Pavements	万平方米	10 000 sq.m	2517
排水管道长度	Length of Sewage Pipes	公里	km	10213
园林绿化	**Greening**			
绿化覆盖面积	Area of Green Coverage Areas	公顷	hectare	46780
绿地面积	Area of Green Areas	公顷	hectare	42661
公园绿地面积	Area of Park Green Areas	公顷	hectare	10465
公园数	Number of Parks and Zoos	个	unit	236
公园面积	Area of Parks and Zoos	公顷	hectare	7943
城市每人平均公园绿地面积	Per Capita Park Green Area	平方米	sq.m	18
建成区绿化覆盖率	Green Coverage Rate of Developed Areas	%	%	43

6-9 环境保护基本情况
BASIC CONDITIONS OF ENVIRONMENTAL PROTECTION

项　目	Item	单位	Unit	2021 年	2020 年
二氧化硫排放总量	Sulphur Dioxide Emission	吨	ton	4577.07	4830.65
氮氧化物排放总量	Discharge Amount of Nitrogen Oxides	吨	ton	9648.50	48233.01
烟（粉）尘排放总量	Soot（Dust）Emission	吨	ton	7474.07	10470.56
工业固体废物排放总量	Industrial Solid Wastes Discharged	吨	ton	0.00	0.00
化学需氧量排放总量	Discharge Amount of Chemical Oxygen Demand	吨	ton	41151.57	40793.42
氨氮排放总量	Discharge Amount of Ammonia and Nitrogen	吨	ton	2024.49	2312.66
废水排放总量	Waste Water Discharged	万吨	10 000 tons	30841.15	30654.75

注：2021 年生态环境统计数据为初报数据，氮氧化物和烟（粉）尘排放总量未含机动车数据。
Note：The statistical data of ecological environment in 2021 are preliminary data, and the total emissions of nitrogen oxides and smoke (dust) do not include motor vehicle data.

6-10 环境质量状况
ENVIRONMENT CONDITION

项　目	Item	单位	Unit	2021 年	2020 年	2021 年比 2020 年增（+）减（-）% 2021 Compared to 2020（+/-）
市区空气质量优良率	Urban air quality good rate	%	%	84.90	86.30	-1.40
一、二类海水水质面积比例	The proportion of Grade I and Ⅱ waters	%	%	99.00	98.80	0.20
市区区域环境噪声平均等效声级	The Average Equivalent Sound Level of the Urban Regional Environmental Noise	分贝（A）	db（A）	57.00	58.70	-2.90
市区道路交通噪声平均等效声级	The Average Equivalent Sound Level of the Urban Road Traffic Noise	分贝（A）	db（A）	68.60	70.00	-2.00

6-11 工业“三废”排放情况

DISCHARGE CONDITIONS OF INDUSTRIAL WASTE WSTER, WASTE GAS AND SOLID WASTE

项 目	Item	单位	Unit	2021 年	2020 年	2021 年比 2020 年增（+）减（-）% 2021 Compared to 2020（+/-）
工业废水排放总量	Industrial Waste Water Discharged	万吨	10 000 tons	6513.76	5695.03	14.38
废水治理设施数	Number of Facilities for Treatment of Waste Water	套	set	465	468	-0.64
废水治理设施处理能力	Capacity of Facilities for Treatment of Waste Water	万吨 / 日	10 000 tons/day	42.47	43.45	-2.25
进入城市污水处理厂量	Volume Handled by Sewage Treatment Plant	万吨	10 000 tons	5768.10	4956.96	16.36
化学需氧量排放量	Discharge Amount of Chemical Oxygen Demand	吨	ton	2015.04	2710.47	-25.65
氨氮排放量	Discharge Amount of Ammonia and Nitrogen	吨	ton	47.94	75.96	-36.88
工业废气排放总量	Industrial Waste Air Discharged	万标立方米	10 000 cu.m	4918.97	4205.95	16.95
废气治理设施数	Number of Facilities for Treatment of Waste Air	套	set	2555	2462	3.77
其中：脱硫设施数	of which：Desulphurization Facilities	套	set	167	194	-13.91
废气治理设施处理能力	Capacity of Facilities for Treatment of Waste Air	万标立方米 / 时	10 000 cu.m	23358.45	34484.05	-32.26
二氧化硫去除量	Sulphur Dioxide Removed	吨	ton	149244.40	205478.96	-27.36
二氧化硫排放量	Sulphur Dioxide Emission	吨	ton	2896.73	3316.69	-12.66
烟（粉）尘排放量	Soot（Dust）Emission	吨	ton	2723.53	5857.54	-53.50
工业固体废物产生量	Industrial Solid Wastes Produced	万吨	10 000 tons	828.46	716.95	15.55
其中：危险废物	of which: Hazardous Wastes	吨	ton	23.82	17.69	34.65
工业固体废物综合利用量	Industrial Solid Wastes Comprehensive Utilized	万吨	10 000 tons	737.81	625.69	17.91
工业固体废物排放量	Industrial Solid Wastes Discharged	万吨	10 000 tons	0	0	-
其中：危险废物	of which: Hazardous Wastes	吨	ton	0	0	-

注：1. 2021 年生态环境统计数据为初报数据。
2. 2021 年生态环境统计口径变化，导致工业废气中脱硫设施数量、废气处理能力、主要污染物排放量等变化幅度较大。

Notes：1. The statistical data of ecological environment in 2021 are preliminary data.
2. The variation of the statistical caliber of ecological environment in 2021 leads to the large variation of the quantity of desulphurization facilities in the industrial waste gas, the capability of disposing exhaust gas and the emission of major pollutants.

主要统计指标解释

供水综合生产能力　指按供水设施取水、净化、送水、出厂输水干管等环节设计能力计算的综合生产能力。

年末供水管道长度　指从送水泵至用户水表之间所有管道的长度。不包括新安装尚未使用的管道。

用水普及率　指城市用水人口数与城市人口总数的比率。计算公式：

$$用水普及率=\frac{城市用水人口数}{城市人口总数}\times 100\%$$

全年供水总量　指报告期供水企业（单位）供出的全部水量。包括有效供水量和漏损水量。

全年供气总量　指全年燃气企业（单位）向用户供应的燃气数量。包括销售量和损失量。

用气普及率　指报告期末使用燃气的城市人口数与城市人口总数的比率。计算公式为：

$$用气普及率=\frac{城市用气人口数}{城市人口总数}\times 100\%$$

年末道路长度　指年末道路长度和与道路相通的广场、桥梁、隧道的长度，按车行道中心线计算。在统计时只统计路面宽度在 3.5 米（含 3.5 米）以上的各种铺装道路，包括开放型工业区和住宅区道路在内。

工业废气排放量　指报告期内企业厂区内燃料燃烧和生产工艺过程中产生的各种排入大气的含有污染物的气体的总量，以标准状态（273K，101325Pa）计算。

工业废水排放量　指经过企业厂区所有排放口排到企业外部的工业废水量。包括生产废水、外排的直接冷却水、超标排放的矿井地下水和与工业废水混排的厂区生活污水，不包括外排的间接冷却水（清污不分流的间接冷却水应计算在内）。

工业废水排放达标量　指各项指标都达到国家或地方排放标准的外排工业废水量，包括未经处理外排达标的和经过处理后外排达标的和两部分。国家排放标准见 GB8978—88。

工业固体废物产生量　指企业在生产过程中产生的固体状、半固体状和高浓度液体状废弃物的总量，包括危险废物、冶炼废渣、粉煤灰、炉渣、煤矸渣、尾矿、放射性废物和其他废物等；不包括矿山开采的剥离废石和掘进废石（煤矸石和呈酸性或碱性的废石除外）酸性或碱性废石是指采掘的废石其流经水、雨淋水的 pH 值小于 4 或 pH 值大于 10.5 者。

工业粉尘排放量　指企业在生产工艺过程中排放的能在空气中悬浮一定时间的固体颗粒物排放量。如钢铁企业的耐火材料粉尘、焦化企业的筛焦系统粉尘、烧结机的粉尘、石灰窑的粉尘、建材企业的水泥粉尘等。不包括电厂排入大气的烟尘。

化学需氧量（COD）　测量有机和无机物质化学分解所消耗氧的质量浓度的水污染指数。

Explanatory Notes on Main Statistical Indicators

Production Capacity of Water Supply　refers to the designed comprehensive production capacity of water facilities, covering the 4 links of water collection, purification, conveyance, and outflow through trunk pipelines.

Length of Water Supply Pipelines at the Year-end refers to the total length of all the pipelines between the water pumps and the user water meters, excluding pipelines newly installed but not used yet.

Coverage Rate of Urban Population with Access to Tap Water refers to the ratio of the urban population with access to tap water to the total urban population. The formula is：

Coverage rate of urban population with access to tap water =（Urban population with access to tap water）/（Urban population）× 100%

Annual Volume of Water Supply refers to the total volume of water supplied by water-works（units）during the reference period, including both the effective water supply and loss during the water supply.

Annual Volume of Gas Supply refers to the total volume of gas provided to users by gas-producing enterprises（units）in a year, including the volume sold and the volume lost.

Coverage Rate of Urban population with Access to Gas refers to the ratio of the urban population with access to gas to the total urban population at the end of the reference period. The formula is：

Coverage rate of urban population with access to gas =（Urban population with access to gas/Urban population）× 100%

Length of Paved Roads at the Year-end refers to the length of roads with paved surface including squares bridges and tunnels connected with roads by the end of the year. Length of the roads is measured by the central lines for vehicles for paved roads with a width of 3.5 meters and over, including roads in open-ended factory compounds and residential quarters.

Industrial Waste Air Emission refers to discharge into atmosphere of waste air containing pollutants generated from fuel burning and production process in enterprises within a given period of time. It is calculated at standard status（273K, 101325Pa）.

Waste Water Discharged by Industry refers to the volume of waste water discharged by industrial enterprises through all their outlets, including waste water from production process, directly cooled water, groundwater from mining wells which does not meet discharge standards and sewage from households mixed with waste water produced by industrial activities, but excluding indirectly cooled water discharged（It should be included if the discharge is not separated with waste water）.

Industrial Waste Water Meeting Discharge Standards refers to volume of industrial waste water discharge which, with or without treatment, reaches national or local standards with regard to all pollutants. National Discharge standards see GB8978–88.

Industrial Solid Wastes Produced refers to total volume of solid, semi-solid and high concentration liquid residues produced by industrial enterprises from production process in a given period of time, including hazardous wastes, slag, coal ash, gangue, tailings, radioactive residues and other wastes, but excluding stones stripped or dug out in mining（gangue and acid or alkaline stones not included）, A stone is acid or alkaline depending on the pH value of the water below 4 or above 10.5 when the stone is in, or soaked by, the water.

Industrial Dust Emission refers to volume of dust emitted by production process of enterprises and suspended in the air for a given period of time, including dust from refractory material of iron and steel works, dust from coke-screening systems and sintering machines of coke plants, dust from lime kilns and dust from cement production in building material enterprises, but excluding soot and dust emitted from power plants.

Chemical Oxygen Demand（COD） refers to index of water pollution measuring the mass concentration of oxygen consumed by the chemical breakdown of organic and inorganic matter.

能源消耗 7

CONSUMPTION OF ENERGY

简要说明

一、本篇资料的主要内容

本篇资料主要反映了全市规模以上工业主要能源消费与库存情况，主要包括规模以上工业主要能源消费与库存、规模以上工业主要能源分行业消费量、重点耗能工业企业能源加工转换、规模以上工业主要能源工业消费量等方面的资料。

二、本篇资料的来源

本篇资料来源于规模以上工业能源统计年报，由市统计局能源统计处整理提供。

Brief Introduction

Ⅰ. Main Content

Data in this chapter show the consumption and stock of major energy of industry above designated size, including consumption and stock of major energy of industry above designated size, major energy consumption of industry above designated size grouped by sector, energy conversion of major energy-consuming industrial enterprises and major energy consumption of industry above designated size, etc.

Ⅱ. Source of Data

Data in this chapter are based on the annual report of energy consumed by industrial enterprises above designated size. The data are provided by the Division of Energy Statistics of Qingdao Municipal Bureau of Statistics.

7-1　规模以上工业主要能源消费与库存（2021 年）
CONSUMPTION AND STOCK OF MAJOR ENERGY OF INDUSTRY ABOVE DESIGNATED SIZE（2021）

名　称	Name	单位	Unit	年初库存 Stock at Year-beginning	工业生产消费量 Consumption for Industrial Production	年末库存 Stock at Year-end
原　煤	Raw Coal	吨	ton	969782.02	10794979.73	1209854.31
焦　炭	Coke	吨	ton	43341.70	1658661.53	70447.38
焦炉煤气	Coking Gas	万立方米	10 000 cu.m		25637.50	
高炉煤气	Blast Furnace Gas	万立方米	10 000 cu.m		598044.90	
原　油	Crude Oil	吨	ton	444293.00	14740355.00	420815.00
汽　油	Petrol	吨	ton	1065.10	16876.27	1038.21
煤　油	Kerosene	吨	ton		38.89	
柴　油	Diesel Oil	吨	ton	1382.45	54945.16	1265.81
燃料油	Fuel Oil	吨	ton	13169.94	64867.56	9634.20
液化石油气	Liquefied Petroleum Gas	吨	ton	8.11	380500.13	55454.51
炼厂干气	Refinery Dry Gas	吨	ton		409294.00	
热　力	Heat	百万千焦	million kJ		26409885.49	
电　力	Electricity	万千瓦时	10 000 kW · h		2210582.49	

补充资料：2021 年综合能源消费量 1591.9 万吨标准煤。
Supplementary Information：The comprehensive energy consumption in 2021 will be 15.919 million tons of standard coal.

7-2 规模以上工业主要能源分行业消费量(2021年)
MAJOR ENERGY CONSUMPTION OF INDUSTRY ABOVE DESIGNATED SIZE BY SECTOR（2021）

名　称	Name	原煤（吨）Raw Coal（ton）	焦炭（吨）Coke（ton）	焦炉煤气（万立方米）Coking Cas（10 000 cu.m）	原油（吨）Crude Oil（ton）	汽油（吨）Petrol（ton）
总　计	**Total**	**10794980**	**1658662**	**25637**	**14740355**	**16876**
采掘业	Mining					
制造业	Manufacturing	1542230	1647682	6076	14740355	16099
电力煤气及水生产供应业	Production and Supply of Electricity，Gas and Water	9252750	10979	19562		777

7-2 续表
Continued

名　称	Name	煤油（吨）Kerosene（ton）	柴油（吨）Diesel Oil（ton）	燃料油（吨）Fuel Oil（ton）	液化石油气（吨）Liquefied Petroleum Gas（ton）	热　力（百万千焦）Heat（millon kJ）	电　力（万千瓦时）Electricity（10 000 kW・h）
总　计	**Total**	**39**	**54945**	**64868**	**380500**	**26409885**	**2210582**
采掘业	Mining		251				4386
制造业	Manufacturing	39	52828	62195	380500	22787209	1937091
电力煤气及水生产供应业	Production and Supply of Electricity，Gas and Water		1866	2673		3622676	269106

7-3 重点耗能工业企业能源加工转换(2021年)

ENERGY CONVERSION OF MAJOR ENERGY-CONSUMING INDUSTRIAL ENTERPRISES (2021)

名称	Name	单位	Unit	能源消费合计 Total Energy Consumption	#加工转换投入 Conversion Input	火电 Thermal Power	供热 Heating	炼油 Petroleum Refining	制气 Gas Production	能源加工转换产出 Conversion Output of Energy
原煤	Raw Coal	吨	ton	10522994	9627283	5048945	4551219		27119	
洗精煤	Dressing Coal	吨	ton	1942190	1942190					
煤制品	Coal Products	吨	ton	68764	68764		68764			
焦炭	Coke	吨	ton	1645138	11935	1032	10903			1460917
其他焦化产品	Other Coking Products	吨	ton	192553						74998
焦炉煤气	Coking Gas	万立方米	10 000 cu.m	19562	19562	19562				25638
高炉煤气	Blast Furnace GAS	万立方米	10 000 cu.m	584782	179361	179361				
原油	Raw Oil	吨	ton	14740355	14735341			14735341		
汽油	Petrol	吨	ton	276	38		38			4358115
煤油	Kerosene	吨	ton							846738
柴油	Diesel Oil	吨	ton	2057	541	369	173			3553495
燃料油	Fuel Oil	吨	ton	17763	17618	832	1696	15090		1859679
液化石油气	Liquefied Petroleum Gas	吨	ton	375109						1100260
炼厂干气	Refinery Dry Gas	吨	ton	409294	3519	352	3167			409294
其他石油制品	Other Petroleum Products	吨	ton	1432119	794680		100	794580		1146948
热力	Heat	百万千焦	million kJ	12428891	2358224	2358224				91726298
电力	Electricity	万千瓦时	10 000 kW·h	824562						1686807
其他燃料	Other Fuel	吨标准煤	ton SCE	28102	28102	12266	15836			
能源合计	**Total**	**吨标准煤**	**ton SCE**	**42188131**	**33497578**	**5251286**	**3831161**	**22486898**	**24887**	**28856515**

7-4 规模以上工业主要能源工业消费量(2021年)

MAJOR ENERGY CONSUMPTION Of INDUSTRY ABOVE DESIGNATED SIZE（2021）

行　业	Sector
总　计	**Total**
煤炭开采和洗选业	Mining and Washing of Coal
石油和天然气开采业	Extraction of Petroleum and Natural Gas
黑色金属矿采选业	Mining of Ferrous Metal Ores
有色金属矿采选业	Mining of Non-ferrous Metal Ores
非金属矿采选业	Mining and Processing of Non-metal Ores
开采辅助活动	Auxiliary Activities of Mining
其他采矿业	Mining of Other Ores
农副食品加工业	Processing of Food from Agricultural Products
食品制造业	Manufacture of Foods
酒、饮料和精制茶制造业	Manufacture of Liquor, Beverages and Refined Tea
烟草制品业	Manufacture of Tobacco
纺织业	Manufacture of Textile
纺织服装、服饰业	Manufacture of Textile Wearing Apparel
皮革、毛皮、羽毛及其制品和制鞋业	Manufacture of Leather, Fur, Feathre & Its Products Footwear
木材加工和木、竹、藤、棕、草制品业	Processing of Timber, Manufacture of Wood, Bamboo, Rattan, Palm and Straw Products
家具制造业	Manufacture of Furniture
造纸和纸制品业	Manufacture of Paper and Paper Products
印刷和记录媒介复制业	Printing, Reproduction of Recording Media
文教、工美、体育和娱乐用品制造业	Manufacture of Articles for Culture, Arts&Crafts, Sports and Entertainment
石油加工、炼焦和核燃料加工业	Processing of Petroleum, Coking, Processing of Nucleus Fuel
化学原料和化学制品制造业	Manufacture of Chemical Raw Material and Chemical Products
医药制造业	Manufacture of Medicines
化学纤维制造业	Manufacture of Chemical Fibres
橡胶和塑料制品业	Manufacture of Rubber and Plastic
非金属矿物制品业	Manufacture of metallic Mineral Products
黑色金属冶炼和压延加工业	Smelting and Pressing of Ferrous Metals
有色金属冶炼和压延加工业	Smelting and Pressing of Non-ferrous Metals
金属制品业	Manufacture of Metal Products
通用设备制造业	Manufacture of General Purpose Machinery
专用设备制造业	Manufacture of Special Purpose Machinery
汽车制造业	Manufacture of Vehicle
铁路、船舶、航空航天和其他运输设备制造业	Manufacture of Transport Equipment for Railway, Shipping, Aerospace and other uses
电气机械和器材制造业	Manufacture of Electrical Machinery and Equipment
计算机、通信和其他电子设备制造业	Manufacture of Computer, Communication Equipment and Other Electronic Equipment
仪器仪表制造业	Manufacture of Measuring Instrument
其他制造业	Manufacture of Other Products
废弃资源综合利用业	Recycling and Disposal of Waste Resources
金属制品、机械和设备修理业	Manufacture of Metal Products, Machinery and Equipment
电力、热力生产和供应业	Production and Supply of Electric Power and Heat Power
燃气生产和供应业	Production and Supply of Gas
水的生产和供应业	Production and Supply of Water

原煤（吨）Raw Coal (ton)	洗精煤（吨）Dressing Coal (ton)	其他洗煤（吨）Other Dressing Coal (ton)	煤制品（吨）Coal Products (ton)	焦炭（吨）Coke (ton)
10794980	**1942190**	**48428**	**68772**	**1658662**
56675				1008
11273				
3210				
6				
20483				
547381		48428		
20				
123783				963
201685				12857
577662	1942190			1632188
11				666
41				
9252750			68764	10979

7-4 续表 1
Continued

行　业	Sector
总　计	**Total**
煤炭开采和洗选业	Mining and Washing of Coal
石油和天然气开采业	Extraction of Petroleum and Natural Gas
黑色金属矿采选业	Mining of Ferrous Metal Ores
有色金属矿采选业	Mining of Non-ferrous Metal Ores
非金属矿采选业	Mining and Processing of Non-metal Ores
开采辅助活动	Auxiliary Activities of Mining
其他采矿业	Mining of Other Ores
农副食品加工业	Processing of Food from Agricultural Products
食品制造业	Manufacture of Foods
酒、饮料和精制茶制造业	Manufacture of Liquor, Beverages and Refined Tea
烟草制品业	Manufacture of Tobacco
纺织业	Manufacture of Textile
纺织服装、服饰业	Manufacture of Textile Wearing Apparel
皮革、毛皮、羽毛及其制品和制鞋业	Manufacture of Leather, Fur, Feathre & Its Products Footwear
木材加工和木、竹、藤、棕、草制品业	Processing of Timber, Manufacture of Wood, Bamboo, Rattan, Palm and Straw Products
家具制造业	Manufacture of Furniture
造纸和纸制品业	Manufacture of Paper and Paper Products
印刷和记录媒介复制业	Printing, Reproduction of Recording Media
文教、工美、体育和娱乐用品制造业	Manufacture of Articles for Culture, Arts&Crafts, Sports and Entertainment
石油加工、炼焦和核燃料加工业	Processing of Petroleum, Coking, Processing of Nucleus Fuel
化学原料和化学制品制造业	Manufacture of Chemical Raw Material and Chemical Products
医药制造业	Manufacture of Medicines
化学纤维制造业	Manufacture of Chemical Fibres
橡胶和塑料制品业	Manufacture of Rubber and Plastic
非金属矿物制品业	Manufacture of metallic Mineral Products
黑色金属冶炼和压延加工业	Smelting and Pressing of Ferrous Metals
有色金属冶炼和压延加工业	Smelting and Pressing of Non-ferrous Metals
金属制品业	Manufacture of Metal Products
通用设备制造业	Manufacture of General Purpose Machinery
专用设备制造业	Manufacture of Special Purpose Machinery
汽车制造业	Manufacture of Vehicle
铁路、船舶、航空航天和其他运输设备制造业	Manufacture of Transport Equipment for Railway, Shipping, Aerospace and other uses
电气机械和器材制造业	Manufacture of Electrical Machinery and Equipment
计算机、通信和其他电子设备制造业	Manufacture of Computer, Communication Equipment and Other Electronic Equipment
仪器仪表制造业	Manufacture of Measuring Instrument
其他制造业	Manufacture of Other Products
废弃资源综合利用业	Recycling and Disposal of Waste Resources
金属制品、机械和设备修理业	Manufacture of Metal Products, Machinery and Equipment
电力、热力生产和供应业	Production and Supply of Electric Power and Heat Power
燃气生产和供应业	Production and Supply of Gas
水的生产和供应业	Production and Supply of Water

焦炉煤气 （万立方米） Coking Gas （10 000 cu.m）	高炉煤气 （万立方米） Blast Furnace GAS （10 000 cu.m）	原油 （吨） Crude Oil （ton）	汽油 （吨） Petrol （ton）	煤油 （吨） Kerosene （ton）
25637	**598045**	**14740355**	**16876**	**39**
			1102	
			398	
			31	
			476	
			450	
			191	
			28	
			105	
			325	
			539	
			219	
		14740355	23	
			621	
			176	
			13	
			1407	
6076	13263		810	
	405421		41	
			85	
			1226	7
			1895	29
			1413	
			897	
			1263	2
			978	
			434	
			787	
			63	
			106	
19562	179361		91	
			242	
			444	

7-4 续表 2
Continued

行 业	Sector
总 计	**Total**
煤炭开采和洗选业	Mining and Washing of Coal
石油和天然气开采业	Extraction of Petroleum and Natural Gas
黑色金属矿采选业	Mining of Ferrous Metal Ores
有色金属矿采选业	Mining of Non-ferrous Metal Ores
非金属矿采选业	Mining and Processing of Non–metal Ores
开采辅助活动	Auxiliary Activities of Mining
其他采矿业	Mining of Other Ores
农副食品加工业	Processing of Food from Agricultural Products
食品制造业	Manufacture of Foods
酒、饮料和精制茶制造业	Manufacture of Liquor，Beverages and Refined Tea
烟草制品业	Manufacture of Tobacco
纺织业	Manufacture of Textile
纺织服装、服饰业	Manufacture of Textile Wearing Apparel
皮革、毛皮、羽毛及其制品和制鞋业	Manufacture of Leather，Fur，Feathre & Its Products Footwear
木材加工和木、竹、藤、棕、草制品业	Processing of Timber, Manufacture of Wood, Bamboo, Rattan, Palm and Straw Products
家具制造业	Manufacture of Furniture
造纸和纸制品业	Manufacture of Paper and Paper Products
印刷和记录媒介复制业	Printing，Reproduction of Recording Media
文教、工美、体育和娱乐用品制造业	Manufacture of Articles for Culture，Arts&Crafts，Sports and Entertainment
石油加工、炼焦和核燃料加工业	Processing of Petroleum，Coking，Processing of Nucleus Fuel
化学原料和化学制品制造业	Manufacture of Chemical Raw Material and Chemical Products
医药制造业	Manufacture of Medicines
化学纤维制造业	Manufacture of Chemical Fibres
橡胶和塑料制品业	Manufacture of Rubber and Plastic
非金属矿物制品业	Manufacture of metallic Mineral Products
黑色金属冶炼和压延加工业	Smelting and Pressing of Ferrous Metals
有色金属冶炼和压延加工业	Smelting and Pressing of Non-ferrous Metals
金属制品业	Manufacture of Metal Products
通用设备制造业	Manufacture of General Purpose Machinery
专用设备制造业	Manufacture of Special Purpose Machinery
汽车制造业	Manufacture of Vehicle
铁路、船舶、航空航天和其他运输设备制造业	Manufacture of Transport Equipment for Railway，Shipping，Aerospace and other uses
电气机械和器材制造业	Manufacture of Electrical Machinery and Equipment
计算机、通信和其他电子设备制造业	Manufacture of Computer，Communication Equipment and Other Electronic Equipment
仪器仪表制造业	Manufacture of Measuring Instrument
其他制造业	Manufacture of Other Products
废弃资源综合利用业	Recycling and Disposal of Waste Resources
金属制品、机械和设备修理业	Manufacture of Metal Products，Machinery and Equipment
电力、热力生产和供应业	Production and Supply of Electric Power and Heat Power
燃气生产和供应业	Production and Supply of Gas
水的生产和供应业	Production and Supply of Water

柴油 （吨） Diesel Oil （ton）	燃料油 （吨） Fuel Oil （ton）	液化石油气 （吨） Liquefied Petroleum Gas （ton）	炼厂干气 （吨） Refinery Dry Gas （ton）
54945	**64868**	**380500**	**409294**
15			
236			
2363	525	510	
317		30	
66		200	
218		875	
126		1	
459	232		
78			
51			
650			
463	718		
266		4	
55	15090	734	409294
2060	583	375109	
148			
27			
2043	319	283	
28616	44102	1766	
58		2	
675			
2099	62	552	
1005		50	
655			
2186		30	
6385	564	142	
1062		199	
557		11	
11		1	
51			
6			
72		1	
1682	2673		
33			
151			

7-4 续表 3
Continued

行 业	Sector
总 计	**Total**
煤炭开采和洗选业	Mining and Washing of Coal
石油和天然气开采业	Extraction of Petroleum and Natural Gas
黑色金属矿采选业	Mining of Ferrous Metal Ores
有色金属矿采选业	Mining of Non-ferrous Metal Ores
非金属矿采选业	Mining and Processing of Non–metal Ores
开采辅助活动	Auxiliary Activities of Mining
其他采矿业	Mining of Other Ores
农副食品加工业	Processing of Food from Agricultural Products
食品制造业	Manufacture of Foods
酒、饮料和精制茶制造业	Manufacture of Liquor，Beverages and Refined Tea
烟草制品业	Manufacture of Tobacco
纺织业	Manufacture of Textile
纺织服装、服饰业	Manufacture of Textile Wearing Apparel
皮革、毛皮、羽毛及其制品和制鞋业	Manufacture of Leather，Fur，Feathre & Its Products Footwear
木材加工和木、竹、藤、棕、草制品业	Processing of Timber, Manufacture of Wood, Bamboo, Rattan, Palm and Straw Products
家具制造业	Manufacture of Furniture
造纸和纸制品业	Manufacture of Paper and Paper Products
印刷和记录媒介复制业	Printing，Reproduction of Recording Media
文教、工美、体育和娱乐用品制造业	Manufacture of Articles for Culture，Arts&Crafts，Sports and Entertainment
石油加工、炼焦和核燃料加工业	Processing of Petroleum，Coking，Processing of Nucleus Fuel
化学原料和化学制品制造业	Manufacture of Chemical Raw Material and Chemical Products
医药制造业	Manufacture of Medicines
化学纤维制造业	Manufacture of Chemical Fibres
橡胶和塑料制品业	Manufacture of Rubber and Plastic
非金属矿物制品业	Manufacture of metallic Mineral Products
黑色金属冶炼和压延加工业	Smelting and Pressing of Ferrous Metals
有色金属冶炼和压延加工业	Smelting and Pressing of Non-ferrous Metals
金属制品业	Manufacture of Metal Products
通用设备制造业	Manufacture of General Purpose Machinery
专用设备制造业	Manufacture of Special Purpose Machinery
汽车制造业	Manufacture of Vehicle
铁路、船舶、航空航天和其他运输设备制造业	Manufacture of Transport Equipment for Railway，Shipping，Aerospace and other uses
电气机械和器材制造业	Manufacture of Electrical Machinery and Equipment
计算机、通信和其他电子设备制造业	Manufacture of Computer，Communication Equipment and Other Electronic Equipment
仪器仪表制造业	Manufacture of Measuring Instrument
其他制造业	Manufacture of Other Products
废弃资源综合利用业	Recycling and Disposal of Waste Resources
金属制品、机械和设备修理业	Manufacture of Metal Products，Machinery and Equipment
电力、热力生产和供应业	Production and Supply of Electric Power and Heat Power
燃气生产和供应业	Production and Supply of Gas
水的生产和供应业	Production and Supply of Water

其他石油制品 （吨） Other Petroleum Products （ton）	热　力 （百万千焦） Heat （million kJ）	电　力 （万千瓦时） Electricity （10 000 kW·h）	其他燃料 （吨标准煤） Other Fuel （ton SCE）
1437221	**26409885**	**2210582**	**29250**
		3569	
		817	
	3364075	93855	28928
	642474	43911	
	2009824	20930	
	0		
	1834539	48315	
	277349	10208	
	1601	6826	181
	0	5142	
	0	9516	120
	382669	13376	
	47461	12347	
	2341	15148	
1382450	1802	123331	
54702	6208512	347339	
	373882	18110	
	14980	7286	
	3048041	208983	
	26121	140369	
	2350234	209545	
	0	22257	
11	114494	103527	
	116640	82052	
	109456	39634	
48	524959	129015	
10	803041	80868	21
	493443	70359	
	39271	65268	
	0	5011	
	0	3547	
	0	664	
	0	351	
	3536323	194808	
	86353	11385	
	0	62912	

主要统计指标解释

工业企业能源消费量 工业企业能源消费包括工业企业在生产过程中作为燃料、动力、原料、辅助材料使用的能源以及工艺用能、非生产用能；作为能源加工转换企业，还要包括能源加工转换的投入量。工业企业能源消费量具体包括：

（1）用于本企业产品生产、工业性作业和其他生产性活动的能源。

（2）用于技术更新改造措施、新技术研究和新产品试制以及科学试验等方面的能源。

（3）用于经营维修、建筑及设备大修理、机电设备和交通运输工具等方面的能源。

（4）用于劳动保护的能源。

（5）其他非生产消费的能源。

不包括：

（1）由仓库发到车间，但在报告期最后一天没有消费的能源。这部分能源应在办理假退料手续后计入库存量。

（2）拨到外单位，委托外单位加工用的能源。

（3）调出本单位或借给外单位的能源。

工业生产能源消费 是指工业企业为进行工业生产活动所使用的能源。主要包括：

（1）用于本企业产品生产、工业性作业的能源，包括用作原料、材料、燃料、动力：作为能源加工转换企业，还包括用作加工转换的能源。

（2）产品生产过程中作为辅助材料使用的能源。

（3）生产工艺过程使用的能源。

（4）新技术研究、新产品试制、科学试验使用的能源。

（5）为了工业生产活动而在进行的各种修理过程中使用的能源。

（6）生产区内的劳动保护用能等。

Explanatory Notes on Main Statistical Indicators

Energy Consumption of Industrial Enterprises include energy in the production process as fuel, power, raw materials, supplementary materials, and for use of technology and non-production. As energy processing and conversion enterprises, also include energy processing and conversion of inputs. These specifically include : (1) Energy for the enterprise product, industrial production operations and other activities. (2) Energy for technical upgrading measures and new technology research and new product production and scientific experiments. (3) Energy for operation maintenance, construction and equipment overhaul, electrical and mechanical equipment and transport, and other aspects. (4) Energy for the protection of labor. (5) Energy for Other non-production and consumption. And these exclude : (1) Energy from the warehouse to the workshop, but out of consumption on the last day of the reporting period. This part of the energy should leave retreat materials handling procedures included stock. (2) Energy transferred to other units, entrusted with the processing. (3) Energy transferred out of the unit or loans to other units.

Energy Consumption for Industrial Production refers to energy for industrial enterprises in industrial production activities. These mainly include : (1) Energy for the enterprise products, industrial operations, including energy as raw materials, materials, fuels, and Power. As energy processing and conversion enterprises, also include energy for processing and conversion. (2) Energy as supplementary material in product process. (3) Energy used in production process. (4) Energy for new technologies, new product production, and scientific experiment. (5) Energy in process of repairing for industrial production activities. (6) Energy for labor protection in production areas and so on.

8 财政、金融和保险业

GOVERNMENT FINANCE, FINANCIAL AND INSURANCE

简 要 说 明

一、本篇资料的主要内容

本篇资料主要反映了全市财政收支、金融和保险方面的情况，主要包括财政收入、财政支出、金融机构存贷款、保险业务开展等方面的资料。

二、本篇资料的来源

1. 财政部分的资料来源于市财政局。

2. 金融方面的资料来源于中国人民银行青岛市中心支行。

3. 保险方面的资料来源于中国银行保险监督管理委员会青岛监管局。

本篇资料由市统计局国民经济核算处整理提供。

Brief Introduction

Ⅰ. Main Content

Data in this chapter mainly reflects the city's fiscal revenue and expenditure, finance and insurance, mainly including fiscal revenue, fiscal expenditure, deposits and loans of financial institutions, and insurance business development.

Ⅱ. Source of Data

1. The financial information comes from the Qingdao Municipal Finance Bureau.

2.The financial information comes from the Qingdao City Center Branch of the People' s Bank of China.

3. The insurance information comes from the Qingdao Supervision Bureau of the China Banking and Insurance Regulatory Commission.

The data in this article is compiled and provided by the National Economic Accounting Office of Qingdao Statistics Bureau.

8-1 主要年份地方财政收支

MAFOR YEAR'S REVENUE AND EXPENDRRURE OF LOCAL GOVERNMENT FINANCE

单位：万元（10 000 yuan）

年份 Year	财政收入 Revenue of Government Finance	财政支出 Expenditure of Government Finance
1949	1527	306
1952	19809	2226
1957	29875	3556
1962	32869	4327
1965	47682	6280
1970	95778	7825
1975	90220	11966
1978	130749	19427
1980	124835	20064
1985	165155	41996
1988	201206	93931
1990	242303	133875
1991	259377	137716
1992	275589	155696
1993	182348	211938
1994	227490	277331
1995	294771	376982
1996	379674	469569
1997	476804	564787
1998	580434	678575
1999	680089	740937
2000	800120	878702
2001	987080	1097848
2002	1006616	1243880
2003	1201398	1471747
2004	1305136	1646214
2005	1763412	2030622
2006	2257663	2367875
2007	2925798	3211777
2008	3424359	3694111
2009	3769896	4335754
2010	4526138	5323888
2011	5661400	6580605
2012	6701820	7659801
2013	7889313	10142273
2014	8952450	10747138
2015	10063220	12228664
2016	11000303	13528516
2017	11572389	14030252
2018	12319138	15597764
2019	12417359	15759729
2020	12538548	15846485
2021	13682971	17067635

注：1. 1993 年以后实行新制度，财政收入数与历年不可比。
2. 2002 年以后，财政收入、支出为一般预算数。

Notes：1. Since 1993，new regulations have been adopted in calculating revenue of government finance，the figures are not comparable with those over the years.
2. Since 2002，revenue of government finance and expenditure of government finance refer to general budgetary revenue and expenditure.

8-2 分市、区公共财政预算收入（2021年）
PULBIC FINANCE BUDGET REVENUE BY CITY AND DISTRICL (2021)

单位：万元（10 000 yuan）

市、区名称	Region	一般公共预算收入 Public Finance Budget Revenue	#增值税 Value-added Tax	#营业税 Business Tax	#企业所得税 Enterprise Income Tax
全　市	**Whole Municipality**	**13682971**	**3629995**		**1922765**
市南区	Shinan District	914174	299566		149362
市北区	Shibei District	1185774	274141		164402
李沧区	Licang District	646856	181723		82554
崂山区	Laoshan District	2001556	530137		452215
黄岛区（西海岸新区）	Huangdao District (West Coast New Area)	2833137	736457		467039
城阳区	Chengyang District	1639261	469415		231492
即墨区	Jimo District	1160170	323272		101793
胶州市	Jiaozhou	1154571	356712		84556
平度市	Pingdu	664772	166727		49396
莱西市	Laixi	600366	243545		64470

8-2 续表
Continued

单位：万元（10 000 yuan）

市、区名称	Region	# 个人所得税 Personal Income Tax	# 城市维护建设税 Urban Maintenance and Development Tax	# 基金预算收入 Funds Budgetary Revenue
全　市	**Whole Municipality**	**676918**	**654071**	**11927276**
市南区	Shinan District	134464	45915	
市北区	Shibei District	44698	54777	
李沧区	Licang District	20317	31339	
崂山区	Laoshan District	162267	130473	1383363
黄岛区（西海岸新区）	Huangdao District (West Coast New Area)	125670	152921	2635754
城阳区	Chengyang District	52716	72478	2001240
即墨区	Jimo District	26653	52114	1218382
胶州市	Jiaozhou	31052	54208	1004930
平度市	Pingdu	17657	24478	281025
莱西市	Laixi	61424	35368	451768

8-3 分市、区公共财政预算支出（2021 年）

PUBLIC FINANCE BUDGET REVENUE BY CITY AND DISTRICT (2021)

单位：万元（10 000 yuan）

市、区名称	Region	一般公共预算支出 Public Finance Budget Revenue	#一般公共服务支出 General Public Services	#公共安全 Public Security	#教育 Education	#科学技术 Science and Technology	#文化体育与传媒 Culture, Sport and Media
全 市	**Whole Municipality**	**17067635**	**1991186**	**1095451**	**3088039**	**513252**	**252504**
市南区	Shinan District	538378	85105	28030	114473	10613	3198
市北区	Shibei District	691773	133584	28904	191942	23127	6105
李沧区	Licang District	543412	57308	15933	127464	14828	6105
崂山区	Laoshan District	1387505	136942	55099	189970	101029	5830
黄岛区（西海岸新区）	Huangdao District (West Coast New Area)	2622995	395911	95211	549006	101160	26158
城阳区	Chengyang District	1392826	181922	39874	347067	86305	15951
即墨区	Jimo District	1278462	188769	55425	346736	15689	14748
胶州市	Jiaozhou	1294948	173632	68900	323911	20545	19776
平度市	Pingdu	1171638	124241	47534	297058	18481	6795
莱西市	Laixi	904329	97844	36354	144832	3217	7091

8-3 续表
Continued

单位：万元（10 000 yuan）

市、区名称	Region	#社会保障和就业 Social Security and Employment	#医疗卫生 Health Care	#节能环保 Environment Protection	#城乡社区事务 Urban and Rural Community Affairs	#农林水事务 Affairs of Agriculture Forest and Irrigation	#基金预算支出 Funds Budgetary Expenditure
全　市	**Whole Municipality**	**2431109**	**1244611**	**177057**	**2448340**	**852668**	**14804981**
市南区	Shinan District	87940	35325	12045	94480	3613	7898
市北区	Shibei District	131622	34318	8784	80719	520	114311
李沧区	Licang District	70235	53155	9311	147198	1852	419488
崂山区	Laoshan District	64868	54401	4269	341818	63220	975042
黄岛区（西海岸新区）	Huangdao District（West Coast New Area）	368181	169877	16740	326265	117835	3683446
城阳区	Chengyang District	134479	89491	2237	177717	53733	2370500
即墨区	Jimo District	213556	92252	18336	109534	89570	1225001
胶州市	Jiaozhou	174910	112913	30309	147355	90497	1918404
平度市	Pingdu	218618	101707	20693	81414	180790	407399
莱西市	Laixi	186301	81278	13467	39504	101451	610850

8-4 主要年份金融系统人民币存贷款（年末余额）
MAJOR YEAR'S DEPOSITS AND LOANS OF FINANCIAL INSTITUTIONS（YEAR-END BALANCE）

单位：万元（10 000 yuan）

年份 Year	存款合计 Total Deposits	# 企业存款 Deposits by Enterprises	# 储蓄存款 Savings Deposits	贷款合计 Total Loans
1949	693	239	28	278
1952	9093	4308	1838	3322
1957	10372	3359	4037	30690
1962	20040	8579	3279	73601
1965	27331	11830	6347	64555
1970	38264	13024	7576	126382
1975	60622	22568	15637	207006
1978	66523	21004	21455	297184
1980	120644	38105	38609	379666
1985	344760	99736	155604	452142
1990	1235562	321542	655895	1535751
1991	1553564	411417	824428	1871462
1992	2076667	612868	1044165	2352449
1993	2747294	835617	1372239	2940658
1994	3769019	1399110	1918734	3610564
1995	5324026	2030382	2687888	4777864
1996	6991289	2630958	3499219	5941281
1997	7385092	2885632	4060259	6508776
1998	8183471	3018063	4591012	7239231
1999	9160001	3454570	4978045	8945730
2000	10560624	4386316	5353215	9564293
2001	12323942	4955336	6187409	10798871
2002	15225733	5819655	7449408	13044792
2003	18920868	7027227	9084693	16783917
2004	22462592	7924690	10894941	18472613
2005	26975372	8226661	13431016	20394792
2006	32453583	10144296	15676197	25779442
2007	38915882	13213434	17020383	30970553
2008	47353803	14641948	21233637	37483209
2009	63019764	21001185	25278658	48735326
2010	76592065	27271963	29123256	58862263
2011	86384994	49189415	31985099	69477500
2012	94348924	50978985	37576007	79465532
2013	109695588	60367185	41405946	88607439
2014	113703085	60791933	44358964	97200532
2015	125330268	45526577	50235905	107718528
2016	140071344	50912759	53263262	118916821
2017	143877550	53835435	53941843	132647913
2018	155321863	57270448	59137089	151941934
2019	172829678	66873600	67552370	173318261
2020	198218001	76209031	80309469	202109625
2021	215823413	82945990	90282352	232534611

注：本表数据来源于人民银行，自 2015 年起，人民银行报表指标变化，企业存款指标暂用非金融企业存款，储蓄存款指标暂用住户存款，口径与以前年度不一致。

Note：The data in this table comes from the People's Bank of China. Since 2015, the report index of the People's Bank of China has changed, the enterprise deposit index is temporarily used as the deposit of the enterprise, the savings deposit index is temporarily used for household deposit, the caliber is not consistent with the previous year.

8-5 金融系统人民币存贷款（年末余额）
DEPOSITS AND LOANS OF FINANCIAL INSTITUTIONS（YEAR-END BALANCE）

单位：万元（10 000 yuan）

项目	Item	2021 年	比年初增减数 Incremental/Reductions Compared to the Beginning of the Year
一、存款总计	Total Deposits	215823413	17605411
住户存款	Household Deposits	90282352	9972883
非金融企业存款	Non-Financial Corporate Deposits	82945990	6740449
广义政府存款	General Government Deposits	27957740	-776231
非银行业金融机构存款	Non-Banking Financial Institutions' s Deposits	12108593	1791592
二、贷款总计	Total Loans	232534611	30424985
住户贷款	Household Loans	76769199	10322401
#短期贷款	Short-Term Loans	10395204	2548676
中长期贷款	Medium And Long-Term Loans	66373996	7773724
非金融企业及机关团体贷款	Non-Financial Enterprises And Institutions/ Organizations' Loans	155449316	19998869
#短期贷款	Short-Term Loans	45278701	4075313
中长期贷款	Medium&Long-term Loans	96720081	11779127
票据融资	Notes Financing	11936352	4047254
非银行业金融机构贷款	Non-Banking Financial Institution' s Loans	0	0

注：自 2015 年起，人民银行报表中指标发生变化，本表数据按照新指标提供。
Note：Since 2015，the indexes in the People' s Bank of China' s statements have changed，the data in the table are provided according to the new indexes.

8-6 国内保险业务（2000—2021年）
DOMESTIC INSURANCE BUSINESS（2000—2021）

项目	Item	2000年	2005年	2010年	2011年	2012年
风险保障金额	**Total domestic insurance Value**	**38357485**	**91691581**	**309244255**	**380829634**	**447476690**
国内业务收入	**Domestic Business Income**	**220780**	**495701**	**1538526**	**1457269**	**1602881**
1. 保费收入	Premium Income	218714	495701	1538526	1457269	1602881
#财产险	Property Insurance	85161	159746	492190	556257	644269
农业险	Agriculture Insurance	18	12	3261	3587	5046
人身险	Personal Insurance	133535	335943	1043075	897425	953566
国内业务支出	**Domestic Business Expenditure**	**94877**	**214148**	**497832**	**463751**	**592167**
1 . 赔款支出	Indemnity Expenditure	62275	111385	279019	307564	360085
#财产险	Property Insurance	58361	92700	250966	286214	328877
农业险	Agriculture Insurance	5	11	2808	1087	1833
人身险	Personal Insurance	3909	18674	25245	20263	29375
2 . 给付支出	Mature Payment	27955	32739	109318	156188	154922
3 . 退保	Surrender	4647	70024	109496	69275	77159

注：1. 本表由青岛银保监局提供，风险保障金额2012年之前为国内保险总值。
2. 因部分保险机构正在进行风险处置，2021年保险业相关数据暂不包括这部分机构。

Notes：1. This table is provided by Qingdao Banking and Insurance Regulatory Bureau. The amount of risk protection before 2012 is the total value of domestic insurance.
2. As some insurance institutions are in the process of risk disposal, insurance industry data in 2021 do not include those of these institutions.

单位：万元（10 000 yuan）

2013年	2014年	2015年	2016年	2017年	2018年	2019年	2020年	2021年
491953749	**611632799**	**836499657**	**1687559828**	**2232390824**	**2337365406**	**2759993215**	**3149621411**	**4706405207**
1789854	**2031421**	**2441172**	**3359013**	**3967170**	**4393970**	**4868673**	**5183142**	**4618400**
1789854	2031421	2441172	3359013	3967170	4393970	4868673	5183142	4618400
744470	872805	920229	1046908	1062116	1269489	1243160	1451301	1404366
6824	8395	12100	12734	15670	18043	24523	28263	37427
1038560	1150220	1508843	2299371	2889384	3106438	3600989	3703578	3176607
757404	**1031415**	**1236281**	**1522375**	**1704218**	**1919252**	**1882881**	**1788966**	**1949551**
432494	492693	539320	681211	733493	917964	937025	1045920	1194932
392860	442168	492573	526586	554513	756987	706639	831317	935922
3820	5519	9724	16337	18232	10985	14019	24474	19531
35814	45006	37023	138288	160749	149992	216368	190129	239478
194592	274790	340786	455300	470266	493511	498555	379492	428880
130318	263932	356175	376777	500459	507777	447301	363553	325739

主要统计指标解释

财政收入　指国家财政参与社会产品分配所取得的收入，是实现国家职能的财力保证。财政收入所包括的内容几经变化，目前主要包括：

（1）税收收入：包括增值税、营业税、企业所得税、个人所得税、资源税、城市维护建设税、房产税、印花税、城镇土地使用税、土地增值税、车船税、耕地占用税、契税、烟叶税、其他税收收入。

（2）非税收入:包括专项收入、行政事业性收费收入、罚没收入、国有资本经营收入、国有资源有偿使用收入、捐赠收入、政府住房基金收入、其他收入。

财政支出　国家财政将筹集起来的资金进行分配使用，以满足经济建设和各项事业的需要，主要包括：

（1）一般公共服务支出：反映政府提供一般公共服务的支出。

（2）公共安全:反映政府维护社会公共安全方面的支出,有关事务包括武装警察、公安、国家安全、检察、法院、司法行政、监狱、劳教、国家保密、缉私警察等。

（3）教育支出：反映政府教育事务支出。有关具体教育事务包括教育行政管理、学前教育、小学教育、初中教育、普通高中教育、普通高等教育、初等职业教育、中专教育、技校教育、职业高中教育、高等职业教育、广播电视教育、留学生教育、特殊教育、干部继续教育、教育机关服务等。

（4）科学技术：反映政府用于科学技术方面的支出。

（5）文化体育与传媒：反映政府在文化、文物、体育、广播电视、新闻出版等方面的支出。

（6）社会保障和就业:反映政府在社会保障与就业方面的支出。有关事项包括社会保障与就业管理事务、民政管理事务、财政对社会保险基金的补助、补充全国社会保障基金、行政事业单位离退休、企业改革补助、就业补助、抚恤、退役安置、社会福利、残疾人事业、城市居民最低生活保障、其他城镇社会救济、农村社会救济、自然灾害生活补助、红十字事务等。

（7）医疗卫生支出：反映政府医疗卫生方面的支出。具体包括医疗卫生管理事务支出、医疗服务支出、医疗保障支出、疾病预防控制支出、卫生监督支出、妇幼保健支出、农村卫生支出等。

（8）环境保护：反映政府环境保护支出。具体包括：环境保护管理事务支出、环境监测与监察支出、污染治理支出、自然生态保护支出、天然林保护工程支出、退耕还林支出、风沙荒漠治理支出、退牧还草支出、已垦草原退耕还草支出。

（9）城乡社区事务：反映政府城乡社区事务支出。具体包括：城乡社区管理事务支出、城乡社区规划与管理支出、城乡社区公共设施支出、城乡社区住宅支出、城乡社区环境卫生支出、建设市场管理与监督支出等。

（10）农林水事务：反映政府农林水事务方面的支出。具体包括农业、林业、水利、扶贫支出、农业综合开发支出等。

存款　指企业、机关、团体或居民根据资金必须收回的原则，把货币资金存入银行或其他信贷机构保管并取得一定利息的一种信用活动形式。根据存款对象或性质的不同可划分为住户存款、非金融企业存款、财政性存款、机关团体存款、非银行业金融机构存款等科目。它是银行信贷资金的主要来源。

贷款　指银行或其他信贷机构根据资金必须归还的原则，按一定利率，为企业、个人等提供资金的一种信用活动形式。我国银行贷款分为短期贷款、中长期贷款、融资租赁、票据融资、各项垫款等。

保费　指投保人为取得保险人在约定范围内所承担赔偿责任而支付给保险人的费用。

Explanatory Notes on Main Statistical Indicators

Government Revenue　refers to the revenue of the government finance by means of participating in the distribution of the social products, which is the financial resources for ensuring the government to function. The contents of government revenue have been changed several times. Now it includes the following main items:

(1) Various tax revenues, including value added tax, business tax, enterprise income tax, personal income tax, resources tax, fixed assets investment direction regulating tax, tax on city maintenance and construction, real estate tax, stamp tax, tax on use of urban land, land value added tax, vehicle and vessel tax, tax on occupancy of cultivated land, property tax, tobacco leaf tax, and other tax revenues.

(2) Non-tax income: including special income, administrative fee income, fine and confiscated income, state-owned capital operating income, income from the paid use of state-owned resources, donation income, government housing fund income, and other income.

Government Expenditure refers to the distribution and use of the funds the government finance has raised, so as to meet the needs of economic construction and various causes. It includes the following main items:

(1) Expenditure for general public services: It reflects the expenditure from the government for general public services.

(2) Expenditure on public security: It reflects the expenditure from the government towards safeguarding the public security, including the related affairs of armed police, public security, state security, procuratorial administration, law court, judicial administration, jail , reeducation through labor, state confidentiality, anti-smuggling Patrol, etc.

(3) Expenditure on education: It reflects the expenditure from the government on education, including the related affairs of educational administration management, preschool education, primary education, junior secondary educate, regular senior secondary educate, regular higher education, primary vocational education, specialized secondary educate, technical educate, vocational senior secondary educate, vocational higher education, radio and television education, foreign student educate, special education, cadre continuing education, education institution services,etc.

(4) Expenditure on science and technology: It reflects the expenditure from the government on science and technology.

(5) Expenditure on culture, sport and media: It reflects the expenditure from the government on culture, cultural relics, sport, radio and television, publication, etc.

(6) Expenditure on social security and employment:It reflects the expenditure from the government on social security and employment, including the related affairs of management of social security and employment, civil administration, subsidies to social insurance funds, supplement to national social security funds, retirees of government agencies and institutions, subsidies to enterprises reform, subsidies to employment, pension, settling down demobilized servicemen, social security, disabled person administration, minimum living allowance in urban area, other social relief in urban area, social relief in rural area, subsidies to natural disaster, Red Cross business, etc.

(7) Expenditure on health care: It reflects the expenditure from the government on health care, including expenditure on management of health care, medical services, medical security, disease control and prevention, public health supervision, rural health care,etc.

(8) Expenditure on environment protection: It reflects the expenditure from the government on environment protection, including expenditure on management of environment protection, environment monitoring and supervisory, pollution government, natural ecological protection, project of natural forest protection, returning farmland to forest, sandstorm and wilderness government, returning grazing land to grassland, returning cultivated grassland to grassland, etc.

(9) Expenditure on urban and rural community affairs: It reflects the expenditure from the government on urban and rural community affairs, including expenditure on management of urban and rural community affairs, plan and management of urban and rural community, public utility of urban and rural community, residential buildings of urban and rural community, environmental sanitation of urban and rural community, management and supervision of markets construction, etc.

(10) Expenditure on agriculture, forest and irrigation: It reflects the expenditure from the government on agriculture, forest and irrigation, including expenditure on agriculture, forest, irrigation, poverty alleviation, comprehensive development of agriculture, etc.

Deposit refers to a form of credit activity in which enterprises, agencies, organizations or residents deposit monetary funds in banks or other credit institutions for safekeeping and obtain a certain amount of interest based on the principle that funds must be recovered. According to the different deposit objects or nature, it can be divided into accounts such as household deposits, non-financial enterprise deposits, fiscal deposits, government agency deposits, and non–banking financial institutions deposits. It is the main source of bank credit funds.

Loan refers to a form of credit activity in which banks or other credit institutions provide funds for enterprises and individuals at a certain interest rate based on the principle that funds must be returned. Bank loans in my country are divided into short–term loans, medium and long–term loans, financial leasing, bill financing, and various advances.

Premium is the fee paid by the insurant to the insurer to obtain the obligation of compensation from the insurance within the agreed terms.

价格指数 9

PRICE INDICES

简 要 说 明

一、本篇资料的主要内容

本篇资料主要包括工业生产者出厂、工业生产者购进、固定资产投资、房地产、居民消费、商品零售等价格指数。

二、本篇资料的来源

1. 工业生产者出厂、工业生产者购进、固定资产投资、房地产价格指数分别来源于生产、投资、房地产价格统计调查月报，由国家统计局青岛调查队生产价格调查处整理提供。

2. 居民消费、商品零售价格指数来源于消费价格统计调查月报，由国家统计局青岛调查队消费价格调查处整理提供。

Brief Introduction

Ⅰ. Main Content

Data in this chapter mainly include producer price indices for manufactured goods, purchasing price indices for industrial producers, price indices of investment in fixed assets, real estate price indices, consumer price indices and retail price indices.

Ⅱ. Source of Data

1. Data on producer price indices for manufactured goods, purchasing price indices for industrial producers price indices of investment in fixed assets, real estate price indices are based on monthly report of price survey on production, investment, real estate, and provided by the Division of Production Price Survey of NBS Survey Office in Qingdao.

2. Data on consumer price indices and retail price indices are based on monthly report of consumer price survey, and provided by the Division of Consumer Price Survey of NBS Survey Office in Qingdao.

9-1 主要年份居民消费和商品零售价格指数（以上年价格为 100）
MAJOR YEAR'S CONSUMER AND RETAIL PRICE INDICES（PRECEDING YEAR=100）

年 份 Year	居民消费价格指数 Consumer Price Index	# 食品类 Food	# 衣着类 Clothing	# 服务项目价格指数 Services Price Index	商品零售价格指数 Retail Price Index
1951	110.5	105.2	112.4		110.5
1952	99.8	99.6	98.7		99.8
1957	101.4	101.3	101.4	99.3	101.4
1962	102.6	102.0	100.2	99.9	102.6
1965	101.2	101.3	98.8	96.9	101.2
1970	98.9	99.7	100.0	99.5	98.9
1975	100.3	100.1	100.0	100.0	100.3
1978	100.5	100.2	99.8	100.0	100.5
1980	105.2	108.5	100.3	100.6	105.5
1985	110.4	115.2	102.3	102.7	110.9
1988	120.7	125.2	117.3	118.3	120.9
1990	104.5	103.4	103.4	118.8	103.6
1991	107.0	107.0	112.1	109.6	106.8
1992	111.4	115.1	108.6	119.9	110.8
1993	123.9	120.9	119.0	158.5	119.8
1994	126.9	135.2	130.1	117.9	122.8
1995	116.2	118.1	122.8	123.2	114.2
1996	112.6	110.1	104.3	130.4	106.0
1997	104.0	101.2	102.3	120.8	100.2
1998	100.0	93.7	94.5	136.2	94.9
1999	100.2	96.7	97.1	115.6	96.6
2000	103.3	100.0	108.3	112.0	99.7
2001	101.0	100.6	98.0	108.7	98.9
2002	98.9	97.8	100.2	101.0	99.5
2003	101.4	104.3	98.4	101.7	98.3
2004	102.1	104.0	103.6	104.7	99.0
2005	102.3	102.1	108.3	101.4	99.3
2006	100.9	101.7	99.4	100.8	99.7
2007	104.5	111.6	99.4	102.4	102.7
2008	104.7	111.7	103.9	99.8	103.9
2009	100.5	101.6	101.4	100.6	98.6
2010	102.2	106.4	101.0	100.4	101.4
2011	105.0	111.1	108.2	103.1	104.5
2012	102.7	104.3	106.3	102.1	101.7
2013	102.5	105.3	104.9	100.7	101.4
2014	102.6	104.4	103.2	101.9	102.3
2015	101.2	101.7	102.8	101.3	100.0
2016	102.5	105.0	100.3	101.8	102.0
2017	102.0	99.6	100.5	103.4	100.8
2018	102.1	103.1	103.8	101.6	101.8
2019	103.3	111.6	100.6	101.7	102.4
2020	102.4	109.8	99.9	100.7	101.5
2021	101.5	99.7	100.6	102.0	101.4

注：1.2016 年起，食品类统计口径有变化，不包括"茶及饮料"和"在外餐饮"两项内容。
2.2016 年起，统计分类"服务项目价格指数"改为"服务价格指数"，增加"养老服务"和"金融服务"两项内容。

Notes：1. Statistical caliber of food category has changed since 2016. The two sections of "Tea and Drinks" and "Catering Service" are not included.
2. The statistical category of "Price Index of Service Item" has been revised to "Price Index of Service" as of 2016 with two additional sections of "Elderly Care Service" and "Financial Service".

9-2 主要年份居民消费和商品零售价格指数(以1950年价格为100)

MAJOR YEAR'S CONSUMER AND RETAIL PRICE INDICES（1950 = 100）

年 份 Year	居民消费价格指数 Consumer Price Index	#食品类 Food	#衣着类 Clothing	#服务项目价格指数 Services Price Index	商品零售价格指数 Retail Price Index
1951	110.5	105.2	112.4		110.5
1952	110.3	104.8	110.9		110.3
1957	119.5	120.7	115.3	91.6	119.5
1962	127.4	128.8	115.1	94.2	127.4
1965	133.3	138.7	108.4	81.5	133.3
1970	129.0	137.6	110.3	76.8	129.0
1975	128.8	138.2	110.0	75.7	128.8
1978	129.1	138.7	109.8	75.7	129.1
1980	137.6	154.1	109.3	76.1	138.1
1985	160.8	196.1	103.8	80.5	162.5
1988	223.8	295.2	133.2	100.8	227.6
1990	269.7	333.3	166.8	155.9	269.7
1991	288.6	356.7	187.0	170.9	288.1
1992	321.5	410.5	203.1	204.9	319.2
1993	398.3	496.3	241.7	324.8	382.4
1994	505.4	671.1	314.4	382.9	469.5
1995	587.3	792.5	386.1	471.8	536.2
1996	661.3	872.6	402.7	615.2	568.4
1997	687.8	883.0	412.0	743.1	569.5
1998	687.8	827.4	389.3	1012.1	540.5
1999	689.2	800.1	378.0	1170.0	522.1
2000	711.9	800.1	409.4	1310.4	520.5
2001	719.0	804.9	401.2	1424.4	514.8
2002	711.1	787.2	402.0	1438.7	512.2
2003	721.1	821.0	395.6	1463.1	503.5
2004	736.2	853.9	409.8	1531.9	498.5
2005	753.1	871.8	443.8	1553.4	495.0
2006	759.9	886.6	441.2	1565.8	493.5
2007	794.1	989.5	438.5	1603.4	506.8
2008	831.4	1105.3	455.6	1600.2	526.6
2009	835.6	1123.0	462.0	1609.8	519.2
2010	854.0	1194.9	466.6	1616.2	526.5
2011	896.7	1327.5	504.9	1666.3	550.2
2012	920.9	1384.6	536.7	1701.3	559.6
2013	943.9	1458.0	563.0	1713.2	567.4
2014	968.4	1522.2	581.0	1745.8	580.5
2015	980.0	1548.1	597.3	1768.5	580.5
2016	1004.5	1625.5	599.1	1800.3	592.1
2017	1024.6	1619.0	602.1	1861.5	596.8
2018	1046.1	1669.2	625.0	1891.3	607.6
2019	1080.6	1862.8	628.7	1923.4	622.2
2020	1106.5	2045.4	628.1	1936.9	631.5
2021	1123.1	2039.3	631.9	1975.6	640.3

注：1. 2016年起，食品类统计口径有变化，不包括"茶及饮料"和"在外餐饮"两项内容。
2. 2016年起，统计分类"服务项目价格指数"改为"服务价格指数"，增加"养老服务"和"金融服务"两项内容。

Notes：1. Statistical caliber of food category has changed since 2016. The two sections of "Tea and Drinks" and "Catering Service" are not included.
2. The statistical category of "Price Index of Service Item" has been revised to "Price Index of Service" of 2016 with two additional sections of "Elderly Care Service" and "Financial Service".

9-3 主要年份生产投资价格指数（以上年价格为 100）

MAJOR YEAR'S PRICE INDICES FOR PRODUCTION AND INVESTMENT（PRECEDING YEAR=100）

年 份 Year	工业生产者 出厂价格指数 Producer Price Indices for Industrial Producers	工业生产者 购进价格指数 Purchasing Price Indices for Industrial Producers	房屋销售 价格指数 Sales Price Indices of Houses	房屋租赁 价格指数 Renting Price Indices of Houses	物业管理 价格指数 Property Management Price Indices	固定资产 投资价格指数 Price Index for Investment in Fixed Assets
1990	104.33	108.64				
1991	101.68	108.10				
1992	105.46	107.13				
1993	115.49	126.91				
1994	121.62	120.30				
1995	112.70	114.25				
1996	103.81	103.25				
1997	100.22	101.93				
1998	94.96	92.77	100.1	94.0		
1999	96.93	95.88	103.7	104.3		
2000	101.89	106.81	102.3	95.8		
2001	98.00	97.81	104.1	107.0		
2002	97.37	96.78	107.6	94.4		
2003	100.97	106.51	114.6	99.4		
2004	102.92	113.62	115.2	98.6		105.8
2005	101.39	106.52	110.9	103.3	100.2	103.1
2006	101.08	105.80	106.9	110.1	99.8	102.6
2007	101.50	106.69	106.5	108.3	100.4	104.1
2008	105.33	115.91	105.1	106.5	102.1	111.0
2009	95.78	90.35	100.3	103.5	100.4	94.6
2010	103.75	112.21		103.0	100.5	104.9
2011	104.90	109.39				107.0
2012	98.61	97.00				100.0
2013	98.82	96.53				100.1
2014	99.20	97.40				99.9
2015	97.04	94.24				97.1
2016	98.77	97.28				99.8
2017	104.40	110.73				107.3
2018	104.22	105.22				106.6
2019	100.0	98.4				

注：2010 年之前工业生产者出厂价格为工业品出厂价格；工业生产者购进价格为主要原材料、燃料、动力购进价格；根据国家制度规定 2019 年起不编制固定资产投资价格指数；根据国家有关规定 2020 年起不再编制工业生产者价格指数。

Note：Producers Prices at works were the prices of industrial products at words before 2010. Producers purchasing price refers to the purchasing price of main raw materials, fuels and power.According to the national system, the fixed asset investment price index will not be compiled from 2019 ; according to the relevant national regulations, the industrial producer price index will no longer be compiled from 2020.

9-4 工业生产者出厂价格指数（以上年价格为 100）
PRODUCER PRICE INDICES FOR INDUSTRIAL PRODUCERS（PRECEDING YEAR=100）

类　别	Item	2000 年	2005 年	2009 年	2010 年
总指数	**General Index**	**101.89**	**101.39**	**95.78**	**103.75**
其中：轻工业	Light Industry	98.50	99.78	97.21	100.80
重工业	Heavy Industry	105.62	104.32	93.45	107.57
其中：生产资料	**Means of Production**	**105.03**	**103.24**	**94.25**	**106.43**
采掘	Excavation	95.67	114.74	93.44	130.94
原料	Raw Materials	113.82	106.91	90.67	115.24
加工	Processing	97.58	101.45	95.34	103.50
生活资料	**Means of Livelihood**	**98.25**	**99.13**	**97.45**	**99.61**
食品	Food	96.59	98.80	98.21	105.06
衣着	Clothing	99.37	101.48	102.03	101.56
一般日用品	Articles for Daily Use	104.52	101.97	99.39	99.96
耐用消费品	Durable Consumer Goods	97.70	97.43	94.52	93.23

注：根据国家有关规定 2020 年起不再编制工业生产者价格指数。
Note：According to relevant national regulations, the industrial producer price index will no longer be compiled from 2020.

2011年	2012年	2013年	2014年	2015年	2016年	2017年	2018年	2019年
104.90	**98.61**	**98.82**	**99.20**	**97.04**	**98.77**	**104.40**	**104.22**	**100.0**
103.46	99.70	99.11	99.62	99.85	98.74	101.13	101.27	101.6
105.89	97.87	98.62	98.91	95.10	98.79	106.46	106.01	98.9
105.54	**97.55**	**98.58**	**98.87**	**95.23**	**98.60**	**106.34**	**105.86**	**99.0**
132.07	93.35	91.72	100.65	95.12				
111.52	99.05	99.26	98.87	88.59	93.92	112.92	114.50	95.8
103.49	97.20	98.50	98.84	97.06	99.60	104.96	103.95	99.8
103.82	**100.42**	**99.21**	**99.76**	**100.07**	**99.12**	**100.69**	**100.95**	**101.8**
109.71	99.91	95.34	98.34	102.53	102.59	100.55	100.55	104.8
107.44	102.03	102.74	100.34	100.39	100.93	101.54	100.14	101.6
108.02	101.64	101.42	101.01	99.59	100.12	101.63	101.54	100.3
94.34	98.79	98.41	99.65	98.26	94.58	99.78	101.32	100.3

9-5 工业生产者购进价格指数（以上年价格为 100）
PURCHASING PRICE INDICES FOR INDUSTRIAL PRODUCERS（PRECEDING YEAR=100）

类　别	Item	2000 年	2005 年	2010 年	2011 年
总指数	**General Index**	**106.81**	**106.52**	**112.21**	**109.39**
燃料、动力类	Fuel and Power	113.82	117.34	115.43	111.29
黑色金属材料类	Ferrous Metals	102.66	107.84	111.97	113.08
#钢材	Rolled-steel	105.44	106.57	108.67	107.95
其他	Others	101.1	112.88	122.64	129.01
有色金属材料及电线类	Nonferrous Metals and Electric Wire	106.75	108.06	122.65	108.45
化工原料类	Raw Chemical Materials	106.9	112.47	111.04	113.79
木材及纸浆类	Timber and Paper Pulp	108.98	103.8	117.06	103.78
建筑材料及非金属矿类	Building Materials and Nonmetals	99.5	115.54	107.61	116.71
其他工业原材料及半成品	Other Industrial Raw Materials and Semi-finished Goods	105.32	97.87	106.41	103.31
农副产品	Agricultural Products	92.73	101.55	121.30	115.04
纺织原料类	Textile Materials	104.03	98.15	112.90	111.11

注：根据国家有关规定 2020 年起不再编制工业生产者价格指数。
Note：According to relevant national regulations, the industrial producer price index will no longer be compiled from 2020.

2012年	2013年	2014年	2015年	2016年	2017年	2018年	2019年
97.00	**96.53**	**97.40**	**94.24**	**97.28**	**110.73**	**105.22**	**98.4**
100.64	95.18	97.65	88.51	89.94	112.91	112.55	95.3
93.20	93.76	95.81	87.26	97.23	117.41	104.02	100.0
92.33	92.87	96.87	89.99	96.89	119.10	108.75	99.1
94.64	96.57	92.49	78.70	98.41	110.30	86.82	103.4
93.64	96.23	96.24	92.34	96.29	114.82	103.94	97.7
96.72	96.47	99.51	96.44	101.00	107.63	101.55	94.2
93.12	98.79	102.42	98.33	99.93	125.23	111.21	89.3
102.48	100.13	97.36	95.52	100.91	115.06	115.97	107.8
98.05	96.65	96.25	96.95	97.50	106.42	102.41	100.5
98.21	98.54	97.62	99.75	101.53	105.92	99.70	103.6
95.61	99.60	97.38	95.86	99.81	110.09	105.80	97.1

9-6 按工业行业分工业生产者出厂价格指数
PRODUCER PRICE INDICES FOR INDUSTRIAL PRODUCERS BY SECTOR

（上年价格 = 100）

行业	Sector
工业生产者出厂价格指数	**Producer Price Indices for Manufactured Manufactured Goods**
黑色金属矿采选业	Mining of Ferrous Metal Ores
有色金属矿采选业	Mining of Non-ferrous Metal Ores
非金属矿采选业	Mining and Processing of Non–metal Ores
农副食品加工业	Processing of Food from Agricultural Products
食品制造业	Manufacture of Foods
酒、饮料和精制茶制造业	Manufacture of Liquor，Beverages and Refined Tea
纺织业	Manufacture of Textile
纺织服装、服饰业	Manufacture of Textile Wearing Apparel
皮革、毛皮、羽毛及其制品和制鞋业	Industry of Leather，Furs，Down and Related Products，and Shoes Making
木材加工和木、竹、藤、棕、草制品业	Processing of Timber, Manufacture of Wood, Bamboo, Rattan, Palm and Straw Products
家具制造业	Manufacture of Furniture
造纸和纸制品业	Manufacture of Paper and Paper Products
印刷和记录媒介复制业	Printing，Reproduction of Recording Media
文教、工美、体育和娱乐用品制造业	Industry of Culture and Education，Arts and Crafts，and Entertainment Products Manufacturing
石油、煤炭及其他燃料加工业	Oil, coal and other fuel processing industries
化学原料和化学制品制造业	Manufacture of Chemical Raw Material and Chemical Products
医药制造业	Manufacture of Medicines
化学纤维制造业	Manufacture of Chemical Fibres
橡胶和塑料制品业	Industry of Rubber and Plastic Products
非金属矿物制品业	Manufacture of metallic Mineral Products
黑色金属冶炼和压延加工业	Smelting and Pressing of Ferrous Metals
有色金属冶炼和压延加工业	Smelting and Pressing of Non-ferrous Metals
金属制品业	Manufacture of Metal Products
通用设备制造业	Manufacture of General Purpose Machinery
专用设备制造业	Manufacture of Special Purpose Machinery
汽车制造业	Vehicle Manufacturing Industry
铁路、船舶、航空航天和其他运输设备制造业	Maufacturing Industry of Railroads，Vessels，Aerospace and Other Transportation Equipment
电气机械和器材制造业	Manufacture of Electrical Machinery and Equipment
计算机、通信和其他电子设备制造业	Computer，Communications and Other Electronic Equipment Manufacturing
仪器仪表制造业	Instruments Manufacturing Industry
其他制造业	Other Manufacturing Industry
金属制品、机械和设备修理业	Industry of Metal Products, and Repair of Machinery and Equipment
电力、热力生产和供应业	Production and Supply of Electric Power and Heat Power
燃气生产和供应业	Production and Supply of Gas
水的生产和供应业	Production and Supply of Water

注：2019 年国民经济行业分类调整，本表中 2011—2019 年数据采用新国民经济行业分类 GB/T 4754-2017。
根据国家有关规定 2020 年起不再编制工业生产者价格指数。

Note：Classification of national economic industries was adjusted in 2019. The new national economic industries classification by GB/T 4754-2017 applies to data from 2011 to 2019 in this table.
According to relevant national regulations, the industrial producer price index will no longer be compiled from 2020.

(preceding year = 100)

2011年	2012年	2013年	2014年	2015年	2016年	2017年	2018年	2019年
104.90	**98.61**	**98.82**	**99.20**	**97.04**	**98.77**	**104.40**	**104.22**	**100.0**
104.33	99.93	100.00	99.86	100.00				
111.39	102.48	98.72	95.57	89.94				
145.13	89.33	87.06	102.14	94.85				
111.34	98.69	93.46	97.58	102.47	102.80	101.12	101.41	104.8
112.52	103.11	103.08	101.78	100.66	100.30	101.40	98.67	99.4
104.14	105.89	100.48	98.76	99.01	99.97	99.54	100.85	107.2
105.09	96.15	100.18	100.27	99.41	97.60	103.84	103.58	101.0
105.43	101.66	104.17	101.74	100.84	100.83	102.17	100.28	102.5
104.79	102.59	101.83	98.56	99.72	99.81	100.15	99.82	99.6
108.13	103.21	99.67	100.96	100.35				
101.11	102.00	100.02	100.00	99.91	98.46	98.72	100.48	99.3
105.71	95.59	96.13	101.96	99.78	99.58	115.83	104.86	96.7
110.06	107.10	108.65	96.97	95.96	98.45	101.11	102.77	97.5
100.61	101.47	100.47	100.00	99.96	99.88	101.90	100.54	101.2
114.95	104.26	99.49	97.38	76.03	91.60	114.48	121.44	97.8
114.60	89.61	98.04	99.70	96.53	95.20	119.17	113.72	94.2
107.33	95.05	105.08	127.56	100.73	104.83	101.06	100.95	102.6
123.72	92.56	95.65	96.69	90.31	89.56	117.03	98.53	96.4
114.68	99.67	95.40	95.50	94.93	97.60	100.62	100.10	99.4
108.19	98.39	99.82	100.91	101.62	99.08	114.14	120.19	100.1
111.00	86.47	93.52	94.45	83.44	99.13	117.16	108.23	99.7
108.26	89.14	93.87	94.43	87.95	95.29	125.17	102.35	98.0
99.79	99.82	104.14	96.62	96.59	103.64	106.15	105.34	99.4
101.39	100.07	103.87	101.02	100.37	98.78	103.45	104.80	103.4
101.69	101.26	99.99	99.81	99.72	98.36	100.00	101.23	101.0
99.27	98.97	98.59	102.49	101.04	101.46	100.93	99.83	100.9
99.17	99.66	97.65	100.96	100.03	99.29	100.16	99.79	97.3
103.10	98.40	98.82	99.24	98.61	98.96	102.82	102.36	99.8
84.65	95.43	94.31	98.88	96.31	90.16	102.17	100.06	97.7
102.01	98.72	98.01	98.43	97.05	100.00	100.09	100.15	100.2
95.16	98.52	99.94	100.12	99.89	100.87	104.20	105.84	108.8
102.17	98.43	88.75	91.69	90.21				
101.49	104.36	99.81	99.15	98.10	97.59	97.05	97.83	96.6
107.34	103.32	102.54	109.38	98.88	101.26	96.32	108.74	104.7
100.15	100.25	100.05	100.34	103.46	108.78	100.00	113.81	100.0

9-7 固定资产投资价格指数（以上年价格为 100）
PRICE INDICES FOR INVESTMENT IN FIXED ASSETS（PRECEDING YEAR=100）

项目名称	Item	2005	2009	2010	2011	2012	2013	2014	2015	2016	2017	2018
总计	**Total**	**103.1**	**94.6**	**104.9**	**107.0**	**100.0**	**100.1**	**99.9**	**97.1**	**99.8**	**107.3**	**106.6**
建筑安装、装饰工程	Construction and Installation Project	103.7	92.1	107.5	110.1	99.8	100.0	99.6	95.5	99.6	110.7	109.5
其中：人工费	Labor Cost	112.7	104.9	112.0	115.9	110.4	107.8	104.8	103.1	101.6	103.0	104.9
材料费	Materials Expenses	101.0	87.5	107.0	109.6	96.7	97.6	97.7	92	98.8	114.9	112.4
机械使用费	Expenses on Machinery Use	104.2	100.0	104.3	105.0	102.3	101.0	100.8	100.9	100.1	101.2	102.0
设备、工器具购置	Purchase of Equipment, Tools and Instruments	99.7	98.0	100.2	101.8	99.2	99.3	99.9	99.2	98.7	100.6	101.5
其他费用	Others	105.5	98.5	102.2	103.0	102.0	101.4	101.4	101.2	102.2	102.0	99.9

注：根据国家制度规定 2019 年起不编制固定资产投资价格指数。

Note：According to national regulations, starting from 2019, no fixed asset investment price index will be compiled.

9-8 住宅销售价格指数(2021 年)(上年同期 =100)
SALES PRICE INDICES FOR RESIDENCE（2021）（PRECEDING YEAR=100）

项 目	Item	2021
新建住宅销售价格指数	**Sales Price Indices for Newly Constructed Residence**	
一月	January	102.9
二月	February	103.4
三月	March	104.4
四月	April	104.6
五月	May	105.1
六月	June	105.1
七月	July	105.4
八月	August	105.4
九月	September	104.9
十月	October	105.0
十一月	November	104.7
十二月	December	104.4
二手住宅销售价格指数	**Sales Price Indices for Second-hand Residence**	
一月	January	97.9
二月	February	98.8
三月	March	99.7
四月	April	100.2
五月	May	100.7
六月	June	100.8
七月	July	101.3
八月	August	101.0
九月	September	101.2
十月	October	101.5
十一月	November	101.4
十二月	December	101.2

9-9 居民消费价格分类指数(2021 年)(上年 =100)
CONSUMER PRICE INDICES BY CATEGORY（2021）（PRECEDING YEAR=100）

项　　目	Item	指数 Indices
居民消费价格总指数	**Consumer Price Index**	**101.5**
非食品烟酒价格指数	Price index of non-food cigarettes and alcohol	101.8
服务价格指数	Price index of services	102.0
鲜活食品价格指数	Price index of fresh food	97.4
消费品价格指数	Consumer Goods Price Index	101.2
扣除鲜菜鲜果价格指数	Price Index Without Fresh Vegetables and Fresh Fruits	101.4
一、食品烟酒	**Food，cigarettes and liquor**	**100.8**
1. 食品	Food	99.7
（1）粮食	Grain	101.4
（2）薯类	Potatoes	96.7
（3）豆类	Beans	109.2
（4）食用油	Cooking Oil	108.4
（5）菜及食用菌	Vegetables and Edible Fungi	105.6
（6）畜肉类	Livestock Products	83.4
（7）禽肉类	Poultry Products	96.3
（8）水产品	Aquatic Products	107.9
（9）蛋类	Eggs	113.1
（10）奶类	Dairy Products	100.8
（11）干鲜瓜果类	Dried and Fresh Melons and Fruits	101.9
（12）糖果糕点类	Candy and Pastry	101.0
（13）调味品	Flavoring	104.3
（14）其他食品类	Other Foods	99.3
2. 茶及饮料	Tea and Beverages	101.9
3. 烟酒	Tobacco Liquor	100.6
4. 在外餐饮	Catering service	103.9

注：2021 年起，居民消费价格调查目录进行了调整，新调查目录与国际标准更为接近。

Note：Since 2021, the consumption price investigation directory has been adjusted, and the new investigation directory is basically consistent with the household consumption expenditure catalogue.

9-9 续表
Continued

项　目	Item	指数 Indices
二、衣着	**Clothing**	**100.6**
1. 服装	Garments	100.4
2. 鞋类	Shoes	101.5
三、居住	**Residence**	**101.1**
1. 租赁房房租	Rents	101.0
2. 住房保养维修及管理	Maintenance and management of house	103.6
3. 水电燃料	Water, Electricity and Fuels	100.4
4. 自有住房	Private Housing	100.8
四、生活用品及服务	**Article of daily use and service**	**98.9**
1. 家具及室内装饰品	Furniture and interior decoration	100.5
2. 家用器具	Home appliances	98.2
3. 家用纺织品	Home textile	101.6
4. 家庭日用杂品	Daily Use Household Articles	97.9
5. 个人护理用品	Personal-care supply	97.3
6. 家庭服务	Household Services	101.9
五、交通通信	**Transportation and Communication**	**106.1**
1. 交通	Transportation	107.6
2. 通信	Communication	101.7
六、教育文化娱乐	**Education, culture and entertainment**	**102.7**
1. 教育	Education	100.3
2. 文化娱乐	Culture and Entertainment	106.7
七、医疗保健	**Health Care**	**100.5**
1. 药品及医疗器具	Medicine and medical apparatus	100.0
2. 医疗服务	Medical service	100.8
八、其他用品及服务	**Other articles and services**	**98.2**
1. 其他用品	Other articles	98.3
2. 其他服务	Other services	98.0

9-10 商品零售价格分类指数（2021 年）（上年 =100）
RETAIL PRICE INDEXES BY CATEGORY（2021）（PRECEDING YEAR=100）

项 目	Item	指数 Indices
商品零售价格总指数	**Retail Price Indexes**	**101.4**
一、食品	**Food**	**100.7**
1. 粮食	Grain	101.4
2. 薯类	Potatoes	96.7
3. 豆类	Beans	109.2
4. 食用油	Edible oil	108.4
5. 菜及食用菌	Vegetables and Edible Fungi	105.6
6. 畜肉类	Stock meat	83.4
7. 禽肉类	Poultry meat	96.3
8. 水产品	Aquatic Products	107.9
9. 蛋类	Eggs	113.1
10. 奶类	Dairy	100.8
11. 干鲜瓜果类	Dried and Fresh Melon, and Fruits	101.9
12. 糖果糕点类	Sweets and cakes	101.0
13. 调味品	Flavoring	104.3
14. 其他食品类	Other food	99.3
15. 餐饮业零售	Catering Services and Retail Trades	103.9
二、饮料、烟酒	**Beverages, Tobacco and Liquor**	**100.9**
1. 茶及饮料	Tea and Beverages	101.9
2. 卷烟	Cigarettes	100.0
3. 酒类	Liquor	101.2
三、服装、鞋帽	**Clothing**	**100.6**
1. 服装	Garments	100.4
2. 鞋帽袜	Footgear and Hats	101.3
3. 其他衣着配件	Other clothing and accessories	101.3
四、纺织品	**Textiles**	**101.4**
1. 服装材料	Clothing material	98.7
2. 床上用品	Blend Cloth	101.9
五、家用电器及音像器材	**Household Appliances, Music and Video Equipment**	**99.2**
1. 家庭设备	Household Facilities	98.2
2. 文娱用耐用消费品	Durable Consumer Goods for Cultural and Recreational Use and Services	98.3
3. 专业音像器材	Professional Audio and Video Equipment	128.9

注：2021 年起，居民消费价格调查目录进行了调整，新调查目录与国际标准更为接近。
Note：Since 2021, the consumption price investigation directory has been adjusted, and the new investigation directory is basically consistent with the household consumption expenditure catalogue.

9-10 续表
Continued

项　目	Item	指数 Indices
六、文化办公用品	**Culture and office Articles**	**99.3**
七、日用品	**Articles for Daily Use**	**98.8**
1. 日用百货	General Merchandise for Daily Use	101.5
2. 厨具餐具茶具	Kitchen ware, tableware, tea set	92.1
3. 清洗用品	Cleaning Products	99.3
4. 其他日用品	Other Articles for Daily Use	99.0
八、体育娱乐用品	**Sports and Recreation Articles**	**101.4**
1. 体育户外用品	Sports and outdoors	98.1
2. 娱乐用品	Recreation Articles	101.7
九、交通、通信用品	**Transportation and Communication Appliances**	**100.0**
1. 交通运输机械	Transportation Machines	99.0
2. 通信器材	Communication Equipment	104.8
十、家具	**Furniture**	**99.9**
十一、化妆品	**Cosmetics**	**97.5**
十二、金银饰品	**Gold, Silver and Jewelry**	**97.4**
十三、中西药品及医疗保健用品	**Traditional Chinese and Western Medicals and Health Care Articles**	**100.0**
1. 医疗卫生器具	Medical apparatus	94.2
2. 中药	Herbal medicine	102.1
3. 西药	Western Medicines	99.6
4. 保健器具及用品	Health Care Articles	101.0
十四、书报杂志及电子出版物	**Books, Newspapers, Magazines and Electronic Publications**	**102.9**
1. 教材及参考书	Teaching Material and Reference Books	104.3
2. 书报杂志及音像制品	Books, Newspapers, Magazines and Audio-Video Products	100.0
3. 计算机办公软件	Computer office software	101.1
十五、燃料	**Fuels**	**116.3**
1. 煤炭及制品	Coal and Its Products	127.1
2. 石油及制品	Petroleum and Its Products	115.9
十六、建筑材料及五金电料	**Building Materials and Hardware**	**101.5**
1. 建筑装潢材料	Building Decoration Materials	102.2
2. 五金水暖	Hardware	99.5

主要统计指标解释

居民消费价格指数 是反映一定时期内城乡居民所购买的生活消费品价格和服务项目价格变动趋势和程度的相对数，是对城市居民消费价格指数和农村居民消费价格指数进行综合汇总计算的结果。该指数可以观察和分析消费品的零售价格和服务价格变动对城乡居民实际生活费支出的影响程度。

商品零售价格指数 是反映一定时期内城乡商品零售价格变动趋势和程度的相对数。商品零售价格的变动直接影响到城乡居民的生活支出和国家的财政收入，影响居民购买力和市场供需的平衡，影响到消费与积累的比例关系。因此，该指数可以从一个侧面对上述经济活动进行观察和分析。

工业生产者出厂价格指数 是反映一定时期内全部工业产品出厂价格总水平的变动趋势和程度的相对数，包括工业企业售给本企业以外所有单位的各种产品和直接售给居民用于生活消费的产品。该指数可以观察出厂价格变动对工业总产值及增加值的影响。

工业生产者购进价格指数 是反映工业企业作为生产投入，而从物资交易市场和能源、原材料生产企业购买原材料、燃料和动力产品时，所支付的价格水平变动趋势和程度的统计指标，是扣除工业企业物质消耗成本中的价格变动影响的重要依据。

房地产价格指数 是反映一定时期内房地产价格变动趋势和程度的相对数，包括新建住宅销售价格指数、二手住宅销售价格指数。

Explanatory Notes on Main Statistical Indicators

Consumer Price Indices reflect the trend and degree of changes in prices of consumer goods and services purchased by urban and rural households during a given period. They are obtained by combining the Urban Consumer Price Indices and the Rural Consumer Price Indices. The Indices enable the observation and analysis of the degree of impact of the changes in the prices of retailed goods and services on the actual living expenses of urban and rural residents.

Retail Price Indices reflect the trend and degree of change in retail prices of commodities during a given period. The change in retail prices of commodities directly affect the living expenditure of urban and rural residents, government revenue, purchasing power of residents and the equilibrium of market supply and demand, and the ratio of consumption to accumulation. Therefore, the retail price indices are useful to analyze the changes of the above economic activities.

Producer Price Indices for Industrial Producers reflect the trend and degree of changes in general ex-factory prices of all industrial products during a given period, including sales of industrial products by an industrial enterprise to all units outside the enterprise, as well as sales of consumer goods to residents. It can be used to analyze the impact of ex-factory prices on gross output value and value-added of the industrial sector.

Purchasing Price Indices for Industrial Producers reflect changes in the level and degree of prices paid by industrial enterprises when they purchase production input such as raw materials, fuels and power from the market or from other energy or raw materials producing enterprises. These indices provide important basis for measuring the material consumption of industrial enterprises after removing influence of price changes.

Price Indices for Real Estate reflect the trend and degree of changes in prices of real estate during a given period, including sales price indices for newly constructed residential buildings and secondhand residential buildings.

人民生活 10

PEOPLE'S LIVELI HOODS

简 要 说 明

一、本篇资料的主要内容

本篇资料主要反映了全市居民的家庭收支、居住、家庭消费构成、耐用消费品拥有量等方面的情况。

二、本篇资料的来源

本篇资料中相关数据来源于住户收支与生活状况调查年报，由国家统计局青岛调查队住户调查处整理提供。

Brief Introduction

Ⅰ. Main Content

This section mainly reflects the residents’ household income and expenditure, housing. household consumption structure, quantity of durable consumer goods possessed and other information.

Ⅱ. Source of Data

The relevant data in this article comes from the annual survey of household income and expenditure and living conditions, compiled and provided by the Household Survey Division of NBS Survey office in Qingdao.

10-1 城镇居民收支(1978—2014年)
INCOME AND EXPENDITURE OF URBAN RESIDENTS（1978—2014）

年 份 Year	城镇居民人均可支配收入（元） Annual Per Capita Disposable Income of Urban Households（yuan）	城镇居民人均消费支出（元） Per Capita Consumption Expenditure of Urban Households（yuan）	城镇居民恩格尔系数（%） Engel Coefficient of Urban Residents（%）
1978	336	321	
1979	380	360	
1980	537	495	53.5
1981	500	490	57.8
1982	528	484	61.5
1983	549	510	63.7
1984	665	580	62.8
1985	733	681	58.6
1986	882	806	59.2
1987	1089	996	58.1
1988	1225	1278	55.9
1989	1455	1439	57.8
1990	1624	1507	58.4
1991	1856	1767	57.4
1992	2138	1956	57.0
1993	2668	2445	51.8
1994	3880	3479	53.2
1995	5357	4606	52.5
1996	5602	5079	51.8
1997	6222	5525	48.2
1998	6542	5567	46.4
1999	7255	5985	44.3
2000	7971	6684	42.1
2001	8665	6858	41.5
2002	8641	7356	39.8
2003	9962	8072	38.4
2004	10944	9023	36.7
2005	12725	9909	35.9
2006	15066	11981	33.9
2007	17516	13421	33.7
2008	20034	15055	33.4
2009	21857	16145	33.7
2010	24380	17608	30.9
2011	27861	19382	31.1
2012	31349	20481	30.4
2013	34356	22157	30.8
2014	37346	24122	30.2

注：自2015年开始，全市城乡住户调查统一使用一体化改革后的数据，与原数据相比，城乡居民收支指标的调查范围和口径均存较大变化。原“城市居民人均可支配收入”调整为“城镇居民人均可支配收入”；原“农民人均纯收入”调整为“农村居民人均可支配收入”。

Note：Since 2015, the city's urban and rural household surveys have uniformly used the data after the integration reform. Compared with the original data, the survey scope and caliber of the income indicators of urban and rural residents have changed significantly. The"per capita disposable income of residents in cities was changed to" per capita disposable income of urban residents" , the "per capita net income of farmers" was changed to "per capita disposable income of rural residents..

10-2 农村居民收支(1978—2014 年)
INCOME AND EXPENDITURE OF RURAL RESIDENTS（1978—2014）

年 份 Year	农村居民人均可支配收入（元） Per Capita Disposable Income of Rural Residents（yuan）	农村居民人均消费支出（元） Per Capita Consumption Expenditure of Rural Households（yuan）	农村恩格尔系数（%） Engel Coefficient of Rural Residents（%）
1978	146	109	59.2
1979	153	129	58.3
1980	209	142	55.0
1981	218	163	44.2
1982	273	199	53.0
1983	399	277	52.8
1984	452	304	50.0
1985	567	376	47.8
1986	647	474	46.4
1987	730	462	42.9
1988	820	439	38.8
1989	876	510	38.9
1990	952	494	41.5
1991	1021	546	41.3
1992	1029	572	41.7
1993	1255	743	42.7
1994	1694	1384	54.5
1995	2225	1641	55.7
1996	2625	2173	50.5
1997	2599	2150	52.9
1998	3144	2112	49.5
1999	3349	2135	47.2
2000	3534	2354	42.9
2001	3756	2579	40.8
2002	4003	2768	38.3
2003	4283	2921	37.0
2004	4757	3266	37.6
2005	5384	3625	36.3
2006	6013	4061	35.2
2007	6801	4557	35.6
2008	7666	5083	35.9
2009	8255	5568	34.4
2010	9326	6335	32.8
2011	10934	7285	33.7
2012	12366	8228	33.3
2013	13905	9305	32.1
2014	15434	10277	31.0

注：自 2015 年开始，全市城乡住户调查统一使用一体化改革后的数据，与原数据相比，城乡居民收支指标的调查范围和口径均存较大变化。原“城市居民人均可支配收入”调整为“城镇居民人均可支配收入”；原“农民人均纯收入”调整为“农村居民人均可支配收入”。

Note：Since 2015, the city's urban and rural household surveys have uniformly used the data after the integration reform. Compared with the original data, the survey scope and caliber of the income indicators of urban and rural residents have changed significantly. The"per capita disposable income of residents in cities was changed to" per capita disposable income of urban residents" , the "per capita net income of farmers" was changed to "per capita disposable income of rural residents..

10-3 城乡居民住房面积（1990—2014 年）
HOUSING AREA OF URBAN AND RURAL RESIDENTS（1990—2014）

年 份 Year	城市居民人均现住房建筑面积（平方米） Per Capita Home Floor Area of Urban Residents（square meter）	农村居民人均居住面积（平方米） Per Capita Housing Area of Rural Residents（square meter）
1990	14.16	19.60
1995	17.12	23.03
2000	20.76	25.88
2001	21.86	26.59
2002	22.76	27.00
2003	23.73	27.00
2004	24.22	27.99
2005	22.96	29.54
2006	23.73	30.82
2007	23.72	30.95
2008	26.83	30.73
2009	26.71	31.39
2010	27.42	30.97
2011	27.67	31.73
2012	27.86	32.32
2013	29.12	33.50
2014	29.80	34.20

10-4 全体居民家庭基本情况（2015—2021 年）
BASIC INFORMATION ON ALL HOUSEHOLDS（2015—2021）

指标名称	Name	单位	Unit	2014 年	2015 年
人均可支配收入	**Per Capita Disposable Income**	**元**	**yuan**	**30273**	**32885**
（一）工资性收入	Income from Wages and Salaries	元	yuan	18348	20068
（二）经营净收入	Net Income from Household Operations	元	yuan	6035	6480
（三）财产净收入	Income from Properties	元	yuan	2396	2522
（四）转移净收入	Income from Transfers	元	yuan	3494	3815
人均消费支出	**Per Capita Consumption Expenditure**	**元**	**yuan**	**19653**	**21326**
（一）食品烟酒	Food，Tobacco and Liquor	元	yuan	5970	6459
（二）衣着	Clothing	元	yuan	1944	2096
（三）居住	Residence	元	yuan	4316	4584
（四）生活用品及服务	Household Facilities，Articles and Services	元	yuan	1374	1485
（五）交通通信	Transportation and Communication	元	yuan	2905	3226
（六）教育文化娱乐	Education，Cultural and Recreation Services	元	yuan	1654	1830
（七）医疗保健	Health Care and Medical Services	元	yuan	1002	1115
（八）其他用品和服务	Other Goods and Services	元	yuan	488	531
城镇居民人均现住房建筑面积	**Per Capita Building Space in Urban Areas**	**平方米**	**sq.m**	**–**	**31.5**
农村居民人均现住房建筑面积	**Per Capita Living Space in Rural Areas**	**平方米**	**sq.m**	**–**	**32.4**

注：自 2015 年开始，全市城乡住户调查统一使用一体化改革后的数据，与原数据相比，城乡居民收支指标的调查范围和口径均存较大变化。原“城市居民人均可支配收入”调整为“城镇居民人均可支配收入”；原“农民人均纯收入”调整为“农村居民人均可支配收入”。本表 2014 年数据为新口径，与 2015 年年鉴数据不一致。2014 年农村居民住房为拥有面积，2015 年后改为现住房建筑面积。

Note：Since 2015, the city's urban and rural household surveys have uniformly used the data after the integration reform. Compared with the original data, the survey scope and caliber of the income indicators of urban and rural residents have changed significantly. The"per capita disposable income of residents in cities was changed to" per capita disposable income of urban residents" , the "per capita net income of farmers" was changed to "per capita disposable income of rural residents. Data in 2014 were counted by new gauge and they are different from the data in last year' s yearbook. As for the statistics of rural resident homes, the owned house area was taken in 2014, but in 2015, the construction area was counted.

2016 年	2017 年	2018 年	2019 年	2020 年	2021 年
35680	**38763**	**42019**	**45452**	**47156**	**51223**
21700	23514	25303	27164	28082	30491
7011	7485	8027	8685	8816	9701
2781	3082	3475	3850	4008	4319
4188	4682	5214	5753	6250	6712
23256	**25232**	**27316**	**29501**	**30294**	**32878**
6983	7489	7787	8325	8520	9204
2271	2467	2538	2657	2706	2973
5018	5454	6365	6969	7173	7707
1607	1747	1837	1957	1998	2192
3479	3753	4084	4369	4477	4873
2075	2347	2571	2904	3012	3363
1233	1350	1480	1600	1679	1789
590	625	654	720	729	777
31.7	**32.7**	**32.9**	**31.9**	**33.4**	**32.1**
33.2	**34.8**	**35.9**	**37.0**	**38.0**	**37.4**

10-5 城镇居民家庭基本情况（2015—2021 年）
BASIC CONDITIONS OF URBAN HOUSEHOLDS（2015—2021）

指标名称	Name	单位	Unit	2014 年	2015 年
人均可支配收入	**Per Capita Disposable Income**	**元**	**yuan**	**37346**	**40370**
（一）工资性收入	Income from Wages and Salaries	元	yuan	23034	25040
（二）经营净收入	Net Income from Household Operations	元	yuan	5818	6277
（三）财产净收入	Income from Properties	元	yuan	3436	3580
（四）转移净收入	Income from Transfers	元	yuan	5058	5473
人均消费支出	**Per Capita Consumption Expenditure**	**元**	**yuan**	**24122**	**26052**
（一）食品烟酒	Food，Tobacco and Liquor	元	yuan	7295	7856
（二）衣着	Clothing	元	yuan	2497	2685
（三）居住	Residence	元	yuan	5302	5607
（四）生活用品及服务	Household Facilities，Articles and Services	元	yuan	1686	1819
（五）交通通信	Transportation and Communication	元	yuan	3455	3810
（六）教育文化娱乐	Education，Cultural and Recreation Services	元	yuan	2057	2264
（七）医疗保健	Health Care and Medical Services	元	yuan	1227	1352
（八）其他用品和服务	Other Goods and Services	元	yuan	603	659

注：本表数据为新口径，2014 年数据与 2015 年统计年鉴数据不一致。
Note：The data in this sheet is in line with new statistic caliber, which leads to the inconsistency between the data of 2014 and of 2015.

2016年	2017年	2018年	2019年	2020年	2021年
43598	**47176**	**50817**	**54484**	**55905**	**60239**
26898	28992	30955	32921	33641	36222
6846	7299	7836	8455	8479	9416
3909	4297	4789	5234	5365	5706
5945	6588	7237	7874	8420	8895
28285	**30569**	**32890**	**35266**	**35936**	**38574**
8473	9059	9318	9877	10025	10727
2882	3117	3168	3276	3306	3596
6105	6605	7751	8449	8626	9152
1962	2121	2207	2333	2365	2571
4089	4399	4765	5062	5154	5556
2553	2875	3122	3503	3608	3972
1490	1624	1764	1893	1977	2079
731	769	795	873	876	920

10-6 农村居民家庭基本情况（2015—2021 年）
BASIC CONDITIONS OF RURAL HOUSEHOLDS（2015—2021）

指标名称	Name	单位	Unit	2014 年	2015 年
人均可支配收入	**Per Capita Disposable Income**	**元**	**yuan**	**15434**	**16730**
（一）工资性收入	Income from Wages and Salaries	元	yuan	8517	9337
（二）经营净收入	Net Income from Household Operations	元	yuan	6489	6919
（三）财产净收入	Income from Properties	元	yuan	216	236
（四）转移净收入	Income from Transfers	元	yuan	212	238
人均消费支出	**Per Capita Consumption Expenditure**	**元**	**yuan**	**10277**	**11127**
（一）食品烟酒	Food，Tobacco and Liquor	元	yuan	3188	3442
（二）衣着	Clothing	元	yuan	784	826
（三）居住	Residence	元	yuan	2248	2377
（四）生活用品及服务	Household Facilities，Articles and Services	元	yuan	720	765
（五）交通通信	Transportation and Communication	元	yuan	1751	1965
（六）教育文化娱乐	Education，Cultural and Recreation Services	元	yuan	809	895
（七）医疗保健	Health Care and Medical Services	元	yuan	532	604
（八）其他用品和服务	Other Goods and Services	元	yuan	245	253

注：本表数据为新口径，2014 年数据与 2015 年统计年鉴数据不一致。
Note：The data in this sheet is in line with new statistic caliber，which leads to the inconsistency between the data of 2014 and of 2015's yearbook.

2016年	2017年	2018年	2019年	2020年	2021年
17969	**19364**	**20820**	**22573**	**23656**	**26125**
10074	10882	11684	12580	13151	14536
7381	7913	8487	9270	9720	10495
256	280	310	344	365	458
258	289	339	379	421	636
12006	**12928**	**13885**	**14899**	**15138**	**17021**
3651	3869	4098	4393	4476	4965
905	971	1020	1091	1096	1237
2586	2801	3024	3222	3269	3685
814	885	945	1004	1011	1138
2113	2262	2445	2611	2659	2972
1004	1129	1245	1389	1412	1668
658	717	794	856	880	980
275	294	314	333	336	377

10-7 全体居民家庭消费构成（2015—2021 年）
HOUSEHOLD CONSUMPTION STRUCTURE（2015—2021）

项　目	Item	2014 年		2015 年		2016 年	
		年人均支出金额（元）Per Capita Annual Expenditure（yuan）	占消费支出的比重（%）Percentage to Consumption Expenditure（%）	年人均支出金额（元）Per Capita Annual Expenditure（yuan）	占消费支出的比重（%）Percentage to Consumption Expenditure（%）	年人均支出金额（元）Per Capita Annual Expenditure（yuan）	占消费支出的比重（%）Percentage to Consumption Expenditure（%）
消费支出	**Consumption Expenditure**	**19653**	**100**	**21326**	**100**	**23256**	**100**
（一）食品烟酒	Food，Tobacco and Liquor	5970	30.4	6459	30.3	6983	30.0
（二）衣着	Clothing	1944	9.9	2096	9.8	2271	9.8
（三）居住	Residence	4316	21.9	4584	21.5	5018	21.6
（四）生活用品及服务	Household Facilities，Articles and Services	1374	7.0	1485	7.0	1607	6.9
（五）交通通信	Transportation and Communication	2905	14.8	3226	15.1	3479	15.0
（六）教育文化娱乐	Education，Cultural and Recreation Services	1654	8.4	1830	8.6	2075	8.9
（七）医疗保健	Health Care and Medical Services	1002	5.1	1115	5.2	1233	5.3
（八）其他用品和服务	Other Goods and Services	488	2.5	531	2.5	590	2.5

2017年		2018年		2019年		2020年		2021年	
年人均支出金额（元）Per Capita Annual Expenditure（yuan）	占消费支出的比重（%）Percentage to Consumption Expenditure（%）	年人均支出金额（元）Per Capita Annual Expenditure（yuan）	占消费支出的比重（%）Percentage to Consumption Expenditure（%）	年人均支出金额（元）Per Capita Annual Expenditure（yuan）	占消费支出的比重（%）Percentage to Consumption Expenditure（%）	年人均支出金额（元）Per Capita Annual Expenditure（yuan）	占消费支出的比重（%）Percentage to Consumption Expenditure（%）	年人均支出金额（元）Per Capita Annual Expenditure（yuan）	占消费支出的比重（%）Percentage to Consumption Expenditure（%）
25232	**100**	**27316**	**100**	**29501**	**100**	**30294**	**100**	**32878**	**100**
7489	29.7	7787	28.5	8325	28.2	8520	28.1	9204	28.0
2467	9.8	2538	9.3	2657	9.0	2706	8.9	2973	9.0
5454	21.6	6365	23.3	6969	23.6	7173	23.7	7707	23.5
1747	6.9	1837	6.7	1957	6.6	1998	6.6	2192	6.7
3753	14.9	4084	15.0	4369	14.8	4477	14.8	4873	14.8
2347	9.3	2571	9.4	2904	9.9	3012	10.0	3363	10.2
1350	5.4	1480	5.4	1600	5.4	1679	5.5	1789	5.4
625	2.4	654	2.4	720	2.5	729	2.4	777	2.4

10-8 城镇居民家庭消费构成（2015—2021 年）

COMPOSITION OF URBAN HOUSEHOLDS CONSUMPTION（2015—2021）

项 目	Item	2014 年		2015 年		2016 年	
		年人均支出金额（元）Per Capita Annual Expenditure（yuan）	占消费支出的比重（%）Percentage to Consumption Expenditure（%）	年人均支出金额（元）Per Capita Annual Expenditure（yuan）	占消费支出的比重（%）Percentage to Consumption Expenditure（%）	年人均支出金额（元）Per Capita Annual Expenditure（yuan）	占消费支出的比重（%）Percentage to Consumption Expenditure（%）
消费支出	**Consumption Expenditure**	**24122**	**100**	**26052**	**100**	**28285**	**100**
（一）食品烟酒	Food，Tobacco and Liquor	7295	30.2	7856	30.2	8473	30.0
（二）衣着	Clothing	2497	10.4	2685	10.3	2882	10.2
（三）居住	Residence	5302	22.0	5607	21.5	6105	21.6
（四）生活用品及服务	Household Facilities，Articles and Services	1686	7.0	1819	7.0	1962	6.9
（五）交通通信	Transportation and Communication	3455	14.3	3810	14.6	4089	14.4
（六）教育文化娱乐	Education，Cultural and Recreation Services	2057	8.5	2264	8.7	2553	9.0
（七）医疗保健	Health Care and Medical Services	1227	5.1	1352	5.2	1490	5.3
（八）其他用品和服务	Other Goods and Services	603	2.5	659	2.5	731	2.6

2017年		2018年		2019年		2020年		2021年	
年人均支出金额（元）Per Capita Annual Expenditure (yuan)	占消费支出的比重（%）Percentage to Consumption Expenditure (%)	年人均支出金额（元）Per Capita Annual Expenditure (yuan)	占消费支出的比重（%）Percentage to Consumption Expenditure (%)	年人均支出金额（元）Per Capita Annual Expenditure (yuan)	占消费支出的比重（%）Percentage to Consumption Expenditure (%)	年人均支出金额（元）Per Capita Annual Expenditure (yuan)	占消费支出的比重（%）Percentage to Consumption Expenditure (%)	年人均支出金额（元）Per Capita Annual Expenditure (yuan)	占消费支出的比重（%）Percentage to Consumption Expenditure (%)
30569	**100**	**32890**	**100**	**35266**	**100**	**35936**	**100**	**38574**	**100**
9059	29.6	9318	28.3	9877	28.0	10025	27.9	10727	27.8
3117	10.2	3168	9.6	3276	9.3	3306	9.2	3596	9.3
6605	21.6	7751	23.6	8449	24.0	8626	24.0	9152	23.7
2121	6.9	2207	6.7	2333	6.6	2365	6.6	2571	6.7
4399	14.4	4765	14.5	5062	14.3	5154	14.4	5556	14.4
2875	9.4	3122	9.5	3503	9.9	3608	10.0	3972	10.3
1624	5.3	1764	5.4	1893	5.4	1977	5.5	2079	5.4
769	2.6	795	2.4	873	2.5	876	2.4	920	2.4

10-9 农村居民家庭消费构成（2015—2021 年）
COMPOSITION OF RURAL HOUSEHOLDS CONSUMPTION（2015—2021）

项 目	Item	2014 年		2015 年		2016 年	
		年人均支出金额（元）Per Capita Annual Expenditure（yuan）	占消费支出的比重（%）Percentage to Consumption Expenditure（%）	年人均支出金额（元）Per Capita Annual Expenditure（yuan）	占消费支出的比重（%）Percentage to Consumption Expenditure（%）	年人均支出金额（元）Per Capita Annual Expenditure（yuan）	占消费支出的比重（%）Percentage to Consumption Expenditure（%）
消费支出	**Consumption Expenditure**	**10277**	**100**	**11127**	**100**	**12006**	**100**
（一）食品烟酒	Food，Tobacco and Liquor	3188	31.0	3442	30.9	3651	30.4
（二）衣着	Clothing	784	7.6	826	7.4	905	7.5
（三）居住	Residence	2248	21.9	2377	21.4	2586	21.5
（四）生活用品及服务	Household Facilities, Articles and Services	720	7.0	765	6.9	814	6.8
（五）交通通信	Transportation and Communication	1751	17.0	1965	17.7	2113	17.6
（六）教育文化娱乐	Education，Cultural and Recreation Services	809	7.9	895	8.0	1004	8.4
（七）医疗保健	Health Care and Medical Services	532	5.2	604	5.4	658	5.5
（八）其他用品和服务	Other Goods and Services	245	2.4	253	2.3	275	2.3

2017年		2018年		2019年		2020年		2021年	
年人均支出金额（元）Per Capita Annual Expenditure（yuan）	占消费支出的比重（%）Percentage to Consumption Expenditure（%）	年人均支出金额（元）Per Capita Annual Expenditure（yuan）	占消费支出的比重（%）Percentage to Consumption Expenditure（%）	年人均支出金额（元）Per Capita Annual Expenditure（yuan）	占消费支出的比重（%）Percentage to Consumption Expenditure（%）	年人均支出金额（元）Per Capita Annual Expenditure（yuan）	占消费支出的比重（%）Percentage to Consumption Expenditure（%）	年人均支出金额（元）Per Capita Annual Expenditure（yuan）	占消费支出的比重（%）Percentage to Consumption Expenditure（%）
12928	**100**	**13885**	**100**	**14899**	**100**	**15138**	**100**	**17021**	**100**
3869	29.9	4098	29.5	4393	29.5	4476	29.6	4965	29.2
971	7.5	1020	7.3	1091	7.3	1096	7.2	1237	7.3
2801	21.7	3024	21.8	3222	21.6	3269	21.6	3685	21.6
885	6.8	945	6.8	1004	6.8	1011	6.7	1138	6.7
2262	17.5	2445	17.6	2611	17.5	2659	17.6	2972	17.5
1129	8.7	1245	9.0	1389	9.3	1412	9.3	1668	9.8
717	5.5	794	5.7	856	5.8	880	5.8	980	5.7
294	2.4	314	2.3	333	2.2	336	2.2	377	2.2

10-10 城镇住户每百户家庭主要耐用品拥有量(1980—2021年)

OWNERSHIP OF MAJOR DURABLE CONSUMER GOODS PER 100 URBAN HOUSEHOLDS (1980—2021)

年份 Year	家用电脑(台) Computer (set)	钢琴(架) Piano (set)	空调器(台) Air Conditioner (set)	热水器(台) Water Heater (unit)	洗衣机(台) Washing Machine (set)	电冰箱(台) Household Refrigerator (set)	家用汽车(辆) Automobile (unit)	彩色电视机(台) Color TV (set)	移动电话(部) Cell Phone (unit)	照相机(架) Camera (set)
1980										2
1981					12			1		2
1982					22			2		4
1983					27	1		6		6
1984					30	2		8		8
1985					36	4		18		14
1986					40	5		25		15
1987					52	18		34		18
1988					61	33		47		21
1989					67	50		59		22
1990					66	62		68		26
1991					70	76		82		33
1992		1	0	13	73	83		81		39
1993		2	1	18	83	86		88		50
1994		4	1	17	81	89		92		51
1995		4	3	34	82	89		100		61
1996		5	7	40	83	92		105		63
1997	1	5	9	47	83	93		111	3	63
1998	8	5	17	53	83	92		111	7	69
1999	11	4	22	61	83	94		117	15	69
2000	19	2	25	66	83	94		120	30	70
2001	20	2	24	66	84	93		128	36	69
2002	32	2	38	75	89	93	1	123	80	73
2003	41	3	48	76	91	93	0	125	106	70
2004	46	3	55	79	93	93	2	124	128	68
2005	55	4	69	84	92	95	4	118	153	72
2006	71	8	89	88	97	99	6	125	187	82
2007	75	7	98	93	100	107	8	122	194	83
2008	75	5	94	90	95	103	13	116	191	67
2009	82	7	98	91	96	105	18	118	199	71
2010	86	8	99	91	97	107	20	119	208	71
2011	95	8	103	92	98	108	22	117	219	77
2012	101	9	104	93	98	108	29	115	231	79
2013	105	10	104	93	98	107	32	118	232	79
2014	105	10	104	98	99	105	34	109	235	79
2015	80	9	91	91	91	94	50	101	215	57
2016	86		98	93	90	96	58	100	212	63
2017	80		101	94	91	95	60	100	205	
2018	81		120	101	100	108	62	107	228	
2019	89		126	99	100	111	64	110	233	
2020	82		127	101	100	111	62	105	235	
2021	72		129	99	103	108	67	104	245	

10-11 农村住户每百户家庭主要耐用品拥有量(1985—2021年)

OWNERSHIP OF MAJOR DURABLE CONSUMER GOODS PER 100 RURAL HOUSEHOLDS（1985—2021）

年份 Year	家用电脑（台）Computer（set）	空调器（台）Air Conditioner（set）	热水器（台）Water Heater（unit）	自行车（辆）Bicycle（unit）	洗衣机（台）Washing Machine（set）	电冰箱（台）Household Refrigerator（set）	彩色电视机（台）Color TV（set）	移动电话（部）Cell Phone（unit）	照相机（架）Camera（set）	家用汽车（辆）Automobile（unit）
1985				147	0.3		3		1	
1986				165	1.1	0.3	4.5		1	
1987				148	2.4	0.5	7		2	
1988				154	2.4	1	9		2	
1989				170	3	1	12		2	
1990				164	4	2	13		2	
1991				173	5	4	16		2	
1992				178	5	7	20		2	
1993				203	7	14	26		2	
1994				204	9	21	35		7	
1995				203	16	28	43		6	
1996				198	13	33	46		8	
1997				191	15	36	56		13	
1998				184	17	39	63		15	
1999				185	20	42	74		10	
2000				165	28	47	86		13	
2001				153	28	53	92		13	
2002				152	36	58	98		16	
2003	6	5	33	137	39	60	100	45	16	2
2004	8	8	39	142	48	68	105	68	21	2
2005	14	14	53	138	57	77	109	91	21	5
2006	17	15	54	116	63	87	112	114	14	7
2007	19	19	63	118	70	94	113	132	17	8
2008	25	23	68	124	76	97	114	148	19	9
2009	28	25	71	127	79	99	115	160	21	11
2010	34	30	75	128	82	102	117	170	21	12
2011	44	32	76	114	85	100	112	202	18	15
2012	55	37	85	119	91	102	114	216	21	16
2013	61	45	88	111	93	105	116	221	26	23
2014	61	49	85		93	102	106	225	24	26
2015	46	54	86		92	105	110	219	21	41
2016	56	70	89		96	107	113	226	21	45
2017	52	78	90		98	106	110	223		48
2018	45	93	88		97	109	105	232		43
2019	42	98	96		98	108	104	227		40
2020	45	97	94		98	107	108	231		49
2021	49	101	95		92	109	101	244		55

主要统计指标解释

常住成员　指住户成员中，经常在家居住，或者调查期内居住时间超过一半的人员，以及本住户供养的学生。

可支配收入　指调查户在调查期内获得的、可用于最终消费支出和储蓄的总和，即调查户可以用来自由支配的收入。可支配收入既包括现金，也包括实物收入。按照收入的来源，可支配收入包含四项，分别为：工资性收入、经营净收入、财产净收入和转移净收入。计算公式为：

可支配收入 = 工资性收入 + 经营净收入 + 财产净收入 + 转移净收入

居民人均可支配收入是按居民家庭常住人口计算的平均每人可支配收入

消费支出　指住户用于满足家庭日常生活消费需要的全部支出。根据用途不同，消费支出可划分为食品烟酒、衣着、居住、生活用品及服务、交通通信、教育文化娱乐、医疗保健、其他用品及服务八大类。根据来源不同，消费支出可划分为现金消费支出、实物消费支出（含自产自用、来自单位、来自政府和其他社会组织）。

Explanatory Notes on Main Statistical Indicators

Permanent resident　refers to residents that live usually in home or more than half of the survey period and students that are supported by them.

Disposable income　refers to sum of all income earned within the survey period that can be used for deposit and expense on final consumption, which means the income that can be disposed freely by residents. The disposable income includes not only cash, but also income in kinds, which shall be categorized into four kinds according to source of incomes: salary income, net operating income, net property income, net transfer income. Computing formula is as follows:

Disposable income = salary income + net operating income + net property income + net transfer income

Disposable income per capita of residents is the average disposable income per person calculated based on the number of permanent residents of the family.

Consumer spending　refers to all spending of residents to cover daily life consumption demands. According to different usages, the consumer spending shall be classified into eight categories: food, cigarettes and alcohol, clothing, housing, daily use articles and services, transportation & communication, education, culture & entertainment, medical and health care, other articles and services. According to sources, the consumer spending shall be classified as cash consumer spending, consumer spending in kinds (including self-produced, from the unit, from government and other social organization).

农　业　11

AGRICULTURE

简要说明

一、本篇资料的主要内容

本篇资料主要反映了全市农业生产和农村经济的基本情况，主要包括农林牧渔业总产值、中间消耗、增加值、农村劳动力、耕地、主要农产品产量、农业机械年末拥有量、业机械化和电气化以及农田水利建设等方面的资料。

二、本篇资料的来源

1. 本篇资料中耕地面积资料来源于市自然资源和规划局。

2. 水产品产量等相关资料来源于市海洋发展局。

3. 农业机械化等相关资料来源于市农业农村局。

4. 农田水利灌溉等相关资料来源于市水务管理局。

5. 植树造林等相关资料来源于市园林和林业局。

三、说明

本篇按照国家统计局规定，根据2016年第三次全国农业普查结果对2007年至2017年历史数据进行了核定和修正。

本篇资料由市统计局农村统计处、市统计局国民经济核算处、国家统计局青岛调查队农业农村调查处整理提供。

Brief Introduction

Ⅰ. Main Content

Data in this chapter show the basic conditions of agricultural production and rural economy, mainly including agricultural output, intermediate consumption, value added, rural labor force, cultivated land, output of main agricultural produces, agricultural machinery and electrification in rural areas and basic construction on irrigation and drainage.

Ⅱ. Source of Data

1. Data on area of cultivated land are provided by Qingdao Natural Resources and Planning Bureau.

2. Data on output of aquatic products are provided by Qingdao Marine Development Bureau.

3. Data on Agricultural machinery are provided by Qingdao Rural Agriculture Bureau.

4. Data on farmland water conservancy are provided by Qingdao Water Administration Bureau.

5. Data on forest planting are provided by Qingdao Landscape and Forestry Bureau.

Ⅲ. Explain

This chapter is in accordance with the provisions of the State Statistical Bureau. According to the results of the third national agricultural census in 2016, the historical data from 2007 to 2017 were verified and revised.

The information in this article was compiled and provided by the Rural Statistics Division of the Qingdao Municipal Bureau of Statistics, the National Economic Accounting Division of the Qingdao Municipal Bureau of Statistics, and the Agricultural and Rural Investigation Division of NBS Survey Office in Qingdao.

11-1　农村基本情况（2000-2021 年）
BASIC STATISTICS ON RURAL AREA（2000-2021）

项目	Item	单位	Unit	2000 年	2005 年	2010 年	2011 年	2012 年	2013 年
一、年末实有耕地面积	**Year-end Area of Cultivated Land**	**万公顷**	**10 000 hectares**	**48**	**42**			**53**	**53**
二、农用机械总动力	**Total Agricultural Machinery Power**	**万千瓦**	**10 000 kW**	**459**	**620**	**764**	**784**	**798**	**809**
拖拉机	Tractors	台	unit	126981	163032	200208	202022	206290	206300
三、农村用电量	**Electricity Consumed in Rural Areas**	**万千瓦时**	**10 000 kW · h**	**189651**	**372645**	**426819**	**431646**	**426815**	**359139**
四、农用化肥施用量（折纯）	**Consumption of Chemical Fertilizer（convert to pure amount）**	**万吨**	**10 000 tons**	**33**	**33**	**30**	**29**	**29**	**29**
五、有效灌溉面积	**Pesticide Usage**	**吨**	**ton**						
六、耕地机电灌溉面积	**Cultivated Land Electromechanical Irrigation Area**	**万公顷**	**10 000 hectares**	**30**	**30**	**33**	**33**	**33**	**30**

11-1 续表
Continued

项目	Item	单位	Unit	2014年	2015年	2016年	2017年	2018年	2019年	2020年	2021年
一、年末实有耕地面积	**Year-end Area of Cultivated Land**	万公顷	**10 000 hectares**	**52**	**52**	**52**	**52**	**52**	**52**	**52**	**43**
二、农用机械总动力	**Total Agricultural Machinery Power**	万千瓦	**10 000 kW**	**827**	**854**	**698**	**728**	**738**	**751**	**754.8**	**757.3**
拖拉机	Tractors	台	unit	205065	207809	211689	214799	215668	216496	214845	210358
三、农村用电量	**Electricity Consumed in Rural Areas**	万千瓦时	**10 000 kW · h**	**404380**	**401122**	**385434**	**382437**	**377858**	**388484**	**359584**	**328106**
四、农用化肥施用量（折纯）	**Consumption of Chemical Fertilizer (convert to pure amount)**	万吨	**10 000 tons**	**29**	**28**	**28**	**28**	**27**	**27**	**26**	**25**
五、农药使用量	**Pesticide Usage**	吨	**ton**						**5401**	**5273**	**5107**
六、耕地机电灌溉面积	**Cultivated Land Electromechanical Irrigation Area**	万公顷	**10 000 hectares**	**32**	**32**	**33**	**33**	**33**	**33**	**36**	**33**

注：1. 农机机械总动力 2016 年为新统计口径，扣除农用运输汽车数据。
2. 2020 年起有效灌溉面积改为耕地机电灌溉面积，数据由农业农村局提供。
3. 耕地面积由市自然资源和规划局错年提供，2021 年使用 2020 年国土资源普查数据。

Notes：1. Data of total power of agricultural machinery of 2016 is based on the new statistic caliber, deducted by the data of agricultural vehicle.
2. Starting from 2020, the effective irrigation area will be changed to the electromechanical irrigation area of arable land. The data is provided by the Agriculture and Rural Bureau.
3. The area of arable land is provided by the Municipal Bureau of Natural Resources and Planning each year from the previous year's data. And the data of land and resources census of 2020 was used in 2021.

11-2 分区市农药、化肥使用量
AMOUNT OF PESTICIDES AND FERTILIZERS USED IN DISTRICT CITIES

单位：吨（ton）

市、区名称	Region	农药使用量 Pesticide Usage		化肥施用量（折纯） Fertilizer Application Amount (Converted Pure)	
		2021 年	2020 年	2021 年	2020 年
全市	**Whole Municipality**	**5106**	**5273**	**248970**	**262755**
崂山区	Laoshan District	16	19	324	357
黄岛区（西海岸新区）	Huangdao District (West Coast New Area)	474	492	23057	32630
城阳区	Chengyang District	15	16	469	585
城阳区（不含高新区）	Chengyang District (Excluding High tech District)	15	16	469	585
高新区	High tech District				
即墨区	Jimo District	546	591	31559	31980
胶州市	Jiaozhou	1001	1042	32879	33816
平度市	Pingdu	1643	1670	109617	110977
莱西市	Laixi	1411	1440	51065	52408

11-3 主要年份农、林、牧、渔业总产值（按现价计算）
MAJOR YEAR'S GROSS OUTPUT VALUE OF FARMING, FORESTRY, ANINAL HUSBANDRY AND FISHERY (CURRENT PRICE)

单位：万元（10 000 yuan）

年份 Year	农、林、牧、渔业总产值 Gross Output Value of Farming, Forestry, Animal Husbandry and Fishery	农业产值 Farming	林业产值 Forestry	畜牧业产值 Animal Husbandry	渔业产值 Fishery
1949	16511	14755	325	1200	231
1952	24428	21353	479	1888	708
1957	26189	22717	644	2218	610
1962	15356	13257	230	1243	626
1965	25123	21488	854	2110	671
1970	44078	36889	1851	3817	1521
1975	93213	79208	2144	7923	3938
1978	121497	94397	3112	17293	6695
1980	149436	117547	2953	22215	6721
1985	299139	215729	8986	53894	20530
1987	378981	263066	5949	73271	36695
1989	463952	303679	19134	91885	49254
1990	579877	381287	13801	119208	65581
1991	664779	417111	12875	144909	89884
1992	703433	400471	15252	150942	136768
1993	989763	509601	20845	232143	227174
1994	1424074	763366	23101	356734	280873
1995	1923771	1021413	26765	503999	371594
1996	2317434	1145399	29100	692362	450573
1997	2047712	939922	24052	578443	505295
1998	2386303	1198043	16760	633735	537765
1999	2382320	1169596	17122	618020	577582
2000	2483256	1116397	19102	692782	654975
2001	2615228	1135816	20433	758313	700666
2002	2688532	1110671	23157	796007	758697
2003	2759692	1062576	36183	859915	801018
2004	2967389	1181009	32831	937494	816055
2005	3205057	1265695	25246	1070831	843285
2006	3396096	1360755	23546	1076254	855131
2007	3665342	1460800	20801	1143644	916648
2008	3995027	1723855	24356	1195857	907793
2009	4070777	1771982	22133	1133732	980995
2010	4802184	2197935	19090	1225222	1181911
2011	5345885	2188072	19049	1500469	1426786
2012	5672486	2270097	20221	1510234	1633469
2013	6105875	2547805	21875	1553621	1711549
2014	6279086	2644851	22266	1559709	1739234
2015	6123485	2469656	21789	1529587	1814625
2016	6690910	2844023	27741	1621935	1777293
2017	6978980	3003367	30891	1663278	1830324
2018	7369968	3290651	36575	1631422	1920519
2019	7781197	3600911	43066	1671765	1936932
2020	8071003	3732576	44453	1800325	1933437
2021	8970590	4228955	41462	1836006	2247619

注：2007—2017 年数据为根据第三次农业普查结果核定修正后数据。
Note: The 2007—2017 data are the approved revised data based on the results of the third agricultural census.

11-4 分市、区农、林、牧、渔业总产值(2021年，现价)
GROSS OUTPUT VALUE OF FARMING，FORESTRY，ANIMAL HUSBANDRY AND FISHERY BY REGION（2021，CURRENT PRICE）

单位：万元（10 000 yuan）

市、区名称	Region	农、林、牧、渔业总产值 Gross Output Value of Farming, Forestry, Animal Husbandry and Fishery	农业 Farming	林业 Forestry	畜牧业 Animal Husbandry	渔业 Fishery	服务业 Services
全市	**Whole Municipality**	**8970590**	**4228955**	**41462**	**1836006**	**2247619**	**616548**
崂山区	Laoshan District	139180	30568	102		83941	24569
黄岛区（西海岸新区）	Huangdao District (West Coast New Area)	1746628	539638	7583	221625	868857	108925
城阳区	Chengyang District	359129	43152	1701	21550	286184	6543
城阳区（不含高新区）	Chengyang District (Excluding High tech District)	359129	43152	1701	21550	286184	6543
高新区	High tech District						
即墨区	Jimo District	1652356	513849	3646	291199	695640	148022
胶州市	Jiaozhou	1249206	603283	8367	215448	302822	119287
平度市	Pingdu	2305034	1673131	15662	507039	2439	106763
莱西市	Laixi	1519056	825335	4401	579145	7737	102439

11-5 分市、区农、林、牧、渔业增加值(2021年，现价)

VALUE-ADDED OF FARMING, FORESTRY, ANIMAL HUSBANDRY AND FISHERY BY REGION (2021, CURRENT PRICE)

单位：亿元（100 million yuan）

市、区名称	Region	农、林、牧、渔业增加值 Added Value Of Farming, Forestry, Animal Husbandry and Fishery	农、林、牧、渔专业及辅助性活动 Agriculture, Forestry, Animal Husbandry, Fishery and Supporting Activities
全市	**Whole Municipality**	**500.50**	**30.44**
崂山区	Laoshan District	8.12	1.20
黄岛区（西海岸新区）	Huangdao District (West Coast New Area)	97.38	5.23
城阳区	Chengyang District	20.46	0.31
城阳区（不含高新区）	Chengyang District (Excluding High tech District)		
高新区	High tech District		
即墨区	Jimo District	92.41	7.34
胶州市	Jiaozhou	69.82	5.88
平度市	Pingdu	129.61	5.44
莱西市	Laixi	79.30	4.92

11-6 主要年份耕地面积与播种面积
MAJOR YEAR'S CULTIVATED AND SOWN AREA

单位：万公顷（10 000 hectares）

年份 Year	年末实有耕地面积 Year-end Area of Cultivated Land	农作物播种面积 Sown Area of Farm Crops	#粮食作物 Grain Crops	#经济作物 Economic Crops
1949		93.47	84.00	7.20
1952		97.53	85.07	10.80
1957		97.87	87.07	10.53
1962		81.47	72.53	5.80
1965		82.80	71.80	8.33
1970		80.73	68.27	10.07
1975		79.82	65.84	11.01
1978		77.60	63.60	10.40
1980		75.87	60.33	12.00
1985		78.27	57.33	15.73
1987		76.67	55.87	15.93
1989		74.78	54.28	16.06
1990		76.85	56.99	15.53
1991		76.98	56.89	15.69
1992		76.96	56.37	15.64
1993	56.90	77.75	56.22	15.71
1994		76.61	54.08	16.20
1995		76.54	53.71	15.65
1996	55.01	77.26	54.81	14.90
1997		75.04	52.32	14.40
1998		77.18	53.05	14.54
1999		77.56	50.61	13.24
2000		76.47	45.07	13.98
2001		73.69	41.91	14.54
2002		72.32	40.83	13.95

11-6 续表
Continued

年份 Year	年末实有耕地面积 Year-end Area of Cultivated Land	农作物播种面积 Sown Area of Farm Crops	#粮食作物 Grain Crops	#经济作物 Economic Crops
2003		67.82	36.05	14.50
2004		71.33	41.40	14.11
2005	42.10	75.02	49.93	11.89
2006	41.29	74.86	49.79	11.75
2007	41.31	64.13	39.16	24.98
2008	41.79	65.29	42.56	22.73
2009	41.87	63.72	42.01	21.72
2010		64.10	42.65	21.45
2011		64.53	43.84	20.70
2012	52.81	64.36	43.95	20.40
2013	52.55	66.16	45.69	20.48
2014	52.42	66.70	46.75	19.95
2015	52.22	67.10	47.93	19.17
2016	52	68.19	48.49	19.70
2017	51.86	67.32	47.79	19.54
2018	51.86	68.37	48.11	20.26
2019	51.62	66.73	47.50	19.23
2020	51.62	66.40	46.95	19.45
2021	43.21	66.80	48.01	18.79

注：1. 2009 年前本表数据由市统计局提供。
2. 2010 年起，粮食作物面积由青岛调查队提供，经济作物面积由市统计局提供。
3. 2007—2017 年农作物播种面积为根据第三次农业普查结果核定修正后数据。
4. 耕地面积由市自然资源和规划局错年提供，2021 年使用 2020 年国土资源普查数据。

Notes：1. Those of before 2009 were provided by the National Bureau of Statistics.
2. Since 2010, the area of grain crops has been provided by NBS survey office in Qingdao , and the area of cash crops has been provided by the Municipal Statistics Bureau.
3. Sown Area of Farm Crops from 2007 to 2017 is revised according to the results of the third agricultural census.
4. The area of arable land is provided by the Municipal Bureau of Natural Resources and Planning each year from the previous year's data. And the data of land and resources census of 2020 was used in 2021.

11-7　分市、区耕地面积（2021 年）
AREA OF CULTIVATED LAND BY REGION（2021）

单位：公顷（hectare）

市、区名称	Region	年末耕地面积 Year-end Area of Cultivated Land	#旱田 Dry Farmland
全市	**Whole Municipality**	**432093**	**201328**
崂山区	Laoshan District	587	567
黄岛区（西海岸新区）	Huangdao District（West Coast New Area）	53158	46774
城阳区	Chengyang District	3626	2422
城阳区（不含高新区）	Chengyang District（Excluding High tech District）	3626	2422
高新区	High tech District		
即墨区	Jimo District	76083	59600
胶州市	Jiaozhou	47386	17571
平度市	Pingdu	172348	9195
莱西市	Laixi	80226	65130

注：耕地面积由市自然资源和规划局错年提供，2021 年使用 2020 年国土资源普查数据。
Note：The area of arable land is provided by the Municipal Bureau of Natural Resources and Planning each year from the previous year's data. And the data of land and resources census of 2020 was used in 2021.

11-8 分市、区农作物播种面积（2021 年）
SOWN AREA OF FARM CROPS BY REGION（2021）

单位：万公顷（10 000 hectares）

市、区名称	Region	总播种面积 Total Sown Area	#粮食 Grain	#棉花 Cotton	#花生 Peanut	#烟叶 Tobacco	#蔬菜 Vegetable
全市	**Whole Municipality**	**66.80**	**48.01**	**0.01**	**6.94**	**0.04**	**10.90**
崂山区	Laoshan District	0.04			0.00		0.03
黄岛区（西海岸新区）	Huangdao District（West Coast New Area）	7.55	4.83		1.79	0.03	0.84
城阳区	Chengyang District	0.18	0.09		0.00		0.08
城阳区（不含高新区）	Chengyang District（Excluding High tech District）	0.18	0.09		0.00		0.08
高新区	High tech District						
即墨区	Jimo District	10.03	7.81		1.01		1.10
胶州市	Jiaozhou	9.04	6.34	0.00	0.59	0.00	2.08
平度市	Pingdu	27.33	20.17	0.01	1.99	0.00	4.80
莱西市	Laixi	12.63	8.77		1.55		1.97

11-9 分市、区部分农作物产量（2021 年）
OUTPUT OF FARM CROPS BY REGION（2021）

单位：吨（ton）

市、区名称	Region	粮食 Grain	棉花 Cotton	花生 Peanut	烟叶 Tobacco	蔬菜 Vegetable
全市	**Whole Municipality**	**3127743**	**79**	**339448**	**853**	**6617749**
崂山区	Laoshan District			171		8976
黄岛区（西海岸新区）	Huangdao District（West Coast New Area）	261570		88535	755	587959
城阳区	Chengyang District	5726		167		29045
城阳区（不含高新区）	Chengyang District（Excluding High tech District）	5726		167		29045
高新区	High tech District					
即墨区	Jimo District	445217		42909		657390
胶州市	Jiaozhou	389003	1	25272	46	1105858
平度市	Pingdu	1460114	78	100494	52	2958686
莱西市	Laixi	566113		81901		1269835

11-10　分市、区部分农作物单位面积产量（2021年）
OUTPUT OF FARM CROPS PER HECTARE BY REGION (2021)

单位：千克/公顷（kg/hectares）

市、区名称	Region	粮食 Grain	棉花 Cotton	花生 Peanut	烟叶 Tobacco	蔬菜 Vegetable
全市	**Whole Municipality**	**6515**	**1389**	**4893**	**2402**	**60692**
崂山区	Laoshan District			3795		27249
黄岛区（西海岸新区）	Huangdao District（West Coast New Area）	5417		4937	2447	69891
城阳区	Chengyang District	6324		4656		35274
城阳区（不含高新区）	Chengyang District（Excluding High tech District）	6324		4656		35274
高新区	High tech District					
即墨区	Jimo District	5700		4265		59895
胶州市	Jiaozhou	6137	1335	4274	2880	53286
平度市	Pingdu	7238	1389	5045	1700	61587
莱西市	Laixi	6458		5297		64446

11-11 主要年份农作物总产量
MAJOR YEAR'S OUPTUT OF FARM CROPS

单位：吨（ton）

年份 Year	粮食 Grain	#小麦 Wheat	#玉米 Corn	棉花 Cotton	花生 Peanut	水果 Fruit	蔬菜 Vegetable
1949	723190	158815	25810	1280	71080	9955	356015
1952	967640	200380	58130	6025	115585	13468	284050
1957	921920	210690	141540	3520	90445	18869	625220
1962	628930	104340	53010	1280	35470	8366	524455
1965	917635	180610	135595	6090	88390	16034	465850
1970	1175985	243945	244530	16490	96280	33907	541145
1975	1899540	430135	420095	15390	98495	59206	693970
1978	1900850	514570	510635	8720	114370	82819	921140
1980	2164415	520045	819930	19630	160670	80840	996565
1985	2331060	961055	739455	19335	475270	200515	1253075
1987	2626029	996165	1030926	13819	394296	249655	1489250
1989	2654334	993406	1084441	14638	391782	288757	1664238
1990	2998246	1265157	1210687	17490	413636	292366	1786041
1991	3180893	1421143	1285043	25965	446880	294349	1837265
1992	2675641	1235755	981490	8160	321145	341415	2030327
1993	3164812	1463759	1248780	15344	419109	383368	2705349
1994	3106562	1392977	1252952	8326	494827	423024	3002318
1995	3291587	1480385	1365167	8177	510662	478685	3221507
1996	3390033	1513479	1466668	4001	486574	505711	3405056
1997	2523064	1584478	743199	2000	308233	438398	3333181
1998	3469821	1627261	1484182	4159	546786	529592	4036992
1999	3331124	1501182	1499775	3668	572941	606800	5459140
2000	2780481	1353445	1169649	2077	534174	651591	6649322
2001	2539257	1143679	1178851	3409	579441	675244	6250361
2002	2383802	1085936	1094731	3755	557714	579703	6847570
2003	2221697	931787	1117704	5324	568798	677361	7305618
2004	2650952	1301791	1202063	7216	580290	748516	6720886
2005	3150203	1535471	1478616	4042	503941	737300	5792110
2006	3039266	1548928	1372166	3954	471853	827755	6051239
2007	2319354	1118044	1106106	3546	495458	1366106	6180515
2008	2602592	1234264	1279002	3163	470424	1276385	6164760
2009	2590287	1276029	1228485	3213	467937	1294706	5743437
2010	2553744	1206593	1272970	2411	439872	1267226	5895190
2011	2678626	1213908	1386365	2375	441237	1262896	5948249
2012	2707295	1242299	1396704	2334	456372	1201836	5826702
2013	2791826	1295227	1432355	2057	440426	1217969	5906625
2014	2780244	1302282	1418469	1392	394461	1188690	6134061
2015	2878062	1332125	1497121	1279	342034	1189312	5988945
2016	2940668	1345273	1551200	408	365207	1207498	5915380
2017	2968896	1264073	1670338	420	383668	1187041	6277779
2018	3100964	1376646	1690817	977	384918	1092176	6443615
2019	3026054	1426280	1544645	434	342424	1185951	6261517
2020	3045755	1334205	1635225	136	360029	1164739	6558479
2021	3127743	1429566	1631325	79	339448	1198348	6617749

注：2007— 2017 年数据为根据第三次农业普查结果核定修正后数据。
Note：Agricultural data from 2007 to 2017 are revised according to the results of the third agricultural census.

11-11 续表 1 分市、区部分蔬菜产量（2021 年）
Continued OUTPUT OF SOME VEGETABLES BY CITY AND DISTRICT (2021)

单位：吨（ton）

市、区名称	Region	蔬菜 Vegetable	#大白菜 Cabbage	#芹菜 Celery	#胡萝卜 Carrot	#马铃薯 Potato
全市	**Whole Municipality**	**6617749**	**1314766**	**149862**	**726426**	**1186353**
崂山区	Laoshan District	8976	3397	31	16	2517
黄岛区（西海岸新区）	Huangdao District (West Coast New Area)	587959	272866	23837	1004	109369
城阳区	Chengyang District	29045	3642	847	657	1886
城阳区（不含高新区）	Chengyang District (Excluding High tech District)	29045	3642	847	657	1886
高新区	High tech District					
即墨区	Jimo District	657390	140100	12011	66898	104189
胶州市	Jiaozhou	1105858	275544	57861	5867	411468
平度市	Pingdu	2958686	458409	24960	416978	496746
莱西市	Laixi	1269835	160807	30316	235006	60178

11-11 续表 2 分市、区部分蔬菜产量（2021 年）
Continued OUTPUT OF SOME VEGETABLES BY CITY AND DISTRICT (2021)

单位：吨（ton）

市、区名称	Region	#黄瓜 Cucumber	#西红柿 Tomato	#大葱 Green onion	#蒜头 Garlic	#食用菌 Edible fungi
全市	**Whole Municipality**	**392968**	**484604**	**763351**	**90008**	**38803**
崂山区	Laoshan District	469	153	173	12	9
黄岛区（西海岸新区）	Huangdao District (West Coast New Area)	14648	64977	4486	952	6840
城阳区	Chengyang District	5951	5529	347	7	592
城阳区（不含高新区）	Chengyang District (Excluding High tech District)	5951	5529	347	7	592
高新区	High tech District					
即墨区	Jimo District	46809	25740	80898	1127	17857
胶州市	Jiaozhou	23525	19614	55454	791	1557
平度市	Pingdu	44070	130483	609396	77488	8057
莱西市	Laixi	257498	238108	12596	9631	3891

11-12 分市、区猪、羊及家禽存养量（2021年）
HOGS, SHEEP, GOATS AND POULTRY IN STOCK BY REGION (2021)

单位：万头、万只（10 000 head）

市、区名称	Region	年末生猪存养量 Hogs in Stock (year-end)	#母猪 Sow	牛 Cattle and Buffaloes	#奶牛 Cows	年末羊存养量 Sheep and Goats in Stock (year-end)	年末家禽存栏 Poultry stock at the end of the year	#蛋禽 Poultry
全市	**Whole Municipality**	**177.90**	**16.32**	**15.37**	**9.93**	**19.99**	**4551.93**	**1302.96**
崂山区	Laoshan District							
黄岛区（西海岸新区）	Huangdao District (West Coast New Area)	24.41	2.08	0.95	0.02	2.79	408.45	114.45
城阳区	Chengyang District	0.83	0.10	0.13	0.13	0.10	19.98	17.58
城阳区（不含高新区）	Chengyang District (Excluding High tech District)							
高新区	High tech District							
即墨区	Jimo District	31.34	1.84	2.62	1.79	1.79	1193.18	483.80
胶州市	Jiaozhou	25.85	2.74	0.86	0.15	3.28	362.51	191.37
平度市	Pingdu	48.18	4.05	1.15	0.37	8.83	1263.58	238.57
莱西市	Laixi	47.28	5.52	9.66	7.47	3.21	1304.23	257.18

11-13 分市、区肉、蛋、奶产量（2021年）
OUTPUT OF MEAT, EGGS AND MILK BY REGION (2021)

单位：万吨（10 000 tons）

市、区名称	Region	肉类产量 Output of Meat	#猪肉 Port	#禽肉 Poultry Meat	禽蛋 Poultry Egg	牛奶 Milk
全市	**Whole Municipality**	**50.40**	**21.32**	**27.08**	**28.87**	**33.25**
崂山区	Laoshan District					
黄岛区（西海岸新区）	Huangdao District (West Coast New Area)	5.51	3.18	2.01	2.61	0.06
城阳区	Chengyang District	0.19	0.14	0.04	0.37	0.52
城阳区（不含高新区）	Chengyang District (Excluding High tech District)					
高新区	High tech District					
即墨区	Jimo District	7.26	3.21	3.80	10.33	6.60
胶州市	Jiaozhou	3.87	3.06	0.54	3.82	0.53
平度市	Pingdu	14.95	6.15	8.34	5.98	1.21
莱西市	Laixi	18.62	5.58	12.35	5.75	24.33

11-14　分市、区渔业养殖面积
AQUACULTURE AREA BY REGION

单位：公顷（hectare）

市、区名称	Region	2021年			2020年		
		养殖面积 Aquaculture Area	#海水 Seawater	#淡水 Fresh Water	养殖面积 Aquaculture Area	#海水 Seawater	#淡水 Fresh Water
全市	**Whole Municipality**	**37254**	**34286**	**2968**	**35214**	**32233**	**2981**
崂山区	Laoshan District	986	986		986	986	
黄岛区（西海岸新区）	Huangdao District (West Coast New Area)	12866	12458	408	12845	12436	409
城阳区	Chengyang District	6165	6012	153	6215	6062	153
城阳区（不含高新区）	Chengyang District (Excluding High tech District)	6165	6012	153	6215	6062	153
高新区	High tech District						
即墨区	Jimo District	13339	13079	260	11186	10916	270
胶州市	Jiaozhou	2442	1751	691	2524	1833	691
平度市	Pingdu	509		509	513		513
莱西市	Laixi	947		947	945		945

11-15　分市、区水产品总产量（2021年）
OUTPUT OF AQUATIC PRODUCTS BY REGION（2021）

单位：吨（ton）

市、区名称	Region	水产品总产量 Output of Aquatic Products	#养殖产量 Aquaculture Output	#捕捞产量 Catch	#鱼类 Fish	#甲壳类 Crust	#贝类 Shellfish	#藻类 Algae
全市	**Whole Municipality**	**1012560**	**814294**	**198266**	**144759**	**54970**	**733828**	**1976**
崂山区	Laoshan District	33314	5426	27888	18307	6218	4239	
黄岛区（西海岸新区）	Huangdao District (West Coast New Area)	350564	287821	62743	73459	12991	227743	1120
城阳区	Chengyang District	231648	199011	32637	10051	6910	195732	
城阳区（不含高新区）	Chengyang District (Excluding High tech District)	231648	199011	32637	10051	6910	195732	
高新区	High tech District							
即墨区	Jimo District	291977	240962	51015	14873	21575	237942	856
胶州市	Jiaozhou	101480	77681	23799	24563	7208	68172	
平度市	Pingdu	1337	1337		1266	68		
莱西市	Laixi	2240	2056	184	2240			

11-16　分市、区植树及造林面积（2021 年）

OUTPUT OF AQUATIC PRODUCTS BY REGION（2021）

市、区名称	Region	当年造林面积（公顷）Area of Afforestation in the Year（hectare）	育苗数量（万株）Number of Seedlings（10 000 trees）	森林抚育作业面积（公顷）Forest Tending Area（hectare）	零星（四旁）植树（万株）Surrounding Tree Planting（10 000 trees）
全市	**Whole Municipality**	**117**	**9579.2**	**5713**	**251.7**
崂山区	Laoshan District		32.0	1133	3.1
黄岛区（西海岸新区）	Huangdao District（West Coast New Area）	100	3908.5	43	
城阳区	Chengyang District		414.0	1000	40.0
城阳区（不含高新区）	Chengyang District（Excluding High tech District）		414.0	1000	40.0
高新区	High tech District				
即墨区	Jimo District		2700.1	2533	
胶州市	Jiaozhou		927.1	776	28.8
平度市	Pingdu	17	1181.7		130.5
莱西市	Laixi		415.8	228	49.3

11-17　分市、区水果产量（2021 年）

AREA OF FORESTATION AND OUTPUT OF FRUITS BY REGION（2021）

单位：吨（ton）

市、区名称	Region	水果总产量 Output of Fruits（ton）	#园林水果 Garden Fruits	#瓜果类水果 Melon Fruits
全市	**Whole Municipality**	**1198348**	**805227**	**393121**
崂山区	Laoshan District	6380	6269	111
黄岛区（西海岸新区）	Huangdao District（West Coast New Area）	129699	105260	24439
城阳区	Chengyang District	18465	17337	1128
城阳区（不含高新区）	Chengyang District（Excluding High tech District）	18465	17337	1128
高新区	High tech District			
即墨区	Jimo District	50465	33881	16584
胶州市	Jiaozhou	73021	57049	15972
平度市	Pingdu	427287	240443	186844
莱西市	Laixi	493031	344988	148043

11-17 续表
Continued

单位：吨（ton）

市、区名称	Region	#苹果 Apple	#梨 Pear	#桃 Peach	#葡萄 Grape	#杏 Apricot	#山楂 Hawthorn	#西瓜 Watermelon	#甜瓜 Muskmelon
全市	**Whole Municipality**	**260743**	**123488**	**166550**	**165403**	**10894**	**2208**	**205977**	**115000**
崂山区	Laoshan District	77	59	1680	95	1273			
黄岛区（西海岸新区）	Huangdao District (West Coast New Area)	38510	3980	25831	5339	287	52	14741	1457
城阳区	Chengyang District	1009	208	5051	4020	3961	1		
城阳区（不含高新区）	Chengyang District (Excluding High tech District)	1009	208	5051	4020	3961	1		
高新区	High tech District								
即墨区	Jimo District	8217	3082	14562	3685	179	38	11076	1538
胶州市	Jiaozhou	17602	4489	21950	4309	5145	70	14551	264
平度市	Pingdu	65621	26868	46175	71630	48	281	143727	1273
莱西市	Laixi	129708	84801	51301	76324		1765	21882	110468

11-18 分市、区果园、茶园面积和茶叶产量（2021年）
AREA OF ORCHARD AND TEA GARDEN AND PRODUCTION OF TEA BY CITY AND DISTRICT (2021)

单位：公顷（hectare），吨（ton）

市、区名称	Region	果园面积 Area of Orchards	#苹果园 Apple Orchard	#梨园 Pear Orchard	#葡萄园 Vineyard	#桃园 Peach Orchard	茶园面积 Area of Tea Plantations	茶叶产量 Tea Yield
全市	**Whole Municipality**	**31824**	**8085**	**3700**	**4838**	**6725**	**4711**	**4955**
崂山区	Laoshan District	618	3	3	3	59	1199	1340
黄岛区（西海岸新区）	Huangdao District (West Coast New Area)	5428	1003	150	197	1324	3072	3057
城阳区	Chengyang District	925	37	6	142	193	31	49
城阳区（不含高新区）	Chengyang District (Excluding High tech District)	925	37	6	142	193	31	49
高新区	High tech District							
即墨区	Jimo District	1821	301	219	155	927	308	495
胶州市	Jiaozhou	1782	451	166	116	665	43	8
平度市	Pingdu	11444	2557	1087	2129	1796	17	5
莱西市	Laixi	9806	3733	2068	2096	1762	40	2

11-19 主要年份主要农业机械拥有量
MAJOR YEAR'S OWNERSHIIP OF AGRICULTURAL MACHINERY

年份 Year	农业机械总动力（万千瓦） Total Agricultural Machinery Power（10 000 kW）	农用拖拉机 Agricultural Tractors		大、中型机引农具（万台） Large and Medium Towing Farm Machinery（10 000 sets）	排灌机械 Drainage and Irrigation Machinery	
		混合台 set	千瓦 kW		台 set	万千瓦 10 000 kW
1949						
1952						
1957	0.22	59	2.2	0.01		
1962	2.47	254	11.47	0.06		
1965	3.49	296	13.2	0.08		
1970	10.40	602	7 963	0.07		
1975	43.94	6447	103 476	0.48		
1978	75.45	15576	309 287	1.02		
1980	110.44	24278	502 731	1.72		
1985	174.76	33097	506 217	1.71	67794	54.92
1990	253.52	55363	680 903	2.03	105574	74.63
1991	250.58	57404	691 332	2.20	134900	73.77
1992	253.94	57182	684 182	2.28	124800	82.68
1993	261.24	56335	678 161	2.34	144460	78.96
1994	278.41	58698	688 886	2.39	147259	80.81
1995	289.23	56391	657 025	2.28	138625	73.98
1996	303.57	59698	680 447	2.32	148313	81.53
1997	326.72	66841	744 424	2.42	155629	88.09
1998	364.21	87226	894 985	2	156565	86.68
1999	411.44	105743	1 075 907	3	170875	96.20
2000	459.21	126981	1 253 210	3	182646	108.26
2001	496.27	141409	1 394 114	4	178437	104.18
2002	534.92	152920	1 537 544	5	182799	107.35
2003	560.94	160676	1 666 185	5	192930	109.44
2004	599	168061	1 818 276	5	192144	110
2005	620	163032	1757177	6	188689	112
2006	651	171155	1890402	6	192010	116
2007	680	173326	1958047	7	195050	118
2008	697	176156	2034453	8	208711	134
2009	719	180171	2266697	9	207648	134
2010	764	200208	2331867	10	190770	123
2011	784	202022	2649283	10	189834	127
2012	798	206290	2759004	10	190134	127
2013	809	206309	2968332	10	190433	127
2014	827	205065	2960438	10	190584	128
2015	854	207809	3176870	10	191152	128
2016	698	211689	3372681	10	191283	128
2017	728	214799	3550005	11	191417	128
2018	738	215668	3668505	0.8	232943	
2019	752	216496	3769281	1.7	232952	
2020	755	214845	3789730			
2021	757	210358				

注：1. 大、中型机引农具 2018 年为新统计口径，只统计功率 58.8 千瓦以上机引农具。
2. 2020 年起，农业农村局不再提供大、中型机引农具及排灌机械数据。
3. 2021 年起，农业农村局不再提供农用拖拉机的功率数据。

Notes：1. Large and medium type agricultural tools are the new statistical caliber in 2018, and only the statistical power is 58.8 kilowatts or more.
2. Starting in 2020, the Bureau of Agriculture and Rural Affairs will no longer provide data on large and medium-sized mechanically-introduced agricultural tools and irrigation and drainage machinery.
3. Starting in 2020, the Bureau of Agriculture and Rural Affairs would have no longer provided data of power on agricultural tractors.

11-20 主要年份农业机械化用电量、化肥施用量

MAJOR YEAR'S MECHANIZATION, ELECTRICITY AND CHEMICAL FERTILIZER CONSUMPTION

年份 Year	耕地机电灌溉面积（公顷） Cultivated Land Electromechanical Irrigation Area（hectare）	配套机电井（眼） Number of Electromechanical Well（unit）	机耕面积（公顷） Area of Motorized Cultivation（hectare）	机播面积（公顷） Area of Motorized Planting（hectare）	机收面积（公顷） Area of Motorized Harvesting（hectare）	农村用电量（万千瓦时） Electricity Consumption in Rural Area（10 000kW·h）	化肥施用量（折纯万吨） Chemical Fertilizer Consumption（convert to 10 000tons）
1949	8340						
1952	14980						
1957	59353		12800	13			0.19
1962	55213	191	65680	927	927	55	0.10
1965	80000	125	11433	573	247	128	0.55
1970	147613	3947	143700	2527	133	1208	1.76
1975	233980	12820	248867	54507	953	2522	2.77
1978	276660	21017	329213	178533	15060	13975	3.64
1980	296606	22472	444800	187980	55333	20492	12.06
1985	302647	42925	366786	148433	56447	41524	11.66
1990	274680	56821	426680	220593	143133	67616	20.47
1991	281500	58987	431293	254266	192946	81200	22.53
1992	281610	62100	438533	270453	207780	88024	22.60
1993	284080	63954	439300	260287	225807	102501	28.04
1994	286750	64877	436820	262846	238693	121307	28.73
1995	287020	64651	435213	271707	250267	134284	31.45
1996	289320	65237	438947	280480	235933	143740	31.36
1997	292130	66783	442213	308267	266147	150971	28.99
1998	294120	64109	442920	359447	285513	153113	32.0
1999	294790	64734	440967	396180	286367	169337	32.6
2000	295190	65179	439980	346480	292787	189651	32.5
2001	296980	65547	436576	382870	265730	228069	31.7
2002	294310	65588	433660	364680	267690	256453	31.1
2003	292410	65406	415790	404980	256600	299425	31.9
2004	292520	65501	415220	454800	314680	330609	32.5
2005	296450	65303	409610	493240	367740	372644	33.0
2006	303070	65981	403980	493750	398700	413762	32.6
2007	305760	66400	400480	499590	429630	425715	33.9
2008	313920	66828	404080	517540	455120	424292	31.1
2009	322710	67027	404080	538220	481176	426306	30.2
2010	328960	67242	578726	558611	499248	426819	29.9
2011	331690	62104	600451	567947	547108	431646	29.4
2012	333850	62112	610382	627701	566653	426815	29.1
2013	302790	170008	410601	627701	566653	359138	29.1
2014	321670	169491	411355	590798	545360	404380	28.9
2015	323400	155074	417991	640022	600696	401122	28.5
2016	327600	135057	362912	561022	511000	385434	28.37
2017	329620	139342	360085	566264	516763	382437	27.83
2018	331240	136785	359238	578082	531733	377858	27.05
2019	329390	136963	353624	563689	527199	388484	26.71
2020	355077		334148	563410	516895	359584	26.28
2021	332085		325956	571213	515677	328106	24.90

注：1.2020 年起有效灌溉面积改为耕地机电灌溉面积，数据由农业农村局提供。
2.2020 年起，部门不再提供配套机电井数据。

Notes：1. Starting from 2020, the effective irrigation area will be changed to the electromechanical irrigation area of arable land. The data is provided by the Agriculture and Rural Bureau.
2. Starting from 2020, the department will no longer provide supporting electromechanical well data.

11-21 分市、区农业机械化和电气化（2021年）

MECHANIZATION AND ELECTRIFICATION IN AGRICULTURE BY REGION（2021）

市、区名称	Region	农村用电量（万千瓦小时）Electricity Consumed in Rural Areas（10 000 kW·h）	机耕作业面积 Area of Motorized Cultivation（hectare）	机播地面积 Area of Motorized Planting（hectare）	机收面积 Area of Motorized Harvesting（hectare）
			面积 Area（公顷）(hectare)		
全市	**Whole Municipality**	**328105**	**325956**	**571213**	**515677**
崂山区	Laoshan District	9962			
黄岛区（西海岸新区）	Huangdao District（West Coast New Area）	30969	28920	59852	50250
城阳区	Chengyang District	34577	878	868	877
城阳区（不含高新区）	Chengyang District（Excluding High tech District）	34577	878	868	877
高新区	High tech District				
即墨区	Jimo District	63018	48139	87935	82671
胶州市	Jiaozhou	95374	38363	75741	70509
平度市	Pingdu	57982	146778	238721	216385
莱西市	Laixi	36223	62878	108080	94985

11-22 分市、区农用化肥施用量（2021年）

CONSUMPTION OF CHEMICAL FERTILIZERS BY REGION（2021）

单位：吨（ton）（折纯）（convert to pure amount）

市、区名称	Region	农用化肥施用量 Consumption of Chemical Fertilizers	氮肥 Nitrogenous Fertilizer	磷肥 Phosphate Fertilizer	钾肥 Potash Fertilizer	复合肥 Compound Fertilizer	附：平均每公顷耕地施用化肥量（折纯千克）Annotation：Consumption of Chemical Fertilizer Per Hectare（convert to pure volume）
全市	**Whole Municipality**	**248971**	**30749**	**9664**	**15179**	**193379**	**576**
崂山区	Laoshan District	324	5	1	1	318	553
黄岛区（西海岸新区）	Huangdao District（West Coast New Area）	23057	3777	1983	4969	12327	434
城阳区	Chengyang District	469	48	24	22	376	129
城阳区（不含高新区）	Chengyang District（Excluding High tech District）	469	48	24	22	376	129
高新区	High tech District						
即墨区	Jimo District	31559	7622	1768	1814	20353	415
胶州市	Jiaozhou	32879	5037	753	3384	23706	694
平度市	Pingdu	109617	5405	1917	2902	99393	636
莱西市	Laixi	51065	8855	3218	2087	36906	637

11-23 分市、区农田水利情况（2021 年）
FARMLAND WATER CONSERVANCY BY REGION（2021）

市、区名称	Region	耕地机电灌溉面积（公顷） Cultivated Land Electromechanical Irrigation Area（hectare）	机电灌溉面积占耕地面积比重（%） Proportion of Electromechanical Irrigation Area in Cultivated Land Area（%）
全市	**Whole Municipality**	**332085**	**76.9**
崂山区	Laoshan District		
黄岛区（西海岸新区）	Huangdao District（West Coast New Area）	20017	37.7
城阳区	Chengyang District	892	24.6
城阳区（不含高新区）	Chengyang District（Excluding High tech District）	892	24.6
高新区	High tech District		
即墨区	Jimo District	63750	83.8
胶州市	Jiaozhou	18600	39.3
平度市	Pingdu	173159	100.5
莱西市	Laixi	55667	69.4

11-24 分市、区主要农业机械拥有量（2021 年）

OWNERSHIP OF MAJOR AGRICULTURAL MACHINERY BY RGION（2021）

市、区名称	Region	农业机械总动力（万千瓦）Agricultural Machinery Power（10 000 kW）	平均每公顷耕地拥有量（千瓦）Power Per Hectare of Cultivated Land（kW）	大中型拖拉机（台）Large and Medium Tractors（set）	小型拖拉机（台）Small Tractors（set）
全市	**Whole Municipality**	**757.3**	**17.5**	**46579**	**163779**
崂山区	Laoshan District				
黄岛区（西海岸新区）	Huangdao District（West Coast New Area）	84.1	15.8	2855	44429
城阳区	Chengyang District	26.2	72.2	55	189
城阳区（不含高新区）	Chengyang District（Excluding High tech District）	26.2	72.2	55	189
高新区	High tech District				
即墨区	Jimo District	101.4	13.3	4600	33735
胶州市	Jiaozhou	112.1	23.7	5335	19134
平度市	Pingdu	283.3	16.4	25448	33723
莱西市	Laixi	138.1	17.2	8286	32569

11-24 续表

Continued

市、区名称	Region	机引犁（部）Towing Ploughs（unit）	机引耙（部）Towing Rakes（unit）	粮食加工机械（台）Grain Processing Machinery（set）	油料加工机械（部）Oil Processing Machinery（unit）	棉花加工机械（部）Cotton Processing Machinery（unit）	饲草料加工机械（台套）Forage processing machinery（unit）
全市	**Whole Municipality**	**160580**	**32230**	**25700**	**9142**	**132**	**22784**
崂山区	Laoshan District						
黄岛区（西海岸新区）	Huangdao District（West Coast New Area）	32937	109	1117	256		2999
城阳区	Chengyang District	1196	197	1602	515	17	338
城阳区（不含高新区）	Chengyang District（Excluding High tech District）	1196	197	1602	515	17	338
高新区	High tech District						
即墨区	Jimo District	19966	1680	3259	1472		1481
胶州市	Jiaozhou	15159	5242	3070	2125		3596
平度市	Pingdu	21937	16500	4372	1424	6	7663
莱西市	Laixi	69385	8502	12280	3350	109	6707

主要统计指标解释

农业总产值　是以货币表现的农、林、牧、渔业全部产品的总量，它反映一定时期内农业生产的总规模和总成果。

农、林、牧、渔业的统计范围是：

（1）农业包括农作物种植业和其他农业。农作物种植业包括谷物、豆类、薯类、棉、油料、糖料、麻类、烟叶、蔬菜、药材、瓜类和其他农作物的种植，以及茶园、桑园、果园的生产经营。其他农业包括采集野生植物的果实、纤维、树胶、树脂、油料以及柴草、野生药材、菌类等及农民家庭兼营的商品性工业。

（2）林业包括林木的栽培（不包括茶园、桑园和果园的栽培、管理和收获等活动）、林产品的采集和村及村以下合作经济组织和农户的竹木采伐。

（3）畜牧业包括除渔业养殖以外的一切动物饲养和放牧，以及野生动物的捕猎和饲养。

（4）渔业包括水生动物和海藻类植物的养殖和捕捞。

（5）农、林、牧、渔专业及辅助性活动指对农业提供的各种专业及辅助性生产活动，不包括各种科学技术和专业技术服务。

粮食产量　指稻谷、小麦、玉米、高粱等谷物及薯类和豆类的全社会产量。包括国有经济经营的、集体统一经营的和农民家庭经营的粮食产量，还包括工矿企业办的农场和其他生产单位的产量。其产量计算方法，豆类按去豆荚后的干豆计算；薯类（不包括芋头、木薯和马铃薯）按 5 公斤鲜薯折 1 公斤粮食计算；马铃薯作为蔬菜统计；其他粮食一律按脱粒后的原粮计算。

水产品产量　指人工养殖的水产品和天然生长的水产品的捕捞量。包括海水的鱼类、虾蟹类、贝类和藻类以及内陆水域的鱼类、虾蟹类和贝类，不包括淡水生植物。

猪、牛、羊肉产量　指当年出栏并已屠宰、除去头蹄下水后带骨头肉（即胴体重）的重量。其统计范围为全社会。

农用化肥施用量　指本年内实际用于农业生产的化肥数量，包括氮肥、磷肥、钾肥和复合肥。化肥施用量要求按折纯量计算数量。折纯量是指把氮肥、磷肥、钾肥分别按含氮、含五氧化二磷、含氧化钾的百分之百成分进行折算后的数量。复合肥按其所含主要成分折算。

公式：折纯量 = 实物量 × 某种化肥有效成分含量的百分比

农业机械总动力　指用于农、林、牧、渔业生产的各种动力机械的动力总和。动力机械包括耕作、排灌、种植、植物保护、收获、农产品加工、运输、畜牧、渔业、农田水利等各种机械。不包括专门用于乡办工业、基本建设、非农业运输、科学试验和教学等非农业生产方面用的动力机械与作业机械的数量。

Explanatory Notes on Main Statistical Indicators

Gross Output Value of Agriculture　refers to the total volume of products of farming, forestry, animal husbandry, and fishery expressed in the monetary terms. It reflects the overall scale and achievements of agricultural production during a given period of time.

The scope of statistics on farming, forestry, animal husbandry, and fishery are as follows:

(1) Farming includes cultivation of farm crops and other agricultural activities. Cultivation of farm crops include cultivation of grain crops, legume crops, tuber-crops, cotton, oil-bearing crops, sugar crops, and cultivation and management of tea plantations,

mulberry fields and orchards. Other agricultural activities include harvesting wild fruits, fiber, tree gum, resin, oil-bearing plants, firewood, wild medicinal herbs, fungus, and rural-household commodity industries.

(2) Forestry refers to planting trees of various kinds (excluding tea plantations, mulberry fields and orchards), collection of forestry products and cutting and felling of bamboo and trees by villages and other cooperative organizations under village level.

(3) Animal husbandry refers to raising and grazing of all kinds of farm animals except fishing and aquatic cultivating, and hunting and rising of wild animals.

(4) Fishery refers to cultivation and catching of fish and other aquatic products and cultivation and collection of seaweed and other aquatic plants.

(5) Agriculture, forestry, animal husbandry, and fishery professions and auxiliary activities refer to various professional and auxiliary production activities provided to agriculture, excluding various scientific and technical and professional technical services.

Grain Output refers to the total output of rice, wheat, corn, sorghum, millet and other miscellaneous grains as well as tubers and bean in the whole country including grains produced by states farms, collective unit, industrial enterprises and mines, output of beans refers to dry beans without pods, the output of tubers (excluding taros, cassava and potatoes) was converted into that of grain at the ratio 5 : 1, i. e. 5 kilograms of fresh tubers was equivalent to 1 kilogram of grain. Statistics of potatoes as vegetables. Output of all other grains refers to husked grain..

Output of Aquatic Products refers to catches of both artificially cultured and naturally grown aquatic products, including fish, shrimps, crabs and shellfish in sea and inland water as well as seaweed. Freshwater plants are not included.

Output of Pork, Beef, and Mutton refers to the meat of slaughtered hogs, cattle, sheep and goats with head, feet, and offal taken away. Data refers to the production of the whole country.

Consumption of Chemical Fertilizers in Agriculture refers to the quantity of chemical fertilizers applied in agriculture in the year, including nitrogenous fertilizer, phosphate fertilizer, potash fertilizer, and compound fertilizer. The consumption of chemical fertilizers in required in calculation to convert the gross weight into weight containing 100% effective component (e. g. 100% nitrogen content in nitrogenous fertilizer, 100% phosphorous pent oxide contents in phosphate fertilizer, 100% potassium oxide contents in potash fertilizer). Compound fertilizer is converted with its major component. The formula is :

Volume of effective component = physical quantity × effective component of certain chemical fertilizer (%)

Total Power of Agriculture Machinery Refers to the total mechanical power of machinery used in farming forestry animal husbandry and fishery, including machines used for ploughing, irrigation and drainage, crop growing, plant protection, harvesting, farm product processing, transport, stock breeding, fishery and water conservancy, Machinery employed for non agricultrual purposes such as township industry, capital construction, non-agricultrual transport, scientific experiments and for teaching is excluded.

工　业 12

INDUSTRY

简 要 说 明

一、本篇资料的主要内容

本篇资料主要反映了全市工业生产和基本效益情况，主要包括工业企业单位数、历年工业总产值、规模以上工业、国有控股工业、国有工业、集体工业、外商投资和港澳台投资工业、大中型工业企业的主要经济指标、相关的财务分析指标和主要工业产品产量等方面的内容。

二、本篇资料的来源

本篇中规模以上工业资料来源于工业统计年报，由市统计局工业统计处整理提供。

Brief Introduction

Ⅰ. Main Content

Data in this chapter show the basic condition of industrial production and benefit in Qingdao, mainly including the number of industrial enterprises, gross industrial output value and indices, the output of major industrial products and major economic and relevant financial indicators of industrial enterprises. Industrial enterprises include enterprises above designated size, state share-holding enterprises, state owned enterprises, collective owned enterprises, foreign funded enterprises, enterprises with funds from Hong Kong, Macao and Taiwan, large and medium sized enterprises.

Ⅱ. Source of Data

Data on industry above designated size are based on the annual report of industrial statistics, and prepared by the Division of Industry Statistics of Qingdao Municipal Bureau of Statistics.

12-1 规模以上工业企业单位数
NUMBER OF INDUSTRIAL ENTERPRISES ABOVE DESIGNATEO SIZE

单位：个（unit）

项 目	Item	1985 年	1990 年	1995 年	2000 年	2005 年	2006 年
总 计	**Total**	**2411**	**2997**	**4987**	**1504**	**3697**	**4567**
一、按经济类型分	**Grouped by Economic Types**						
国有企业	State-owned	502	568	1084	179	76	74
集体企业	Collective-owned	1907	2386	2731	226	87	72
其他经济类型企业	Other Economic Types	2	43	1172	1099	3534	4421
#外商及港澳台商投资企业	Foreign Funded Enterprises and Enterprises with Funds from Hong Kong, Macao and Taiwan		35	1027	593	1658	1952
二、按轻重工业分	**Grouped by Light and Heavy Industries**						
轻工业	Light Industry	1398	1730	2858	891	1942	2313
重工业	Heavy Industry	1013	1267	2129	613	1755	2254
三、按企业规模分	**Grouped by Size of Enterprises**						
大型企业	Large	26	42	89	202	51	51
中型企业	Medium	80	168	216	229	441	469
小型企业	Small	2305	2787	4480	1073	3205	4047
四、按行业分	**Grouped by sectors**						
黑色金属矿采选业	Miring of Non-ferrous Metal Ores		4	6	1	2	5
有色金属矿采选业	Mining of Non-ferrous Metal Ores	2	7	9	7	5	5
非金属矿采选业	Mining and Processing of Non-metal Ores	43	70	87	29	34	31
食品制造业	Manufacture of Foods	244	324	437	170	121	137
#粮食及饲料加工	Processing of Gren and Feed	62	57	60	27		
饮料制造业	Manufacture of Beverage	31	44	74	23	29	28
#饮料酒	Beverage Liquor	20	28	27	19	20	25

12-1 续表 1
Continued

单位：个（unit）

项　目	Item	2007 年	2008 年	2009 年	2010 年	2011 年
总　计	**Total**	**5032**	**5628**	**5895**	**5674**	**4727**
一、按经济类型分	**Grouped by Economic Types**					
国有企业	State-owned	63	65	163	61	147
集体企业	Collective-owned	72	61	59	53	31
其他经济类型企业	Other Economic Types	4897	5502	5673	5560	4549
# 外商及港澳台商投资企业	Foreign Funded Enterprises and Enterprises with Funds from Hong Kong，Macao and Taiwan	2091	2217	2244	2037	1618
二、按轻重工业分	**Grouped by Light and Heavy Industries**					
轻工业	Light Industry	2489	2704	2805	2635	2131
重工业	Heavy Industry	2543	2924	3090	3039	2596
三、按企业规模分	**Grouped by Size of Enterprises**					
大型企业	Large	53	48	50	52	50
中型企业	Medium	489	519	502	525	516
小型企业	Small	4490	5061	5343	5097	4161
四、按行业分	**Grouped by sectors**					
黑色金属矿采选业	Miring of Non-ferrous Metal Ores	7	23	22	12	12
有色金属矿采选业	Mining of Non-ferrous Metal Ores	5	6	6	4	
非金属矿采选业	Mining and Processing of Non–metal Ores	33	30	26	26	23
食品制造业	Manufacture of Foods	156	158	174	167	127
# 粮食及饲料加工	Processing of Gren and Feed					
饮料制造业	Manufacture of Beverage	33	40	42	42	36
# 饮料酒	Beverage Liquor					

12-1 续表 2
Continued

单位：个（unit）

项　目	Item	1985年	1990年	1995年	2000年	2005年	2006年
烟草制品业	Manufacture of Tobacco	2	2	5	3	2	2
纺织业	Manufacture of Textile	169	225	330	132	300	327
纺织服装、鞋、帽制造业	Manufacture of Textile Wearing Apparel. Footware and Caps	171	194	322	95	272	339
皮革、毛皮、羽毛（绒）及其制品业	Manufacture of Leather, Fur, Feather and Related Products	56	64	161	64	167	194
木材加工制品业	Processing of Wood and Wood Prodncts	71	89	116	19	40	53
家具制造业	Manufacture of Furniture	61	72	88	10	72	103
造纸及纸制品业	Manufacture of Paper and Paper Products	66	74	110	56	102	128
印刷业和记录媒介的复制	Printing, Reproduction of Recording Media	61	81	215	23	44	59
文教体育用品制造业	Manufacture of Articles For Culture, Education and Sport Activities	31	27	93	48	89	91
石油、煤炭及其他燃料加工业	Oil, coal and other fuel processing industries	2	3	13	5	10	6
化学原料及制品	Manufacture of Raw Chemical Materials and Chemical Products	106	156	278	81	178	233
医药制造业	Manufacture of Medicines	16	14	39	20	30	46
化学纤维制造业	Manufacture of Chemical Fibres	2	4	26	15	14	13
橡胶制品业	Manufacture of Rubber	53	57	143	48	116	170
塑料制品业	Manufacture of Plastics	103	131	237	64	153	179
非金属矿物制品业	Manufacture of metallic Mineral Products	230	245	275	62	161	218
黑色金属压延加工业	Smelting and Pressing of Ferrous Metals	11	13	31	15	41	45
有色金属压延加工业	Smelting and Pressing of Non-ferrous Metals	6	8	19	9	28	40
金属制品业	Manufacture of Metal Products	161	186	372	88	186	250
通用设备制造业	Manufacture of General Purpose Machinery	320	398	320	94	299	397
交通运输制造业	Manufacture of Electrical Machinery and Equipment	104	114	358	52	151	194
电气机械及器材制造业	Manufacture of Electrical tion Machinery and Equipment	86	96	211	79	214	249
通信设备、计算机及其他电子设备制造业	Manufacture of Communication Equipment, Computers and Other Electronic Equipment	32	31	79	34	123	140
仪器仪表及文化、办公用机械制造业	Manufacture of Measuring Instruments and Machinery for Cultural Activity and Office Work	28	33	70	20	40	44
水的生产和供应业	Production and Supply of Water	8	12	12	8	10	10
电力、热力的生产和供应业	Production and Supply of Electric Power and Heat Power	10	16	20	17	27	32
燃气生产和供应业	Production and Supply of Gas	1	4	3	2	5	6
其他工业	Other Industrial Sectors	46	48	209	63	166	534

12-1 续表 3
Continued

单位：个（unit）

项　目	Item	2007 年	2008 年	2009 年	2010 年	2011 年
烟草制品业	Manufacture of Tobacco	2	2	2	1	1
纺织业	Manufacture of Textile	340	330	322	287	229
纺织服装、鞋、帽制造业	Manfacture of Testilee Wearing Apparel. Footware and Caps	362	418	434	392	295
皮革、毛皮、羽毛（绒）及其制品业	Manufacture of Leather, Fur, Feather and Related Products	197	209	210	211	160
木材加工制品业	Processing of Woon and Wood Prodncts	64	66	68	68	49
家具制造业	Manufacture of Furniture	119	130	133	117	97
造纸及纸制品业	Manufacture of Paper and Paper Producls	126	133	133	138	101
印刷业和记录媒介的复制	Printing, Reproduction of Recording Media	63	74	79	92	58
文教体育用品制造业	Manufacture of Articles For Culture, Education and Sport Activities	97	96	99	90	75
石油、煤炭及其他燃料加工业	Oil, coal and other fuel processing industries	7	7	9	8	7
化学原料及制品	Manufacture of Raw Chemical Materials and Chemical Products	261	276	275	262	231
医药制造业	Manufacture of Medicines	48	49	56	52	44
化学纤维制造业	Manufacture of Chemical Fibres	12	13	14	12	10
橡胶制品业	Manufacture of Rubber	183	211	214	196	187
塑料制品业	Manufacture of Plastics	199	227	234	233	169
非金属矿物制品业	Manufacture of metallic Mineral Products	259	311	320	327	303
黑色金属压延加工业	Smelting and Pressing of Ferrous Metals	39	24	27	31	29
有色金属压延加工业	Smelting and Pressing of Non-ferrous Metals	40	41	40	35	34
金属制品业	Manufacture of Metal Products	271	347	376	361	294
通用设备制造业	Manufacture of General Purpose Machinery	473	535	592	597	521
交通运输制造业	Manufacture of Electrical Machinery and Equipment	217	264	290	296	263
电气机械及器材制造业	Manufacture of Electrication Machinery and Equipment	274	303	300	281	230
通信设备、计算机及其他电子设备制造业	Manufacture of Communication Equipment, Computers and Other Eleetronic Equipment	152	163	168	167	124
仪器仪表及文化、办公用机械制造业	Manufacture of Measuring Instruments and Machinery for Cultural Activity and Office Work	47	47	55	54	39
水的生产和供应业	Production and Supply of Water	10	13	14	14	11
电力、热力的生产和供应业	Production and Supply of Electric Power and Heat Power	34	36	39	38	36
燃气生产和供应业	Production and Supply of Gas	7	13	13	14	11
其他工业	Other Industrial Sectors	895	1033	1109	1049	921

12-1 续表 4
Continued

单位：个（unit）

项　目	Item	2012 年	2013 年	2014 年	2015 年	2016 年
总　计	**Total**	**4817**	**4917**	**4790**	**4876**	**4431**
一、按经济类型分	**Grouped by Economic Types**					
国有企业	State-owned	144	140	132	141	128
集体企业	Collective-owned	28	24	19	15	11
其他经济类型企业	Other Economic Types	4645	4753	4639	4720	4292
# 外商及港澳台商投资企业	Foreign Funded Enterprises and Enterprises with Funds from Hong Kong，Macao and Taiwan	1599	1551	1445	1361	1205
二、按轻重工业分	**Grouped by Light and Heavy Industries**					
轻工业	Light Industry	2153	2190	2080	2095	1875
重工业	Heavy Industry	2664	2727	2710	2781	2556
三、按企业规模分	**Grouped by Size of Enterprises**					
大型企业	Large	98	97	91	89	85
中型企业	Medium	596	599	568	566	516
小微型企业	Small & Micro–Enterprises	4123	4221	4131	4221	3830
四、按行业分	**Grouped by sectors**					
黑色金属矿采选业	Mining of Ferrous Metal Ores	10	11	8	7	1
有色金属矿采选业	Mining of Non–ferrous Metal Ores					
非金属矿采选业	Mining and Processing of Non–metal Ores	14	13	7	6	5
农副食品加工业	Processing of Food from Agricultural Products	454	468	444	458	419
食品制造业	Manufacture of Foods	129	123	109	116	115
酒、饮料和精制茶制造业	Manufacture of Liquor，Beverages and Refined Tea	34	35	34	38	33
烟草制品业	Manufacture of Tobacco	1	1	1	1	
纺织业	Manufacture of Textile	181	175	146	133	111
纺织服装、服饰业	Manufacture of Textile Wearing Apparel	312	283	249	244	206
皮革、毛皮、羽毛及其制品和制鞋业	Manufacture of Leather, Fur, Feather & Its Products Footwear	177	148	124	116	89
木材加工和木、竹、藤、棕、草制品业	Processing of Timbers, Manufacture of Wood, Bamboo, Rattan, Palm and Straw Products	34	40	32	34	31
家具制造业	Manufacture of Furniture	103	107	96	98	88
造纸和纸制品业	Manufacture of Paper and Paper Producls	100	71	54	52	50
印刷和记录媒介复制业	Printing, Reproduction of Recording Media	80	121	150	156	137

注：国家统计局根据《国民经济行业分类》（GB/T 4754–2017），对《三次产业划分规定（2012）》中行业类别进行了对应调整，其中“石油加工、炼焦和核燃料加工业”更名为“石油、煤炭及其他燃料加工业”，并将 2011 版《国民经济行业分类》4500 中部分内容和 4120 全部内容调到此类。

Note：According to the national economic industry classification (GB/ T 4754–2017), the National Bureau of Statistics carries out a corresponding adjustment to the three industries according to the classification of the national economy (GB/ T 4754–2017), in which the petroleum processing, coking and nuclear fuel processing industry is changed to petroleum, coal and other fuel processing industries, and the content of part of the content and 4120 of the 2011 edition of the national economy industry category 4500 are transferred to this category.

12-1 续表 5
Continued

单位：个（unit）

项 目	Item	2017 年	2018 年	2019 年	2020 年	2021 年
总 计	**Total**	**3569**	**3508**	**3536**	**3856**	**4280**
一、按经济类型分	**Grouped by Economic Types**					
国有企业	State-owned	131	145	175	189	226
集体企业	Collective-owned	5	4	5	5	4
其他经济类型企业	Other Economic Types	3433	3359	3356	3662	4050
#外商及港澳台商投资企业	Foreign Funded Enterprises and Enterprises with Funds from Hong Kong, Macao and Taiwan	1037	938	868	825	817
二、按轻重工业分	**Grouped by Light and Heavy Industries**					
轻工业	Light Industry	1522	1448	1400	1469	1597
重工业	Heavy Industry	2047	2060	2136	2387	2683
三、按企业规模分	**Grouped by Size of Enterprises**					
大型企业	Large	78	76	86	77	73
中型企业	Medium	459	383	386	396	391
小微型企业	Small & Micro-Enterprises	3032	3049	3064	3383	3816
四、按行业分	**Grouped by sectors**					
黑色金属矿采选业	Miring of Ferrous Metal Ores					
有色金属矿采选业	Mining of Non-ferrous Metal Ores		1	1	2	2
非金属矿采选业	Mining and Processing of Non-metal Ores	2	1	2	2	1
农副食品加工业	Processing of Food from Agricultural Products	338	331	304	295	319
食品制造业	Manufacture of Foods	111	115	123	142	159
酒、饮料和精制茶制造业	Manufacture of Liquor, Beverages and Refined Tea	18	17	13	13	18
烟草制品业	Manufacture of Tobacco					
纺织业	Manufacture of Textile	91	93	103	134	140
纺织服装、服饰业	Manufacture of Texitile Wearing Apparel	152	144	132	121	126
皮革、毛皮、羽毛及其制品和制鞋业	Manufacture of Leather, Fur, Feather & Its Products Footwear	58	47	39	36	31
木材加工和木、竹、藤、棕、草制品业	Processing of Timbers, Manufacture of Wood, Bamboo, Rattan, Palm and Straw Products	27	22	28	43	52
家具制造业	Manufacture of Furniture	65	64	59	61	64
造纸和纸制品业	Manufacture of Paper and Paper Products	40	40	43	64	57
印刷和记录媒介复制业	Printing, Reproduction of Recording Media	110	101	88	66	97

12-1 续表 6
Continued

单位：个（unit）

项　目	Item	2012 年	2013 年	2014 年	2015 年	2016 年
文教、工美、体育和娱乐用品制造业	Manufacture of Articles for Culture, Arts & Crafts, Sports and Entertainment	263	335	348	345	310
石油、煤炭及其他燃料加工业	Oil, coal and other fuel processing industries	8	8	9	9	9
化学原料和化学制品制造业	Manufacture of Chemical Raw Material and Chemical Products	224	240	246	249	223
医药制造业	Manufacture of Medicines	45	49	50	54	47
化学纤维制造业	Manufacture of Chemical Fibres	9	8	8	8	6
橡胶和塑料制品业	Manufacture of Rubber and Plastic	350	345	331	310	281
非金属矿物制品业	Manufacture of metallic Mineral Products	325	333	330	338	315
黑色金属冶炼和压延加工业	Smelting and Pressing of Ferrous Metals	105	93	87	83	73
有色金属冶炼和压延加工业	Smelting and Pressing of Non-ferrous Metals	37	36	38	39	30
金属制品业	Manufacture of Metal Products	399	389	380	388	348
通用设备制造业	Manufacture of General Purpose Machinery	362	382	395	402	383
专用设备制造业	Manufacture of Special Purpose Machinery	312	322	314	336	311
汽车制造业	Manufacture of Vehicle	136	141	145	158	154
铁路、船舶、航空航天和其他运输设备制造业	Manufacture of Transport Equipment for Railway, Shipping, Aerospace and other uses	145	146	152	168	156
电气机械和器材制造业	Manufacture of Electrical Machinery and Equipment	202	212	217	226	211
计算机、通信和其他电子设备制造业	Manufactute of Computer, Communication Equipment and Other Electronic Equipment	137	136	141	147	140
仪器仪表制造业	Manufacture of Measuring Instrument	41	49	52	58	50
其他制造业	Manufacture of Other Products	18	17	13	15	16
废弃资源综合利用业	Recycling and Disposal of Waste Resources	4	6	6	5	6
金属制品、机械和设备修理业	Maintenance of Metal Products, Machinery and Equipment	7	7	7	6	5
电力、热力生产和供应业	Production and Supply of Electric Power and Heat Power	36	39	40	43	42
燃气生产和供应业	Production and Supply of Gas	12	13	12	14	14
水的生产和供应业	Production and Supply of water	11	15	15	16	16

12-1 续表 7
Continued

单位：个（unit）

项 目	Item	2017 年	2018 年	2019 年	2020 年	2021 年
文教、工美、体育和娱乐用品制造业	Manufacture of Articles for Culture, Arts & Crafts, Sports and Entertainment	222	179	131	103	107
石油、煤炭及其他燃料加工业	Oil, coal and other fuel processing industries	9	8	10	10	13
化学原料和化学制品制造业	Manufacture of Chemical Raw Material and Chemical Products	176	171	165	164	172
医药制造业	Manufacture of Medicines	35	34	40	43	50
化学纤维制造业	Manufacture of Chemical Fibres	7	8	7	8	8
橡胶和塑料制品业	Manufacture of Rubber and Plastic	250	252	268	331	362
非金属矿物制品业	Manufacture of metallic Mineral Products	228	218	234	296	344
黑色金属冶炼和压延加工业	Smelting and Pressing of Ferrous Metals	27	30	25	31	32
有色金属冶炼和压延加工业	Smelting and Pressing of Non-ferrous Metals	23	24	29	31	33
金属制品业	Manufacture of Metal Products	289	278	295	343	402
通用设备制造业	Manufacture of General Purpose Machinery	301	316	318	325	369
专用设备制造业	Manufacture of Special Purpose Machinery	233	245	243	275	320
汽车制造业	Manufacture of Vehicle	156	168	200	236	253
铁路、船舶、航空航天和其他运输设备制造业	Manufacture of Transport Equipment for Railway, Shipping, Aerospace and other uses	150	155	164	168	191
电气机械和器材制造业	Manufacture of Electrical Machinery and Equipment	184	186	184	197	211
计算机、通信和其他电子设备制造业	Manufactute of Computer, Communication Equipment and Other Electronic Equipment	128	114	117	114	130
仪器仪表制造业	Manufacture of Measuring Instrument	46	49	59	67	73
其他制造业	Manufacture of Other Products	10	11	11	16	14
废弃资源综合利用业	Recycling and Disposal of Waste Resources	3	3	3	2	5
金属制品、机械和设备修理业	Maintenance of Metal Products, Machinery and Equipment	6	6	3	7	8
电力、热力生产和供应业	Production and Supply of Electric Power and Heat Power	43	44	58	64	71
燃气生产和供应业	Production and Supply of Gas	14	15	14	17	17
水的生产和供应业	Production and Supply of water	17	18	23	29	29

12-2　分市、区规模以上工业企业数（2021 年）
NUMBER OF ALL INDUSTRIAL ENTERPRISES BY REGION（2021）

单位：个（unit）

市、区名称	Region	规模以上 Above Designated	按轻重工业分 Grouped by Light and Heavy Ind		按企业规模分 Grouped by Size of Enterprises		
			轻工业 Light Industry	重工业 Heavy Industry	大型企业 Large	中型企业 Medium	小微型企业 Small& Micro-Enterprises
全市	**Whole Municipality**	**4280**	**1597**	**2683**	**73**	**391**	**3816**
市南区	Shinan District	11	5	6	1	3	7
市北区	Shibei District	58	12	46	2	11	45
李沧区	Licang District	110	25	85		6	104
崂山区	Laoshan District	106	44	62	5	12	89
黄岛区（西海岸新区）	Huangdao District（West Coast New Area）	988	282	706	30	100	858
城阳区	Chengyang District	818	302	516	10	78	730
城阳区（不含高新区）	Chengyang District（Excluding High tech District）	670	274	396	9	57	604
高新区	High tech District	148	28	120	1	21	126
即墨区	Jimo District	569	249	320	9	63	497
胶州市	Jiaozhou	790	311	479	5	61	724
平度市	Pingdu	474	198	276	6	34	434
莱西市	Laixi	355	168	187	4	23	328

12-2　续表
Continued

单位：个（unit）

市、区名称	Region	按经济类型分 Grouped by Economic Types			
		国有企业 State-owned	集体企业 Collective-owned	其他经济 Others	#外资及港澳台商企业 Foreign Funded Enterprises and Enterprises with Funds from Kong Kong，Macao and Taiwan
全市	**Whole Municipality**	**226**	**4**	**4050**	**817**
市南区	Shinan District	3		8	
市北区	Shibei District	15	1	42	11
李沧区	Licang District	13		97	11
崂山区	Laoshan District	11		95	26
黄岛区（西海岸新区）	Huangdao District（West Coast New Area）	80		908	199
城阳区	Chengyang District	40		778	206
城阳区（不含高新区）	Chengyang District（Excluding High tech District）	24		646	170
高新区	High tech District	16		132	36
即墨区	Jimo District	14		555	106
胶州市	Jiaozhou	14		776	116
平度市	Pingdu	22	3	449	81
莱西市	Laixi	13		342	61

12-3 历年全部工业总产值
GROSS INDUSTRIAL OUTPUT VALUE OVER THE YEARS

单位：万元（10 000 yuan）

年 份 Year	工业总产值 Gross Industrial Output Value	轻工业产值 Light Industry	重工业产值 Heavy Industry
1949	21605	18494	3111
1950	34010	28720	5290
1951	53538	44600	8938
1952	84295	69258	15037
1953	115222	74716	40506
1954	126064	80604	45460
1955	118935	86956	31979
1956	144833	93809	51024
1957	142920	101202	41718
1958	217648	92407	125241
1959	282610	84376	198234
1960	291451	77043	214408
1962	120738	64233	56505
1963	139542	83630	55912
1964	177273	108884	68389
1965	215536	141765	73771
1966	252896	152304	100592
1967	287739	163627	124112
1968	299814	175791	123489
1969	296814	188860	107954
1970	345212	202903	142309

注：本表按当年价格计算，1995年开始工业总产值按新规定计算。
Note：The data in this form are calculated at current price. Since 1995，new regulations have been adopted in calculating gross industrial output value.

12-3 续表 1
Continued

单位：万元（10 000 yuan）

年　份 Year	工业总产值 Gross Industrial Output Value	轻工业产值 Light Industry	重工业产值 Heavy Industry
1971	365770	216172	149598
1972	378266	230309	147957
1973	377943	245371	132572
1974	237219	154054	83165
1975	402541	261418	141123
1976	439793	278514	161279
1977	490669	296728	193941
1978	565503	336817	228686
1979	625227	379276	245951
1980	677690	442078	235612
1981	707434	479954	227480
1982	732705	474767	257938
1983	816793	513759	303034
1984	918364	569080	349284
1985	1113891	699524	414367
1986	1316230	833864	482366
1987	1703830	1065873	637957
1988	2481594	1451215	1030379
1989	3191643	1857019	1334624
1990	3571845	2057968	1513878

12-3 续表 2
Continued

单位：万元（10 000 yuan）

年 份	Year	工业总产值 Gross Industrial Output Value	轻工业产值 Light Industry	重工业产值 Heavy Industry
1991	1991	3986427	2318257	1668170
1992	1992	4826834	2835728	1991106
1993	1993	5929236	3422107	2507129
1994	1994	8456974	4931262	3525712
1995	1995	9412635	5579637	3832998
1996	1996	11173672	6793007	4380665
1997	1997	13704735	8620710	5084025
1998	1998	15794106	10153634	5640472
1999	1999	16822436	10918827	5903609
2000	2000	19408338	12433214	6975124
2001	2001	22398464	14368582	8029882
2002	2002	25794324	14811106	10983218
2003	2003	31195595	17306539	13889056
2004	2004	39590783	21473202	18117581
2005	2005	50017829	24697792	25320037
2006	2006	59188120	28686826	30501294
2007	2007	74306364	33463071	40843293
2008	2008	89467300	37871227	51596073
2009	2009	102556155	42715781	59840374
2010	2010	116148345	44954630	71193715
2011	2011	132779629	50854938	81924691

12-3 续表 3
Continued

单位：万元（10 000 yuan）

年 份	Year	工业总产值 Gross Industrial Output Value	轻工业产值 Light Industry	重工业产值 Heavy Industry
2012	2012	153063174	60516341	92546833
2013	2013	168971805	66799317	102172488
2014	2014	174442125	67683545	106758580
2015	2015	180194299	71176748	109017551
2016	2016	174157133	68552071	105605062
2017	2017	130197343	48954201	81243142
2018	2018	113897787	39054621	74843166
"一五"时期合计	"First Five-Year Plan" Period	647974	437287	210687
"二五"时期合计	"Second Five-Year Plan" Period	1077075	388406	688669
1963-1965 年合计	1963-1965	532351	334279	198072
"三五"时期合计	"Third Five-Year Plan" Period	1481941	883485	598456
"四五"时期合计	"Fourth Five-Year Plan" Period	1761739	1107324	654415
"五五"时期合计	"Fifth Five-Year Plan" Period	2798882	1733413	1065469
"六五"时期合计	"Sixth Five-Year Plan" Period	4289187	2737084	1552103
"七五"时期合计	"Seventh Five-Year Plan" Period	12265142	7265939	4999204
"八五"时期合计	"Eighth Five-Year Plan" Period	32612106	19087323	13524783
"九五"时期合计	"Ninth Five-Year Plan" Period	76903287	48919392	27983895
"十五"时期合计	"Tenth Five-Year Plan" Period	168996995	92657221	76339774
"十一五"时期合计	"Eleventh Five-Year Plan" Period	175336465	73641456	101695009
"十二五"时期合计	"Twelfth Five-Year Plan" Period	809490422	317030889	492420143

12-4　规模以上工业企业主要指标（2021 年）
MAIN INDICATORS OF INDUSTRIAL ENTERPRISES ABOVE DESIGNATED SIZE（2021）

项　目	Indicator	企业单位数（个）Number of Enterprises（unit）
总　计	**Total**	**4280**
按注册登记类型分	**Grouped by Status of Registration**	
国有及国有控股企业	State-owned and State-holding Enterprises	254
集体企业	Collective-owned Enterprises	4
股份有限公司	Share-holding Corporations Ltd	102
外商投资企业	Foreign Funded Enterprises	628
港澳台商投资企业	Invested by HongKong, Macao and Taiwan	189
按轻重工业分	**Grouped by Light and Heavy Industries**	
轻工业	Light Industry	1597
重工业	Heavy Industry	2683
按企业规模分	**Grouped by Size of Enterprises**	
大型企业	Large	73
中型企业	Medium	391
小微型企业	Small & Micro-Enterprises	3816
按所在地分	**Grouped by Location**	
市南区	Shinan District	11
市北区	Shibei District	58
李沧区	Licang District	110
崂山区	Laoshan District	106
黄岛区（西海岸新区）	Huangdao District（West Coast New Area）	988
城阳区	Chengyang District	818
城阳区（不含高新区）	Chengyang District（Excluding High tech District）	670
高新区	High tech District	148
即墨区	Jimo District	569
胶州市	Jiaozhou	790
平度市	Pingdu	474
莱西市	Laixi	355
按行业分	**Grouped by sector**	
煤炭开采和洗选业	Mining and Washing of Coal	
石油和天然气开采业	Extraction of Petroleum and Natural Gas	
黑色金属矿采选业	Mining of Ferrous Metal Ores	
有色金属矿采选业	Mining of Non-ferrous Metal Ores	2
非金属矿采选业	Mining and Processing of Non-metal Ores	1
开采辅助活动	Auxiliary Activities of Mining	
其他采矿业	Mining of Other Ores	

单位：万元（10 000 yuan）

资产合计 Total Assets	流动资产年合计 Total Current Assets	固定资产净值 Net Value of Fixed Assets
129504092	**80287657**	**21546487**
48708607	28869345	10345126
250925	165556	45832
34374823	19609199	2024517
19229034	13395354	3396438
7383524	4898342	1497583
36808472	21323149	4398077
92695620	58964508	17148409
41902409	26384169	6432552
37002478	23681603	6986893
50599205	30221885	8127042
983857	332570	448332
4171412	2350746	859493
3422310	2181996	498760
6137420	4211243	539348
50098785	28894070	8821149
24276668	16565729	3320024
19158541	13268359	2577568
5118127	3297369	742457
12540708	7802704	2046905
12927137	9141945	1875330
8425455	4454414	1900385
6520341	4352240	1236761

12-4 续表 1
Continued

项 目	Indicator	营业收入 Revenue from Principal Business
总 计	**Total**	**115429470**
按注册登记类型分	**Grouped by Status of Registration**	
国有及国有控股企业	State-owned and State-holding Enterprises	40782052
集体企业	Collective-owned Enterprises	718417
股份有限公司	Share-holding Corporations Ltd	17289580
外商投资企业	Foreign Funded Enterprises	23177339
港澳台商投资企业	Invested by HongKong, Macao and Taiwan	6350420
按轻重工业分	**Grouped by Light and Heavy Industries**	
轻工业	Light Industry	35309592
重工业	Heavy Industry	80119878
按企业规模分	**Grouped by Size of Enterprises**	
大型企业	Large	39379048
中型企业	Medium	33933960
小微型企业	Small & Micro-Enterprises	42116462
按所在地分	**Grouped by Location**	
市南区	Shinan District	361096
市北区	Shibei District	4432425
李沧区	Licang District	4036010
崂山区	Laoshan District	4089295
黄岛区（西海岸新区）	Huangdao District（West Coast New Area）	42789889
城阳区	Chengyang District	18479798
城阳区（不含高新区）	Chengyang District（Excluding High tech District）	14949880
高新区	High tech District	3529919
即墨区	Jimo District	14437040
胶州市	Jiaozhou	11744222
平度市	Pingdu	9416023
莱西市	Laixi	5643673
按行业分	**Grouped by sector**	
煤炭开采和洗选业	Mining and Washing of Coal	
石油和天然气开采业	Extraction of Petroleum and Natural Gas	
黑色金属矿采选业	Mining of Ferrous Metal Ores	
有色金属矿采选业	Mining of Non ferrous Metal Ores	
非金属矿采选业	Mining and Processing of Non-metal Ores	
开采辅助活动	Auxiliary Activities of Mining	
其他采矿业	Mining of Other Ores	

单位：万元（10 000 yuan）

营业成本 Cost of Principal Business	营业税金及附加 Taxes and Extra Charges on Principal Business	利润总额 Total Profits	全部从业人员年平均人数（人） Annual Average Employed Persons (person)
98383602	**1865095**	**5780290**	**689001**
34765983	1569754	2286097	129256
655887	2465	-29229	3592
14450008	130546	1187740	80367
19533020	106640	1535163	156065
5396700	27466	328165	43363
30112687	196864	1664183	269853
68270915	1668232	4116107	419148
34285109	220814	2274808	168394
27543442	1469598	2116280	211328
36555051	174683	1389203	309279
349504	10145	-7254	3066
4108643	19749	135443	14588
3233050	382421	214750	17445
3233648	26247	286245	23039
35990775	1159587	2681018	187128
15189339	86690	1272185	136830
12459936	69570	902379	111689
2729403	17120	369806	25141
12971257	49711	446644	96216
10205346	48799	364690	94276
8241983	59908	265647	71880
4860059	21837	120923	44533

12-4 续表 2
Continued

项　目	Indicator	企业单位数(个) Number of Enterprises (unit)
农副食品加工业	Processing of Food from Agricultural Products	319
食品制造业	Manufacture of Foods	159
酒、饮料和精制茶制造业	Manufacture of Liquor，Beverages and Refined Tea	18
烟草制品业	Manufacture of Tobacco	
纺织业	Manufacture of Textile	140
纺织服装、服饰业	Manufacture of Textile Wearing Apparel	126
皮革、毛皮、羽毛及其制品和制鞋业	Processing of Leather, Fur, Feather & Its Products Footwear	31
木材加工和木、竹、藤、棕、草制品业	Processing of Timber, Manufacture of Wood, Bamboo, Rattan, Palm and Straw Products	52
家具制造业	Manufacture of Furniture	64
造纸和纸制品业	Manufacture of Paper and Paper Products	57
印刷和记录媒介复制业	Printing, Reproduction of Recording Media	97
文教、工美、体育和娱乐用品制造业	Manufacture of Articles for Culture, Arts & Crafts, Sports and Entertainment	107
石油、煤炭及其他燃料加工业	Oil, coal and other fuel processing industries	13
化学原料和化学制品制造业	Manufacture of Chemical Raw Material and Chemical Products	172
医药制造业	Manufacture of Medicines	50
化学纤维制造业	Manufacture of Chemical Fibres	8
橡胶和塑料制品业	Manufacture of Rubber and Plastic	362
非金属矿物制品业	Manufacture of metallic Mineral Products	344
黑色金属冶炼和压延加工业	Smelting and Pressing of Ferrous Metals	32
有色金属冶炼和压延加工业	Smelting and Pressing of Nonferrous Metals	33
金属制品业	Manufacture of Metal Products	402
通用设备制造业	Manufacture of General Purpose Machinery	369
专用设备制造业	Manufacture of Special Purpose Machinery	320
汽车制造业	Manufacture of Vehicle	253
铁路、船舶、航空航天和其他运输设备制造业	Manufacture of Transport Equipment for Railway, Shipping, Aerospace and other uses	191
电气机械和器材制造业	Manufacture of Electrical Machinery and Equipment	211
计算机、通信和其他电子设备制造业	Manufacture of Compute, Communication Equipment and Other Electronic Equipment	130
仪器仪表制造业	Manufacture of Measuring Instrument	73
其他制造业	Manufacture of Other Products	14
废弃资源综合利用业	Recycling and Disposal of Waste Resources	5
金属制品、机械和设备修理业	Manufacture of Metal Products, Machinery and Equipment	8
电力、热力生产和供应业	Production and Supply of Electric Power and Heat Power	71
燃气生产和供应业	Production and Supply of Gas	17
水的生产和供应业	Production and Supply of Water	29

单位：万元（10 000 yuan）

资产合计 Total Assets	流动资产合计 Total Current Assets	固定资产净值 Net Value of Fixed Assets
4719796	3590943	602610
3680591	2522560	714855
3735286	1989218	324747
1048016	726870	178241
1754194	1004144	183217
259208	194880	49012
257215	179568	47659
529974	431710	53316
436324	291984	78046
849832	567189	200034
870057	578380	137989
2953595	2292052	520341
7986174	3992683	2239445
2040516	1220291	372919
85526	43239	18168
6398970	3775957	1572559
5961192	4633573	844437
2800451	1165871	866484
592993	205452	221188
6324381	4003828	899705
7606908	5541396	1100374
8545548	6275968	865430
8758334	6491203	1370943
15658801	10495230	2042254
16980048	8489986	1008741
6747672	4931807	759465
1772702	1281215	118124
158384	107382	32343
36986	24307	5360
64712	59295	3417
6198792	2052089	2284238
1607286	330516	945576
1975960	769641	835478

12-4　续表 3
Continued

项　目	Indicator	营业收入 Revenue from Principal Business
农副食品加工业	Processing of Food from Agricultural Products	9469356
食品制造业	Manufacture of Foods	2930397
酒、饮料和精制茶制造业	Manufacture of Liquor，Beverages and Refined Tea	2655113
烟草制品业	Manufacture of Tobacco	
纺织业	Manufacture of Textile	1639242
纺织服装、服饰业	Manufacture of Textile Wearing Apparel	1625899
皮革、毛皮、羽毛及其制品和制鞋业	Processing of Leather, Fur, Feather & Its Products Footwear	361411
木材加工和木、竹、藤、棕、草制品业	Processing of Timber, Manufacture of Wood, Bamboo, Rattan, Palm and Straw Products	298351
家具制造业	Manufacture of Furniture	615059
造纸和纸制品业	Manufacture of Paper and Paper Products	568420
印刷和记录媒介复制业	Printing, Reproduction of Recording Media	961472
文教、工美、体育和娱乐用品制造业	Manufacture of Articles for Culture, Arts & Crafts, Sports and Entertainment	1034309
石油、煤炭及其他燃料加工业	Oil, coal and other fuel processing industries	7298561
化学原料和化学制品制造业	Manufacture of Chemical Raw Material and Chemical Products	7029866
医药制造业	Manufacture of Medicines	1197791
化学纤维制造业	Manufacture of Chemical Fibres	70761
橡胶和塑料制品业	Manufacture of Rubber and Plastic	5011888
非金属矿物制品业	Manufacture of metallic Mineral Products	4355817
黑色金属冶炼和压延加工业	Smelting and Pressing of Ferrous Metals	4021012
有色金属冶炼和压延加工业	Smelting and Pressing of Nonferrous Metals	1067594
金属制品业	Manufacture of Metal Products	6631258
通用设备制造业	Manufacture of General Purpose Machinery	6375215
专用设备制造业	Manufacture of Special Purpose Machinery	5521959
汽车制造业	Manufacture of Vehicle	12316680
铁路、船舶、航空航天和其他运输设备制造业	Manufacture of Transport Equipment for Railway, Shipping, Aerospace and other uses	7937326
电气机械和器材制造业	Manufacture of Electrical Machinery and Equipment	11924096
计算机、通信和其他电子设备制造业	Manufacture of Compute, Communication Equipment and Other Electronic Equipment	7757692
仪器仪表制造业	Manufacture of Measuring Instrument	1178070
其他制造业	Manufacture of Other Products	151735
废弃资源综合利用业	Recycling and Disposal of Waste Resources	107381
金属制品、机械和设备修理业	Manufacture of Metal Products, Machinery and Equipment	58044
电力、热力生产和供应业	Production and Supply of Electric Power and Heat Power	1771582
燃气生产和供应业	Production and Supply of Gas	1031590
水的生产和供应业	Production and Supply of Water	419141

单位：万元（10 000 yuan）

营业成本 Cost of Principal Business	营业税金及附加 Taxes and Extra Charges on Principal Business	利润总额 Total Profits	全部从业人员年平均人数（人） Annual Average Employed Persons (person)
8941231	13237	97435	43466
2307296	14492	201333	18147
2095553	77000	241410	15941
1463889	6861	47126	16679
1426911	9709	51873	33189
323219	1865	-19506	10611
270747	1462	-2815	3560
519672	2702	19197	8731
521627	1543	5510	4632
807366	4359	48992	10760
875416	4947	38565	16547
5290512	1345610	617013	2325
5818415	26091	554125	22456
556403	12487	230740	10578
60251	518	3818	752
4291079	21680	185651	48923
3698287	23202	208174	27202
3627021	13036	212301	8509
975437	5092	23530	2671
5703172	29829	401215	43117
5257122	27095	309940	58178
4304421	25856	443663	42114
11293266	45101	282501	49536
6696324	46702	512206	54727
10104613	40366	673066	56110
6961114	22623	264399	42378
800688	7264	145390	11468
134784	1023	7055	4188
103161	1384	940	89
40665	323	7566	664
1867392	13322	-209360	13103
821286	2684	144684	2531
404855	14334	25874	4736

12-5 按行业分国有控股工业企业主要指标（2021 年）
MAIN INDICATORS OF STATE-HOLDING INDUSTRIAL ENTERPRISES BY INDUSTRIAL SECTOR（2021）

项　目	Indicator	企业单位数（个）Number of Enterprises (unit)
总　计	**Total**	**226**
煤炭开采和洗选业	Mining and Washing of Coal	
石油和天然气开采业	Extraction of Petroleum and Natural Gas	
黑色金属矿采选业	Mining of Ferrous Metal Ores	
有色金属矿采选业	Mining of Non-ferrous Metal Ores	2
非金属矿采选业	Mining and Processing of Non-metal Ores	1
开采辅助活动	Auxiliary Activities of Mining	
其他采矿业	Mining of Other Ores	
农副食品加工业	Processing of Food from Agricultural Products	2
食品制造业	Manufacture of Foods	5
酒、饮料和精制茶制造业	Manufacture of Liquor， Beverages and Refined Tea	3
烟草制品业	Manufacture of Tobacco	
纺织业	Manufacture of Textile	
纺织服装、服饰业	Manufacture of Textile Wearing Apparel	1
皮革、毛皮、羽毛及其制品和制鞋业	Manufacture of Leather, Fur, Feather & Its Products Footwear	
木材加工和木、竹、藤、棕、草制品业	Processing of Timber, Manufacture of Wood, Bamboo, Rattan, Palm and Straw Products	2
家具制造业	Manufacture of Furniture	
造纸和纸制品业	Manufacture of Paper and Paper Products	1
印刷和记录媒介复制业	Printing, Reproduction of Recording Media	2
文教、工美、体育和娱乐用品制造业	Manufacture of Articles for Culture, Arts & Crafts, Sports and Entertainment	
石油、煤炭及其他燃料加工业	Oil, coal and other fuel processing industries	2
化学原料和化学制品制造业	Manufacture of Chemical Raw Material and Chemical Products	10
医药制造业	Manufacture of Medicines	4
化学纤维制造业	Manufacture of Chemical Fibres	
橡胶和塑料制品业	Manufacture of Rubber and Plastic	5
非金属矿物制品业	Manufacture of metallic Mineral Products	13
黑色金属冶炼和压延加工业	Smelting and Pressing of Ferrous Metals	7
有色金属冶炼和压延加工业	Smelting and Pressing of Non-ferrous Metals	5
金属制品业	Manufacture of Metal Products	11
通用设备制造业	Manufacture of General Purpose Machinery	15
专用设备制造业	Manufacture of Special Purpose Machinery	17
汽车制造业	Manufacture of Vehicle	8
铁路、船舶、航空航天和其他运输设备制造业	Manufacture of Transport Equipment for Railway, Shipping, Aerospace and other uses	17
电气机械和器材制造业	Manufacture of Electrical Machinery and Equipment	8
计算机、通信和其他电子设备制造业	Manufacture of Computer, Communication Equipment and Other Electronic Equipment	9
仪器仪表制造业	Manufacture of Measuring Instrument	3
其他制造业	Manufacture of Other Products	
废弃资源综合利用业	Recycling and Disposal of Waste Resources	1
金属制品、机械和设备修理业	Manufacture of Metal Products, Machinery and Equipment	2
电力、热力生产和供应业	Production and Supply of Electric Power and Heat Power	45
燃气生产和供应业	Production and Supply of Gas	6
水的生产和供应业	Production and Supply of Water	19

单位：万元（10 000 yuan）

资产合计 Total Assets	流动资产合计 Total Current Assets	固定资产净值 Net Value of Fixed Assets
46351210	**27497969**	**9724741**
261463	179591	50367
3430523	1799270	249600
2023455	531332	945564
804414	447356	133560
869529	478697	323516
433031	353448	55102
2343106	805420	796184
373379	43577	190001
903964	638448	214535
612462	462282	87582
2113713	1629738	237787
4261583	3499567	489243
12877054	8503427	1680446
833612	540128	126796
2857821	2364046	109783
317854	286959	17267
4969496	1683595	2017360
1045885	148889	644189
1816027	682431	788011

12-5 续表
Continued

项 目	Indicator	营业收入 Revenue from Principal Business
总 计	**Total**	**39098549**
煤炭开采和洗选业	Mining and Washing of Coal	
石油和天然气开采业	Extraction of Petroleum and Natural Gas	
黑色金属矿采选业	Mining of Ferrous Metal Ores	
有色金属矿采选业	Mining of Non-ferrous Metal Ores	
非金属矿采选业	Mining and Processing of Non-metal Ores	
开采辅助活动	Auxiliary Activities of Mining	
其他采矿业	Mining of Other Ores	
农副食品加工业	Processing of Food from Agricultural Products	
食品制造业	Manufacture of Foods	135135
酒、饮料和精制茶制造业	Manufacture of Liquor， Beverages and Refined Tea	2401216
烟草制品业	Manufacture of Tobacco	
纺织业	Manufacture of Textile	
纺织服装、服饰业	Manufacture of Textile Wearing Apparel	
皮革、毛皮、羽毛及其制品和制鞋业	Manufacture of Leather, Fur, Feather & Its Products Footwear	
木材加工和木、竹、藤、棕、草制品业	Processing of Timber, Manufacture of Wood, Bamboo, Rattan, Palm and Straw Products	
家具制造业	Manufacture of Furniture	
造纸和纸制品业	Manufacture of Paper and Paper Products	
印刷和记录媒介复制业	Printing, Reproduction of Recording Media	
文教、工美、体育和娱乐用品制造业	Manufacture of Articles for Culture, Arts & Crafts, Sports and Entertainment	
石油、煤炭及其他燃料加工业	Oil, coal and other fuel processing industries	
化学原料和化学制品制造业	Manufacture of Chemical Raw Material and Chemical Products	1776988
医药制造业	Manufacture of Medicines	348628
化学纤维制造业	Manufacture of Chemical Fibres	
橡胶和塑料制品业	Manufacture of Rubber and Plastic	391429
非金属矿物制品业	Manufacture of metallic Mineral Products	351821
黑色金属冶炼和压延加工业	Smelting and Pressing of Ferrous Metals	2832364
有色金属冶炼和压延加工业	Smelting and Pressing of Non-ferrous Metals	185858
金属制品业	Manufacture of Metal Products	1047166
通用设备制造业	Manufacture of General Purpose Machinery	365351
专用设备制造业	Manufacture of Special Purpose Machinery	1274683
汽车制造业	Manufacture of Vehicle	7540726
铁路、船舶、航空航天和其他运输设备制造业	Manufacture of Transport Equipment for Railway, Shipping, Aerospace and other uses	6288484
电气机械和器材制造业	Manufacture of Electrical Machinery and Equipment	533002
计算机、通信和其他电子设备制造业	Manufacture of Computer, Communication Equipment and Other Electronic Equipment	3788370
仪器仪表制造业	Manufacture of Measuring Instrument	157475
其他制造业	Manufacture of Other Products	
废弃资源综合利用业	Recycling and Disposal of Waste Resources	
金属制品、机械和设备修理业	Manufacture of Metal Products, Machinery and Equipment	
电力、热力生产和供应业	Production and Supply of Electric Power and Heat Power	1498568
燃气生产和供应业	Production and Supply of Gas	387992
水的生产和供应业	Production and Supply of Water	365770

单位：万元（10 000 yuan）

营业成本 Cost of Principal Business	营业税金及附加 Taxes and Extra Charges on Principal Business	利润总额 Total Profits	全部从业人员年平均人数（人） Annual Average Employed Persons (person)
33289503	**1563433**	**2193988**	**119289**
114784	913	10795	1040
1924682	70519	216329	13439
1338790	7446	300067	4005
133407	4208	81582	2628
376321	1992	-16879	3282
310697	1759	15659	1155
2497298	11483	191631	6360
139805	4110	19194	1048
879768	6510	100814	5583
329726	1437	-3014	2820
1027658	4725	71988	5661
7119846	25736	119388	9699
5348710	34971	437325	26521
479722	4638	18857	5093
3458294	9646	110192	8191
111602	868	13642	1440
1672683	10302	-240347	11210
263035	1828	105883	1049
371909	13869	10320	4318

12-6 按行业分规模以上外商投资和港澳台商投资工业企业主要指标（2021年）
MAIN INDICATORS OF FOREIGN FUNDED ENTERPRISES AND ENTERPRISES WITH FUNDS FROM HONG KONG, MACAO AND TAIWAN ABOVE DESIGNATED SIZE BY INDUSTRIAL SECTOR（2021）

项　目	Indicator	企业单位数（个）Number of Enterprises（Unit）
总　计	**Total**	**817**
煤炭开采和洗选业	Mining and Washing of Coal	
石油和天然气开采业	Extraction of Petroleum and Natural Gas	
黑色金属矿采选业	Mining of Ferrous Metal Ores	
有色金属矿采选业	Mining of Non-ferrous Metal Ores	
非金属矿采选业	Mining and Processing of Non-metal Ores	
开采辅助活动	Auxiliary Activities of Mining	
其他采矿业	Mining of Other Ores	
农副食品加工业	Processing of Food from Agricultural Products	73
食品制造业	Manufacture of Foods	35
酒、饮料和精制茶制造业	Manufacture of Liquor, Beverages and Refined Tea	7
烟草制品业	Manufacture of Tobacco	
纺织业	Manufacture of Textile	39
纺织服装、服饰业	Manufacture of Textile Wearing Apparel	39
皮革、毛皮、羽毛及其制品和制鞋业	Manufacture of Leather, Fur, Feather & Its Products Footwear	12
木材加工和木、竹、藤、棕、草制品业	Processing of Timber, Manufacture of Wood, Bamboo, Rattan, Palm and Straw Products	5
家具制造业	Manufacture of Furniture	16
造纸和纸制品业	Manufacture of Paper and Paper Products	11
印刷和记录媒介复制业	Printing, Reproduction of Recording Media	15
文教、工美、体育和娱乐用品制造业	Manufacture of Articles for Culture, Arts & Crafts, Sports and Entertainment	33
石油、煤炭及其他燃料加工业	Oil, coal and other fuel processing industries	1
化学原料和化学制品制造业	Manufacture of Chemical Raw Material and Chemical Products	44
医药制造业	Manufacture of Medicines	11
化学纤维制造业	Manufacture of Chemical Fibres	2
橡胶和塑料制品业	Manufacture of Rubber and Plastic	54
非金属矿物制品业	Manufacture of metallic Mineral Products	34
黑色金属冶炼和压延加工业	Smelting and Pressing of Ferrous Metals	7
有色金属冶炼和压延加工业	Smelting and Pressing of Non-ferrous Metals	2
金属制品业	Manufacture of Metal Products	54
通用设备制造业	Manufacture of General Purpose Machinery	69
专用设备制造业	Manufacture of Special Purpose Machinery	50
汽车制造业	Manufacture of Vehicle	61
铁路、船舶、航空航天和其他运输设备制造业	Manufacture of Transport Equipment for Railway, Shipping, Aerospace and other uses	26
电气机械和器材制造业	Manufacture of Electrical Machinery and Equipment	32
计算机、通信和其他电子设备制造业	Manufacture of Computer, Communication Equipment and Other Electronic Equipment	48
仪器仪表制造业	Manufacture of Measuring Instrument	11
其他制造业	Manufacture of Other Products	4
废弃资源综合利用业	Recycling and Disposal of Waste Resources	
金属制品、机械和设备修理业	Manufacture of Metal Products, Machinery and Equipment	2
电力、热力生产和供应业	Production and Supply of Electric Power and Heat Power	6
燃气生产和供应业	Production and Supply of Gas	9
水的生产和供应业	Production and Supply of Water	5

单位：万元（10 000 yuan）

资产合计 Total Assets	流动资产合计 Total Current Assets	固定资产净值 Net Value of Fixed Assets
26612558	**18293695**	**4894021**
1695847	1365728	194630
2298593	1594625	472361
215834	153066	35638
391233	295949	58924
457782	354074	45796
137266	96251	35110
48977	38938	8177
152888	122040	23114
167305	119122	38715
290260	206322	46143
585810	376923	92641
2487838	1356105	539044
345007	244500	81177
1045102	592446	405536
756188	487249	210266
220354	174347	35148
1213825	852638	261902
1922355	1410628	397606
1741473	1310211	268376
3129470	2500640	472932
2082137	1620412	208734
2427130	1283314	246120
1454222	980618	308018
428241	351683	21237
114818	68926	28911
244069	57992	136919
319066	147806	132798
152178	66071	70002

12-6 续表
Continued

项　目	Indicator	营业收入 Revenue from Principal Business
总　计	**Total**	**29527759**
煤炭开采和洗选业	Mining and Washing of Coal	
石油和天然气开采业	Extraction of Petroleum and Natural Gas	
黑色金属矿采选业	Mining of Ferrous Metal Ores	
有色金属矿采选业	Mining of Non-ferrous Metal Ores	
非金属矿采选业	Mining and Processing of Non-metal Ores	
开采辅助活动	Auxiliary Activities of Mining	
其他采矿业	Mining of Other Ores	
农副食品加工业	Processing of Food from Agricultural Products	3381861
食品制造业	Manufacture of Foods	1623803
酒、饮料和精制茶制造业	Manufacture of Liquor, Beverages and Refined Tea	188034
烟草制品业	Manufacture of Tobacco	
纺织业	Manufacture of Textile	560016
纺织服装、服饰业	Manufacture of Textile Wearing Apparel	648751
皮革、毛皮、羽毛及其制品和制鞋业	Manufacture of Leather, Fur, Feather & Its Products Footwear	247718
木材加工和木、竹、藤、棕、草制品业	Processing of Timber, Manufacture of Wood, Bamboo, Rattan, Palm and Straw Products	29465
家具制造业	Manufacture of Furniture	194262
造纸和纸制品业	Manufacture of Paper and Paper Products	181564
印刷和记录媒介复制业	Printing, Reproduction of Recording Media	340331
文教、工美、体育和娱乐用品制造业	Manufacture of Articles for Culture, Arts & Crafts, Sports and Entertainment	544526
石油、煤炭及其他燃料加工业	Oil, coal and other fuel processing industries	
化学原料和化学制品制造业	Manufacture of Chemical Raw Material and Chemical Products	2418699
医药制造业	Manufacture of Medicines	249164
化学纤维制造业	Manufacture of Chemical Fibres	
橡胶和塑料制品业	Manufacture of Rubber and Plastic	1012772
非金属矿物制品业	Manufacture of metallic Mineral Products	623783
黑色金属冶炼和压延加工业	Smelting and Pressing of Ferrous Metals	504091
有色金属冶炼和压延加工业	Smelting and Pressing of Non-ferrous Metals	
金属制品业	Manufacture of Metal Products	1894988
通用设备制造业	Manufacture of General Purpose Machinery	2132926
专用设备制造业	Manufacture of Special Purpose Machinery	1499485
汽车制造业	Manufacture of Vehicle	3659617
铁路、船舶、航空航天和其他运输设备制造业	Manufacture of Transport Equipment for Railway, Shipping, Aerospace and other uses	812542
电气机械和器材制造业	Manufacture of Electrical Machinery and Equipment	3650129
计算机、通信和其他电子设备制造业	Manufacture of Computer, Communication Equipment and Other Electronic Equipment	1921883
仪器仪表制造业	Manufacture of Measuring Instrument	431964
其他制造业	Manufacture of Other Products	107607
废弃资源综合利用业	Recycling and Disposal of Waste Resources	
金属制品、机械和设备修理业	Manufacture of Metal Products, Machinery and Equipment	
电力、热力生产和供应业	Production and Supply of Electric Power and Heat Power	48843
燃气生产和供应业	Production and Supply of Gas	500883
水的生产和供应业	Production and Supply of Water	46722

单位：万元（10 000 yuan）

营业成本 Cost of Principal Business	营业税金及附加 Taxes and Extra Charges on Principal Business	利润总额 Total Profits	全部从业人员年平均人数（人） Annual Average Employed Persons (person)
24929721	**134107**	**1863328**	**199428**
3212041	4015	49974	13901
1200172	9107	151807	6548
132453	2576	9786	1636
487380	3359	19410	6724
582667	3491	12380	12640
227454	1188	-21169	7099
26308	173	-536	385
166626	1059	5653	3521
162771	761	1606	1410
279640	1763	23455	3888
459518	2759	20550	9572
2057855	9332	98932	7466
138446	3169	49353	1425
831702	5540	44979	11352
503922	3798	48297	3714
471382	964	16398	1089
1551570	9452	235115	11834
1743636	8748	131846	17113
1210507	6537	99360	10526
3216489	22229	169582	18044
623880	6387	119030	8812
3044097	14995	316126	13570
1655297	6972	119326	19008
274646	2661	77099	2355
99432	772	2570	3627
22426	512	19965	264
460500	613	28118	873
28526	705	9190	324

12-7 按行业分大中型工业企业主要指标（2021年）

MAIN INDICATORS OF LARGE AND MEDIUM-SIZED INDUSTRIAL ENTERPRISES BY INDUSTRIAL SECTOR (2021)

项 目	Indicator	企业单位数（个） Number of Enterprises (Unit)
总 计	**Total**	**464**
煤炭开采和洗选业	Mining and Washing of Coal	
石油和天然气开采业	Extraction of Petroleum and Natural Gas	
黑色金属矿采选业	Mining of Ferrous Metal Ores	
有色金属矿采选业	Mining of Non-ferrous Metal Ores	
非金属矿采选业	Mining and Processing of Non-metal Ores	
开采辅助活动	Auxiliary Activities of Mining	
其他采矿业	Mining of Other Ores	
农副食品加工业	Processing of Food from Agricultural Products	31
食品制造业	Manufacture of Foods	14
酒、饮料和精制茶制造业	Manufacture of Liquor, Beverages and Refined Tea	4
烟草制品业	Manufacture of Tobacco	
纺织业	Manufacture of Textile	10
纺织服装、服饰业	Manufacture of Textile Wearing Apparel	28
皮革、毛皮、羽毛及其制品和制鞋业	Manufacture of Leather, Fur, Feather & Its Products Footwear	8
木材加工和木、竹、藤、棕、草制品业	Processing of Timber, Manufacture of Wood, Bamboo, Rattan, Palm and Straw Products	3
家具制造业	Manufacture of Furniture	8
造纸和纸制品业	Manufacture of Paper and Paper Products	1
印刷和记录媒介复制业	Printing, Reproduction of Recording Media	6
文教、工美、体育和娱乐用品制造业	Manufacture of Articles for Culture, Arts & Crafts, Sports and Entertainment	13
石油、煤炭及其他燃料加工业	Oil, coal and other fuel processing industries	2
化学原料和化学制品制造业	Manufacture of Chemical Raw Material and Chemical Products	18
医药制造业	Manufacture of Medicines	9
化学纤维制造业	Manufacture of Chemical Fibres	
橡胶和塑料制品业	Manufacture of Rubber and Plastic	23
非金属矿物制品业	Manufacture of metallic Mineral Products	12
黑色金属冶炼和压延加工业	Smelting and Pressing of Ferrous Metals	4
有色金属冶炼和压延加工业	Smelting and Pressing of Non-ferrous Metals	2
金属制品业	Manufacture of Metal Products	25
通用设备制造业	Manufacture of General Purpose Machinery	50
专用设备制造业	Manufacture of Special Purpose Machinery	32
汽车制造业	Manufacture of Vehicle	34
铁路、船舶、航空航天和其他运输设备制造业	Manufacture of Transport Equipment for Railway, Shipping, Aerospace and other uses	30
电气机械和器材制造业	Manufacture of Electrical Machinery and Equipment	38
计算机、通信和其他电子设备制造业	Manufacture of Computer, Communication Equipment and Other Electronic Equipment	34
仪器仪表制造业	Manufacture of Measuring Instrument	8
其他制造业	Manufacture of Other Products	1
废弃资源综合利用业	Recycling and Disposal of Waste Resources	
金属制品、机械和设备修理业	Manufacture of Metal Products, Machinery and Equipment	
电力、热力生产和供应业	Production and Supply of Electric Power and Heat Power	12
燃气生产和供应业	Production and Supply of Gas	2
水的生产和供应业	Production and Supply of Water	2

单位：万元（10 000 yuan）

资产合计 Total Assets	流动资产合计 Total Current Assets	固定资产净值 Net Value of Fixed Assets
78904887	**50065772**	**13419445**
1993818	1505146	221902
2228965	1586332	416944
3531497	1872797	270790
309766	235963	40071
1203857	649746	105571
167591	119802	36216
66150	27065	27878
259453	231031	14689
195776	143210	35897
481102	302117	79055
5723169	2451890	1836839
1429781	880811	243617
4214868	2253834	1120769
840526	600167	166329
2293020	750310	806421
2700215	1748830	386093
4946245	3585091	684997
4808682	3626324	381206
5784583	4324961	786305
13472019	9170883	1797963
8327752	5548487	849055
5214767	3865361	553173
1104081	737133	67109
3085485	1228968	1151123

12-7 续表
Continued

项 目	Indicator	营业收入 Revenue from Principal Business
总 计	**Total**	**73313008**
煤炭开采和洗选业	Mining and Washing of Coal	
石油和天然气开采业	Extraction of Petroleum and Natural Gas	
黑色金属矿采选业	Mining of Ferrous Metal Ores	
有色金属矿采选业	Mining of Non-ferrous Metal Ores	
非金属矿采选业	Mining and Processing of Non-metal Ores	
开采辅助活动	Auxiliary Activities of Mining	
其他采矿业	Mining of Other Ores	
农副食品加工业	Processing of Food from Agricultural Products	3882956
食品制造业	Manufacture of Foods	1529708
酒、饮料和精制茶制造业	Manufacture of Liquor，Beverages and Refined Tea	2559893
烟草制品业	Manufacture of Tobacco	
纺织业	Manufacture of Textile	569189
纺织服装、服饰业	Manufacture of Textile Wearing Apparel	1049937
皮革、毛皮、羽毛及其制品和制鞋业	Manufacture of Leather, Fur, Feather & Its Products Footwear	232655
木材加工和木、竹、藤、棕、草制品业	Processing of Timber, Manufacture of Wood, Bamboo, Rattan, Palm and Straw Products	43554
家具制造业	Manufacture of Furniture	348432
造纸和纸制品业	Manufacture of Paper and Paper Products	
印刷和记录媒介复制业	Printing, Reproduction of Recording Media	232335
文教、工美、体育和娱乐用品制造业	Manufacture of Articles for Culture, Arts & Crafts, Sports and Entertainment	458558
石油、煤炭及其他燃料加工业	Oil, coal and other fuel processing industries	
化学原料和化学制品制造业	Manufacture of Chemical Raw Material and Chemical Products	4409669
医药制造业	Manufacture of Medicines	817086
化学纤维制造业	Manufacture of Chemical Fibres	
橡胶和塑料制品业	Manufacture of Rubber and Plastic	2129357
非金属矿物制品业	Manufacture of metallic Mineral Products	571544
黑色金属冶炼和压延加工业	Smelting and Pressing of Ferrous Metals	2592239
有色金属冶炼和压延加工业	Smelting and Pressing of Non-ferrous Metals	
金属制品业	Manufacture of Metal Products	3154770
通用设备制造业	Manufacture of General Purpose Machinery	3972478
专用设备制造业	Manufacture of Special Purpose Machinery	2993359
汽车制造业	Manufacture of Vehicle	9585339
铁路、船舶、航空航天和其他运输设备制造业	Manufacture of Transport Equipment for Railway, Shipping, Aerospace and other uses	6714927
电气机械和器材制造业	Manufacture of Electrical Machinery and Equipment	9807527
计算机、通信和其他电子设备制造业	Manufacture of Computer, Communication Equipment and Other Electronic Equipment	6348378
仪器仪表制造业	Manufacture of Measuring Instrument	532903
其他制造业	Manufacture of Other Products	
废弃资源综合利用业	Recycling and Disposal of Waste Resources	
金属制品、机械和设备修理业	Manufacture of Metal Products, Machinery and Equipment	
电力、热力生产和供应业	Production and Supply of Electric Power and Heat Power	1046957
燃气生产和供应业	Production and Supply of Gas	
水的生产和供应业	Production and Supply of Water	

单位：万元（10 000 yuan）

营业成本 Cost of Principal Business	营业税金及附加 Taxes and Extra Charges on Principal Business	利润总额 Total Profits	全部从业人员年平均人数（人） Annual Average Employed Persons (person)
61828551	**1690412**	**4391087**	**379722**
3703976	5540	19920	24131
1121408	7843	160460	6840
2037776	71608	224407	14708
508161	2279	28213	5037
910919	6411	53456	22669
203509	1478	1223	7835
36819	541	-2168	1259
285336	1737	15211	4053
184797	1221	20245	2807
378621	2283	24418	8086
3661415	14666	397116	10766
309893	9947	201662	6518
1808182	10768	95100	21136
481020	2753	36036	5341
2255215	11528	195133	6505
2630565	15149	355347	17194
3275166	15554	221110	31464
2314426	14449	297655	18736
8844510	33000	263993	26165
5695316	39472	426661	41582
8240055	34777	584879	42013
5705275	17960	244223	32525
350063	3612	84119	4642
1198002	7311	-194153	7699

12-8　按行业分规模以上工业企业主要经济效益指标（2021 年）
MAIN INDICATORS ON ECONOMIC BENEFIT OF INDUSTRIAL ENTERPRISES ABOVE DESIGNATED SIZE BY INDUSTRIAL SECTOR （2021）

项　目	Indicator	总资产贡献率（%） Ratio of Total Assets to Industrial Output Value（%）
总　计	**Total**	**7.55**
煤炭开采和洗选业	Mining and Washing of Coal	
石油和天然气开采业	Extraction of Petroleum and Natural Gas	
黑色金属矿采选业	Mining of Ferrous Metal Ores	
有色金属矿采选业	Mining of Non-ferrous Metal Ores	
非金属矿采选业	Mining and Processing of Non-metal Ores	
开采辅助活动	Auxiliary Activities of Mining	
其他采矿业	Mining of Other Ores	
农副食品加工业	Processing of Food from Agricultural Products	3.38
食品制造业	Manufacture of Foods	8.01
酒、饮料和精制茶制造业	Manufacture of Liquor，Beverages and Refined Tea	10.49
烟草制品业	Manufacture of Tobacco	
纺织业	Manufacture of Textile	7.12
纺织服装、服饰业	Manufacture of Textile Wearing Apparel	5.3
皮革、毛皮、羽毛及其制品和制鞋业	Manufacture of Leather, Fur, Feather & Its Products Footwear	-5.8
木材加工和木、竹、藤、棕、草制品业	Processing of Timber, Manufacture of Wood, Bamboo, Rattan, Palm and Straw Products	1.19
家具制造业	Manufacture of Furniture	7.04
造纸和纸制品业	Manufacture of Paper and Paper Products	3.54
印刷和记录媒介复制业	Printing, Reproduction of Recording Media	9.28
文教、工美、体育和娱乐用品制造业	Manufacture of Articles for Culture, Arts & Crafts, Sports and Entertainment	5.94
石油、煤炭及其他燃料加工业	Oil, coal and other fuel processing industries	73.15
化学原料和化学制品制造业	Manufacture of Chemical Raw Material and Chemical Products	9.16
医药制造业	Manufacture of Medicines	15.95
化学纤维制造业	Manufacture of Chemical Fibres	6.83
橡胶和塑料制品业	Manufacture of Rubber and Plastic	4.6
非金属矿物制品业	Manufacture of metallic Mineral Products	6.07
黑色金属冶炼和压延加工业	Smelting and Pressing of Ferrous Metals	9.77
有色金属冶炼和压延加工业	Smelting and Pressing of Non-ferrous Metals	6.07
金属制品业	Manufacture of Metal Products	8.32
通用设备制造业	Manufacture of General Purpose Machinery	5.72
专用设备制造业	Manufacture of Special Purpose Machinery	7.05
汽车制造业	Manufacture of Vehicle	5.95
铁路、船舶、航空航天和其他运输设备制造业	Manufacture of Transport Equipment for Railway, Shipping, Aerospace and other uses	4.68
电气机械和器材制造业	Manufacture of Electrical Machinery and Equipment	5.03
计算机、通信和其他电子设备制造业	Manufacture of Computer, Communication Equipment and Other Electronic Equipment	5.2
仪器仪表制造业	Manufacture of Measuring Instrument	11.05
其他制造业	Manufacture of Other Products	7.22
废弃资源综合利用业	Recycling and Disposal of Waste Resources	35.99
金属制品、机械和设备修理业	Manufacture of Metal Products, Machinery and Equipment	16.14
电力、热力生产和供应业	Production and Supply of Electric Power and Heat Power	-1.53
燃气生产和供应业	Production and Supply of Gas	11.32
水的生产和供应业	Production and Supply of Water	3.02

单位：万元（10 000 yuan）

资产负债率（%） Assets-Liability Ratio（%）	流动资产周转次数（次/年） Number of Times of Annual of Turnover Current Assets（time/year）	工业成本费用利润率（%） Ratio of Profits to Industrial Costs（%）
56.77	**1.44**	**5.3**
68.72	2.64	1.04
64.26	1.16	7.36
49.06	1.33	9.57
58.43	2.26	2.94
52.46	1.62	3.25
60.6	1.85	-5.32
74.12	1.66	-0.93
68.93	1.42	3.29
60.35	1.95	0.98
64.19	1.7	5.33
52.48	1.79	3.88
47.95	3.18	11.57
48.17	1.76	8.55
41.42	0.98	23.86
60.82	1.64	5.73
56.05	1.33	3.79
65.67	0.94	5.03
65.96	3.45	5.57
55.16	5.2	2.26
51.08	1.66	6.44
54.46	1.15	5.1
56.31	0.88	8.61
63.71	1.9	2.35
60.04	0.76	6.81
51.47	1.4	5.91
44.71	1.57	3.47
44.66	0.92	13.92
69.07	1.41	4.68
70.51	4.42	0.89
40.86	0.98	14.94
77.1	0.86	-10.28
49.54	3.12	15.93
61.47	0.54	5.51

12-9 按行业分国有控股工业企业主要经济效益指标（2021 年）
MAIN INDICATORS ON ECONOMIC BENEFIT OF STATE-OWNED AND STATE-HOLDING INDUSTRIAL ENTERPRISES BY INDUSTRIAL SECTOR （2021）

项　目	Indicator	总资产贡献率（%） Ratio of Total Assets to Industrial Output Value（%）
总　计	**Total**	**9.89**
煤炭开采和洗选业	Mining and Washing of Coal	
石油和天然气开采业	Extraction of Petroleum and Natural Gas	
黑色金属矿采选业	Mining of Ferrous Metal Ores	
有色金属矿采选业	Mining of Non-ferrous Metal Ores	
非金属矿采选业	Mining and Processing of Non-metal Ores	
开采辅助活动	Auxiliary Activities of Mining	
其他采矿业	Mining of Other Ores	
农副食品加工业	Processing of Food from Agricultural Products	
食品制造业	Manufacture of Foods	5.44
酒、饮料和精制茶制造业	Manufacture of Liquor， Beverages and Refined Tea	10.15
烟草制品业	Manufacture of Tobacco	
纺织业	Manufacture of Textile	
纺织服装、服饰业	Manufacture of Textile Wearing Apparel	
皮革、毛皮、羽毛及其制品和制鞋业	Manufacture of Leather, Fur, Feather & Its Products Footwear	
木材加工和木、竹、藤、棕、草制品业	Processing of Timber, Manufacture of Wood, Bamboo, Rattan, Palm and Straw Products	
家具制造业	Manufacture of Furniture	
造纸和纸制品业	Manufacture of Paper and Paper Products	
印刷和记录媒介复制业	Printing, Reproduction of Recording Media	
文教、工美、体育和娱乐用品制造业	Manufacture of Articles for Culture, Arts & Crafts, Sports and Entertainment	
石油、煤炭及其他燃料加工业	Oil, coal and other fuel processing industries	
化学原料和化学制品制造业	Manufacture of Chemical Raw Material and Chemical Products	16.86
医药制造业	Manufacture of Medicines	13.87
化学纤维制造业	Manufacture of Chemical Fibres	0.00
橡胶和塑料制品业	Manufacture of Rubber and Plastic	-0.35
非金属矿物制品业	Manufacture of metallic Mineral Products	6.91
黑色金属冶炼和压延加工业	Smelting and Pressing of Ferrous Metals	10.42
有色金属冶炼和压延加工业	Smelting and Pressing of Non-ferrous Metals	6.90
金属制品业	Manufacture of Metal Products	13.69
通用设备制造业	Manufacture of General Purpose Machinery	0.50
专用设备制造业	Manufacture of Special Purpose Machinery	5.45
汽车制造业	Manufacture of Vehicle	5.95
铁路、船舶、航空航天和其他运输设备制造业	Manufacture of Transport Equipment for Railway, Shipping, Aerospace and other uses	4.54
电气机械和器材制造业	Manufacture of Electrical Machinery and Equipment	3.65
计算机、通信和其他电子设备制造业	Manufacture of Computer, Communication Equipment and Other Electronic Equipment	5.15
仪器仪表制造业	Manufacture of Measuring Instrument	5.88
其他制造业	Manufacture of Other Products	
废弃资源综合利用业	Recycling and Disposal of Waste Resources	
金属制品、机械和设备修理业	Manufacture of Metal Products, Machinery and Equipment	
电力、热力生产和供应业	Production and Supply of Electric Power and Heat Power	-3.17
燃气生产和供应业	Production and Supply of Gas	11.88
水的生产和供应业	Production and Supply of Water	2.26

单位：万元（10 000 yuan）

资产负债率（%） Assets-Liability Ratio（%）	流动资产周转次数（次/年） Number of Times of Annual of Turnover Current Assets（time/year）	工业成本费用利润率（%） Ratio of Profits to Industrial Costs（%）
61.09	**1.42**	**6.10**
37.02	0.75	8.60
48.60	1.33	9.42
54.63	3.34	20.15
38.63	0.78	30.78
0.00	0.00	0.00
79.39	0.82	-4.04
66.51	1.00	4.70
67.02	3.52	7.25
49.97	4.27	11.73
66.97	1.64	10.62
81.83	0.79	-0.83
73.06	0.78	5.95
68.91	2.15	1.61
61.44	0.74	7.36
59.72	0.99	3.53
39.33	1.60	2.94
50.49	0.55	9.55
79.80	0.89	-13.40
44.19	2.61	36.30
62.87	0.54	2.39

12-10 按行业分规模以上外商及港澳台商投资工业企业主要经济效益指标(2021年)

MAIN INDICATORS ON ECONOMIC BENEFIT OF FOREIGN FUNDED ENTERPRISES AND ENTERPRISES WITH FUNDS FROM HONG KONG, MACAO AND TAIWAN ABOVE DESIGNATED SIZE BY INDUSTRIAL SECTOR (2021)

项　目	Indicator	总资产贡献率(%) Ratio of Total Assets to Industrial Output Value(%)
总　计	**Total**	**9.10**
煤炭开采和洗选业	Mining and Washing of Coal	
石油和天然气开采业	Extraction of Petroleum and Natural Gas	
黑色金属矿采选业	Mining of Ferrous Metal Ores	
有色金属矿采选业	Mining of Non-ferrous Metal Ores	
非金属矿采选业	Mining and Processing of Non-metal Ores	
开采辅助活动	Auxiliary Activities of Mining	
其他采矿业	Mining of Other Ores	
农副食品加工业	Processing of Food from Agricultural Products	4.14
食品制造业	Manufacture of Foods	9.21
酒、饮料和精制茶制造业	Manufacture of Liquor, Beverages and Refined Tea	9.45
烟草制品业	Manufacture of Tobacco	
纺织业	Manufacture of Textile	7.34
纺织服装、服饰业	Manufacture of Textile Wearing Apparel	4.66
皮革、毛皮、羽毛及其制品和制鞋业	Manufacture of Leather, Fur, Feather & Its Products Footwear	-13.70
木材加工和木、竹、藤、棕、草制品业	Processing of Timber, Manufacture of Wood, Bamboo, Rattan, Palm and Straw Products	-2.44
家具制造业	Manufacture of Furniture	5.90
造纸和纸制品业	Manufacture of Paper and Paper Products	4.55
印刷和记录媒介复制业	Printing, Reproduction of Recording Media	11.90
文教、工美、体育和娱乐用品制造业	Manufacture of Articles for Culture, Arts & Crafts, Sports and Entertainment	4.47
石油、煤炭及其他燃料加工业	Oil, coal and other fuel processing industries	
化学原料和化学制品制造业	Manufacture of Chemical Raw Material and Chemical Products	6.13
医药制造业	Manufacture of Medicines	21.46
化学纤维制造业	Manufacture of Chemical Fibres	
橡胶和塑料制品业	Manufacture of Rubber and Plastic	6.21
非金属矿物制品业	Manufacture of metallic Mineral Products	8.89
黑色金属冶炼和压延加工业	Smelting and Pressing of Ferrous Metals	9.26
有色金属冶炼和压延加工业	Smelting and Pressing of Non-ferrous Metals	
金属制品业	Manufacture of Metal Products	21.22
通用设备制造业	Manufacture of General Purpose Machinery	8.39
专用设备制造业	Manufacture of Special Purpose Machinery	7.99
汽车制造业	Manufacture of Vehicle	7.72
铁路、船舶、航空航天和其他运输设备制造业	Manufacture of Transport Equipment for Railway, Shipping, Aerospace and other uses	7.50
电气机械和器材制造业	Manufacture of Electrical Machinery and Equipment	14.87
计算机、通信和其他电子设备制造业	Manufacture of Computer, Communication Equipment and Other Electronic Equipment	9.21
仪器仪表制造业	Manufacture of Measuring Instrument	22.47
其他制造业	Manufacture of Other Products	4.58
废弃资源综合利用业	Recycling and Disposal of Waste Resources	
金属制品、机械和设备修理业	Manufacture of Metal Products, Machinery and Equipment	
电力、热力生产和供应业	Production and Supply of Electric Power and Heat Power	11.70
燃气生产和供应业	Production and Supply of Gas	10.21
水的生产和供应业	Production and Supply of Water	8.74

单位：万元（10 000 yuan）

资产负债率（%） Assets-Liability Ratio（%）	流动资产周转次数（次/年） Number of Times of Annual of Turnover Current Assets（time/year）	工业成本费用利润率（%） Ratio of Profits to Industrial Costs（%）
49.73	**1.61**	**6.72**
68.50	2.48	1.50
65.31	1.02	10.33
59.09	1.23	5.47
37.33	1.89	3.61
51.08	1.83	1.95
50.21	2.57	-8.32
81.99	0.76	-1.78
62.06	1.59	3.01
45.22	1.52	0.89
50.76	1.65	7.41
46.96	1.44	3.94
48.30	1.78	4.28
44.23	1.02	24.80
36.64	1.71	4.69
38.55	1.28	8.43
35.73	2.89	3.37
53.16	2.22	14.19
47.02	1.51	6.59
51.97	1.14	7.02
38.44	1.46	4.87
50.33	0.50	17.03
48.56	2.84	9.32
45.23	1.96	6.61
48.34	1.23	21.75
79.13	1.56	2.31
42.92	0.84	66.60
56.31	3.39	5.80
48.72	0.71	24.80

12-11 按行业分大中型工业企业主要经济效益指标（2021 年）

MAIN INDICATORS ON ECONOMIC BENEFIT OF LARGE AND MEDIUM-SIZED INDUSTRIAL ENTERPRISES BY INDUSTRIAL SECTOR (2021)

项　　目	Indicator	总资产贡献率（%） Ratio of Total Assets to Industrial Output Value（%）
总　计	**Total**	**9.37**
煤炭开采和洗选业	Mining and Washing of Coal	
石油和天然气开采业	Extraction of Petroleum and Natural Gas	
黑色金属矿采选业	Mining of Ferrous Metal Ores	
有色金属矿采选业	Mining of Non-ferrous Metal Ores	
非金属矿采选业	Mining and Processing of Non-metal Ores	
开采辅助活动	Auxiliary Activities of Mining	
其他采矿业	Mining of Other Ores	
农副食品加工业	Processing of Food from Agricultural Products	2.17
食品制造业	Manufacture of Foods	9.95
酒、饮料和精制茶制造业	Manufacture of Liquor，Beverages and Refined Tea	10.30
烟草制品业	Manufacture of Tobacco	
纺织业	Manufacture of Textile	11.56
纺织服装、服饰业	Manufacture of Textile Wearing Apparel	6.83
皮革、毛皮、羽毛及其制品和制鞋业	Manufacture of Leather, Fur, Feather & Its Products Footwear	2.31
木材加工和木、竹、藤、棕、草制品业	Processing of Timber, Manufacture of Wood, Bamboo, Rattan, Palm and Straw Products	0.35
家具制造业	Manufacture of Furniture	11.28
造纸和纸制品业	Manufacture of Paper and Paper Products	
印刷和记录媒介复制业	Printing, Reproduction of Recording Media	14.36
文教、工美、体育和娱乐用品制造业	Manufacture of Articles for Culture, Arts & Crafts, Sports and Entertainment	5.92
石油、煤炭及其他燃料加工业	Oil, coal and other fuel processing industries	
化学原料和化学制品制造业	Manufacture of Chemical Raw Material and Chemical Products	9.02
医药制造业	Manufacture of Medicines	19.40
化学纤维制造业	Manufacture of Chemical Fibres	
橡胶和塑料制品业	Manufacture of Rubber and Plastic	3.33
非金属矿物制品业	Manufacture of metallic Mineral Products	5.83
黑色金属冶炼和压延加工业	Smelting and Pressing of Ferrous Metals	10.81
有色金属冶炼和压延加工业	Smelting and Pressing of Non-ferrous Metals	
金属制品业	Manufacture of Metal Products	14.96
通用设备制造业	Manufacture of General Purpose Machinery	5.80
专用设备制造业	Manufacture of Special Purpose Machinery	7.71
汽车制造业	Manufacture of Vehicle	7.57
铁路、船舶、航空航天和其他运输设备制造业	Manufacture of Transport Equipment for Railway, Shipping, Aerospace and other uses	4.43
电气机械和器材制造业	Manufacture of Electrical Machinery and Equipment	8.75
计算机、通信和其他电子设备制造业	Manufacture of Computer, Communication Equipment and Other Electronic Equipment	5.91
仪器仪表制造业	Manufacture of Measuring Instrument	9.78
其他制造业	Manufacture of Other Products	
废弃资源综合利用业	Recycling and Disposal of Waste Resources	
金属制品、机械和设备修理业	Manufacture of Metal Products, Machinery and Equipment	
电力、热力生产和供应业	Production and Supply of Electric Power and Heat Power	-4.17
燃气生产和供应业	Production and Supply of Gas	
水的生产和供应业	Production and Supply of Water	

单位：万元（10 000 yuan）

资产负债率（%） Assets-Liability Ratio （%）	流动资产周转次数（次/年） Number of Times of Annual of Turnover Current Assets（time/year）	工业成本费用利润率（%） Ratio of Profits to Industrial Costs （%）
54.98	**1.46**	**6.43**
72.65	2.58	0.51
67.58	0.96	11.68
49.13	1.37	9.17
55.89	2.41	5.13
50.27	1.62	5.25
71.64	1.94	0.54
59.98	1.61	-4.71
73.47	1.51	4.74
57.42	1.62	9.60
40.39	1.52	5.65
49.42	1.80	9.88
34.92	0.93	32.70
54.03	0.94	4.49
53.02	0.95	6.73
64.48	3.45	8.13
46.31	1.80	12.68
53.48	1.11	5.87
53.71	0.83	10.83
61.04	2.22	2.83
61.71	0.73	6.71
51.72	1.77	6.27
42.33	1.64	3.94
42.11	0.72	18.61
73.19	0.85	-15.20

12-12　主要年份规模以上工业主要产品产量
OUTPUT OF MAIN PRODUCTS OF INDUSTRIES ABOVE DESIGNATED SIZE IN MAJOR YEARS

年　份 Year	原盐 （万吨） Salt （10 000 tons）	发电量 （亿千瓦小时） Electricity （100 million kW·h）	饮料酒 （万吨） Beverage Liquor （10 000 tons）	#啤酒 Beer	卷烟 （万箱） Cigarettes （10 000 cases）	罐头 （吨） Canned Food （ton）	化学纤维 （吨） Chemical Fiber （ton）	纱 （吨） Yarn （ton）
1949	15.16	1.21	0.18	0.12	2.36			27447
1952	35.08	2.11	0.37	0.18	12.27			59674
1957	44.34	2.92	0.96	0.58	23.41			50699
1962	38.60	3.86	1.58	0.79	16.59		28	17939
1965	41.34	6.80	2.04	1.34	31.34		205	68082
1970	29.96	10.57	3.39	2.55	42.16		621	85591
1975	34.52	10.98	5.30	2.98	36.00		357	79516
1978	60.68	13.63	6.25	3.75	44.00	4743	1413	85233
1980	41.19	12.50	8.49	4.84	48.79	3521	2116	83389
1985	47.34	26.97	13.76	10.05	51.81	6400	1747	91839
1988	53.28	29.35	26.61	15.58	57.01	27200	3393	107720
1990	35.70	40.22	29.18	19.61	61.94		2900	100381
1991	31.39	54.60	36.75	27.38	56.19	130510	5200	96271
1992	46.24	58.63	44.59	37.01	59.37	3200	6000	99043
1993	48.88	59.39	54.74	45.92	63.46	1900	27100	91351
1994	53.02	59.62	60.00	50.92	69.20	2300	21400	86744
1995	50.84	64.69	60.85	54.16	70.96	4609	20973	79492
1996	41.39	83.02	61.79	54.40	73.04	1719	22945	66832
1997	34.11	95.12	66.64	56.06	88.32	554	26300	70402
1998	19.08	79.65	47.33	42.79	77.10		23858	66504
1999	30.30	82.00	126.21	120.10	149.00	379	29967	56431
2000	41.83	90.84	211.47	206.50	148.10	225	65362	69561
2001	31.40	85.73	279.37	274.28	142.95	99	89989	72933
2002	42.50	89.70	323.20	320.60	138.10	11690	91394	70888
2003	36.85	87.69	353.90	351.80	148.00		101752	65919
2004	34.36	89.01	393.30	390.60	147.10	10889	115187	71931
2005	10.00	98.63	439.70	435.20	150.70	10097	95887	72140
2006	15.30	124.54	101.60（本地）	95.60(本地）	95.16(本地）	1668	72381	56128
2007	19.23	155.30	118.10(本地）	112.50（本地）	100.08（本地）	1850	68746	47850
2008	15.90	164.58	132.07(本地）	124.75(本地）	100.02（本地）	1510	51751	43102
2009	5.90	172.66	137.21(本地）	127.12(本地）	100.08(本地）	4706	59852	38566
2010	11.25	181.93	144.66(本地）	141.65（本地）	102.55（本地）	1092	68654	35278
2011		173.69	164.04（本地）	156.50（本地）	104.51（本地）	41204	38640	18556
2012		174.72	174.03(本地）	163.95（本地）	106.03（本地）	35026	32371	19404
2013	1.28	180.11	194.22（本地）	185.17（本地）	108.36（本地）	30203	23647	33687
2014		178.29	169.85（本地）	164.59（本地）	112.06（本地）	23970	22053	32336
2015		173.53	162.66（本地）	157.83（本地）	111.48（本地）	36179	17419	27721
2016		175.40	168.82(本地）	164.27（本地）		53139	14839	33416
2017		181.80	163.41(本地）	159.97（本地）		85942	11565	26493
2018		192.40	165.81(本地）	162.44（本地）		43893	5545	28948
2019		181.03	177.82（本地）	174.80（本地）		5940	39091	40562
2020		172.47	180.84（本地）	178.17（本地）		2699	11855	30269
2021		187.90	202.46(本地）	199.57(本地）		1398	17383	60779

注：1998 年以前为乡及乡以上工业。
Note：Before 1998，the data refer to those at and above county level.

12-12 续表 1
Continued

年 份 Year	布 (万米) Cloth (10 000 m)	印染布 (万米) Printed Fabric (10 000 m)	机制纸及纸板(万吨) Machine-made Paper and Paperboards (10 000 tons)	硫酸 (万吨) Sulfuric Acid (10 000 tons)	烧碱 (万吨) Caustic Soda (10 000 tons)	纯碱 (万吨) Soda Ash (10 000 tons)
1949	10608	2947	0.98		0.01	
1952	30069	13658	0.44		0.17	
1957	27806	16053	1.54		0.74	
1962	7444	7375	1.45	0.06	0.89	
1965	29538	13670	2.22		1.66	5.32
1970	33660	21994	3.14	0.04	2.14	12.01
1975	31242	22828	3.10	0.53	2.36	9.15
1978	36877	25797	4.55	1.32	3.61	14.04
1980	34937	22900	5.25	4.11	4.33	18.18
1985	34998	17679	6.20	3.34	5.52	26.03
1988	35890	21213	7.42	4.88	6.62	31.12
1990	34066	21446	6.02	4.86	6.73	30.48
1991	34076	19999	5.99	5.62	5.99	29.50
1992	33682	21534	5.95	6.70	5.62	34.60
1993	35912	16606	8.84	6.96	6.07	40.43
1994	43241	16387	12.36	8.33	6.48	43.36
1995	41170	17864	11.06	9.69	7.90	43.20
1996	39023	16881	11.31	10.12	7.30	46.91
1997	43615	15722	7.78	10.16	8.45	50.55
1998	40440	9864	6.91	10.33	9.25	52.80
1999	39576	4340	7.77	12.56	8.96	53.70
2000	41783	3526	10.96	12.96	10.24	56.20
2001	40640	3402	23.05	13.03	11.44	58.47
2002	47609	5592	29.92	5.00	13.80	60.70
2003	35922	10131	31.76	4.50	13.53	62.50
2004	50111	7718	36.38	14.70	14.86	60.80
2005	51307	16027	31.95	14.80	16.10	62.50
2006	55093	20867	15.50	7.00	15.90	63.95
2007	44251	18708	24.04	9.22	14.91	71.02
2008	48399	58907	22.41	13.02	12.78	72.03
2009	31048	27998	34.59	1.40	12.24	68.21
2010	17457	29631	35.43	4.07	13.87	69.35
2011	49617	28449	32.28	5.06	13.20	70.07
2012	48987	32478	22.27	7.22	13.71	63.35
2013	51646	34381	17.95	4.32	11.06	61.66
2014	44593	33653	18.26			67.85
2015	28040	25458	18.29			68.95
2016	24973	28661	18.17		11.33	
2017	23550	21530	17.39		33.89	
2018	46737	22647	14.58		35.36	
2019	11354	27528	11.52		35.11	
2020	16207	31116	26.21		39.17	
2021	23090	35830	19.44		69.01	

12-12 续表 2
Continued

年 份 Year	合成氨 （万吨） Synthetic Ammonia （10 000 tons）	化学肥料 （万吨） Chemical Fertilizer （10 000 tons）	化学农药 （吨） Chemical Pesticide （ton）	油漆 （吨） Paint （ton）	染料 （吨） Dye （ton）
1949				30	599
1952				480	2855
1957			1226	1247	4307
1962		0.45	213	910	3560
1965		1.42	2	4727	8667
1970	0.98	5.89	2313	6380	9347
1975	3.46	12.46	4439	7016	5967
1978	7.17	23.66	9714	8786	5877
1980	7.24	7.82	8333	14556	2159
1985	6.31	5.16	2000	26055	4448
1988	8.72	9.41	2400	28943	5527
1990	7.56	7.55	2500	29075	5119
1991	8.52	8.04	2800	33548	5263
1992	10.45	7.85	3400	35058	4821
1993	10.70	8.02	3600	33054	4550
1994	13.04	12.39	3600	29437	5097
1995	14.98	12.62	4934	37772	7185
1996	18.67	12.62	4976	26762	7668
1997	16.94	12.52	4600	19743	11189
1998	22.36	15.30	6755	17594	8274
1999	26.09	20.19	4480	3730	7866
2000	24.64	20.04	3758	693	9306
2001	35.53	28.07	3915	1349	9757
2002	20.30	9.80	4020	1701	9826
2003	21.55	9.70	2039	2106	10734
2004	30.30	19.60	5061	1955	3961
2005	33.80	22.10	6524	1687	13979
2006	33.30	21.30	12544		26544
2007	28.22	25.70	16433	2957	28269
2008	17.93	21.51	12848	12105	18263
2009	17.71	21.23	49684		24893
2010	16.84	14.10	16450		41383
2011	10.78	9.26	23286		
2012	7.71	6.98	28801		
2013	6.48	5.10	27715		
2014			27160		
2015			36853		
2016		14.33	34993		
2017		7.38	18911		
2018		8.08	8507		
2019		8.50	17524		
2020		8.60	11938		
2021		8.65	14167		

12-12 续表 3
Continued

年 份 Year	化学原料药（吨）Chemical Medicines (ton)	水泥（万吨）Cement (10 000 tons)	平板玻璃（万重量箱）Plate Glass (10 000 weight cases)	耐火材料（万吨）Refractory Material (10 000 tons)	粗钢（万吨）Crude Steel (10 000 tons)	钢材（万吨）Rolled-steel (10 000 tons)
1949						0.06
1952				0.78	0.36	0.41
1957				3.39	1.77	4.30
1962		2.09		2.41	4.59	2.94
1965		6.59		2.91	11.72	8.43
1970		7.35	16.31	3.23	19.38	14.56
1975	55	20.93	19.44	4.88	21.25	20.01
1978	185	35.40	8.86	5.93	31.06	27.61
1980	123	44.66	70.13	5.38	37.14	32.82
1984	7228	70.27	91.25	7.98	37.81	32.43
1985	4222	82.70	77.00	4.35	37.51	32.68
1988	7655	141.00	108.81	4.56	50.17	38.26
1990	6913	139.48	83.13	3.91	54.55	38.04
1991	4754	165.66	96.90	3.71	56.96	39.02
1992	5743	191.50	120.00	3.86	63.75	50.09
1993	6566	221.30	148.71	3.55	61.75	44.88
1994	4238	246.50	145.12	3.06	60.82	46.95
1995	1993	213.82	426.40	3.88	67.27	49.60
1996	5505	181.45	423.60	3.54	72.02	50.60
1997	1693	208.04	570.85	2.45	75.71	51.06
1998	910	131.51	509.38	0.99	84.02	64.93
1999	1691	149.41	576.50	0.59	108.10	86.58
2000	2131	137.52	556.58	0.62	101.17	93.35
2001	2534	148.67	421.51	0.51	124.45	119.77
2002	2712	140.30	405.40	0.45	145.90	142.20
2003	3288	154.90	361.40	0.47	204.80	204.30
2004	4394	181.19	163.30	0.69	225.70	230.97
2005	4430	210.80	297.50	1.04	309.70	330.30
2006	32232	232.72	418.74	1.21	325.82	375.52
2007	14139	425.53	397.79	2.38	327.00	365.55
2008	17910	363.57	599.87	3.65	300.19	350.14
2009	19086	397.66	681.02	18.46	307.89	349.63
2010	26170	442.66	662.04	8.17	300.04	333.46
2011	29337	588.08	510.05	20.02	318.27	325.89
2012	49290	556.57	494.54	33.44	252.78	274.67
2013	49081	575.66	610.21	42.34	235.53	230.39
2014	50713	597.35	612.40	39.37	214.43	212.79
2015	45923	532.36	534.99	41.13	154.56	140.63
2016	2248	600.56	576.16	108.76	188.04	191.37
2017	2775	525.42	557.44	109.84	280.97	291.85
2018	1809	284.47	561.51	27.97	309.70	319.90
2019	2616	442.47	393.64	12.18	319.25	336.19
2020	745	414.03	1003.97	19.54	335.19	389.20
2021	806	522.43	998.18	25.53	325.00	544.82

12-12 续表 4
Continued

年　份 Year	金属切削机床（台） Metal-cutting Machine Tools （unit）	锻压机械（台） Metal Forming Machinery （unit）	交流电动机（万千瓦） AC Motors （10 000 kW）
1949			0.02
1952	105		0.50
1957	76		3.61
1962	167	77	3.85
1965	526	111	6.48
1970	2353	531	14.53
1975	3213	788	15.56
1978	2558	379	21.72
1980	595	444	20.11
1985	900	607	26.08
1988	1336	737	39.60
1990	1049	440	34.28
1991	869	764	44.17
1992	1018	982	61.08
1993	1532	919	64.13
1994	1505	860	37.71
1995	972	2563	39.18
1996	1084	584	22.65
1997	449	416	20.74
1998	280		6.43
1999	251		11.10
2000	384		38.70
2001	472	2477	42.72
2002	588		68.25
2003	990		95.63
2004	1287		96.13
2005	1347		63.50
2006	3636		702.02
2007	3392	1869	119.23
2008	8381	1230	96.89
2009	668		728.03
2010	1120		101.10
2011	1194		74.08
2012	1014		104.48
2013	2689		126.82
2014	2563		114.46
2015	618		104.30
2016	588		98.70
2017	610		202.79
2018	204		230.86
2019	584		110.03
2020	466		173.94
2021	387		243.72

12-12 续表 5
Continued

年　份 Year	钢芯铝绞线（吨） Steel-cored Aluminum Stranded Wire （ton）	家用电冰箱 （万台） Home Refrigerators （10 000 sets）	家用洗衣机 （万台） Home Washing Machines （10 000 sets）	彩色电视机 （万部） Color TV Sets （10 000 sets）
1949				
1952				
1957				
1962				
1965	250			
1970	34			
1975	188			
1978	684			
1980	1232			
1985	2327	1.66	0.48	6.60
1988	1571	15.22	42.38	17.00
1990	1880	27.41	45.86	18.50
1991	2463	31.51	45.70	22.27
1992	2248	54.84	46.31	28.07
1993	1144	50.48	56.59	36.08
1994	287	62.50	71.34	60.15
1995	1659	107.91	64.34	60.53
1996	2265	193.80	100.94	56.68
1997	2616	257.10	171.95	124.86
1998	1725	219.23	183.67	96.83
1999	2805	259.60	256.30	285.20
2000	4202	311.10	318.50	379.40
2001	4498	396.30	367.89	455.40
2002	5825	518.20	408.6	593.20
2003	4940	598.30	471.5	671.70
2004	6608	815.03	575.06	957.90
2005	116592	908.80	614.9	1324.30
2006	46974	1290.00	649.4	1205.60
2007	22564	1421.40	769.4	1243.10
2008	29507	723.19	407.54	836.66
2009		827.21	488.72	1064.70
2010		801.22	580.87	1111.19
2011		718.54	604.55	1154.20
2012		575.01	583.6	1439.98
2013		524.35	606.65	1512.05
2014		610.07	590.95	1714.93
2015		872.09	595.11	1736.20
2016		882.22	606.74	2111.71
2017		818.65	603.4	1703.01
2018		886.58	601.72	1695.18
2019		731.81	513.71	1580.42
2020		822.01	575.41	1774.86
2021		888.81	730.78	1986.73

12-13 规模以上工业主要产品产量
OUTPUT OF MAJOR INDUSTRIAL PRODUCTS OF INDUSTRY ABOVE DESIGNATED SIZE

产品名称	Name	计量单位	Unit	2021 年	增长（±%）Increase（±%）
冶金工业产品	**Products of Metallurgical Industry**				
粗钢	Crude Steel	万吨	10 000 tons	325.00	-2.98
钢材	Rolled-steel	万吨	10 000 tons	544.82	5.43
耐火材料制品	Refractory Material	万吨	10 000 tons	25.53	26.86
电力工业产品	**Products of Electricity Industry**				
发电量	Electricity	亿千瓦小时	100 million kW · h	187.90	4.90
化学工业产品	**Products of Chemical Industry**				
原油加工量	Processing Amount of Crude Oil	万吨	10 000 tons	1473.50	9.96
汽油	Petrol	万吨	10 000 tons	435.80	17.50
柴油	Diesel Oil	万吨	10 000 tons	355.35	7.10
燃料油	Fuel Oil	万吨	10 000 tons	185.97	52.60
化学农药	Chemical Pesticides	万吨	10 000 tons	1.42	18.67
塑料制品	Plastic	万吨	10 000 tons	48.48	12.64
化学药品（原料）	Chemical drugs	万吨	10 000 tons	0.08	3.56

12-13 续表 1
Continued

产品名称	Name	计量单位	Unit	2021 年	增长（±%） Increase（±%）
橡胶轮胎外胎	Rubber Tire Casing	万条	10 000 tires	5033.77	2.10
机械工业产品	**Products of Machinery Industry**				
工业锅炉	Industrial Boiler	蒸发量吨	ton （evaporation amunt）	31015.80	38.97
交流电动机	AC Motors	万千瓦	10 000 kW	243.72	35.48
金属切削机床	Metal-cutting Machine	台	set	387	-1.78
改装汽车	Refitted Motor Vehicles	辆	set	44260	-38.06
民用钢质船舶	Civil Steel Ships	载重吨	syn-ton	2681232	3.24
电子产品	**Electronic Products**				
彩色电视机	Color TV sets	万台	10 000 sets	1986.73	11.94
电子元件	Electronic Component	亿只	10 000 Units	341.23	29.31
建材工业产品	**Products of Construction Industry**				
水泥	Cement	万吨	10 000 tons	522.43	19.07
平板玻璃	Plate Glass	万重量箱	10 000 weight cases	998.18	-0.42

12-13 续表 2
Continued

产品名称	Name	计量单位	Unit	2021 年	增长（±%）Increase（±%）
纺织工业产品	**Products of Textile Industry**				
纱	Yarn	吨	ton	60778.85	153.35
布	Cloth	万米	10 000 m	23090.27	29.12
印染布	Printed Fabric	万米	10 000 m	35830.32	15.61
化学纤维	Chemical Fibers	吨	ton	17383.10	46.63
轻工产品	**Products of Light Industry**				
机制纸及纸板	Machine-made Paper and Paperboards	万吨	10 000 tons	19.44	-25.83
家用洗衣机	Home Washing Machines	万台	10 000 sets	730.78	27.00
糖果	Sugar	吨	ton	966.09	-1.72
食用植物油	Vegetable Oil	万吨	10 000 tons	100.21	-1.68
饮料酒	Beverage Liquor	万千升	10 000 KL	200.06	11.96
# 白酒	White Spirit	万千升	10 000 KL	2.15	2.81
# 啤酒	Beer	万千升	10 000 KL	197.20	12.01
塑料制品	Plastic Products	万吨	10 000 tons	48.48	12.64
家具	Furniture	万件	10 000 articles	1037.71	17.78
家用电冰箱	Home Refrigerators	万台	10 000 sets	888.81	8.13
皮革鞋靴	Leather Shoes	万双	10 000 pairs	799.73	-21.28
服装	Clothing	万件	10 000 articles	44264.32	-4.64

12-14　规模以上工业主要产品生产能力
PRODUCTION CAPACITY OF MAJOR PRODUCTS OF INDUSTRY ABOVE DESIGNATED SIZE

产品名称	Name	计量单位	Unit	2021 年生产能力 Production Capacity of 2021	2020 年生产能力 Production Capacity of 2020
发电设备容量总计 / 发电量	Total Capacity of Generation Equipment	万千瓦 / 万千瓦小时	10 000 kW/ 10 000 kW · h	445	450
化学纤维	Chemical Fiber	吨	ton	36350	36990
棉纺锭 / 纺纱量	Knitting Spindle	锭 / 吨	spindle/ton	141858	144532
棉布织机 / 布	Cotton Cloth Loom	台 / 万米	set/10 000 m	1974	2428
焦炭	Coke	吨	ton	1700000	1700000
农用氮、磷、钾化学肥料总计（折纯）	Chemical Fertilizer	吨	ton	80100	110000
水泥	Cement	吨	ton	7702000	7310000
平板玻璃	Plate Glass	重量箱	weight cases	11241440	11241440
生铁	Pig Iron	吨	ton	4350000	3220000
粗钢	Crude Steel	吨	ton	4275000	3125000
钢材	Rolled-steel	吨	ton	6970540	5610150
金属切削机床	Metal-cutting Machine	台	set	966	2293
家用电冰箱	Home Refrigerators	台	set	10916400	10453300
房间空气调节器	Air Conditioner	台	set	16930000	15806755
移动通信手持机（手机）	Cell Phone	台	set	3600000	7000000
彩色电视机	Color TV Sets	台	set	28079000	19953200

主要统计指标解释

工业总产值 是以货币表现的工业企业在一定时期内生产的已出售或可供出售工业产品总量，它是反映一定时间内工业生产的总规模和总水平。

资产总计 指企业拥有或控制的能以货币计量的经济资源，包括各种财产、债权和其他权利。资产按其流动性（即资产的变现能力和支付能力）划分为：流动资产、长期投资、固定资产、无形资产、递延资产和其他资产。

负债合计 指企业所承担的能以货币计量，将以资产或劳务偿付的债务，偿还形式包括货币、资产或提供劳务。负债一般按偿还期长短分为流动负债和长期负债。

利润总额 指企业生产经营活动的最终成果，是企业在一定时期内实现的盈亏相抵后的利润总额（亏损以“–”号表示），它等于营业利润加上补贴收入加上投资收益加上营业外净收入再加上以前年度损益调整。

Explanatory Notes on Main Statistical Indicators

Gross Industrial Output Value is the total volume of final industrial products produced and industrial services provided during a given period. It reflects the total achievements and overall scale of industrial production during a given period

Total Assets refers to the economic resources that can be measured in currency owned or controlled by an enterprise, including various properties, claims and other rights. Assets are divided into: current assets, long–term investments, fixed assets, intangible assets, deferred assets and other assets according to their liquidity(that is, the ability to realize assets and payment capabilities) .

Total Liabilities refers to the debts that an enterprise bears that can be measured in currency and will be repaid in assets or services. The form of repayment includes currency, assets or the provision of services. Liabilities are generally divided into current liabilities and long–term liabilities according to the length of the repayment period.

Total Profits refer to the final achievements of production and operation of the enterprises, represented by the total profits after deducting losses(loss is expressed by the negative figure) . It is the sum of profits from operation, income from subsidies, investment earnings, net income from activities other than operation, and adjustment of profits and losses of previous years.

服务业 13

SERVICE ENTERPRISES

简要说明

一、本篇资料的主要内容

本篇资料主要反映了全市规模以上服务业企业主要财务状况，规模以上服务业企业分行业财务状况，规模以上服务业企业分登记注册类型财务状况，分区市规模以上服务业企业财务状况等方面的内容。

二、本篇资料的来源

本篇中规模以上服务业企业资料来源于规模以上服务业统计年报，由市统计局服务业统计处整理提供。

Brief Introduction

Ⅰ. Main Content

This document mainly reflects the major financial indicators of service enterprises above designated size in the city, the financial indicators of service enterprises above designated size by industry, the financial indicators of service enterprises above designated size by registration type, and the financial indicators of service enterprises above designated size in regional cities content.

Ⅱ. Source of Data

The data of service enterprises above designated size in this chapter are derived from the annual statistical report of service industries above designated size, which are compiled and provided by the Service Statistics Department of the Municipal Statistics Bureau.

13-1 规模以上服务业企业主要财务状况
MAIN FINANCIAL INDICATORS OF SERVICE ENTERPRISES ABOVE THE DESIGNATED

单位：亿元（100 million yuan）

项　目	Item	2021	2020	2021 年比 2020 年增长（%）Growth Rate in 2021 Over 2020（%）
营业收入	Business Revenue	3803.38	2550.90	49.10
营业成本	Business Costs	3329.79	2112.02	57.66
税金及附加	Tax and Extra Charges on Business	16.10	12.23	31.64
销售费用	Sales Expenses	80.23	72.32	10.94
管理费用	Management Expenses	217.36	185.20	17.37
财务费用	Financial Expenses	77.70	66.40	17.02
营业利润	Business Profits	209.67	196.55	6.68
利润总额	Total Profits	213.25	202.48	5.32
所得税费用	Income Taxes Payable	41.24	39.43	4.59
应付职工薪酬	Employee Compensation Payable	474.56	375.41	26.41
应交增值税	Value-added Tax Payable	53.16	40.14	32.44

注：增速按可比口径计算。
Note：The growth rates are calculated on comparable coverage.

13-2 规模以上其他营利性服务业企业主要财务状况
MAIN FINANCIAL INDICATORS OF OTHER FOR-PROFIT SERVICE ENTERPRISES ABOVE THE DESIGNATED

单位：亿元（100 million yuan）

项　目	Item	2021	2020	2021 年比 2020 年增长（%）Growth Rate in 2021 Over 2020（%）
营业收入	Business Revenue	1170.03	943.69	23.98
营业成本	Business Costs	906.54	710.80	27.54
税金及附加	Tax and Extra Charges on Business	6.78	5.58	21.51
销售费用	Sales Expenses	47.12	41.41	13.79
管理费用	Management Expenses	109.89	98.74	11.29
财务费用	Financial Expenses	15.41	14.41	6.94
营业利润	Business Profits	50.99	55.64	-8.36
利润总额	Total Profits	50.05	62.01	-19.29
所得税费用	Income Taxes Payable	9.30	9.75	-4.62
应付职工薪酬	Employee Compensation Payable	225.10	172.47	30.52
应交增值税	Value-added Tax Payable	26.37	23.02	14.55

注：增速按可比口径计算。
Note：The growth rates are calculated on comparable coverage.

13-3 规模以上服务业企业分登记注册类型财务状况（2021 年）
FINANCIAL INDICATORS OF SERVICE ENTERPRISES ABOVE DESIGNATED SIZE BY REGISTRATION TYPE（2021）

单位：亿元（100 million yuan）

类 别	Category	企业单位数（个）Number of Enterprises（unit）	营业收入 Business Revenue	营业成本 Business Costs	税金及附加 Tax and Extra Charges on Business
总计	**Total**	**2513**	**3803.38**	**3329.79**	**16.10**
按登记注册类型分	**by Status of Registration**				
内资企业	**Domestic Funded Enterprises**	**2384**	**3307.54**	**2945.61**	**14.65**
国有企业	State-owned Enterprises	68	82.44	66.51	0.42
集体企业	Collective-owned Enterprises	10	2.89	1.94	0.07
股份合作企业	Cooperative Enterprises	1			
有限责任公司	Limited Liability Corporations	682	1519.20	1381.95	8.78
股份有限公司	Share-holding Corporations Limited	61	292.26	250.99	1.46
私营企业	Private Enterprises	1548	1405.79	1241.05	3.86
其他企业	Other Enterprises	13	4.65	3.09	0.02
港、澳、台商投资企业	**Enterprises with Funds from Hong Kong, Macao and Taiwan**	**48**	**149.64**	**118.51**	**0.57**
合资经营企业（港或澳、台资）	Joint-ventures Enterprises	26	62.99	41.81	0.22
合作经营企业（港或澳、台资）	Cooperative Enterprises	1			
港澳台商独资经营企业	Enterprises with Sole Investment	19	71.60	64.29	0.31
港澳台商投资股份有限公司	Share-holding Corporations Ltd. With Funds from Hong Kong, Macao and Taiwan	2			
其他企业	Other Enterprises				
外商投资企业	**Foreign Funded Enterprises**	**81**	**346.19**	**265.69**	**0.88**
中外合资经营企业	Joint-venture Enterprises	37	174.38	136.07	0.41
中外合作经营企业	Cooperation Enterprises	3	0.43	0.19	0.03
外资企业	Foreign Investment	39	168.31	126.64	0.43
其他企业	Other Enterprises	1			

13-3 续表 1
Continued

单位：亿元（100 million yuan）

类　别	Category	销售费用 Selling Expenses	管理费用 Management Expenses	财务费用 Financial Expenses	营业利润 Business Profits
总计	**Total**	**80.23**	**217.36**	**77.70**	**209.67**
按登记注册类型分	**by Status of Registration**				
内资企业	**Domestic Funded Enterprises**	**71.36**	**190.18**	**74.40**	**137.03**
国有企业	State-owned Enterprises	1.03	7.78	3.76	3.78
集体企业	Collective-owned Enterprises	0.07	0.71	0.01	0.34
股份合作企业	Cooperative Enterprises				
有限责任公司	Limited Liability Corporations	29.14	78.17	61.40	68.15
股份有限公司	Share-holding Corporations Limited	8.50	15.35	2.78	40.69
私营企业	Private Enterprises	32.52	86.61	6.45	24.01
其他企业	Other Enterprises	0.10	1.38	0.01	0.06
港、澳、台商投资企业	**Enterprises with Funds from Hong Kong, Macao and Taiwan**	**3.37**	**5.98**	**2.12**	**19.06**
合资经营企业（港或澳、台资）	Joint-ventures Enterprises	1.52	2.63	1.43	15.50
合作经营企业（港或澳、台资）	Cooperative Enterprises				
港澳台商独资经营企业	Enterprises with Sole Investment	0.95	2.89	0.65	2.78
港澳台商投资股份有限公司	Share-holding Corporations Ltd. With Funds from Hong Kong, Macao and Taiwan				
其他企业	Other Enterprises				
外商投资企业	**Foreign Funded Enterprises**	**5.52**	**21.20**	**1.18**	**53.58**
中外合资经营企业	Joint-venture Enterprises	1.39	9.20	0.57	26.49
中外合作经营企业	Cooperation Enterprises	0.15	0.11	0.00	-0.01
外资企业	Foreign Investment	3.98	11.80	0.61	26.92
其他企业	Other Enterprises				

13-3 续表 2
Continued

单位：亿元（100 million yuan）

类别	Category	利润总额 Total Profits	所得税费用 Income Taxes Payable	应付职工薪酬 Total Wages Payable	应交增值税 Value-added Tax Payable
总计	**Total**	**213.25**	**41.24**	**474.56**	**53.16**
按登记注册类型分	**by Status of Registration**				
内资企业	**Domestic Funded Enterprises**	**137.13**	**28.74**	**422.15**	**47.66**
国有企业	State-owned Enterprises	3.44	1.16	13.14	1.55
集体企业	Collective-owned Enterprises	0.35	0.08	0.69	0.05
股份合作企业	Cooperative Enterprises				
有限责任公司	Limited Liability Corporations	72.35	16.95	223.05	22.59
股份有限公司	Share-holding Corporations Limited	41.37	5.48	46.34	4.87
私营企业	Private Enterprises	19.53	5.04	137.14	18.54
其他企业	Other Enterprises	0.08	0.02	1.76	0.06
港、澳、台商投资企业	**Enterprises with Funds from Hong Kong, Macao and Taiwan**	**19.21**	**4.52**	**9.49**	**1.64**
合资经营企业（港或澳、台资）	Joint-ventures Enterprises	15.57	3.66	6.18	1.18
合作经营企业（港或澳、台资）	Cooperative Enterprises				
港澳台商独资经营企业	Enterprises with Sole Investment	2.76	0.79	2.39	0.24
港澳台商投资股份有限公司	Share-holding Corporations Ltd. With Funds from Hong Kong, Macao and Taiwan				
其他企业	Other Enterprises				
外商投资企业	**Foreign Funded Enterprises**	**56.92**	**7.99**	**42.92**	**3.87**
中外合资经营企业	Joint-venture Enterprises	29.49	6.53	23.97	1.51
中外合作经营企业	Cooperation Enterprises	0.01	0.03	0.13	0.01
外资企业	Foreign Investment	27.24	1.39	18.66	2.32
其他企业	Other Enterprises				

13-4 规模以上服务业企业分行业财务状况（2021年）

FINANCIAL INDICATORS OF SERVICE ENTERPRISES ABOVE DESIGNATED SIZE BY SECTOR (2021)

行　业	Category	企业单位数（个）Number of Enterprises（unit）	营业收入 Business Revenue	营业成本 Business Costs	税金及附加 Tax and Extra Charges on Business
总计	**Total**	**2513**	**3803.38**	**3329.79**	**16.10**
按行业分	**Grouped by Sector**				
交通运输、仓储和邮政业	Transport, Storage and Postal Services	830	2264.19	2159.85	5.95
信息传输、软件和信息技术服务业	Information Transmission, Software and Information Technology Services	231	530.81	383.94	1.65
房地产业	Real Estate	189	120.12	86.77	2.67
租赁和商务服务业	Leasing and Business Services	638	435.93	376.68	2.73
科学研究和技术服务业	Scientific Research and Technical Services	310	290.05	205.30	1.57
水利、环境和公共设施管理业	Management of Water Conservancy, Environment and Public Facilities	44	38.34	29.72	0.29
居民服务、修理和其他服务业	Households' service, Repair and Other Services	60	26.73	18.27	0.13
教育	Education	19	10.87	7.21	0.05
卫生和社会工作	Health and Social Work	72	37.30	25.37	0.02
文化、体育和娱乐业	Culture, Sports and Entertainment	120	49.04	36.68	1.04

单位：亿元（100 million yuan）

销售费用 Selling Expenses	管理费用 Management Expenses	财务费用 Financial Expenses	营业利润 Business Profits	利润总额 Total Profits	所得税费用 Income Taxes Payable	应付职工薪酬 Total Wages Payable	应交增值税 Value-added Tax Payable
80.23	**217.36**	**77.70**	**209.67**	**213.25**	**41.24**	**474.56**	**53.16**
16.94	70.76	42.70	119.45	120.97	25.93	174.93	18.36
25.98	24.19	2.47	60.43	62.85	5.46	70.35	10.54
3.02	18.13	16.96	2.59	5.14	1.82	31.00	5.35
11.66	34.79	11.77	5.00	7.96	3.49	61.20	7.88
9.73	43.87	1.13	17.48	19.80	2.66	88.72	7.76
0.34	4.41	0.73	3.74	4.04	0.71	11.99	0.79
3.68	2.84	−0.11	1.95	2.15	0.58	6.80	1.01
0.71	2.48	0.09	0.23	0.13	0.07	4.84	0.23
3.66	7.72	0.62	−0.59	−0.42	0.25	12.28	0.11
4.51	8.17	1.34	−0.61	−9.37	0.27	12.45	1.13

13-5 规模以上服务业企业分市、区财务状况（2021年）

FINANCIAL INDICATORS OF SERVICE ENTERPRISES ABOVE DESIGNATED SIZE BY REGION（2021）

行　业	Category	企业单位数（个）Number of Enterprises（unit）	营业收入 Business Revenue	营业成本 Business Costs	税金及附加 Tax and Extra Charges on Business
全市	**Total**	**2513**	**3803.38**	**3329.79**	**16.10**
市南区	Shinan District	500	1384.10	1243.39	2.47
市北区	Shibei District	293	352.56	348.61	2.08
李沧区	Licang District	228	89.67	77.82	0.76
崂山区	Laoshan District	288	649.92	540.26	2.76
黄岛区（西海岸新区）	Huangdao District（West Coast New Area）	582	735.83	586.42	3.29
城阳区	Chengyang District	260	232.43	197.88	1.81
城阳区（不含高新区）	Chengyang District（Excluding High tech District）	185	166.06	143.86	1.06
高新区	High tech District	75	66.37	54.02	0.75
即墨区	Jimo District	92	112.70	97.79	0.54
胶州市	Jiaozhou	169	202.66	200.32	2.17
平度市	Pingdu	63	30.09	25.67	0.17
莱西市	Laixi	38	13.41	11.64	0.04

注：截至汇总，省统计局尚未反馈年报最终数据，故表中数据为初步情况。
Note：Up to the summary, the provincial Bureau of Statistics has not given back the final data of the annual report, so the data in the table are preliminary.

单位：亿元（100 million yuan）

销售费用 Selling Expenses	管理费用 Management Expenses	财务费用 Financial Expenses	营业利润 Business Profits	利润总额 Total Profits	所得税费用 Income Taxes Payable	应付职工薪酬 Total Wages Payable	应交增值税 Value-added Tax Payable
80.23	**217.36**	**77.70**	**209.67**	**213.25**	**41.24**	**474.56**	**53.16**
23.20	54.72	7.43	56.85	58.73	8.69	120.39	8.28
9.04	25.22	19.52	13.67	14.08	2.32	70.31	5.67
1.70	9.64	3.15	1.03	1.51	0.50	17.76	0.94
18.84	42.50	3.62	43.30	38.52	4.70	89.84	11.90
12.92	42.61	16.27	111.65	113.63	21.01	98.41	11.04
6.95	19.25	7.06	6.87	8.00	1.57	36.48	5.00
2.75	13.82	3.85	6.45	7.12	1.19	26.09	3.38
4.20	5.43	3.20	0.41	0.88	0.38	10.39	1.62
2.66	7.80	5.35	-0.87	-0.07	0.91	8.51	1.52
4.10	11.26	14.79	-23.25	-22.20	1.30	28.75	3.07
0.69	2.64	0.42	0.81	1.10	0.25	3.04	0.23
0.15	1.71	0.09	-0.31	-0.05	0.00	1.08	0.34

13-6 规模以上其他营利性服务业企业分行业财务状况(2021年)

FFINANCIAL INDICATORS OF OTHER FOR-PROFIT SERVICE ENTERPRISES ABOVE DESIGNATED SIZE BY SECTOR (2021)

行　业	Category	企业单位数(个) Number of Enterprises (unit)	营业收入 Business Revenue	营业成本 Business Costs	税金及附加 Tax and Extra Charges on Business
总计	**Total**	**1345**	**1170.03**	**906.54**	**6.78**
按行业分	**Grouped by Sector**				
互联网和相关服务	Internet and Related Services	20	26.22	21.39	0.08
软件和信息技术服务业	Software and Information Technology Services	197	342.06	248.23	1.23
租赁业	Leasing	28	11.83	9.83	0.05
商务服务业	Business Services	610	424.10	366.85	2.68
研究和试验发展	Research and Experimental Development	36	34.76	21.83	0.24
专业技术服务业	Professional Technical Service Industry	254	247.90	178.34	1.30
科技推广和应用服务业	Technology Promotion and Application Service Industry	20	7.39	5.14	0.03
居民服务业	Services to Households	21	7.21	4.27	0.02
机动车、电子产品和日用产品修理业	Motor Vehicle, Electronic Products and Consumer Products Repair	15	14.08	9.49	0.09
其他服务业	Other Services	24	5.43	4.52	0.03
新闻和出版业	News and Publication	9	13.96	8.73	0.16
广播、电视、电影和影视录音制作业	Production of Radio, Television, Film and Video Recording	47	14.95	12.02	0.11
文化艺术业	Culture and Arts	18	8.92	5.75	0.13
体育	Sports	21	5.44	5.49	0.33
娱乐业	Entertainment	25	5.76	4.69	0.32

注：根据核算最新划定标准，规上其他营利性服务业新增科学研究和技术服务业行业门类。

Note: According to the latest accounting standards, the new scientific research and technical service industry categories of other for-profit service industries are stipulated.

单位：亿元（100 million yuan）

销售费用 Selling Expenses	管理费用 Management Expenses	财务费用 Financial Expenses	营业利润 Business Profits	利润总额 Total Profits	所得税费用 Income Taxes Payable	应付职工薪酬 Total Wages Payable	应交增值税 Value-added Tax Payable
47.12	**109.89**	**15.41**	**50.99**	**50.05**	**9.30**	**225.10**	**26.37**
1.16	1.58	0.00	1.03	1.30	0.04	2.07	0.66
16.38	18.64	1.28	26.15	28.21	2.27	53.86	7.93
0.32	1.28	0.33	0.03	0.15	0.03	1.14	0.36
11.34	33.50	11.45	4.97	7.81	3.46	60.06	7.52
1.06	3.98	-0.04	7.12	9.11	0.71	12.97	0.82
8.01	38.98	1.11	9.87	10.26	1.90	74.42	6.80
0.66	0.91	0.06	0.49	0.44	0.04	1.34	0.14
0.46	1.51	0.06	0.87	0.96	0.27	2.01	0.09
3.16	0.67	-0.19	0.95	1.03	0.29	2.15	0.72
0.07	0.66	0.01	0.13	0.16	0.02	2.64	0.20
1.06	1.92	0.02	2.60	2.90	0.00	3.52	0.50
1.10	1.84	0.18	-0.17	0.06	0.07	1.36	0.15
0.51	1.51	0.41	1.26	-8.10	0.19	2.56	0.23
0.85	1.16	0.39	-2.09	-2.08	–	3.61	0.15
0.99	1.73	0.33	-2.20	-2.15	0.01	1.41	0.11

13-7 规模以上其他营利性服务业企业分市、区财务状况（2021 年）

FFINANCIAL INDICATORS OF OTHER FOR-PROFIT SERVICE ENTERPRISES ABOVE DESIGNATED SIZE BY REGION（2021）

行　业	Category	企业单位数（个）Number of Enterprises（unit）	营业收入 Business Revenue	营业成本 Business Costs	税金及附加 Tax and Extra Charges on Business
全市	**Total**	**1345**	**1170.03**	**906.54**	**6.78**
市南区	Shinan District	241	284.69	219.93	1.49
市北区	Shibei District	165	123.46	96.50	0.69
李沧区	Licang District	128	47.21	39.07	0.32
崂山区	Laoshan District	194	318.36	230.88	1.64
黄岛区（西海岸新区）	Huangdao District（West Coast New Area）	290	205.13	169.03	0.94
城阳区	Chengyang District	171	101.08	78.99	1.00
城阳区（不含高新区）	Chengyang District（Excluding High tech District）	109	55.90	45.20	0.29
高新区	High tech District	62	45.18	33.79	0.71
即墨区	Jimo District	40	17.51	11.74	0.15
胶州市	Jiaozhou	66	45.63	36.73	0.45
平度市	Pingdu	27	18.04	16.02	0.06
莱西市	Laixi	23	8.91	7.67	0.03

单位：亿元（100 million yuan）

销售费用 Selling Expenses	管理费用 Management Expenses	财务费用 Financial Expenses	营业利润 Business Profits	利润总额 Total Profits	所得税费用 Income Taxes Payable	应付职工薪酬 Total Wages Payable	应交增值税 Value-added Tax Payable
47.12	**109.89**	**15.41**	**50.99**	**50.05**	**9.30**	**225.10**	**26.37**
11.82	28.56	3.70	11.88	14.62	2.60	65.87	5.70
4.33	11.73	2.97	6.16	6.53	1.05	25.78	3.11
0.89	5.01	1.50	0.35	0.60	0.31	7.99	0.34
12.90	29.35	0.69	27.17	21.45	2.72	61.68	8.74
8.35	16.99	1.02	2.33	3.49	0.98	33.53	3.32
5.30	10.79	3.76	2.12	2.79	0.92	19.48	2.39
1.26	6.12	0.68	1.63	1.89	0.55	10.55	0.94
4.04	4.68	3.09	0.48	0.90	0.36	8.92	1.46
1.50	2.54	1.62	-0.95	-1.89	0.16	4.75	0.24
1.60	2.55	0.15	1.85	2.16	0.47	4.58	1.16
0.36	1.23	-0.03	0.29	0.30	0.10	0.82	0.17
0.08	1.13	0.03	-0.13	0.01	0.00	0.64	0.32

主要统计指标解释

营业收入 指企业经营主要业务和其他业务所确认的收入总额。营业收入合计包括"主营业务收入"和"其他业务收入"。根据会计"利润表"中"营业收入"项目的本年累计数填报。

营业成本 指企业经营主要业务和其他业务所发生的成本总额。包括企业（单位）在报告期内从事销售商品、提供劳务等日常活动发生的各种耗费。包括"主营业务成本"和"其他业务成本"。根据会计"利润表"中"营业成本"项目的本年累计数填报。

税金及附加 指企业因从事生产经营活动按税法规定应缴纳的消费税、城市维护建设税、资源税、教育费附加及房产税、土地使用税、车船使用税、印花税等相关税费。根据会计"利润表"中"税金及附加"项目的本年累计数填报。

销售费用 指企业在销售商品和材料、提供劳务的过程中发生的各种费用，包括保险费、包装费、展览费和广告费、商品维修费、预计产品质量保证损失、运输费、装卸费等以及为销售本企业商品而专设的销售机构（含销售网点、售后服务网点等）的职工薪酬、业务费、折旧费等经营费用。

管理费用 指企业为组织和管理企业生产经营所发生的费用，包括企业在筹建期间内发生的开办费、董事会和行政管理部门在企业经营管理中发生的，或者应当由企业统一负担的公司经费等。根据会计"利润表"中"管理费用"项目的本年累计数填报。

财务费用 指企业为筹集生产经营所需资金等而发生的筹资费用，包括企业生产经营期间发生的利息支出（减利息收入）、汇兑损失（减汇兑收益）以及相关的手续费等。根据会计"利润表"中"财务费用"项目的本年累计数填报。

利润总额 指企业在一定会计期间的经营成果，是生产经营过程中各种收入扣除各种耗费后的盈余，反映企业在报告期内实现的盈亏总额。根据会计"利润表"中"利润总额"项目的本年累计数填报。执行《企业会计准则》或《小企业会计准则》的企业，利润总额为营业利润加上营业外收入，减去营业外支出后的金额；执行其他企业会计制度的企业，利润总额为营业利润加上投资收益、营业外收入，再减去营业外支出后的金额。

应交增值税 指按照税法规定，以销售货物、服务、无形资产、不动产或提供加工、修理修配劳务的增值额和货物进口金额为计税依据而课征的一种流转税。

Explanatory Notes on Main Statistical Indicators

Business Revenue refers to the total income of the business recognized by business and other business. Total operating revenue includes the main business income and other operating income. Fill in according to the cumulative number of the current year's "Business Revenue" item in the "profit statement" of accounting.

Business Costs refers to the total amount of costs incurred by an enterprise in operating its main business and other businesses. Including the enterprise (unit) in the reporting period engaged in selling goods, providing labor services and other daily activities of all kinds of consumption. Include "main business cost" and "other business cost" . The current year' s cumulative counting is reported according to the operating cost item in the accounting "income statement" .

Taxes and surcharges refers to the excise duty, urban maintenance and construction tax, resource tax, education surcharge, property tax, land use tax, vehicle and vessel use tax, stamp tax and other related taxes and fees that the enterprise should pay in accordance with the tax law for its production and business activities. Fill in according to the cumulative number of the current year' s "Taxes and surcharges" item in the "profit statement" of accounting.

Sales expense refers to the various expenses incurred by the enterprise in the process of selling goods and materials and providing labor services, including insurance, packaging, exhibition and advertising fees, product maintenance fees, estimated product quality assurance losses, transportation fees, loading and unloading fees, etc. Operating expenses such as employee salaries, business expenses, depreciation expenses and other operating expenses of specialized sales organizations (including sales outlets, after-sales service outlets, etc.) that sell the products of the enterprise.

Management Cost refers to the costs of organizing and managing enterprise operation, including the operational cost of the board of directors and the executive body in management that shall be borne by the enterprise. Fill in according to the cumulative number of the current year' s "Management Cost " item in the "profit statement" of accounting.

Financial Cost refers to the cost from raising fund for production and operation, including expenditure of interests, loss of momentary exchange and related charges. Fill in according to the cumulative number of the current year' s "Financial Cost" item in the "profit statement" of accounting.

Total Profits refers to the operating results of an enterprise in a certain accounting period. It is the surplus after deducting various expenses from various incomes in the production and operation process, reflecting the total profit and loss realized by the enterprise during the reporting period. Fill in according to the cumulative number of the current year' s "Total Profits" item in the "profit statement" of accounting. For companies that implement the "Accounting Standards for Business Enterprises" or "Accounting Standards for Small Businesses," the total profit is the amount of operating profit plus non-operating income, minus non-operating expenses ; for companies implementing other corporate accounting systems, the total profit is the operating profit plus Investment income, nonoperating income, minus the amount of non-operating expenses.

VAT payable refers to a transfer tax levied on the basis of tax on the value added of goods, services, intangible assets, real estate or the provision of processing, repair and repair services and the amount of import of goods, as stipulated in the tax law.

建筑业 14

CONSTRUCTION

简要说明

一、本篇资料的主要内容

本篇资料主要反映了全市建筑业基本情况，主要包括建筑业总产值、增加值、建筑企业生产指标、财务指标、重点建筑企业名单等方面的内容。

二、本篇资料的来源

本篇资料来源于建筑业统计年报，由市统计局固定资产投资统计处整理提供。

Brief Introduction

Ⅰ. Main Content

Data in this chapter show the basic conditions of construction of the whole city, mainly including the gross output value of construction, value added, major production and financial indicators and list of key enterprises of construction, etc.

Ⅱ. Source of Data

Data in this chapter are based on the annual report of construction industry, and complied by the Division of Investment and Construction Statistics of Qingdao Municipal Bureau of Statistics.

14-1 建筑业企业生产情况（2021 年）
PRODUCTION SITUATION OF CONSTRUCTION ENTERPRISES（2021）

项 目	Item	单位	Unit	合计 Total	#中央 of which：Central Enterprises	国有企业 State-owned Enterprises	集体企业 Collective Enterprises	其他所有制企业 Other Ownership Enterprises
施工企业单位数	Number of Construction Enterprises	个	unit	889	13	19	7	863
建筑业总产值	Gross Output Value of Construction	万元	10 000 yuan	32972735	6789684	376537	10793	32585405
#建筑工程	of which：Construction	万元	10 000 yuan	28291365	5321836	340166	10793	27940406
安装工程	Installation	万元	10 000 yuan	3480438	1225420	7491		3472947
建筑业增加值	Value Added of Construction	万元	10 000 yuan	12147300				
全年竣工产值	Output Value of Buildings Completed in the Year	万元	10 000 yuan	11684026	963962	29878	8657	11645491
施工房屋面积	Floor Space of Buildings under Construction	万平方米	10 000 sp.m	21906	4847	44	11	21851
#新开工	of which：Newly Operating	万平方米	10 000 sp.m	7126	852	37	6	7083
竣工房屋面积	Floor Space of Buildings Completed	万平方米	10 000 sp.m	4508	210		2	4506
#住宅	of which：Residential Buildings	万平方米	10 000 sp.m	2527	123			2527
计算建筑业劳动生产率平均人数	Average Number of Persons for Calculating the Labor Productivity	人	person	638808	97733	2844	355	635609

14-2 建筑业企业财务状况（2021年）
FINANCIAL SITUATION OF CONSTRUCTION ENTRPRISES（2021）

项　目	Item	单位	Unit	合计 Total
流动资产	Circulating Funds	万元	10 000 yuan	27922937
#存货	of which：Inventory	万元	10 000 yuan	3824085
年末固定资产原价	Original Value of Fixed Assets（year-end）	万元	10 000 yuan	2253316
本年固定资产折旧	Depreciation of Fixed Assets in the Year	万元	10 000 yuan	161091
年末资产合计	Total Assets（year-end）	万元	10 000 yuan	33225430
年末负债合计	Total Liabilities（year-end）	万元	10 000 yuan	26455774
所有者权益合计	Total Owners' Equity	万元	10 000 yuan	6769791
#实收资本	Paid-in Capitals	万元	10 000 yuan	3592883
主营业务收入	Revenue from Principal Business	万元	10 000 yuan	30753016
主营业务成本	Cost of Principal Business	万元	10 000 yuan	27778703
主营业务税金及附加	Taxes and Extra Charges on Principal Business	万元	10 000 yuan	92908
管理费用	Management Expenses	万元	10 000 yuan	795083
利润总额	Total Profits	万元	10 000 yuan	729848
利税总额	Total Pre-tax Profits	万元	10 000 yuan	1284091
年末应收工程款	Account Receivable（year-end）	万元	10 000 yuan	7707691

#中央 of which : Central Enterprises	国有企业 State-owned Enterprises	集体企业 Collective Enterprises	其他所有制企业 Other Ownership Enterprises
8051646	661653	3965	27257319
592460	78119	493	3745473
846429	98470	1492	2153355
56476	8187	7	152897
9629463	788278	6503	32430648
8402901	631257	2177	25822340
1226562	157022	4326	6608443
594165	96463	2328	3494092
9635966	518470	10921	30223625
9010364	423909	10576	27344218
13619	1128	37	91743
132067	19063	258	775762
190818	30573	94	699181
260039	49905	447	1233740
1695612	205784	1050	7500857

14-3 建筑业企业主要经济效益指标（2021 年）
MAIN INDICATORS ON ECONOMIC BENEFIT OF CONSTRUCTION ENTERPRISES（2021）

项 目	Item	单位 Unit	合计 Total	#中央 of which: Central Enterprises	国有企业 State-owned Enterprises	集体企业 Collective Enterprises	其他所有制企业 Other Ownership Enterprises
建筑业劳动生产率	**Labor Productivity of Construction**						
按总产值计算	In Terms of Gross Output Value	元/人 yuan/person	516160	694718	1323970	304028	512664
竣工率	**Rate of Buildings completed**						
按产值计算	In Terms of Gross output Value	%	35.4	24.2	17.9	60.8	33.3
产值工资率	Ratio of Wages to Gross Output Value	%	14.9	15.8	14.5	25.8	14.5
资金利润率	Ratio of Profit to Funds	%	2.5	2.2	4.1	1.8	2.1
产值利润率	Ratio of Profit to Gross Output Value	%	2.2	2.7	8.1	1.9	1.6
流动比率	Current Ratio	%	112.7	103.1	110.7	138.0	112.7
资产负债率	Assets-Liability Ratio	%	79.6	87.3	80.1	37.5	78.6

14-4 建筑业增加值（2021 年）
VALUE ADDED OF CONSTRUCTION（2021）

单位：亿元（100 million yuan）

市、区名称	Region	增加值 Value Added
全市	**Whole Municipal**	**1214.73**
市南区	Shinan District	74.89
市北区	Shibei District	136.01
李沧区	Licang District	45.36
崂山区	Laoshan District	127.08
黄岛区（西海岸新区）	Huangdao District（West Coast New Area）	344.00
城阳区（含高新区）	Chengyang District（Including High tech District）	112.91
即墨区	Jimo District	136.06
胶州市	Jiaozhou	131.33
平度市	Pingdu	31.58
莱西市	Laixi	81.61

14-5 重点建筑企业一览表(2021年)
LIST OF KEY CONSTRUCTION ENTERPRISES(2021)

序号 Precedence	企业单位名称	Name	所在地区 Location	资质等级 Qualification Criteria
1	青建集团股份公司	Qingjian Group Co., Ltd.	市北区 Shibei District	A001
2	中铁建工集团山东有限公司	China Railway Construction Engineering Group Shandong Co., Ltd.	城阳区 Chengyang District	A101
3	中建八局第四建设有限公司	Fourth Construction of China Construction Eight Bureau Co., Ltd.	崂山区 Laoshan District	A001
4	荣华建设集团有限公司	Ronghua Construction Group Co., Ltd.	莱西市 Laixi	A001
5	中青建安建设集团有限公司	Zhongqing Jianan Construction Group Co., Ltd.	市北区 Shibei District	A001
6	中铁二十局集团第四工程有限公司	Fourth Engineering of China Railway twenty Bureau Group Co., Ltd.	崂山区 Laoshan District	A002
7	中启胶建集团有限公司	Zhongqi Rubber Construction Group Co., Ltd.	胶州市 Jiaozhou	A001
8	山东兴华建设集团有限公司	Shandong Xinghua Construction Group Co., Ltd.	黄岛区 Huangdao District	A001
9	荣泰建设集团有限公司	Rongtai Construction Engineering Group Co., Ltd.	黄岛区 Huangdao District	A001
10	青岛亿联建设集团股份有限公司	Qingdao Elink Construction Group Co., Ltd.	黄岛区 Huangdao District	A001
11	中铁十七局集团第一工程有限公司	China Railway No.17 Bureau Group First Engineering Co.,Ltd.	黄岛区 Huangdao District	A003
12	中交一航局第二工程有限公司	Second Engineering Company Co., Ltd. of China Communications Central Airlines	市南区 Shinan District	A104
13	东亚装饰股份有限公司	East Asia Decoration Limited by Share Ltd.	市北区 Shibei District	B103
14	青岛中嘉建设集团有限公司	Qingdao Zhongjia Construction Group Co., Ltd.	市北区 Shibei District	A101
15	青岛海骊住居科技股份有限公司	Qingdao Hailizhuju Technology Co., Ltd.	胶州市 Jiaozhou	B103
16	青岛海川建设集团有限公司	Qingdao Hai Chuan Construction Group Co., Ltd.	市北区 Shibei District	A001
17	青岛建设集团股份有限公司	Qingdao Construction Group Co., Ltd.	市南区 Shinan District	B103
18	中建筑港集团有限公司	Zhongjian Zhu Gang Group Co., Ltd.	市北区 Shibei District	A104
19	中诚祥建设集团有限公司	Zhongchengxiang Construction Engineering Co., Ltd.	李沧区 Licang District	A101
20	青岛新华友建工集团股份有限公司	Qingdao Xinhuayou Construction Engineering Group Limited by Share Ltd.	崂山区 Laoshan District	A101
21	青岛博海建设集团有限公司	Qingdao Bohai Construction Group Co., Ltd.	市南区 Shinan District	A001
22	中建八局发展建设有限公司	China Construction Eight Engineering Division Co., Ltd.	黄岛区 Huangdao District	A101
23	青建国际集团有限公司	Qingjian International Group Limited	市北区 Shibei District	A101
24	青岛瑞源工程集团有限公司	Qingdao Ruiyuan Engineering Group Co., Ltd.	黄岛区 Huangdao District	A105
25	青岛市房屋建设集团股份有限公司	Qingdao Housing Construction Group Limited by Share Ltd.	市北区 Shibei District	A101
26	中铁二十五局集团第五工程有限公司	The 5th Engineering Co., Ltd. of China Railway 25th Bureau Group	崂山区 Laoshan District	A110
27	青岛营上建设集团有限公司	Qingdao Yingshang Construction Group Co., Ltd.	即墨区 Jimo District	A101
28	中铁十局集团青岛工程有限公司	China Railway Ten Bureau Group Qingdao Engineering Co., Ltd.	市北区 Shibei District	A110
29	德才装饰股份有限公司	Decai Decoration Limited by Share Ltd.	崂山区 Laoshan District	B103
30	中国石油天然气第七建设有限公司	China Petroleum and Natural Gas Seventh Construction Co., Ltd.	崂山区 Laoshan District	A109
31	青岛颐金建设装饰集团有限公司	Qingdao Yijin Construction Decoration Group Co., Ltd.	市南区 Shinan District	B103
32	青岛即建建设集团有限公司	Qingdao JiJian Construction Group Co., Ltd.	即墨区 Jimo District	A101
33	青岛胶城建设集团有限公司	Qingdao Rubber City Construction Group Co., Ltd.	胶州市 Jiaozhou	A101
34	青岛土木建工集团有限公司	Qingdao Civil Engineering Group Co., Ltd.	黄岛区 Huangdao District	A101

14-5 续表 1
Continued

序 号 Precedence	企业单位名称	Name	所在地区 Location	资质等级 Qualification Criteria
35	山东电力建设第三工程有限公司	Third Engineering Co., Ltd. of Shandong Electric Power Construction	崂山区 Laoshan District	A006
36	青岛温泉建设集团有限公司	Qingdao Hot Spring Construction Group Co., Ltd.	即墨区 Jimo District	A101
37	青岛艺高城市建设工程有限公司	Qingdao Yi Gao City Construction Engineering Co., Ltd.	市北区 Shibei District	A201
38	青岛滨海建设集团有限公司	Qingdao Binhai Construction Group Co., Ltd.	黄岛区 Huangdao District	A101
39	青岛中建联合集团有限公司	Qingdao Sino United Group Co., Ltd.	崂山区 Laoshan District	A101
40	中铁十四局集团青岛工程有限公司	Qingdao Engineering Co., Ltd. of China Railway 14th Bureau Group Co., Ltd.	城阳区 Chengyang District	A110
41	青岛恒生源集团建设有限公司	Qingdao Hengshengyuan Group Construction Co., Ltd.	即墨区 Jimo District	A101
42	青岛平建建筑安装股份有限公司	Qingdao Pingjian Construction and Installation Co., Ltd.	平度市 Pingdu	A101
43	山东高速莱钢绿建发展有限公司	Laigang Lvjian Development Co. Ltd of Shandong Hi-speed Group	崂山区 Laoshan District	A101
44	青岛第一市政工程有限公司	Qingdao First Municipal Engineering Co., Ltd.	市北区 Shibei District	A110
45	中石化第十建设有限公司	Sinopec tenth Construction Company Limited	黄岛区 Huangdao District	A109
46	中即控股有限公司	Zongji Holding Grouping	即墨区 Jimo District	A101
47	青岛德泰建设工程有限公司	Qingdao De Tai Construction Engineering Co., Ltd.	黄岛区 Huangdao District	A101
48	山东国建工程集团有限公司	Shandong State Construction Engineering Group Co., Ltd.	崂山区 Laoshan District	A101
49	青岛建祥建设集团有限公司	Qingdao Jian Xiang Construction Group Co., Ltd.	胶州市 Jiaozhou	A101
50	青岛一建集团有限公司	Qingdao Yi Jian Group Co., Ltd.	市北区 Shibei District	A001
51	青岛胶州湾建设集团有限公司	Qingdao Jiaozhou Bay Construction Group Co., Ltd.	胶州市 Jiaozhou	A101
52	中建中新建设工程有限公司	China State Construction Zhongxin Construction Engineering Co.,Ltd	高新区 High tech District	A101
53	青岛福瀛建设集团有限公司	Qingdao Fu ying Construction Group Co., Ltd.	黄岛区 Huangdao District	A101
54	青岛环城建工集团有限公司	Qingdao Ring City Construction Engineering Group Co., Ltd.	黄岛区 Huangdao District	A101
55	青岛城建集团有限公司	Qingdao Urban Construction Group Co., Ltd.	市北区 Shibei District	A110
56	青岛西海岸市政工程有限公司	Qingdao West Coast municipal Group Municipal Engineering Company	黄岛区 Huangdao District	A110
57	青城建工集团有限公司	Qingcheng Construction Group Co., Ltd.	高新区 High tech District	A101
58	青岛港（集团）港务工程有限公司	Harbor Engineering Co., Ltd of Qingdao Port (Group)	黄岛区 Huangdao District	A204
59	青岛营海建设（集团）有限公司	Qingdao Ying hai Construction Group Co., Ltd.	胶州市 Jiaozhou	A101
60	青岛安装建设股份有限公司	Qingdao Installation and Construction Limited by Share Ltd.	市北区 Shibei District	A112
61	青岛前盛业建设工程有限公司	Qingdao Qianshengye Construction Engineering Co., Ltd.	黄岛区 Huangdao District	A101
62	青岛海德工程集团股份有限公司	Qingdao Hyde Road and Bridge Engineering Limited by Share Ltd.	崂山区 Laoshan District	B111
63	青岛建设集团建兴工程有限公司	Qingdao construction group LITE-ON Engineering Co., Ltd.	高新区 High tech District	A101
64	青岛海纳云智能系统有限公司	Qingdao Haina Cloud Intelligent System Co., Ltd	崂山区 Laoshan District	B223
65	青岛建设装饰集团有限公司	Qingdao Construction Decoration Group Co.,Ltd.	市南区 Shinan District	B103

14-5 续表 2
Continued

序 号 Precedence	企业单位名称	Name	所在地区 Location	资质等级 Qualification Criteria
66	青岛元昌盛房建集团有限公司	Qingdao Yuanchangsheng Housing Construction Group Co., Ltd.	胶州市 Jiaozhou	A201
67	青岛泰佳建筑工程有限公司	Qingdao Taijia Construction Engineering Co., LTD	胶州市 Jiaozhou	A201
68	青岛亨通路桥建设有限公司	Qingdao Hengtong Road and Bridge Construction Co. LTD	市北区 Shibei District	A301
69	青岛方圆达建设集团有限公司	Qingdao Fang Yuan Da Construction Group Co.,Ltd.	李沧区 Licang District	A101
70	青岛青房建安集团有限公司	Qingdao Qingfang Jianan Group Co., Ltd.	市南区 Shinan District	A101
71	青岛高新建筑安装工程有限公司	Qingdao High-tech Construction and Installation Engineering Co., Ltd.	崂山区 Laoshan District	A101
72	青岛东捷建设工程有限公司	Qingdao Dong jie Construction Engineering Co., Ltd.	市北区 Shibei District	A101
73	青岛市政空间开发集团有限责任公司	Qingdao Municipal Construction Group Co., Ltd.	市南区 Shinan District	A110
74	青岛交科建设集团有限公司	Qingdao Jiaoke Construction Group Co. LTD	崂山区 Laoshan District	A102
75	山东天诚交通工程有限公司	Shandong Tiancheng Traffic Engineering Co., LTD	崂山区 Laoshan District	A110
76	青岛云川建筑有限公司	Qingdao Yun Chuan Architecture Co., Ltd.	胶州市 Jiaozhou	A210
77	平度市兴业建筑有限公司	Pingdu Xingye Construction Co. LTD	平度市 Pingdu	A201
78	青岛鑫兴泰建筑工程有限公司	Qingdao Xinxingtai Construction Engineering Co., Ltd.	城阳区 Chengyang District	A201
79	青岛建工建安集团有限公司	Qingdao Construction Engineering Jian'an Group Co., Ltd.	崂山区 Laoshan District	A101
80	青岛市崂山区古建建筑工程有限公司	Qingdao Laoshan ancient building engineering Co., Ltd.	崂山区 Laoshan District	A101
81	青岛昆泉建设工程有限公司	Qingdao Kunquan Construction Engineering Co., Ltd.	黄岛区 Huangdao District	A101
82	青岛亿佰建工集团有限公司	Qingdao Yibai Construction Engineering Group Co., Ltd.	黄岛区 Huangdao District	A201
83	青岛兰桂建工有限公司	Qingdao Langui Construction Engineering Co., Ltd.	黄岛区 Huangdao District	A301
84	青岛诚通建筑工程有限公司	Qingdao Chengtong Construction Engineering Co., Ltd.	黄岛区 Huangdao District	A201
85	青岛华山广泰建设集团有限公司	Qingdao Huashan Guangtai Construction Group Co., Ltd.	即墨区 Jimo District	A201
86	青岛交建集团有限公司	Qingdao Construction Group Co. LTD	崂山区 Laoshan District	A102
87	恒华数字科技集团有限公司	Henghua Digital Technology Group Co. LTD	市南区 Shinan District	B123
88	山东世纪阳光建筑科技有限公司	Shandong Century Sunshine Construction Technology Co., Ltd.	市南区 Shinan District	B112
89	青岛巨源建工集团有限公司	Qingdao Juyuan Construction Engineering Group Co., Ltd.	崂山区 Laoshan District	A110
90	青岛隆昌达建设集团有限公司	Qingdao Longchangda Construction Group Co., Ltd.	胶州市 Jiaozhou	A101
91	即墨市七级建筑工程有限公司	Jimo Seventh Grade Construction Engineering Co., Ltd.	即墨区 Jimo District	A201
92	青岛望城三宝建设有限公司	Qingdao Wangcheng Sanbao Construction Co., Ltd.	莱西市 Laixi	A101
93	青岛田横建筑工程有限公司	Qingdao Tianheng Construction Engineering Co., LTD	即墨区 Jimo District	A201
94	青岛嘉恒建设集团有限公司	Qingdao Jiaheng Construction Group Co., Ltd.	市南区 Shinan District	A101
95	青岛林海建设工程有限公司	Qingdao Linhai Construction Engineering Co., LTD	黄岛区 Huangdao District	A210
96	青岛东建建设有限公司	Qingdao Dongjian Construction Co., Ltd.	李沧区 Licang District	A101
97	青岛地矿岩土工程有限公司	Qingdao Geotechnical Engineering Co., Ltd.	市南区 Shinan District	B101
98	中铁二十五局集团轨道交通建设有限公司	China Railway 25th Bureau Group Rail Transit Construction Co. LTD	高新区 High tech District	A310
99	青岛金星科技工程有限公司	Qingdao Jinxing Technology Engineering Co., LTD	市南区 Shinan District	B111
100	青岛恒基伟泰建筑有限公司	Qingdao Hengji Weitai Construction Co. LTD	城阳区 Chengyang District	A201

主要统计指标解释

建筑业统计单位 指从事房屋、构筑物建造和设备安装活动的法人企业。建筑业法人企业应具有建筑业资质并能够独立核算，同时其应具备以下条件：①依法成立，有自己的名称、组织机构和场所，能够承担民事责任；②独立拥有和使用资产，承担负债，有权与其他单位签订合同；③独立核算盈亏，能够编制资产负债表。

建筑业总产值 是以货币形式表现的建筑业企业在一定时期内生产的建筑业产品和提供的服务的总和。建筑业总产值包括：

（1）建筑工程产值：指列入建筑工程预算内的各种工程价值。

（2）安装工程产值：指设备安装工程价值，不包括被安装设备本身的价值。

（3）其他产值：建筑业总产值中除建筑工程、安装工程以外的产值。包括房屋构筑物修理产值、非标准设备制造产值、总包企业向分包企业收取的管理费以及不能明确划分的施工活动所完成的产值。

建筑业增加值 指建筑业企业在报告期内以货币形式表现的建筑业生产经营活动的最终成果。

建筑业现价增加值 按生产法和分配法（收入法）两种方法计算，以收入法的计算结果为准，即从收入的角度出发，根据生产要素在生产过程中应得的收入份额计算。具体计算方法：经济普查年度建筑业增加值按照《经济普查年度 GDP 核算方案》计算，非经济普查年度建筑业增加值按照《非经济普查年度 GDP 核算方案》计算。

Explanatory Notes on Main Statistical Indicators

Statistical Unit in Construction refers to corporate enterprise engaged in the construction of buildings and structures and in the installation of equipment. A corporate construction enterprise should have qualification certificates with independent accounting system, and should meet the following 3 requirements: (1) being set up in line with relevant legal basis, having its full name, organization and location, and capable of taking civil liabilities; (2) independently possessing and using its assets and assuming its liabilities, and entitled to sign contracts with other institutions; (3) making independent accounts of its profits and losses, and capable of compiling its own balance sheet.

Gross Output Value of Construction refers to total of construction products and services, expressed in money terms, produced or rendered by construction and installation enterprises during a given period of time. It includes:

(1) Output value of construction projects, that is the value of projects covered by the project budgets;

(2) Output value of installation projects, that is the value of the installation of equipment, excluding the value of the equipment to be installed;

(3) Output value of others, that is the output value of construction industry excluding that of construction projects and installation projects. It includes: output value of repair of buildings and structures; output value of non-standard equipment manufacturing; overhead expenses received by contracted enterprises to the sub-contracted enterprises and the completed output value of construction activities that have no clear definition.

Added Value Of Construction Industry refers to the final results of construction industry production and operation activities expressed in currency by construction enterprises during the reporting period.

Value Added At Current Price Of Construction Industry Calculate according to the two methods of production method and distribution method (income method) . The calculation result of income method shall prevail, that is, from the perspective of income, it is calculated according to the income share of production factors in the production process. Specific calculation method : The annual added value of the construction industry in the economic census is calculated in accordance with the "Annual GDP Accounting Plan for the Economic Census", and the annual added value of the construction industry in the non-economic census is calculated in accordance with the "Non-economic Census Annual GDP Accounting Plan" .

运输、邮电 15

TRANSPORT, POSTAL AND TELECOMMUNICATION SERVICES

简要说明

一、本篇资料的主要内容

本篇资料主要反映了全市交通运输业和邮电业通讯业发展的基本情况，主要包括客货运输及港口吞吐量、民用汽车拥有量、独立核算运输邮电单位主要财务指标、邮电通讯基本情况、邮政行业发展情况、快递企业发展情况、电信行业基本情况、城市轨道交通发展情况等方面的内容。

二、本篇资料的来源

1. 本篇资料中交通运输邮电资料来源于全市交通运输邮电业统计年报。

2. 交通运输资料来源于青岛市交通运输局、青岛港（集团）有限公司、青岛国际机场集团有限公司、青岛地铁集团有限公司。

3. 邮政业资料来源于青岛市邮政管理局、中国邮政集团公司青岛市分公司。

4. 电信业资料来源于青岛市通信管理局、中国电信集团公司山东省青岛市电信分公司、中国电信股份有限公司青岛分公司、中国联合网络通信有限公司青岛市分公司、中国移动通信集团山东有限公司青岛分公司。

5. 民用汽车拥有量资料来源于青岛市公安局交警支队车辆管理所。

本篇资料由市统计局服务业统计处整理提供。

Brief Introduction

Ⅰ. Main Content

Data in this chapter show the basic conditions of the development of transport, post and.telecommunications in Shandong Province, mainly including the freight traffic and passenger traffic, cargo handled at port, possession of civil motor vehicles, major financial indices and basic conditions of transport postal and telecommunication services, development of the postal services, express company development development of urban rail transit.

Ⅱ. Source of Data

1. Data on transport are based on the annual report of transport.

2. Transportation data comes from Qingdao Municipal Transportation Bureau, Qingdao Port (Group) Co., Ltd.. Qingdao International Airport Group Co.,Ltd., and Qingdao Metro Group Co., Ltd.

3. Data on postal and telecommunication are based on Qingdao Municipal Postal Administration, Qingdao Post Bureau.

4. Data on business of telecommunication services Qingdao Communication Administration,China Telecom Group Corporation Qingdao Branch of Shandong Province,China Telecom Co.,Ltd.Qingdao Branch, China United Network Communications Co.. Ltd. Qingdao Branch,China Mobile Communications Group Shandong Co., Ltd.Qingdao Branch.

5. Date on possession of civil motor vehicles are provided by Qingdao Municipal Public Security Bureau Traffic Police Detachment Vehicle Management Office.

Data in this chapter are prepared and provide by the Division of Industry Statistics of Qingdao Municipal Bureau of Statistics.

15-1 主要年份客货运输及港口吞吐量
MAJOR YEAR'S PASSENGER & FREIGHT TRAFFIC AND HANDLING CAPACITY OF THE PORTS

年份 Year	客运量（万人）Passenger Traffic（10 000 persons）			货运量（万吨）Freight Traffic（10 000 tons）			港口货物吞吐量（万吨）Volume of Freight Handled in Ports（10000 tons）	集装箱吞吐量（万标箱）Containers（10 000 TEU）	航空旅客吞吐量（万人）Air Passenger Throughput（10 000 persons）	航空货邮吞吐量（万吨）Air Cargo and Mail Throughput（10 000 tons）
	铁路 Railways	公路 Highways	海运 Waterways	铁路 Railways	公路 Highways	海运 Waterways				
1949	327	14	9	386	162	22	73			
1952	571	49	13	447	399	44	181			
1957	1054	149	13	747	548	118	269			
1962	3100	141	39	909	524	97	391			
1965	1424	230	19	1257	690	158	524			
1970	1329	373	20	1856	736	232	695			
1975	1803	159	30	2325	817	282	1542			
1978	1986	274	49	2917	1561	528	2081			
1980	1896	713	73	2596	1642	941	1779			
1985	2063	1 894	86	3009	2303	919	2610		2.17	0.06
1988	2083	3 300	234	3418	6486	1160	3153		17.48	0.32
1990	1488	3 639	316	3741	6433	1556	3068		28.12	0.54
1991	1453	4144	366	3774	6896	1789	3194		38.36	0.70
1992	1488	4965	437	3899	6822	1981	3240		54.17	0.57
1993	1499	6436	499	4044	7685	1910	3650		70.77	0.70
1994	1564	6787		4112	8336	1804	4331		92.64	0.88
1995	1480	9785		4205	11788	2185	5165		132.71	1.26
1996	1230	10738		4415	10749	474	6056	81.1	157.61	1.73
1997	1308	11855		4466	11232	544	6944	103.3	178.68	1.96
1998	1549	11754		4028	14311	1792	7044	121.3	184.66	2.15
1999	1674	12103		3919	14550	1926	7282	154.3	203.11	2.89
2000	1780	12145		4256	17234	2998	8661	212.0	243.15	3.44
2001	1678	13686		4778	20906	3432	10423	264.0	281.01	3.62
2002	1530	14516	777	5079	24480	2530	12252	341.0	321.99	4.63
2003	1366	13132	786	4929	27241	2773	14135	424.0	349.10	5.46
2004	1496	16420	862	5119	29937	3503	16303	514.0	480.84	7.55
2005	552	17212	972	2299	31009	4471	18727	630.7	587.96	8.91
2006	810	17752	999	2790	32047	4768	22438	770.0	679.12	10.13
2007	1101	18800	1080	2781	33336	4019	26507	946.6	786.80	11.57
2008	1278	19909	1055	3225	34172	5080	30029	1037.7	820.04	13.05
2009	1425	19612	1145	3772	16297	4332	31668	1027.6	966.01	13.54
2010	1537	20460	1302	5031	17525	4407	35012	1201.0	1110.12	16.37
2011	1693	21560	791	5697	19208	4220	37971	1302.0	1171.64	16.65
2012	1881	22724	414	6126	21312	1791	41465	1450.0	1260.12	17.19
2013	2056	23588	333	6266	23270	1313	45782	1552.0	1451.67	18.62
2014	2301	5588	324	5564	19043	1434	47701	1658.0	1641.18	20.44
2015	2421	5370	288	5486	20073	1456	49749	1743.0	1820.21	20.81
2016	2701	4532	225	5569	20701	1685	51463	1805.0	2050.50	23.69
2017	3179	4534	215	6021	24716	1800	51314	1830.9	2321.06	23.21
2018	3455	4602	161	6280	27453	2502	54250	1931.5	2453.57	22.45
2019	3979	4593	186	6115	29170	2493	57736	2101.2	2555.63	25.63
2020	1240	1844	66	8416	25737	2363	60459	2200.8	1456.16	20.68
2021	1912	3113	119	8494	28407	3068	63029	2371.4	1603.20	23.76

注：1. 从 2014 年公路客、货运量统计口径进行调整，与以前年度不可比。
2. 根据市交通运输局提供数据，对航空部分吞吐量历史数据进行了修正。

Notes：1. In 2014，the Ministry of Transportation made an adjustment to the statistical gauge for highway passenger and freight transportation and the data are not comparable directly.
2. According to the data provided by the Municipal Transportation Bureau, some historical data of aviation throughput have been revised.

15-2 民用车辆拥有量(2021 年底)
POSSESSION OF CIVIL MOTOR VEHICLES（END OF 2021）

单位：辆（unit）

项目	Item	合计 Total 辆数 Number	#个人 of which：Private Vehicles 辆数 Number
一、汽车	**Automobile**	**3537988**	**3051830**
1. 载客汽车	Passenger Vehicles	3023577	2738949
其中：轿车	of which：Sedan	1937247	1783993
2. 载货汽车	Trucks	330943	181829
3. 其他汽车	Other Automobile	19546	10175
二、电车	**Tram**	**125**	
三、摩托车	**Motorcycle**	**128360**	**125902**
四、农用运输车	**Agricultural Camion**		
五、挂车	**Trailer Trucks**	**41205**	**616**
六、其他类型车	**Other Vehicles**		
七、校车	**School Bus**	**2618**	**1**

补充资料：机动车驾驶员（4138459 人），其中：汽车驾驶员（4091983 人）
Supplementary information：Motor drivers（4138459 persons），Of which：Automobile drivers（4091983 persons）

15-3 客货运输及港口吞吐量（2021 年）
PASSENGER & FREICHT TRAFFIC AND HANDLING CAPACITY OF THE PORTS（2021）

项目 Item	货运量（万吨）Freight Traffic（10 000 tons）	货物周转量（亿吨公里）Cargo Turnover（100million tons · km）	客运量（万人）Passenger Traffic（10 000 persons）	旅客周转量（亿人公里）Passenger Turnover（100 million persons-km）	项目 Item	旅客吞吐量（万人）Passenger Throughput（10 000 persons）	货物吞吐量（万吨）Cargo Throughput（10 000 tons）	集装箱（万标箱）Containers（10 000 TEU）
总计 Total	**39969**	**2645.96**	**5144**	**73.60**	**总计 Total**	**1603**	**63053**	**2371**
铁路 Railways	8494	78.09	1912	48.06	机场 Civil Aviation	1603	24	
公路 Highways	28407	662.92	3113	25.41	港口 Ports		63029	2371
水运 Waterways	3068	1904.96	119	0.13				

15-4 规模以上运输邮电单位主要财务指标（2021 年）
MAJOR FINANCIAL INDICATORS OF TRANSPORTATION, POST AND TELECOMMUNICATION UNITS ABOVE DESIGNATED SCALE（2021）

单位：亿元（100 million yuan）

项目	Item	营业收入 Revenue from principal Business	营业成本 Cost of principal Business	营业利润 Operating Profits	营业税金及附加 Business taxes and surtax	利润总额 Total Profits
总　计	**Total**	**2426.73**	**2274.19**	**152.71**	**6.28**	**154.31**
铁路运输业	Railway Transport	17.39	11.90	-1.62	0.06	-1.62
道路运输业	Road Transport	330.78	375.72	12.07	1.89	13.32
水上运输业	Water Transport	148.80	98.40	69.18	1.50	69.15
航空运输业	Air Transport	34.49	49.04	-23.00	0.64	-22.35
管道运输业	Pipeline Transport	15.29	6.20	10.39	0.12	10.44
多式联运和运输代理业	Multimodal Transport and Transport Agent	1437.96	1377.33	32.84	0.51	31.85
装卸搬运和仓储业	Loading And Unloading And Storage	223.93	189.34	19.15	1.06	19.65
邮政业	Post	55.56	51.93	0.45	0.16	0.53
电信、广播电视和卫星传输服务	Telecommunications, Broadcast Television and Satellite Transmission Services	162.53	114.33	33.25	0.34	33.34

注：该表数据来源于规模以上服务业统计年报。
Note：The data in this table comes from the statistical annual report of the service industry above designated size.

15-5 邮政行业基本情况(2021年)
BASIC SITUATION OF THE POSTAL INDUSTRY（2021）

指标名称	Name	计量单位	Unit	本年实际 Actual Situation of the current year	去年实际 Actual Situation of last year
营业网点	Business Outlets	处	unit	4058	3062
其中：快递营业网点	Express Business Outlets	处	unit	1860	2684
邮路总长度	Total Length of Postal Route	公里	km	85716	60587
邮运汽车	Postal Car	辆	unit	445	605
邮筒信箱	Mail Box	个	unit	267	313
平均每一营业网点服务面积	Average Service Area of Each Business Outlet	平方公里	aq.km	3.0	3.7
平均每一营业网点服务人口	Average Service Population of Each Business Outlet	万人	10000 persons	0.3	0.3
平均每人每年发函件数	Average Number of Letters Sent Per Person Per Year	件	articles	8.0	10.8
平均每百人每年订有报刊数	Average Number of Newspapers Per 100 People Per Year	份	copies	2.0	2.0

注：该表数据由青岛市邮政管理局提供。
Note：The data in this table is provided by Qingdao Post Management Bureau.

15-6 邮政行业发展情况
DEVELOPMENT OF THE POSTAL SERVICES

指标名称	Name	计量单位	Unit	2021 年	2020 年
一、邮政行业业务收入	**Postal Services Business Income**	**亿元**	**100 million yuan**	**110.76**	**95.02**
1、邮政寄递服务	Postal Delivery Service	亿元	100 million yuan	2.44	2.57
2、快递业务	Express Service	亿元	100 million yuan	94.87	78.91
二、邮政行业业务总量	**Total Business Volume Of Postal Industry**	**亿元**	**100 million yuan**	**88.01**	**68.63**
1、邮政寄递服务	Postal Delivery Service	万件	10 000 articles	18381	17590
其中：函件	Number Of Letters	万件	10 000 articles	609	923
包裹	Package	万件	10 000 articles	33	30
订销报纸累计数	Cumulative number of newspapers ordered and sold	万份	10 000 copies	13752	13576
订销杂志累计数	Cumulative number of magazines ordered and sold	万份	10 000 copies	611	621
汇兑	Exchange	万笔	10 000 sums	4	6
2、快递业务	Express Service	万件	10 000 articles	77252	58711
其中：同城	Same City	万件	10 000 articles	14322	11978
异地	Different Places	万件	10 000 articles	62242	45999
国际 / 港澳台	International/Hong Kong, Macao And Taiwan	万件	10 000 articles	689	734

注：该表数据由青岛市邮政管理局提供。
Note：The data in this table is provided by Qingdao Post Management Bureau.

15-7 快递企业发展情况
EXPRESS COMPANY DEVELOPMENT

指标名称	Name	计量单位	Unit	2021 年	2020 年
快递业务量	**Express Business Volume**	**万件**	**10 000 articles**	**77252**	**58711**
同城	Same City	万件	10 000 articles	14322	11978
异地	Different Places	万件	10 000 articles	62242	45999
国际及港澳台	International/ Hong Kong, Macao And Taiwan	万件	10 000 articles	689	734
快递业务收入	**Express Revenue**	**亿元**	**100 million yuan**	**94.87**	**78.91**
同城	Same City	亿元	100 million yuan	10.79	9.54
异地	Different Places	亿元	100 million yuan	50.41	42.25
国际及港澳台	International/ Hong Kong, Macao And Taiwan	亿元	100 million yuan	16.35	14.62
其他	Others	亿元	100 million yuan	17.33	12.51

注：该表数据由青岛市邮政管理局提供。
Note：The data in this table is provided by Qingdao Post Management Bureau.

15-8 电信行业基本情况
BASIC SITUATION OF TELECOM INDUSTRY

指标名称	Name	计量单位	Unit	2021 年	2020 年
一、电信业务总量及收入	**Total telecommunications services and revenue**	—			
电信业务总量（上年不变价）	Total telecommunications services（constant price of the previous year）	亿元	100 million yuan	136.30	106.91
电信业务收入	Telecommunications Revenue	亿元	100 million yuan	119.76	111.54
二、电信营业网点（企业自有）	**Telecom Business Outlets (company-owned)**	个	**unit**	**397**	**400**
三、通信能力	**Communication Ability**	—			
固定电话交换机总容量（含农话）	Total Capacity Of Fixed Telephone Exchanges（Including Rural Fixed Telephone）	万门	10 000 line	344	344
其中：市话交换机总容量	Total Local Switch Capacity	万门	10 000 line	40	40
乡村交换机容量	Rural switch capacity	万门	10 000 line	20	20
移动电话交换机容量	Mobile Phone Switch Capacity	万门	10 000 line	3391	3051
移动电话基站数	Number Of Mobile Phone Base Stations	个	unit	78597	76605
其中：4G 移动电话基站数	Number Of 4G Mobile Phone Base Stations	个	unit	49372	46729
其中：5G 移动电话基站数	Number Of 5G Mobile Phone Base Stations	个	unit	14882	9119
（固定）互联网宽带接入端口	Fixed Internet Broadband Access Port	万个	10 000 unit	813	812
其中：FTTH/O 端口	FTTH/O port	万个	10 000 unit	767	764
光缆线路长度	Cable Line Length	公里	km	353655	357084
其中：长途光缆线路长度	Long-Distance Cable Line Length	公里	km	4754	5058
四、电信服务业务	Telecommunications services	—			
固定电话主叫通话时长（含 IP）	Fixed-line Calling Duration of the calling party（including IP）	万分钟	10 000 minutes	76602	88275
固定电话年末用户	Fixed Telephone Year-End User	万户	10 000 households	159	158
其中：新装电话	Newly Installed Telephone	万户	10 000 households	8	6
城市电话用户	Urban Telephone User	万户	10 000 households	122	112
乡村电话用户	Village Phone User	万户	10 000 households	10	19

注：1. 电信业务总量、电信业务收入、（固定）互联网宽带接入端口、FTTH/O 端口、固定电话年末用户、期末移动电话用户数、固定宽带互联网用户数指标为青岛市通信管理局提供；

2. 除注 1 中指标外的其他指标由中国电信集团公司山东省青岛市电信分公司、中国电信股份有限公司青岛分公司、中国联合网络通信有限公司青岛市分公司、中国移动通信集团山东有限公司青岛分公司等企业报表数据汇总。

Notes：1. Business volume of total Telecommunication service, Telecommunication service revenue, and the number of（fixed）Internet broadband access port, FTTH/O port, fixed telephone users at the end of the year, mobile phone users at the end of the period, fixed broadband Internet users, and other indicators are provided by Qingdao Communication Administration Bureau.

2. Indicators other than those in Note 1 are summarized from the statement data of Shandong Qingdao Telecom Branch of China Telecom Corporation, China Telecom Co., LTD. Qingdao Branch, China United Network Communications Co., LTD., Qingdao Branch, Qingdao Branch of China Mobile Communications Group, Shandong Co., LTD., and other enterprises.

15-8 续表
Continued

指标名称	Name	计量单位	Unit	2021年	2020年
住宅电话年末用户	Home Phone Year-End User	万户	10 000 households	7.8	10.1
城市电话用户	Urban Telephone User	万户	10 000 households	5.2	7.0
乡村电话用户	Village Phone User	万户	10 000 households	2.6	3.1
移动电话通话时长	Mobile Phone Call Duration	万分钟	10 000 minutes	3727920.0	3744372.0
其中：去话通话时长	Calling Duration of the calling party	万分钟	10 000 minutes	666362.0	661973.0
移动短信业务量	Mobile SMS service volume	万条	10 000 items	801566.0	1250732.0
期末移动电话用户数	Number of mobile phone users at the end of the period	万户	10 000 households	1295.3	1257.3
其中：3G移动电话用户	3G Mobile Phone Users	万户	10 000 households	50.6	31.2
其中：4G移动电话用户	4G Mobile Phone Users	万户	10 000 households	841.8	1030.3
五、互联网用户数	**Number Of Internet Users**				
固定宽带互联网用户数	Number Of Fixed Broadband Internet Users	万户	10 000 households	498.1	464.3
移动互联网用户数	Number Of Mobile Internet Users	万户	10 000 households	1129.5	1091.5
物联网终端用户	Terminal user of the Internet of things	万户	10 000 households	961.7	792.3
IPTV用户	IPTV subscriber	万户	10 000 households	103.2	108.3
六、互联网通信量	**Internet Traffic**				
固定互联网宽带使用时长	Fixed Internet Broadband Usage Time	亿分钟	100 million households	7316.3	6494.1
固定互联网宽带接入流量	Fixed Internet Broadband Access Traffic	万G	10 000 G	188749.0	41840.8
移动互联网接入流量	Mobile Internet Access Traffic	万G	10 000 G	86465.3	63488.4

15-9　城市轨道交通发展情况
DEVELOPMENT OF URBAN RAIL TRANSIT

指标名称	Name	计量单位	Unit	2021 年	2020 年
客运量	**Passenger Traffic**	万人次	**10 000 person-times**	**24659**	**13909**
日均客运量	**Average Daily Passenger**	万人次	**10 000 person-times**	**68**	**38**
旅客周转量	**Passenger Turnover**	万人公里	**10 000 passenger-km**	**238201**	**119515**
运营车数	**Number Of Vehicles Operated**	辆	**unit**	**1214**	**980**
其中：地铁	Subway	辆	unit	1214	980
轻轨	Subway	辆	unit		
运营线路总数	**Total Number Of Operating Lines**	条	**line**	**6**	**6**
其中：新增运营线路	New Operating Line	条	line	0	2
其中：地铁	Subway	条	line		2
轻轨	Light Rail	条	line		
运营线路总长度	**Total Length Of Operating Line**	公里	**km**	**284**	**246**
其中：新增运营线路长度	New Operating Line Length	公里	km	38	70
其中：地铁	Subway	公里	km	38	70
轻轨	Light Rail	公里	km		
地铁站点总数	**Total Number Of Subway Stations**	个	**unit**	**128**	**106**
其中：换乘站点个数	Number Of Transfer Stations	个	unit	7	4
其中：新增站点个数	Number Of New Sites	个	unit	22	26
其中：新增换乘站点个数	Increase The Number Of Transfer Stations	个	unit	3	1
总开行次数	**Total Number Of Trips**	列次	**train number**	**666720**	**458491**
总运营里程	**Total Operating Mileage**	公里	**km**	**21767244**	**15113048**
列车准点率	**Train On Time Rate**	%	**%**	**100**	**100**

注：该表数据由青岛地铁集团有限公司提供。
（2018 年数据由青岛地铁集团有限公司轨道运营公司提供，为了统一数据口径，2019 年起，数据由青岛地铁集团有限公司提供。）

Note: The data in this table is provided by Qingdao Metro Group Co., Ltd.
(The data for 2018 are provided by Qingdao Metro Group Co., Ltd. Rail Operation Company. In order to unify the data, the data will be provided by Qingdao Metro Group Co., Ltd. from 2019 onwards.)

15-10 按行业分企业信息化及电子商务情况（2021 年）

INFORMATIZATION AND E-COMMERCE OF ENTERPRISES BY INDUSTRIAL SECTOR （2021）

行 业	Industry	企业数（个）Number of Enterprises (unit)	期末使用计算机数（台）Computers Used at the End of Period (unit)	每百人使用计算机数（台）Computers Used Per 100 Persons (unit)
总计	**Total**	**13204**	**639697**	**45**
采矿业	Mining	3	161	42
制造业	Manufacturing	4102	238055	36
电力、热力、燃气及水生产和供应业	Production and Supply of Electricity, Heat, Gas and Water	116	10166	50
建筑业	Construction	850	65168	36
批发和零售业	Wholesale and Retail Trades	3716	83309	64
交通运输、仓储和邮政业	Transport, Storage and Post	818	47782	42
住宿和餐饮业	Hotels and Catering Services	744	13586	28
信息传输、软件和信息技术服务业	Information Transmission, Software and Information Technology Services	228	50621	140
房地产业	Real Estate	1372	39568	56
租赁和商务服务业	Leasing and Business Services	631	25979	42
科学研究和技术服务业	Scientific Research and Technical Services	310	46102	87
水利、环境和公共设施管理业	Management of Water Conservancy, Environment and Public Facilities	43	2487	12
居民服务、修理和其他服务业	Service to Households, Repair and Other Services	60	1801	20
教育	Education	19	2930	68
卫生和社会工作	Health and Social Service	72	6157	60
文化、体育和娱乐业	Culture, Sports and Entertainment	120	5825	65

注：有电子商务交易活动的企业是指通过计算机网络开展电子商务销售或电子商务采购的企业。
Note：Enterprises with E-Commerce Transactions refers to those enterprises which performed sales or purchases through internet.

企业拥有网站数（个）Websites of Enterprises（unit）	每百家企业拥有网站数（个）Websites Per 100 Enterprises（unit）	有电子商务交易活动 With E-Commerce Transactions		电子商务销售额（万元）Sales of E-Commerce（10 000 yuan）	电子商务采购额（万元）Purchases of E-Commerce（10 000 yuan）
		企业数（个）Enterprises（unit）	比重（%）Proportion（%）		
7057	**53**	**6417**	**48.6**	**58543206**	**39630216**
2	67	2	66.7		3
2979	73	2271	55.4	25773916	13888128
50	43	66	56.9	9751	39485
431	51	398	46.8	3871	104195
1417	38	1558	41.9	27446877	21656814
376	46	386	47.2	3647038	2978556
214	29	463	62.2	414649	4068
223	98	155	68.0	680770	340634
602	44	394	28.7	27576	17721
322	51	316	50.1	278759	194072
252	81	215	69.4	90100	381278
14	33	27	62.8	1565	1440
30	50	34	56.7	60376	18577
22	116	9	47.4	22058	720
54	75	52	72.2	4866	2912
69	58	71	59.2	81034	1612

15-11 区（市）企业信息化及电子商务情况（2021年）

INFORMATIZATION AND E-COMMERCE OF ENTERPRISES BY REGION （2021）

区（市）	Region	企业数（个）Number of Enterprises (unit)	期末使用计算机数（台）Computers Used at the End of Period (unit)	每百人使用计算机数（台）Computers Used Per 100 Persons (unit)
全市	**Total**	**13204**	**639697**	**45**
市南区	Shinan District	1344	100196	68
市北区	Shibei District	1022	64760	57
李沧区	Licang District	820	20189	37
崂山区	Laoshan District	836	84485	61
黄岛区（西海岸新区）	Huangdao District (West Coast New Area)	3092	142456	39
城阳区	Chengyang District	1870	98497	48
城阳区（不含高新区）	Chengyang District (Excluding High tech District)	1524	71946	43
高新区	High tech District	346	26551	70
即墨区	Jimo District	1074	39349	32
胶州市	Jiaozhou	1624	48576	33
平度市	Pingdu	892	24673	28
莱西市	Laixi	630	16516	29

注：有电子商务交易活动的企业是指通过计算机网络开展电子商务销售或电子商务采购的企业。

Note: Enterprises with E-Commerce Transactions refers to those enterprises which performed sales or purchases through internet.

企业拥有网站数（个） Websites of Enterprises (unit)	每百家企业拥有网站数（个） Websites Per 100 Enterprises (unit)	有电子商务交易活动 With E-Commerce Transactions		电子商务销售额（万元） Sales of E-Commerce (10 000 yuan)	电子商务采购额（万元） Purchases of E-Commerce (10 000 yuan)
		企业数（个） Enterprises (unit)	比重（%） Proportion (%)		
7057	**53**	**6417**	**48.6**	**58543206**	**39630216**
813	61	554	41.2	12061417	5960805
469	46	504	49.3	1971336	1840305
352	43	397	48.4	2699269	2524894
505	60	542	64.8	18640629	14082817
1531	50	1555	50.3	15038294	11516421
1017	54	962	51.4	1765655	1600222
774	51	777	51.0	1590252	1365802
243	70	185	53.5	175403	234420
668	62	529	49.3	2505444	843668
935	58	837	51.5	3189680	773997
432	48	357	40.0	309928	390824
335	53	180	28.6	361556	96265

主要统计指标解释

货（客）运量 指在一定时期内，各运输部门实际运送的货物（旅客）数量。是反映运输业为国民经济和人民生活服务的数量指标，也是制定和检查运输生产计划，研究运输发展规模和速度的重要指标。货运按吨计算，客运按人计算。货物不论运输距离长短，货物类别，均按实际重量统计；旅客不论行程远近或票价多少，均按一人一次作为客运量统计。半价票、小孩票也按一人统计。

货物（旅客）周转量 指在一定时期内，由各种运输工具运送的货物（旅客）数量与其相应运输距离的乘积之总和，是反映运输业生产总成果的重要指标，也是编制和检查运输生产计划，计算运输效益、劳动生产率以及核算运输单位成本的主要基础资料。通常以吨公里和人公里为计算单位。计算货物周转量通常按发出站与到达站之间的最短距离，也就是计费距离计算。

港口货物吞吐量 指经水运进出沿海主要港区范围，并经过装卸的货物数量，包括邮件及办理托运手续的行李、包裹以及补给运输船舶的燃、物料和淡水。货物吞吐量按货物流向分为进口、出口吞吐量，按货物交流性质分为外贸货物吞吐量和国内贸易货物吞吐量。货物吞吐量的货类构成及其流向，是衡量港口生产能力大小的重要指标。

邮政行业业务总量 指以货币形式表现的邮政企业为社会提供各类邮政通信服务或其他服务的总数量。计算方法为各类邮政通信服务业务的实物量分别乘以相应的不变单价，求出各类业务的货币量后加总求得。该指标反映了一定时期邮政通信业务发展的总成果，是观察邮政通信业务发展变化总趋势的综合性指标。

邮政行业业务收入 指邮政企业和快递企业从事各种邮政业务、快递业务取得的收入总和。

快递业务量 指企业收寄的各类快递业务总数量，由受理用户委托的企业负责统计。包括国内同城快递业务量、国内异地快递业务量、港澳台快递业务量、国际快递业务量。

快递业务收入 指企业从事快递业务取得的收入。快递业务收入 = 国内同城快递业务收入 + 国内异地快递业务收入 + 港澳台快递业务收入 + 国际快递业务收入 + 其他快递业务收入。

电信业务总量 指以货币形式表示的电信企业为社会提供的各类电信服务的总数量。包括固定话音业务总量、固定数据及互联网业务总量、固定增值及其他业务总量、移动话音业务总量、移动数据及互联网业务总量、移动增值及其他业务总量。

电信业务收入 指电信企业经营的基础电信业务和增值电信业务所取得的资费收入，以及电信企业之间网间互联电信业务的结算收入。

长途光缆线路长度 指长途光缆线路的实际长度。架空的光缆按实际杆路长度统计，埋设地下、水底的光缆按沟长统计。

本地网中继光缆线路长度 指本地网内各业务节点之间，从起点至终点所经由的光缆线路实际长度。架空光缆按实际杆路长度统计，埋设地下、水底的光缆按埋设光缆的沟长统计。

移动电话基站数 指为小区服务的无线收发信设备，处理基站与移动台之间的无线通信，在移动交换机与移动台之间起中继作用，监视无线传输质量的全套设备数。

3G 移动电话基站数 指报告期末本电信企业 3G 移动通信网络上实际使用的 NoFe-B 数量。包括 TF-SCFMA 基站、WCFMA 基站和 CFMA2000 基站。

4G 移动电话基站数 指报告期末本电信企业 4G 移动通信网络上实际使用的 Node-B 数量。包括 TD-LTE 基站和 FDD-LTE 基站。

互联网宽带接入用户 指报告期末在电信企业登记注册，通过 xDSL、FTTx+LAN、FTTH/O 以及其他宽带接入方式和普通专线接入公众互联网的用户。互联网宽带接入用户按行政区划分为城市宽带接入用户和农村宽带接入用户；按客户类别分为家庭宽带接入用户和政企宽带接入用户。

移动互联网用户 指报告期内通过移动通信网络接入公众互联网或 WAP 网站的用户。

互联网宽带接入端口 指用于接入互联网用户的各类实际安装运行的宽带接入端口的数量。

网站数 指报告期末企业拥有和维护的，在互联网上可浏览的网站数，不包括企业内网。网站是指在公共互联网上，面向公众使用的，基于 TCP/IP 协议的计算机系统，以域名本身或者“WWW. +域名”为网址的 web 站点，由地址、软件、硬件和内容组成。

电子商务销售金额 指报告期内企业（单位）借助网络订单而销售的商品和服务总额。借助网络订单指通过网络接受订单，付款和配送可以不借助于网络。

电子商务采购金额 指报告期内企业（单位）借助网络订单而采购的商品和服务总额。借助网络订单指通过网络发送订单，付款和配送可以不借助于网络。

电子商务交易平台 指在电子商务活动中为交易双方或多方提供交易撮合及相关服务的信息网络系统的总和。

Explanatory Notes on Main Statistical Indicators

Freight (Passenger) Traffic refers to the volume of freight (passenger) transported with various means. Freight transport is calculated in tons and passenger traffic is calculated in the number of persons. Despite the type of freight and traveling distance, the freight transport is calculated in the actual weight of the goods; and despite the traveling distance and ticket price, the passenger traffic is calculated by the principle that one person can be counted only once in one travel. The passengers who travel with a half price ticket or a child ticket is also calculated as one person. The freight (passenger) traffic provides a quantitative measure to show how the transport industry serves the national economy and people, and is also an important indicator for planning the transport industry and for studying the development scale and speed of the transport industry.

Freight Ton-kilometers (Passenger-kilometers) refer to the sum of the products of the volume of transported cargo (passengers) multiplying by the transport distance. It is an important indicator to reflect the achievement of transportation industry. Normally, the shortest distance between the departure station and the destination station (i.e., the payable distance) is the basis to calculate the freight ton-kilometers. This is an important indicator to show the total results of the transport industry, to prepare and examine the transport plan and to measure the efficiency, the labour productivity and the unit cost of transport.

Volume of Freight Handled in Ports refers to the volume of cargo passing in and out the harbor area of the major coastal ports and having been loaded and unloaded. The volume includes that of the postal matters, registered luggage and fuels, materials and fresh water as supplies of the ships. The volume of freight handled may be classified by direction of flow as freight for import and freight for export, or by nature of cargo as freight for domestic trade and freight for foreign trade. As an important indicator, the volume of freight handled by type of cargo and by main flow direction reflects the production capacity of ports.

Business Volume of Post Services refers to the total amount of post services or other services provided by the post departments for society. The calculation method is that the physical quantity of each type of postal communication service business is multiplied by the corresponding constant unit price, and the monetary quantity of each type of service is obtained and summed up. This indicator reflects the total results of the development of postal communication services in a certain period of time, and is a comprehensive indicator for observing the general trend of development and change of postal communication services.

Postal Services Business Income refers to the total income obtained by postal enterprises and courier enterprises from various postal services and express delivery services.

Business Volume of Express Services refers to the total number of various types of express delivery services received and received by the enterprise, and the enterprises entrusted by the user are responsible for statistics. Including domestic city express business volume, domestic off-site express business volume, Hong Kong, Macao and Taiwan express business volume, international express business volume.

Express Revenue refers to the income obtained by enterprises engaged in express business. Express business income = Income from domestic intra-city express business + Income from domestic long-distance express business +Income from Hong Kong, Macao and Taiwan express business + Income from international express business + other express business income.

Business Volume of Telecommunication Services refers to the total number of telecommunication services provided by telecommunication enterprises in the form of money for the society. Including the total volume of fixed voice services, fixed data and total Internet services, fixed value-added and other services, total mobile voice services, total mobile data and Internet services, mobile value-added and other business.

Telecommunications Service Revenue refers to the income obtained from basic telecommunication service and value-added telecommunication service operated by telecommunication enterprises, as well as the settlement income from telecommunication service of interconnection among telecommunication enterprises.

Long-Distance Cable Line Length refers to the actual length of the long-distance cable line. The overhead optical cable is counted according to the actual length of the pole. The underground and underwater cables are counted according to the length of the trench.

Local Network Trunk Cable Length refers to the actual length of the cable line between the service nodes in the local network and from the starting point to the destination. The overhead optical cable is counted according to the actual length of the pole. The underground and underwater optical cables are counted according to the length of the buried optical cable.

Number of Mobile Phone Base Stations refers to the wireless transceiver device serving the cell, handles the wireless communication between the base station and the mobile station, and acts as a relay between the mobile switch and the mobile station to monitor the total number of devices for wireless transmission quality.

Number of 3G Mobile Phone Base Stations refers to the number of NoFe-B actually used on the 3G mobile communication network of the telecommunications enterprise at the end of the reporting period. It includes TF-SCFMA base station, WCFMA base station, and CFMA2000 base station.

Number of 4G Mobile Phone Base Stations refers to the number of Node-B actually used on the 4G mobile communication network of the telecommunications enterprise at the end of the reporting period. It includes TD-LTE base station and FDD-LTE base station.

Internet Broadband Access Users refer to those who are registered with telecom enterprises at the end of the report period and access the public Internet through xDSL, FTTx+LAN, FTTH/O, and other broadband access methods and ordinary special lines. Internet broadband access users are divided into urban broadband access users and rural broadband access users according to administrative regions. According to the customer category they are divided into home broadband access users and government and enterprise broadband access users.

Mobile Internet Users refer to those who access public Internet or WAP websites through mobile communication networks during the reporting period.

Internet Broadband Access Port refers to the number of broadband access ports that are actually installed and operated for accessing Internet users.

Websites refers to the number of websites owned and maintained by enterprises at the end of the reporting period, excluding the intranet. A website is a web site on the public Internet, accessible to the public, based on the TCP/IP protocol, with the domain name itself or the "WWW.+ domain name" as its URL, consisting of address, software, hardware and content.

E-commerce sales amount refers to the total amount of goods and services sold by an enterprise (unit) through online orders during the reporting period. With the help of a network order refers to the acceptance of orders over the network, payment and distribution can be made without the help of the network.

E-commerce purchase amount refers to the total amount of goods and services purchased by an enterprise (unit) through the help of a network order during the reporting period. With the help of a network order, an order is sent over the network, and payment and distribution can be made without the help of the network.

E-commerce trading platform refers to the sum of information network systems that provide transaction matching and related services for both parties or parties in e-commerce activities.

批发和零售业 16

WHOLESALE AND RETAIL TRADES

简 要 说 明

一、本篇资料的主要内容

本篇资料主要反映了全市批发和零售业经营情况和效益情况，主要包括批发和零售业商品流转及财务情况、亿元以上商品交易市场、社会消费品零售总额等内容。

二、本篇资料的来源

本篇资料来源于批发和零售业统计年报和定期报表统计资料，由市统计局外经贸易统计处整理提供。

Brief Introduction

Ⅰ. Main Content

Data in this chapter show the development of wholesale and retail trade of the whole city, mainly including the circulation and financial indices of commodities in the wholesale and retail trade commodity exchange markets over 100 million yuan, total retail sales of consumer goods, etc.

Ⅱ. Source of Data

Data in this chapter are based on annual report and regular reports of wholesale and retail trade. Data in this chapter are prepared and compiled by the Division of Trade and External Economic Relations Statistics of Qingdao Municipal Bureau of Statistics.

16-1 社会消费品零售总额（1985—2021年）
TOTAL RETAIL SALES OF CONSUMER GOODS（1985—2021）

单位：万元（10 000 yuan）

年 份 Year	消费品零售总额 Total Retail Sales of Consumer Goods	批发和零售业 Wholesale and Retail Trades	住宿和餐饮业 Hotels and Catering Services	其他行业 Others
1985	307222	231477	16996	18753
1986	364091	269418	21384	27118
1987	432569	310658	23319	32617
1988	590538	434572	32304	45449
1989	619941	450812	34083	56303
1990	658264	484770	35568	67863
1991	760562	566767	43320	56812
1992	888411	666911	53045	67392
1993	1381791	1029750	79918	96567
1994	1873212	1346723	126809	202134
1995	2362682	1627640	184925	304133
1996	2687133	1858214	218582	318787
1997	2979302	2084958	239542	357685
1998	3328902	2294750	274412	406348
1999	3710897	2678209	310962	385994
2000	4215480	3067944	381840	397499
2001	4824874	3498744	498046	426179
2002	5464940	4080963	625827	394750
2003	6315866	5169609	830717	315540
2004	7299288	6119422	993279	186587
2005	8479672	7118804	1146604	214264
2006	9885247	8226694	1403617	254936
2007	11805893	9702897	1783908	319089
2008	14456246	12590079	1505564	360603
2009	16728814	13761257	2464719	502838
2010	18923835	16550240	2373595	
2011	22172581	19408076	2764505	
2012	25331596	22147219	3184377	
2013	28650167	25076367	3573800	
2014	32182505	28179596	4002909	
2015	35481601	31012690	4468911	
2016	39141939	34175128	4966811	
2017	43214295	37751718	5462577	
2018	47427204	41340208	6086996	
2019	51265971	44158221	7107750	
2020	52034957	46836540	5198417	
2021	59754345	53434436	6319909	

注：1. 自 2003 年开始消费品零售总额不再包括制造业零售额和农民对非农居民的销售额分组。
2. 自 2005 年起，住宿业从其他行业调整到住宿餐饮业中。
3. 根据第四次经济普查结果，对 1993 年以来的历史数据进行了调整。

Notes：1.Since 2003，retail sales of manufacturing and retail sales of rural residents to urban residents are excluded in total retail sales of consumer goods.
2.Since 2005，hotels is adjusted to hotels and catering services from the others.
3.Historical data since1993 have been adjusted according to results of the Four China Economic Census.

16-2　分市、区社会消费品零售总额（2021年）
TOTAL RETAIL SALES OF CONSUMER GOODS BY REGION（2021）

单位：万元（10 000 yuan）

市、区名称	Region	消费品零售总额 Total Retail Sales of Consumer Goods	按行业分（Grouped by sectors） 批发和零售业 Wholesale and Retail Trades	住宿和餐饮业 Hotels and Catering Services
全　市	**Whole Municipal**	**59754345**	**53434436**	**6319909**
市南区	Shinan District	7313489	6257582	1055907
市北区	Shibei District	7266990	6424830	842159
李沧区	Licang District	4486238	4172916	313322
崂山区	Laoshan District	4518188	4166256	351933
黄岛区（西海岸新区）	Huangdao District（West Coast New Area）	13107837	11660580	1447256
城阳区	Chengyang District	4627018	4106934	520084
城阳区（不含高新区）	Chengyang District（Excluding High tech District）	4443345	3943450	499895
高新区	High tech District	183673	163483	20189
即墨区	Jimo District	5360956	4952854	408102
胶州市	Jiaozhou	6438078	5855053	583025
平度市	Pingdu	3538959	3164941	374018
莱西市	Laixi	3096594	2672492	424102

16-3 限额以上批发和零售业商品销售、库存情况(2021 年)

SALES AND INVENTORIES OF WHOLESALE AND RETAIL COMMODITIES ABOVE DESIGNATED SIZE (2021)

单位：万元(10 000 yuan)

项 目	Item	商品销售额 Commodity Sales	#批发额 Wholesale Amount	零售额 Retail Sales	库存额 Inventory
总 计	**Total**	**171102331.8**	**152996794.9**	**17882945.7**	**7959186.5**
国有企业	State-owned Enterprises	6598558.8	6518750.8	65156.4	510204.1
集体企业	Collective-owned Enterprises	103108.9	103108.9		706.6
其他企业	Other Enterprises	164400664.1	146374935.2	17817789.3	7448275.8
农、林、牧产品批发	Products Wholesale of Agriculture, Forestry and Animal Husbandry Products Wholesale	5442454.3	5422974.6	17441.2	292133.0
食品、饮料及烟草制品批发	Wholesale of Food, Beverages and Tobaccos	13680237.8	13327004.2	333314.1	1033058.1
纺织、服装及家庭用品批发	Retail of Textiles, Garments and Daily Consumer Articles	16666273.8	16262924.0	390616.3	408537.6
文化、体育用品及器材批发	Wholesale of Culture, Sports Appliances and Equipments	1593117.4	1547532.7	43118.6	102190.0
医药及医疗器材批发	Wholesale of Medicines and Medical Appliances	4168884.1	4155136.2	12543.4	312192.4
矿产品、建材及化工产品批发	Wholesale of Mineral Products, Building Materials and Chemical Products	98944905.8	98554950.3	213927.0	3379712.4
机械设备、五金产品及电子产品批发	Wholesale of Machinery, Hardware and Electronic Equipment	9258691.3	9036959.5	213531.2	435009.9
贸易经纪与代理	Trade Broker and Agency	1166097.9	1166097.9		67612.5
其他批发业	Other Wholesale not Classified Elsewhere	2316409.1	2251427.6	64981.5	30141.0
综合零售	Integrated Retail Trade	2726290.1	40258.3	2686031.8	484304.6
食品、饮料及烟草制品专门零售	Retail of Food, Beverages and Tobaccos	289336.3	14228.3	275108.0	35835.8
纺织、服装及日用品专门零售	Retail of Textiles, Garments and Daily Consumer Articles	944131.1	184231.4	759899.7	302284.2
文化、体育用品及器材专门零售	Retail of Culture, Sports Appliances and Equipments	259638.2	6148.9	253489.3	66613.2
医药及医疗器材专门零售	Retail of Medicines and Medical Appliances	913566.2	79785.9	833780.3	92539.0
汽车、摩托车、燃料及零配件专门零售	Retail of Motor Vehicles, Motorcycles, Fuel and Parts	7006881.8	605138.1	6401743.7	482631.9
家用电器及电子产品专门零售	Retail of Household Electric Appliances and Electronic Products	680211.9	81397.6	598814.3	44767.0
五金、家具及室内装饰材料专门零售	Retail of Hardware, Furniture and Decoration Materials	122069.5	1874.6	120194.9	24338.7
货摊、无店铺及其他零售业	Non-shop and Other Retails	4923135.2	258724.8	4664410.4	365285.2

16-4 限额以上批发和零售业商品分类销售额(2021 年)

CLASSIFIED SALES OF WHOLESALE AND RETAIL AND RETAIL COMMODITIES ABOVE DESIGNATED SIZE(2021)

单位：万元(10 000 yuan)

项目	Item	销售额 Total Sales Value	#批发额 Wholesale Value	零售额 Retail Value
销售总额	**Total Sales Value**	**163153629.7**	**145181062.6**	**17972567.1**
1. 粮油、食品类	Grain & Oil and Food	10979378.8	9077346.6	1902032.2
其中：粮油类	Grain and Oil	3572110.2	3293441.8	278668.4
肉禽蛋类	Meat, Poultry and Eggs	3481519.6	3209931.7	271587.9
水产品类	Aquatic Products	744799.4	640074.3	104725.1
蔬菜类	Vegetable and Fruit	385017.6	256824.3	128193.3
干鲜果品类	Dried and Fresh Fruit	958447.3	612000.9	346446.4
2. 饮料类	Beverages	590238.4	162677	427561.4
3. 烟酒类	Tobacco and Liquor	2284400.9	1955430	328970.9
4. 服装、鞋帽、针纺织品类	Clothing, Shoes, Hats and Textiles	3982672.4	2609508.5	1373163.9
(1)服装类	Clothing	1759266.5	918813.5	840453
(2)鞋帽类	Shoes and Hats	755687.6	293043.2	462644.4
(3)针纺织品类	Knitwear and Textiles	1467718.3	1397651.8	70066.5
5. 化妆品类	Cosmetics	407615	141659.8	265955.2
6. 金银珠宝类	Gold, Silver and Jewellery	489600.5	129604.3	359996.2
7. 日用品类	Articles for Daily Use	1184823.8	539661.3	645162.5
其中：可穿戴智能设备	Wearable smart devices	43195.5	27154.4	16041.1
8. 五金、电料类	Hardware and Electrical Materials	770646.4	758213.3	12433.1
9. 体育、娱乐用品类	Sports and Recreation Articles	309336.1	108716.6	200619.5
其中：照相器材类	Photographic Apparatus	177682.6	29736.4	147946.2
10. 书报杂志类	Newspapers and Magazines	201927.3	63857.4	138069.9
11. 电子出版物及音像制品类	E-journals and Video Products	3106	611.8	2494.2
12. 家用电器和音像器材类	Household Appliances and Video Appliances	15496557.3	12434386.6	3062170.7
其中：能效等级为 1 级和 2 级的商品	Products with energy efficiency grades 1 and 2	3277464.9	1305470.8	1971994.1
其中：智能家用电器和音像器材	Smart household appliances and audio-visual equipment	4133370.4	3556464.2	576906.2
13. 中西药品类	Traditional Chinese and Western Medicines	3524666.7	2720810.8	803855.9
其中：西药类	Western Medicines	2933238.5	2312650	620588.5
中草药及中成药类	Traditional Chinese Medicines	175356.1	94309.8	81046.3
14. 文化办公用品类	Cultural and Offices Appliances	1491568.3	1074843.8	416724.5
其中：计算机及其配套产品	Computer and Related Products	1235839.5	876797.1	359042.4
15. 家具类	Furniture	312210.8	224093.7	88117.1
16. 通讯器材类	Communication Appliances	1216043.6	409510.8	806532.8
其中：智能手机	Smart phones	1104769	371776	732993
17. 煤炭及制品类	Coal and Related Products	4881290	4857152.8	24137.2
18. 木材及制品类	Wood and Wooden Products	1388544.7	1388544.7	
19. 石油及制品类	Petroleum and Related Products	36408862	34279236.8	2129625.2
20. 化工材料及制品类	Chemical Materials and Related Products	13252481.3	13252481.3	
其中：化肥类	Fertilizers	401846	401846	
21. 金属材料类	Metal Materials	39346773.8	39346773.8	
22. 建筑及装潢材料类	Building and Decoration Materials	1832747.6	1755225.5	77522.1
23. 机电产品及设备类	Mechanical and Electrical Products	2984773.8	2931183.3	53590.5
其中：农机类	Agricultural Machineries	25393.1	25393.1	
24. 汽车类	Automobiles	7289398.4	2713186.7	4576211.7
其中：新能源汽车	New Energy Vehicles	537215.4	228182.1	309033.3
25. 种子饲料类	Seeds and Feedstuff	3748367.7	3748367.7	
26. 棉麻类	Cotton, Flax	973837.3	961750	12087.3
27. 其他类	Others	7801760.8	7536227.7	265533.1

注：此表为定期报表数据。

Note: The data are from regular reports.

16-5 限额以上批发业财务状况（2021年）

FINANCIAL POSITION OF ENTERPRISES ABOVE DESIGNATED SIZE OF WHOLESALE TRADE（2021）

单位：万元（10 000 yuan）

指标	Indicator	合计 Total	国有经济 State-owned Enterprises	集体经济 Collective-owned Enterprises	外商及港澳台经济 Foreign Funded Enterprises and Enterprises with Funds from Hong Kong，Macao and Taiwan	其他 Other Enterprises
单位数	**Number of Enterprises**	**2994**	**38**	**2**	**88**	**2866**
年末资产负债	**Year-end Assets-Liability**					
资产总计	Total Assets	56998320	2731192		7085038	47143006
流动资产合计	Sub-total of Current Assets	49793380	2291863		6067252	41396957
负债合计	Total Liabilities	46620044	1967317		5568570	39048331
所有者权益合计	Total Owners' Equities	10271067	751106		1516468	8000236
损益及分配	**Loss，Profits and Distribution**					
营业收入	Revenue from Principal Business	136765109	5267626		13797800	117607310
营业成本	Cost of Principal Business	132299567	4890691		13501657	113823557
营业税金及附加	Taxes and Extra Charges on Principal Business	271473	153864		8833	108655
营业利润	Profits from Principal Business	995447	134252		122461	739454
其他业务利润	Profits from other Business	126569	1539		-236	125266
销售费用	Operating Costs	2074082	39429		105710	1928408
管理费用	Management Expenses	953236	56777		74318	813238
财务费用	Financial Expenses	377388	3387		4160	369927
利润总额	Total Profits	1051273	134713		123431	793873
经济效益	**Economic Benefit**					
商品经营费用率 %	Ratio of Operating Costs to Revenue from Principal Business	1.52	0.75		0.77	1.64
商品销售利润率 %	Ratio of Profit to Sales Revenue	0.77	2.56		0.89	0.68

注：限额以上批发业企业中，由于包含了部分视同法人单位，因此财务指标数据资产≠负债+所有者权益。

Note：In wholesale enterprises above designated size, as some deemed legal entities are included, the financial index data asset ≠ liability + owner's equity.

16-6 限额以上零售业财务状况（2021 年）
FINANCIAL POSITION OF ENTERPRISES ABOVE DESIGNATED SIZE OF RETAIL TRADE（2021）

单位：万元（10 000 yuan）

指标	Indicator	合计 Total	国有经济 State-owned Enterprises	集体经济 Collective-owned Enterprises	外商及港澳台经济 Foreign Funded Enterprises and Enterprises with Funds from Hong Kong, Macao and Taiwan	其他 Other Enterprises
单位数	**Number of Enterprises**	**830**	**5**		**50**	**775**
年末资产负债	**Year-end Assets-Liability**					
资产总计	Total Assets	9089602	27725		2174839	6887038
流动资产合计	Sub-total of Current Assets	6729391	20129		1660823	5048440
负债合计	Total Liabilities	7803951	8147		1695037	6100767
所有者权益合计	Total Owners' Equities	1749934	19578		479109	1251247
损益及分配	**Loss, Profits and Distribution**					
营业收入	Revenue from Principal Business	16217886	44562		3567923	12605401
营业成本	Cost of Principal Business	14400071	35642		3052991	11311438
营业税金及附加	Taxes and Extra Charges on Principal Business	45786	160		15894	29732
营业利润	Profits from Principal Business	32328	5817		-15625	42136
其他业务利润	Profits from other Business	169171			39609	129563
销售费用	Operating Costs	1240766	2633		338665	899469
管理费用	Management Expenses	463031	3290		156364	303377
财务费用	Financial Expenses	82515	-35		7862	74687
利润总额	Total Profits	50489	6191		-11973	56271
经济效益	**Economic Benefit**					
商品经营费用率 %	Ratio of Operating Costs to Revenue from Principal Business	7.65	5.91		9.49	7.14
商品销售利润率 %	Ratio of Profit to Sales Revenue	0.31	13.89		-0.34	0.45

注：限额以上批发业企业中，由于包含了部分视同法人单位，因此财务指标数据资产≠负债+所有者权益。

Note: In wholesale enterprises above designated size, as some deemed legal entities are included, the financial index data asset ≠ liability + owner's equity.

16-7 分市、区亿元以上商品交易市场成交情况（2021 年）
BASIC STATISTICS ON COMMODITY EXCHANGE MARKETS OF TRANSACTION VALUE OVER 100 MILLION YUAN BY REGION（2021）

市、区名称	Region	亿元商品交易市场数量（个） Number of Commodity Exchange Markets of Transaction Value over 100 Million Yuan（unit）			亿元商品交易市场成交额（亿元） Turnover of Commodity Exchange Markets of Transaction Value over 100 Million yuan（100 million yuan）		
		合计 Total	#综合市场 Integrated Markets	#专业市场 Special Markets	合计 Total	#综合市场 Integrated Markets	#专业市场 Special Markets
全　市	**Whole Municipal**	**58**	**17**	**41**	**13737184**	**5518155**	**8219029**
市南区	Shinan District						
市北区	Shibei District	7	1	6	763421	430114	333307
李沧区	Licang District	3	1	2	339391	94764	244627
崂山区	Laoshan District	2		2	32956		32956
黄岛区（西海岸新区）	Huangdao District（West Coast New Area）	8	2	6	653474	256678	396796
自贸	Free trade	1		1	43500		43500
城阳区	Chengyang District	1	1		2497243	2497243	
城阳区（不含高新区）	Chengyang District（Excluding High tech District）	1	1		2497243	2497243	
高新区	High tech District						
即墨区	Jimo District	9	1	8	6954057	1603545	5350512
胶州市	Jiaozhou	19	9	10	1810398	464566	1345832
平度市	Pingdu	9	2	7	642744	171245	471499
莱西市	Laixi						

主要统计指标解释

社会消费品零售总额 指各种经济类型的批发和零售业、住宿和餐饮业以及其他行业对城乡居民和社会集团的消费品零售额总和。该指标从2003年开始不再包括制造业零售额和农民对非农居民的零售额。

商品购进总额 指从本企业（单位）以外的单位和个人购进（包括从国外直接进口）作为转卖或加工后转卖的商品金额（含增值税）。这个指标反映批发零售贸易业从国内、国外市场上购进商品的总价。商品购进总额包括：

（1）从工农业生产者购进的商品；

（2）从出版社、报社的出版发行部门购进的图书、杂志和报纸；

（3）从各种类型的批发零售贸易企业（单位）购进的商品；

（4）从其他单位购进的商品，如从机关、团体、企业、单位购进的剩余物资，从餐饮业、服务业购进的商品，从海关、市场管理部门购进的缉私和没收的商品，向居民收购的废旧商品等；

（5）从国（境）外直接进口的商品，但不包括企业（单位）为自身经营用和未通过买卖行为而收入的商品以及销售退回、商品损益等。

商品销售总额 指对本企业（单位）以外的单位和个人出售（包括对国（境）外直接出口）的商品金额（包括售给本单位消费用的商品，含增值税）。这个指标反映批发零售贸易业在国内市场上销售商品以及出口商品的总价。商品销售总额包括：

（1）售给城乡居民和社会集团消费用的商品；

（2）售给工业、农业、建筑业、运输邮电业、批发零售贸易业、餐饮业、服务业等作为生产、经营使用的商品；

（3）售给批发零售贸易业作为转卖或加工后转卖的商品；

（4）对国（境）外直接出口的商品。

不包括：出售本企业（单位）自用的废旧包装用品，未通过买卖行为付出的商品，经本单位介绍，由买卖双方直接结算，本单位只收取手续费的业务，购货退出的商品以及商品损耗和损失等。

Explanatory Notes on Main Statistical Indicators

Total Retail Sales of Consumer Goods refers to the sum of retail sales of consumer goods sold by all sectors of the national economy to urban and rural residents and social groups. Sectors of the national economy include wholesale and retail trade, accommodation and catering trade and others. Since 2003, retail sales of manufacture and retail sales of rural residents to urban residents are excluded in total retail sales.

Total Purchases of Commodities refers to the total value (VAT included) of purchases of commodities by the enterprises (establishments) from other establishments or individuals (including direct import from abroad) for the purpose of re-selling, either with or without further processing of the commodities purchased. This indicator is used to show the total value of purchases of commodities by wholesale and retail establishments from domestic and overseas markets. The total purchases include:

(1) agricultural and industrial products purchased from producers;

(2) books, magazines and newspapers purchased from distribution departments of the publishers;

(3) commodities purchased from wholesale and retail establishments of different status of registration;

(4) commodities purchased from other units, such as surplus materials purchased from government agencies, enterprises or institutions, commodities purchased from catering and service establishments, confiscated goods purchased from customs authorities or

market management agencies, second–hand goods and wastes purchased from residents;

(5) commodities directly imported from abroad. Excluded are commodities purchased by enterprises (establishments) for use in their own business operation, commodities obtained without buying or selling procedures, rejected commodities, etc.

Total Sales of Commodities refers to value of commodities sold by the establishments to other establishments and individuals (including commodities sold to the establishments for consumption, VAT included), including those directly exported to foreign countries. This indicator is used to show the total value of sales of merchandise by wholesale and retail establishments at domestic markets and overseas markets. The total sales include:

(1) commodities sold to urban and rural residents and social groups for their consumption;

(2) commodities sold to establishments in industry, agriculture, construction, transportation, post and telecommunications, wholesale and retail trades, hotels and catering services, and public utility for their production and operation;

(3) commodities sold to wholesale and retail establishments for re–selling, with or without further processing;

(4) commodities for direct export to other countries.

Excluded are selling of waste packaging materials used by the establishments (units) themselves, commodities transferred without buying or selling procedures, commission income from brokerage in transactions for which settlement is directly handled by buyers and sellers, rejected commodities in the purchase, loss in commodities, etc.

住宿、餐饮业和旅游 17

HOTELS，CATERING SERVICES AND TOURISM

简 要 说 明

一、本篇资料的主要内容

本篇资料主要反映了全市住宿和餐饮业的经营情况和效益情况以及旅游的基本情况，主要包括住宿和餐饮业经营情况和财务情况、涉外以及国内旅游基本情况等方面的内容。

二、本篇资料的来源

本篇资料中住宿和餐饮业经营情况和财务情况资料来源于住宿和餐饮业统计年报和定期报表统计资料；旅游资料来源于市文化和旅游局。由市统计局外经贸易统计处整理提供。

Brief Introduction

Ⅰ. Main Content

The information in this chapter mainly reflects the operating conditions and benefits of the accommodation and catering industry in the city, as well as the basic conditions of tourism, mainly including the operating conditions and financial conditions of the accommodation and catering industry, foreign-related and domestic tourism, and other aspects.

Ⅱ. Source of Data

The information on the operating and financial status of the accommodation and catering industry in this article comes from the accommodation and catering industry statistical annual reports and periodic statement statistics; the tourism information comes from the Qingdao Municipal Bureau of Culture and Tourism. Provided by the Foreign Economic and Trade Statistics Department of Qingdao Municipal Bureau of Statistics.

17-1 限额以上住宿和餐饮业经营情况（2021年）
OPERATION OF ACCOMMODATION AND CATERING SERVICES ABOVE DESIGNATED SIZE（2021）

单位：万元（10 000 yuan）

项目	Item	营业额 Turnover	客房收入 Income from Guest Rooms	餐费收入 Catering Income	商品销售收入 Income from Commodity Sales	其他收入 Other Income
总　计	**Total**	**1414119.3**	**306258.3**	**1007161.4**	**29861.2**	**70838.4**
一、住宿业	**Hotels**	**529757.3**	**289023.2**	**179171.3**	**6490.8**	**55072.0**
国有企业	State-owned Enterprises	67053.4	21852.4	28783.3	1179.5	15238.2
集体企业	Collective-owned Enterprises	774.4	692.0	82.4		
其他企业	Other Enterprises	461929.5	266478.8	150305.6	5311.3	39833.8
独立门店	Freestanding Stores	458689.2	234562.1	165852.0	6067.6	52207.5
连锁总店	General Chain Stores	3884.3	2035.0	1521.5	81.9	245.9
连锁直营店	Chain Store	8273.1	6358.1	878.3	43.6	993.1
连锁加盟店	Franchise Store	31286.1	29181.5	1238.8	190.6	675.2
其他	Others	27624.6	16886.5	9680.7	107.1	950.3
五星	Five Star Class	93029.3	36703.7	45541.9	1773.3	9010.4
四星	Four Star class	72107.6	32344.2	30863.4	864.8	8035.2
三星	Three Star class	39806.9	22048.2	13140.8	838.7	3779.2
二星	Two Star class	2518.5	1167.1	1018.9	23.6	308.9
一星	One Star class	3279.4	2618.4	613.6		47.4
其他	Others	319015.6	194141.6	87992.7	2990.4	33890.9
二、餐饮业	**Catering Services**	**884362.0**	**17235.1**	**827990.1**	**23370.4**	**15766.4**
国有企业	State-owned Enterprises	6367.7	2567.7	3731.1	19.9	49.0
集体企业	Collective-owned Enterprises					
其他企业	Other Enterprises	877994.3	14667.4	824259.0	23350.5	15717.4
独立门店	Freestanding Stores	416282.3	13713.5	373221.9	15760.4	13586.5
连锁总店	General Chain Stores	304777.5	22.4	300413.8	3655.3	686.0
连锁直营店	Chain Store	19505.2	1403.4	17100.4	376.9	624.5
连锁加盟店	Franchise Store	58110.5		58109.5	1.0	
其他	Others	85686.5	2095.8	79144.5	3576.8	869.4

17-2 限额以上住宿业财务状况（2021年）
FINANCIAL SITUATION OF HOTELS ABOVE DESIGNATED SIZE（2021）

单位：万元（10 000 yuan）

指标	Indicator	合计 Total	国有经济 State-owned Enterprises	集体经济 Collective-owned Enterprises	外商及港澳台经济 Foreign Funded Enterprises and Enterprises with Funds from Hong Kong, Macao and Taiwan	其他 Other Enterprises
单位数	**Number of Enterprises**	**332**	**19**		**10**	**302**
年末资产负债	**Year-end Assets-Liability**					
资产总计	Total Assets	1371877	132771		181308	1056572
流动资产合计	Sub-total of Current Assets	701630	72560		78986	549776
负债合计	Total Liabilities	1182017	89317		144484	947809
所有者权益合计	Total Owners’ Equities	206689	43454		36823	125593
损益及分配	**Loss，Profits and Distribution**					
营业收入	Revenue from Principal Business	505640	63838		56798	384237
营业成本	Cost of Principal Business	222492	18876		17624	185560
营业税金及附加	Taxes and Extra Charges on Principal Business	6858	914		1812	4132
营业利润	Profits from Principal Business	-58045	-6692		1375	-52741
其他业务利润	Profits from other Business	7176	996		3651	2529
销售费用	Operating Costs	157116	32328		10597	114189
管理费用	Management Expenses	176769	20350		25061	131041
财务费用	Financial Expenses	18556	-122		580	18098
利润总额	Total Profits	-54957	-5497		1487	-50962
其他	**Others**					
应付职工薪酬	Employee Compensation Payable	155704	31563		17194	106821
营业利润率	Operating Profit Margin	-10.87	-8.61		2.62	-13.26

17-3 限额以上餐饮业财务状况（2021年）
FINANCIAL SITUATION OF CATERING SERVICES ABOVE DESIGNATED SIZE (2021)

单位：万元（10 000 yuan）

指标	Indicator	合计 Total	国有经济 State-owned Enterprises	集体经济 Collective-owned Enterprises	外商及港澳台经济 Foreign Funded Enterprises and Enterprises with Funds from Hong Kong, Macao and Taiwan	其他 Other Enterprises
单位数	**Number of Enterprises**	**433**	**4**		**14**	**415**
年末资产负债	**Year-end Assets-Liability**					
资产总计	Total Assets	638059	12296		211870	413893
流动资产合计	Sub-total of Current Assets	330639	11304		58779	260556
负债合计	Total Liabilities	524025	4097		191570	328358
所有者权益合计	Total Owners' Equities	109168	8200		20300	80668
损益及分配	**Loss, Profits and Distribution**					
营业收入	Revenue from Principal Business	849147	6058		283545	559543
营业成本	Cost of Principal Business	491005	3699		147019	340288
营业税金及附加	Taxes and Extra Charges on Principal Business	1132	100		164	869
营业利润	Profits from Principal Business	15157	84		22215	-7142
其他业务利润	Profits from other Business	2957			2065	892
销售费用	Operating Costs	222430	646		82858	138927
管理费用	Management Expenses	109428	2068		26584	80776
财务费用	Financial Expenses	9486	2		5592	3891
利润总额	Total Profits	19789	911		22498	-3621
其他	**Others**					
应付职工薪酬	Employee Compensation Payable	199083	1720		79403	117960
营业利润率	Operating Profit Margin	2.33	15.04		7.93	-0.65

17-4 入境旅游人数(2000—2021年)
NUMBER OF OVERSEA VISITOR ARRIVALS(2000—2021)

项　目	Item	2000年	2005年	2010年	2011年
总　计	**Total**	**237465**	**684407**	**1080511**	**1156391**
一、外国人	**Foreigner**	**177098**	**596177**	**826628**	**809043**
#韩国	Korea	69878	295111	382225	298096
日本	Japan	67215	177121	242082	216755
美国	USA	10384	23284	35539	45842
俄罗斯	Russia	4820	12062	15793	15750
德国	Germany	3820	10646	21626	26178
新加坡	Singapore	6321	6060	13444	16626
英国	UK	2798	5744	17639	23955
加拿大	Canada	1865	4397	9279	12007
法国	France	2491	5166	11766	12019
意大利	Italy	1555	3963	3867	7028
澳大利亚	Australia	1817	4257	8223	15465
菲律宾	Philippines	7947	3459	14140	14259
泰国	Thailand	780	3261	2572	3271
印尼	Indonesia	1 241	2349	7863	8128
新西兰	New Zealand	442	710	1597	6265
二、港澳和台湾同胞	**Chinese Compatriots from Hong Kong, Macao and Taiwan**	**60367**	**88230**	**253883**	**347348**

17-5 入境旅游收入(2000—2021年)
EARNINGS FROM INTERNATIONAL TOURISM(2000—2021)

项　目	Item	2000年	2005年	2010年	2011年
总　计	**Total**	**118164**	**340899**	**399688**	**441171**
旅游购物	Shopping	20742	67047	74104	80823
住宿费	Accommodation	17443	37277	43933	59823
餐饮费	Dining	11223	33557	38747	40191
交通费	Transportation	35252	128112	145551	134425
邮电费	Postal and Telecommunication	5502	18394	19081	16720
文化娱乐费	Culture and Entertainment	6894	20240	24032	36132
游览	Sightseeing			22978	51705
其他	Other Services		36272	31262	21353

注：因新冠疫情影响，2020年、2021年未开展此项统计。
Note：Due to the impact of the new crown epidemic, the statistics were not carried out in 2020 and 2021.

单位：人次（person-time）

2012 年	2013 年	2014 年	2015 年	2016 年	2017 年	2018 年	2019 年	2020 年	2021 年
1270113	**1282814**	**1280526**	**1338702**	**1410494**	**1443715**	**1535733**	**1702568**	**188361**	**222857**
877593	**905415**	**951732**	**996191**	**1042213**	**1056800**	**1118860**	**1258240**	**155124**	**201691**
338383	338191	366584	389832	68010	432430	451046	507854	73266	87137
185613	146080	135179	140762	151832	164095	174147	192257	41274	70244
48431	54178	57907	62771	68010	73905	79392	87014	9079	6567
26432	26519	25356	28529	30534	32540	37053	44720	4896	2646
26311	19014	21723	23425	25456	26636	28646	33256	5874	3536
16316	16305	19975	21310	23713	25257	26060	29001	3942	5043
28385	19496	22817	23812	26133	28006	28942	31577	3582	3816
11678	9727	9483	10659	11592	12544	15473	16849	2245	2278
15595	21422	17828	19388	21836	23507	25035	27218	2708	2335
5622	5679	7705	8747	9234	10627	11559	12904	1563	1182
16644	11149	15339	16798	18839	20304	21491	23344	1679	1008
7546	18630	6668	7300	7891	8489	9837	11300	1327	274
2369	3692	4803	5331	5784	6628	7367	8331	2075	1262
4571	10011	6568	5692	6220	7388	9816	11161	515	403
6448	1452	2549	2872	3352	4230	7367	7965	429	430
392520	**377399**	**328794**	**342511**	**368281**	**386915**	**416873**	**444328**	**33237**	**21166**

单位：万元（10 000 yuan）

2012 年	2013 年	2014 年	2015 年	2016 年	2017 年	2018 年	2019 年
519495	**511158**	**503900**	**566742**	**656966**	**694103**	**798373.5914**	**1084000**
93872	94055	109246	122473	141970	129381	102192	264604
59378	58577	62232	69879	81004	77184	150893	134308
51378	51065	44041	49589	57483	68091	122950	95717
170238	180945	160492	180791	209573	249113	273842	351975
23014	22950	19400	21593	25031	33248	16766	42059
32832	32103	33409	36271	42045	42201	62273	70243
32832	32152	44192	49930	57879	40674	33532	90839
55951	39311	30888	36216	41982	54211	35927	34254

17-6　国内旅游人数及收入（2021 年）
NUMBER OF DOMESTIC TOURISTS AND INCOME（2021）

指　　标	Indicator	单位	Unit	2021 年
国内旅游人数	Number of Domestic Tourists	万人次	10000 person-times	8198.9
1. 过夜旅游者人数	Number of Overnight Tourists	万人次	10000 person-times	3856.7
2. 不过夜旅游者（一日游人数）	Number of Non-overnight（One-day Sightseeing）Tourists	万人次	10000 person-times	4342.2
国内旅游人均花费	Per Capita Expenditure of Domestic Tourist	元	yuan	1721.0
国内旅游收入	Earings from Domestic Tourism	亿元	100 million yuan	1411.0
1. 接待过夜旅游者收入	Earings from Overnight Tourists	亿元	100 million yuan	1004.1
2. 接待不过夜旅游者（一日游）收入	Earnings form Non-overnight（One-day Sightseeing）Tourists	亿元	100 million yuan	406.9

主要统计指标解释

住宿餐饮业营业额 指住宿和餐饮业法人企业、产业活动单位在经营活动中因提供服务或销售商品等取得的收入，包括客房收入、餐费收入、商品销售收入和其他收入。客房收入指住宿和餐饮业法人企业、产业活动单位在经营活动中因提供住宿服务取得的客房收入。餐费收入指住宿和餐饮业法人企业、产业活动单位因为顾客提供就餐服务取得的收入，包括经烹饪、调制加工后出售的各种食品，如主食、炒菜、凉拌菜等的收入。商品销售收入指住宿和餐饮业法人企业、产业活动单位伴随服务而出售商品所取得的收入。其他收入指营业收入中除客房收入、餐费收入、商品销售收入以外的其他收入，包括娱乐、健身和商务服务等。

国内旅游者 是指不以谋求职业、获取报酬为目的，离开惯常居住环境，到国内其他地方从事参观、游览、度假等旅游活动（包括外出探亲、疗养、考察、参加会议和从事商务、科技、文化、教育、宗教活动过程中的旅游活动），出行距离超过 10 公里，出游时间超过 6 小时，但不超过 12 个月的我国大陆居民。

入境旅游者 指来我国参观、访问、旅行、探亲、访友、休养、考察、参加会议和从事经济、科技、文化、教育、体育、宗教等活动的外国人、华侨、港澳和台湾同胞的人数。不包括外国在我国的常驻机构，如领事馆、通讯社、企业办事处的工作人员；来我国常住的外国专家、留学生以及在岸逗留不过夜人员。

Explanatory Notes on Main Statistical Indicators

Business Revenue of Hotels and Catering Services refer to revenue received from providing services or selling commodities by corporate enterprises and establishments engaged in hotel and catering services, including income from hotel rooms, from catering services, from selling of commodities and from other services. Income from hotel rooms refers to income of corporate enterprises and establishments by providing lodging services. Income from catering services refers to income of corporate enterprises and establishments by providing catering services, including selling of cooked or prepared foods such as stable food, cooked dishes or cold dishes. Income from selling of commodities refers to income of corporate enterprises and establishments by selling commodities that accompany the services they provide. Income from other activities refers to income received other than income from hotel rooms, catering services or selling of commodities, such as income from providing recreation, fitness or business services.

Domestic Tourists refers to residents Chinese mainland who are not for the purpose of seeking employment, remuneration, and leaving the usual living environment, elsewhere to engage in domestic visitors, sightseeing, vacation travel (including to go out to visit relatives, infirmary, observing, participate in the meeting and engage in business, science and technology, culture, education, religious activities in the course of tourism activities), trip distance of more than 10 km, trips longer than six hours, but not more than 12 months.

Entrance Tourists refers to foreigners, overseas Chinese, Chinese compatriots from Hong Kong, Macao and Taiwan coming to China for sight-seeing, visits, tours, family reunions, vacations, study tours, conferences and other activities of a business, scientific and technological, cultural, educational and religious nature. It does not include representatives and employees of resident institutions of foreign countries in China such as embassies, consulates, news agencies and offices of foreign companies and organizations, nor does it include long-term foreign experts or students residing in China, or persons in transition without spending a night in China.

教育、科技和文化 18

EDUCATION SCIENCE &
TECHNOLOY AND CULTURE

简要说明

一、本篇资料的主要内容

本篇资料主要反映了全市教育、科技和文化事业基本情况。教育部分主要包括高等教育、中等教育、初等教育、成人教育、职业教育、幼儿园等方面的基本情况。科技部分主要包括科研机构、科学技术奖励。文化部分主要包括文化、文物、广播、电视、报纸杂志出版、图书出版等方面的发展状况。

二、本篇资料的来源

1. 教育部分，技工学校的资料来源于市人力资源和社会保障局，其他资料来源于市教育局。

2. 科技部分，科研机构及科技奖励资料来源于市科技局。

3. 文化部分，图书、杂志、报纸出版有关资料来源于青岛出版集团、海大出版社其他资料来源于市文化和旅游局。

本篇资料由市统计局人口就业和社会科技文化统计处整理提供。

Brief Introduction

Ⅰ. Main Content

Data in this chapter show the basic conditions of education, science & technology and culture. Data on education show the development of higher education secondary education, primary education, adult education, vocational education and kindergartens. Data on science & technology show the basic conditions of science research institutions, scientific and technological achievements and prizes, scientific& technological activities of large and medium- size industrial enterprises. Data on culture show the basic conditions of arts, cultural relics,broadcasting, television and publication of newspapers magazines and books.

Ⅱ. Source of Data

1.In education component, data on the basic conditions of technical schools are provided by Qingdao Municipal Bureau of Human Resources and Social Security, and the other data on education are provided by Qingdao Municipal Bureau of Education.

2.In science & technology component, data on science research institutions and scientific & technological achievements and prizes are provided by Qingdao Municipal Bureau of Science and Technology Data on scientific and technological activities are from the annual report of scientific and technological activities, which is provided by Qingdao Municipal Bureau of Statistics.

3.In the cultural part, the related materials for books, magazines, and newspapers are from Qingdao Publishing Group and Haida Publishing House. Other materials are from the Municipal Bureau of Culture and Tourism.

The information in this article was compiled and provided by the Population, Employment and Social Science, Technology and Culture Statistics Department of Qingdao Bureau of Statistics.

18-1 各级各类学校基本情况（2021 年）
BASIC STATISTICS ON SCHOOLS BY LEVEL AND TYPE OF SCHOOL（2021）

项目	Item	学校数（所）Schools（unit）	毕业生数（人）Graduates（person）	招生数（人）New Students Enrollment（person）	在校学生数（人）Students Enrollment（person）	教职工数（人）Teachers and Staff（person）	#专任教师 of which：Full-time Teachers
研究生	Postgraduates	8	14419	21364	61772		
普通高等学校	Regular Institutions of Higher Education	27	114731	146306	457201	36263	25059
普通中等职业学校	Regular Secondary Vocational School	52	25327	27244	90220	8362	6942
技工学校	Technical Schools	23	7697	11540	35436	2606	1933
普通中学	Regular Secondary Schools	345	123225	145864	445941	46282	39521
#初中	Junior Secondary Schools	260	85359	93084	294018	28644	26298
#高中	Senior Secondary Schools	85	37866	52780	151923	17638	13223
小学	Primary Schools	676	92980	117741	630538	36702	39199
特殊教育学校	Special Education Schools	15	322	486	2475	834	676
幼儿园	Kindergartens	2518	103557	103562	367883	47467	28265
成人高等学校	Adult Institutions of Higher Education	1	66599	92505	186161		

注：1. 普通中等职业学校包含普通中专学校、成人中专学校、职业高中学校。
2. 普通中等职业学校自 2021 年起按照学校类别统计学生数，2020 年以前是按学生身份统计学生数。
3. 因九年一贯制学校的教职工数计入初中，完全中学、十二年一贯制学校的教职工数计入高中，而专任教师是按照教育层次进行归类，存在小学教职工数据小于专任教师数据。

Notes：1.Regular Secondary Vocational Schools include: Secondary Specialized Schools, Adult Secondary Specialized Schools, Vocational High schools.
2.The number of students in regular secondary vocational schools has been counted by school category from 2021, and by student identity before 2020.
3.Because the number of teaching and administrative staff in nine-year schools is included in junior high schools, and the number of full-central schools and 12-year schools is included in senior high schools, while full-time teachers are classified according to education levels, therefore, the data of primary school teaching and administrative staff is less than that of full-time teachers.

18-2 主要年份各级各类学校在校学生数
MAJOR YEAR'S STUDENTS ENROLLMENT OF SCHOOLS BY LEVEL AND TYPE OF SCHOOL

单位：人（person）

年份 Year	普通高等学校 Regular Institutions of Higher Education	中等学校 Secondary Schools	普通中学 Regular Secondary Schools	普通中等职业学校 Regular Secondary Vocational School	技工学校 Technical Schools	中等专业学校 Specialized Secondary Schools	职业中学 Vocational Schools	小学 Primary Schools
1949	1 007	13 804	12 204			1 600		213 470
1952	2 761	27 951	24 181			3 770		413 286
1957	3 133	56 689	51 604			4 985	100	482 397
1962	4 381	62 646	58 639		973	2 791	243	522 921
1965	2 987	99 605	88 187		523	9 405	1 490	788 485
1970	320	222 521	220 262			105	2 154	728 433
1975	1 151	350 309	346 403		762	3 144		928 153
1978	3 465	464 584	457 460		865	4 269	2 000	634 905
1980	6 783	325 935	318 193		1 203	5 195	1 344	816 970
1985	10 631	327 446	279 915		2 111	11 475	33 945	691 341
1988	14 408	352 576	306 943		4 881	11 819	28 933	629 212
1990	15 433	351 365	296 163		5 516	15 118	34 568	632 314
1991	15 491	353 410	298 568		5 803	14 618	34 421	612 772
1992	16 470	367 480	307 903		6 572	14 763	38 242	585 381
1993	23 858	383 043	318 179		7 244	16 877	40 743	583 585
1994	25 018	420 077	347 667		8 094	20 582	43 734	593 419
1995	24 908	450 212	372 335		8 089	23 744	46 044	595 891
1996	26 076	468 561	382 760		8 719	26 951	50 131	607 284
1997	27 434	463 619	362 305		11 131	28 543	61 640	626 749
1998	29 507	442 525	336 918		10 861	28 757	65 989	625 308

注：自 2021 年起中等学校校生学生数包含普通中学、普通中等职业学校和技工学校在校生数。

Note：The number of students enrolled in secondary schools from 2021 includes the number of students enrolled in regular secondary schools, regular secondary vocational schools, and technical schools.

18-2 续表
Continued

单位：人（person）

年份 Year	普通高等学校 Regular Institutions of Higher Education	中等学校 Secondary Schools	普通中学 Regular Secondary Schools	普通中等职业学校 Regular Secondary Vocational School	技工学校 Technical Schools	中等专业学校 Specialized Secondary Schools	职业中学 Vocational Schools	小学 Primary Schools
1999	33 681	459 520	352 238		10 091	26 955	70 236	583 594
2000	46 131	497 391	398 458		9 847	25 192	63 894	534 922
2001	60 728	542 400	443 693		11 346	25 358	62 003	499 147
2002	82 539	575 599	467 628		13 465	27 421	67 085	478 634
2003	168 439	586 704	461 435		21 100	28 948	75 221	467 560
2004	201 739	598 804	436 117		30 253	30 881	101 553	476 897
2005	239 761	569 230	391 148		38 160	33 522	106 400	479 781
2006	260 339	554 308	365 192		40 578	32 051	116 487	483 892
2007	264 917	558 527	360 410		39 950	28 011	130 156	484 775
2008	269 314	582 932	373 884		40 592	25 330	143 126	477 230
2009	275157	564476	377427		36518	22739	127792	465031
2010	284788	535079	380025		32480	24014	98560	462722
2011	291453	505051	373226		31028	25905	74892	479513
2012	296645	489103	369580		27099	27005	65419	484985
2013	300246	484025	365110		28932	28389	61594	496343
2014	313486	479260	362599		29740	28751	58170	516529
2015	322260	467231	355401		30202	33038	48590	536492
2016	340875	470333	356107		30589	32710	50927	547231
2017	346328	490796	372196		33179	32882	52539	550540
2018	397982	500872	385443		32110	31879	51440	569923
2019	415824	521758	408953		32733	30555	49517	583784
2020	430671	546747	430426		33432	33122	49767	603763
2021	457201	571597	445941	90220	35436	-	-	630538

18-3 主要年份普通高等学校基本情况
MAJOR YEAR' S BASIC STATISTICS ON REGULAR INSTTUTIONS OF HIGHER EDUCATION

单位：人（person）

年份 Year	学校数（所） Schools （unit）	毕业生数 Graduates	招生数 New Students Enrollment	在校学生数 Students Enrollment	教职工数 Teachers and Staff	#专任教师 of which : Full-time Teachers
1949	1		250	1 007	779	226
1952	2	262	565	2 761	12 530	308
1957	2	356	755	3 133	1 308	622
1962	5	647	653	4 381	1 866	749
1965	3	741	529	2 987	1 539	623
1970	2	684		320	1 178	486
1975	2	460	473	1 151	1 353	582
1978	4	739	1 782	3 465	2 829	1 176
1980	6	431	1 717	6 783	4 182	1 606
1985	7	1 828	3 823	10 631	5 561	2 181
1988	7	3 496	4 687	14 408	6 875	2 499
1990	7	4 495	4 745	15 433	7 305	2 624
1991	7	4 880	4 954	15 491	7 282	2 489
1992	7	4 458	5 428	16 470	7 344	2 523
1993	7	3 140	9 449	23 858	7 366	2 520
1994	4	7 059	8 042	25 018	7 466	2 650
1995	4	7 828	7 978	24 908	7 545	2 682
1996	4	6 691	7 956	26 076	7 606	2 745
1997	4	7 091	8 503	27 434	7 790	2 813
1998	4	6 912	8 849	29 507	7 662	2 907
1999	4	7 202	11 584	33 681	7 662	2 928
2000	6	7 128	18 427	46 131	8 030	3 278

18-3 续表
Continued

单位：人（person）

年份 Year	学校数（所） Schools （unit）	毕业生数 Graduates	招生数 New Students Enrollment	在校学生数 Students Enrollment	教职工数 Teachers and Staff	#专任教师 of which： Full-time Teachers
2001	6	8 991	22 787	60 728	8 706	4 058
2002	7	13 053	29 731	82 539	9 517	4 723
2003	25	25 747	61 975	168 439	18 911	10 293
2004	25	34 860	70 022	201 739	21 437	12 347
2005	25	46 114	79 725	239 761	23 078	13 894
2006	25	55 931	79 094	260 339	24 881	15 195
2007	25	68 354	78 728	264 917	25 956	16 005
2008	25	75 198	86 878	269 314	26 654	16 805
2009	25	69475	81025	275157	26983	16870
2010	25	70450	82220	284788	28145	16996
2011	22	79466	84434	291453	28151	17120
2012	22	79791	87981	296645	29445	18183
2013	22	78974	85707	300246	28958	18396
2014	22	77503	90127	313486	28944	18587
2015	24	79784	92251	322260	29620	19213
2016	26	86270	100525	340875	30390	20151
2017	25	95006	98983	346238	32013	21231
2018	25	105580	118247	397982	32628	21576
2019	24	103684	126423	415824	34259	22849
2020	27	107147	133158	430671	35540	24321
2021	27	114731	146306	457201	36263	25059

18-4 分市、区普通中学情况(2021年)

BASIC STATISTICS ON REGULAR SECONDARY SCHOOLS BY REGION（2021）

单位：人(person)

市、区名称	Region	普通高中 Regular Senior Secondary Schools				普通初中 Regular Junior Secondary Schools			
		学校数 Schools (unit)	毕业生数 Graduates	招生数 New Students Enrollment	在校生数 Students Enrollment	学校数 Schools (unit)	毕业生数 Graduates	招生数 New Students Enrollment	在校生数 Students Enrollment
合　计	**Whole Municipality**	**85**	**37866**	**52780**	**151923**	**260**	**85359**	**93084**	**294018**
市直属	Municipal Level	25	9879	12953	37606	6	2889	3518	10858
市南区	Shinan District					10	2539	2820	9174
市北区	Shibei District					25	6867	9095	26403
李沧区	Licang District	2	14	7	25	14	3944	5147	14720
崂山区	Laoshan District	3	0	2	5	12	2273	3247	9554
黄岛区(西海岸新区)	Huangdao District (West Coast New Area)	15	5681	9796	25256	41	15018	16990	50587
城阳区(含高新区)	Chengyang District (Including High tech District)	8	2675	4674	12258	19	7663	10299	29594
即墨区	Jimo District	12	5861	7704	21791	32	14385	14396	45711
胶州市	Jiaozhou	7	4377	6075	17823	24	10809	10119	33207
平度市	Pingdu	9	6180	7326	23776	47	12132	11475	36100
莱西市	Laixi	4	3199	4243	13383	30	6840	5978	28110

18-5 分市、区职业中学、小学情况(2021 年)

BASIC STATISTICS ON VOCATIONAL SECONDARY SCHOOLS AND PRIMARY SCHOOLS BY REGION（2021）

单位：人（person）

市、区名称	Region	普通中等职业学校 Regular Secondary Vocational School				小学 Primary School			
		学校数 Schools（unit）	毕业生数 Graduates	招生数 New Students Enrollment	在校生数 Students Enrollment	学校数 Schools（unit）	毕业生数 Graduates	招生数 New Students Enrollment	在校生数 Students Enrollment
全 市	**Whole Municipality**	**52**	**25327**	**27244**	**90220**	**676**	**92980**	**117741**	**630538**
市直属	Municipal Level	30	9980	10354	31712	1	662	1457	6266
市南区	Shinan District					29	4702	6328	34800
市北区	Shibei District					64	9542	11607	65134
李沧区	Licang District					39	5676	8641	45910
崂山区	Laoshan District					25	3829	4949	26796
黄岛区（西海岸新区）	Huangdao District（West Coast New Area）	10	5644	6283	22553	99	16840	22970	118310
城阳区（含高新区）	Chengyang District（Including High tech District）	3	2658	1441	5875	55	10504	14734	78687
即墨区	Jimo District	3	1631	1900	6431	147	14057	15111	86644
胶州市	Jiaozhou	1	1905	1940	8021	66	9834	12851	67606
平度市	Pingdu	2	1104	2595	7223	102	11480	12324	67906
莱西市	Laixi	3	2405	2731	8405	49	5854	6769	32479
高新区	High tech District								

注：1. 市直属中有一所十二年一贯制学校，校数在高中中统计。
2. 自 2021 年起按照学校类别统计学生数，2020 年以前是按学生身份统计学生数。

Notes：1. There is a twelve-year consistent school in the municipality, and the number of schools is counted in high schools.
2. The number of students has been counted by school category from 2021 and by student identity before 2020.

18-6 分市、区中小学教职工情况(2021年)

BASIC STATTSTICS ON TEACHERS AND STAFF IN SECONDARY AND PRIMARY SCHOOLS BY REGION (2021)

单位：人(person)

市、区名称	Region	普通中学 Regular Secondary Schools		普通中等职业学校 Regular Secondary Vocational School		小学 Primary Schools	
		教职工数 Teachers and Staff	#专任教师 of which: Full-time Teachers	教职工数 Teachers and Staff	#专任教师 of which: Full-time Teachers	教职工数 Teachers and Staff	#专任教师 of which: Full-time Teachers
全　市	**Whole Municipality**	**46282**	**39521**	**8362**	**6942**	**36702**	**39199**
市直属	Municipal Level	5300	4004	3249	2523	80	526
市南区	Shinan District	1090	903			2149	2140
市北区	Shibei District	2738	2099			3515	3803
李沧区	Licang District	1739	1275			2221	2469
崂山区	Laoshan District	1491	1058			1694	2012
黄岛区(西海岸新区)	Huangdao District (West Coast New Area)	7398	6690	1666	1385	6367	6589
城阳区(含高新区)	Chengyang District (Including High tech District)	4109	3445	649	634	3895	4203
即墨区	Jimo District	7110	6052	842	742	5479	5970
胶州市	Jiaozhou	4375	4097	615	465	4311	4266
平度市	Pingdu	6558	5892	684	616	4601	4745
莱西市	Laixi	4374	4006	657	577	2390	2476

注：因九年一贯制学校的教职工数计入初中，完全中学、十二年一贯制学校的教职工数计入高中，而专任教师是按照教育层次进行归类，存在小学教职工数据小于专任教师数据的情况。

Note: Because the number of teaching and administrative staff in nine-year schools is included in junior high schools, and the number of full-central schools and 12-year schools is included in senior high schools, while full-time teachers are classified according to education levels, therefore, the data of primary school teaching and administrative staff is less than that of full-time teachers.

18-7 分市、区幼儿园基本情况(2021年)
BASIC STATISTICS ON KINDERGARTENS BY REGION（2021）

单位：人（person）

市、区名称	Region	幼儿园（所）Kindergartens（unit）	幼儿数 Children	教职工数 Teachers and Staff	#专任教师 of which：Full-time teachers
合　计	**Whole Municipality**	**2518**	**367883**	**47467**	**28265**
市直属	Municipal Level				
市南区	Shinan District	68	14852	2491	1312
市北区	Shibei District	222	38961	5469	2529
李沧区	Licang District	121	33352	4348	2086
崂山区	Laoshan District	116	16945	2620	1614
黄岛区（西海岸新区）	Huangdao District（West Coast New Area）	531	77499	9697	5876
城阳区（含高新区）	Chengyang District（Including High tech District）	211	42570	6106	3649
即墨区	Jimo District	441	49492	6111	3780
胶州市	Jiaozhou	288	42740	5577	3355
平度市	Pingdu	375	34104	3166	2565
莱西市	Laixi	145	17368	1882	1499

18-8 科研机构基本情况(1978—2021 年)
BASIC STATISTICS ON SCIENTIFIC RESEARCH INSTITUTIONS（1978—2021）

年 份 Year	独立自然科研结构(个) Independent Institutions of Natural Scientific Research (unit)	独立自然科研结构中科技人员(个) Personnel of Independent Institutions of Natural Scientific Research (person)	完成科研项目(项) Number of Scientific Research Projects Completed (item)	取得科技成果(项) Number of Achievements in S&T (item)
1978	31	2701	306	306
1980			481	297
1982	41	2345	451	451
1983	48	3182	530	530
1984	53	3312	507	507
1985	52	3673	552	552
1986	63	3998	577	577
1988	101	5199	544	510
1990	141	6046	414	931
1991	72	5665	753	753
1992	71	5726	659	659
1993	69	5545	546	546
1994	69	5540	467	467
1995	59	5286	441	441
1996	58	4738	613	613
1997	54	4577	418	418
1998	52	4142	517	517
1999	58	3771	606	606
2000	54	3637	621	621
2001	50	3191	457	457
2002	52	3248	406	406
2003	53	3246	589	589
2004	50	3226	506	506
2005	50	3234	438	438
2006	50	3291	548	548
2007	50	3432	506	506
2008	42	3709	416	416
2009	43	3727	572	572
2010	44	4088	472	472
2011	47	4548	345	345
2012	48	4967	304	304
2013	48	6057	433	433
2014	50	5438	415	415
2015	54	6037	639	639
2016	57	5722	606	606
2017	57	6017	588	588
2018	58	6017	406	406
2019	58	6417	400	400
2020	49	7379	1309	984
2021	31	5492	1349	1356

注：1991 年以后不包括民办科研机构。
Note：Since 1991，private institutions of scientific research are not included.

18-9 独立科学研究机构情况（2021 年）
BASIC STATISTICS ON INDEPENDENT INSHUTIONS OF SCIENTIFIC RESEARCH（2021）

项　目	Item	单位	Unit	总　计 Total	中央属 Central	地方属 Local
机构数	Number of Institutions	个	unit	44	16	28
职工人数	Staff and Workers	人	person	7240	4617	2623
科技人员	Personnel Engaged in S&T	人	person	6363	4191	2172
经费收入	Funding for S&T	万元	10 000 yuan	502282	310182	192101
经费支出	Expenditures for S&T	万元	10 000 yuan	570645	352960	217685

18-10 科学技术奖励情况（2021 年）
AWARD STATISTICS ON SCIENCE AND TECHNOLOGY（2021）

项　目	Item	单位	unit	自然科学奖 Natural Science Prizes Awarded	技术发明奖 Invention Prizes Awarded	科技进步奖 Scientific and Technological Progress Prizes Awarded	国际科技合作奖 International S&T Cooperation Prizes Award	最高奖 Highest Prizes Award
国家级	National Level	项	item					
特等	Special Grade	项	item					
# 一等	First Prize	项	item					
二等	Second Prize	项	item					
省级	Provincial Level	项	item	12	4	85	0	1
# 一等	First Prize	项	item			15		
二等	Second Prize	项	item	12	3	34		
三等	Third Prize	项	item	0	1	36		
市级	Municipal Level	项	item					
# 一等	First Prize	项	item					
二等	Second Prize	项	item					
三等	Third Prize	项	item					

注：1. 国际科技合作奖、最高奖不分等级。
　　2. 国家级科学技术奖励最终结果暂未公布。

Notes：1. There is no grade in international scientific and technological cooperation prizes award and highest prizes award.
　　2. The final result of the national science and technology award has not been announced yet.

18-11　文化、文物事业机构、人员数
NUMBER OF CULTURAL AND CULTURAL RELIC INSTITUTIONS AND PERSONNEL

项目	Item	文化机构数（个）Number of Cultural Institutions（unit）		文化人员数（人）Number of Cultural Personnel（Person）	
		2021 年	2020 年	2021 年	2020 年
一、艺术事业	**Art**				
1.艺术表演团体	Art Performance Troupes	5	6	318	378
2.艺术表演场所	Art Centers	7	1	134	15
3.艺术研究机构	Art Research Institutions	1	1	38	24
4.艺术展览机构	Art Exhibition Institutions	2	1	38	20
5.其他	Others				
二、图书馆事业	**Libraries**				
公共图书馆	Public Libraries	11	12	272	272
#县(区)级图书馆	County Libraries	10	11	263	177
三、群众文化事业	**Nass Culture**				
1.群众艺术馆	Nass Art Centers				
2.文化馆	Cultural Palaces	11	12	225	211
3.文化站	Cultural Centers	137	138	607	619
4.其他	Others				

18-12 文化部门艺术剧团情况(2021 年)
STATISTICS ON ART TROUPES OF CULTURAL DEPARTMENT（2021）

项 目	Item	剧团(院)数(个) Number of Troupes (theatres) (unit)	职工人数(人) Staff and Workers (person)	演出场次(场) Number of Performances (show)	观众人数(万人次) Number of Spectators (10000 person-times)	演出收入(万元) Income from Ticket Sales (10000 yuan)	#财政补贴(万元) Appropriation Funds (10000 yuan)
总 计	**Total**	**8**	**838**	**1446**	**64.1**	**2487.8**	**12538.7**
一、按单位性质分	**Divided by unit nature**						
事业	Career	5	318	764	36.1	1014.7	5499.2
企业	Enterprise	3	520	682	28	1473.1	7039.5
二、按艺术门类分	**By category of art**						
1. 话剧院	Theatre Drama Troupes	1	118	300	8.0	621.2	1689.7
2. 交响乐团	Symphony orchestra	1	151	64	5.5	220	3317.4
3. 地方戏曲剧团	Local opera troupe	4	167	700	30.6	794.7	2181.8
4. 京剧院	Peking opera theatre	1	87	100	8.0	225.0	1175.9
5. 综合性艺术表演团体	Comprehensive art performance group	1	315	282	12	626.9	4173.9

18-13 图书馆、文化馆情况
STATISTICS ON LIBRARIES AND CULTURAL CENTERS

项 目	Item	单位	Unit	2021 年 全市合计 Total	2021 年 #市区 Urban Area	2020 年 全市合计 Total	2020 年 #市区 Urban Area
公共图书馆	**Public Libraries**	个	**unit**	**11**	**8**	**12**	**9**
工作人员	Staff and Workers	人	person	272	226	272	216
藏书册数	Collcetion Books	千册	1000 copies	8896.6	7774	8402	7365
阅览席位	Seating Capacity of Reading Rooms	张	piece	5984	4663	5984	4663
读者人数	Readers	万人次	10 000 person/times	378.27	291.9	233.55	201.74
文化馆	**Cultural Centers**	个	**unit**	**11**	**8**	**12**	**9**

主要统计指标解释

普通高等学校 指通过国家普通高等教育招生考试,招收高中毕业生为主要培养对象,实施高等学历教育的全日制大学、独立设置的学院、独立学院和高等专科学校、高等职业学校及其他普通高教机构。

大学、独立设置的学院主要实施本科及本科层次以上的教育。独立学院主要实施本科层次的教育。高等专科学校、高等职业学校实施专科层次的教育。其他普通高教机构是指承担国家普通招生计划任务不计校数的机构，包括普通高等学校分校、大专班等。

科技活动人员 指直接从事科技活动、专门从事科技活动管理和为科技活动提供直接服务，累计的实际工作时间占全年制度工作时间 10% 及以上的人员。

独立自然科研机构 按照《科学研究和技术服务业非企业单位调查表》表 1 “机构概况” 填报。其中,机构类别为 “1. 县以上政府部门属自然科学与技术领域研究与开发机构（理、工、农、医类）” 全部包含，机构类别为 “4. 县属研究与开发机构” “5. 其他事业单位” 的从事的国民经济行业代码分类中的 731、732、733、734。

取得科技成果 按照《科技研究和技术服务业非企业单位调查表》表 9 “科技产出”，未包含科技论文。

文化事业机构 指从事专业文化工作和为专业文化工作服务的独立建制的单独核算的单位。不包括这些单位另外举办独立核算的其他机构和各部门的业余文化组织。

Explanatory Notes on Main Statistical Indicators

Colleges and Universities refers to full-time universities, independently established colleges, independent colleges and technical colleges, higher vocational schools and other general higher education institutions that have passed the national general higher education enrollment examination and recruited high school graduates as the main training objects.

Universities and independent colleges mainly implement education at the undergraduate level and above. Independent colleges mainly implement education at the undergraduate level. Higher technical colleges and higher vocational schools implement college-level education. Other general higher education institutions refer to institutions that undertake the tasks of the national general enrollment plan without counting the number of schools, including general higher education branch schools, college classes, etc.

Personnel Engaged in S&T Activities refer to personnel directly engaged in S&T activities, in the management of S&T activities, and in providing direct service to S&T activities, who spend over 10% of the total working hours in a year in S&T activities.

The independent research institutions The independent research institutions fill in tables in accordance with the "Institutional profile" (Table 1) from the document Survey of non-enterprise units in scientific research and technology services. If the category of institutions is "1. Government departments at or above the county level belonging to natural science and technology research and development institutions (science, industry, agriculture and medicine)" , it covers all. And if the categories of institutions are respectively "4. research and development institutions at county level" , or "5. Other institutional organization" , the codes are 731 732 733 734 respectively according to the National economy industry code classification.

Scientific and technological achievements are filled according to Table 9 (scientific and technological output) of *Survey of non-enterprise units in scientific research and technology services*, with scientific and technical papers excluded.

Cultural Institutions refer to entities with independent structure and independent accounting that engage in or serve professional cultural work, and do not include other institutions and amateur cultural organizations of various departments that conduct independent accounting.

体育、卫生和民政、司法 19

SPORTS，PUBLIC HEALTH AND CIVIL AFFAIRS，JUDICIAL AFFAIRS

简要说明

一、本篇资料的主要内容

本篇资料反映了全市体育、卫生、民政、司法等社会事业的基本情况。体育部分主要包括主要年份运动员、教练员、裁判员发展人数、体育运动破纪录、获奖情况。卫生部分主要包括各类卫生机构及其人员、床位数。民政部分主要包括婚姻登记、社会救济、社会福利事业基本情况、殡葬服务情况。司法部分主要包括律师、公证、调解、社会治安基本情况。

二、本篇资料的来源

1. 体育部分来源于市体育局。

2. 卫生部分来源于市卫健委。

3. 民政部分来源于市民政局。

4. 司法部分，社会治安资料来源于市公安局，其他资料来源于市司法局。

本篇资料由市统计局人口就业和社会科技文化统计处整理提供。

Brief Introduction

Ⅰ. Main Content

Data in this chapter show the basic conditions of sports, public health, civil affairs and judicial affairs Data on sports are mainly including the number of athletes, coaches and referees, conditions of record and awards. Data on public health are mainly including the number of health institutions, personnel and beds. Data on civil affairs are mainly including the conditions of marriage registration, social relief, social welfare and funeral services. Data on judicial affairs are mainly including the conditions of lawyers, notarization, mediation and social order.

Ⅱ. Source of Data

1. Data on sports are provided by Qingdao Municipal Bureau of Physical.

2. The health part comes from the Qingdao Municipal Health Commission.

3. Data on civil affairs are provided by Qingdao Municipal Bureau of Civil Affairs.

4. In judicial affairs component, data on social order are provided by Qingdao Municipal Bureau of Public Security and the other data are provided by Qingdao Municipal Bureau of Justice.

The information in this article was compiled and provided by the Population, Employment and Social Science, Technology and Culture Statistics Department of Qingdao Bureau of Statistics.

19-1 体育事业情况(2000—2021年)

STATISTICS ON SPORTS（2000—2021）

单位：人（person）

项 目	Item	2000年	2005年	2010年	2011年	2012年	2013年	2014年	2015年	2016年	2017年	2018年	2019年	2020年	2021年
体育部门职工人数	**Staff and Workers in Sports Commissions**	**849**	**834**	**1015**				**847**	**795**	**857**	**654**	**682**	**784**	**780**	**832**
#运动员	Athletes	90	87	287				287	259		284	1123	2259	2787	2100
教练员	Coaches	174	235	170	136					120	133	134	131	133	271
重点体校	Key Sports School	126	117	115	129						1061	1370	881	980	1248
业余体校	Spare Time Sports Schools	142	223								1537	1846	1702	1807	1810
体育专业队	Professional Sports Teams	135	132	192	87	84	42	38	17	17	5	5			
优秀运动员	Excellent Athletes	90	87	146	57										
优秀运动队专职教练员	Full-time Coaches of Excellent Sports Teams	18	23	97	54				89	120					
等级裁判员发展人数	**Certified Referees**	**1114**	**275**	**212**	**510**	**558**	**512**	**514**	**490**	**167**		**511**	**347**	**519**	**530**
#二级	Second Grades	451	275	169	510	484	463	514	490	116		319	122	236	437
三级	Third Grades	616											90	283	
等级运动员发展人数	**Certified Athletes**	**343**	**260**	**229**	**436**	**362**	**362**	**283**	**259**		**176**	**327**	**829**	**328**	**625**
#二级	Second Grades	209	260	229	436	256	362	283	259		176	290	730	328	568
三级	Third Grades	46													
少年级	Junior Grades	88													

19-1 续表
Continued

项 目	Item	单位	Unit	2013年	2014年	2015年	2016年	2017年	2018年	2019年	2020年	2021年
全年获得奖牌数	**Number of Medals Won in the Year**	枚	**piece**	**659**	**576.5**	**596**	**729.5**	**3032**	**849**	**1507.5**	**666.5**	**1242**
#国家级金牌	Golden Medals at National Level	枚	piece	90	48	51	101	104	76	142	40	81
国家级银牌	Silver Medals at National Level	枚	piece	44	21	44	56	91	81	127	32	81
省级金牌	Golden Medals at Provincial Level	枚	piece	174.5	202.5	149	219.5	214.5	264	428.5	372.5	321
省级银牌	Silver Medals at Provincial Level	枚	piece	111.5	121.5	126	135	140	161	289	222	385
体育运动比赛记录	**Records Broken the National Records**											
项目	Number of Events	项	item						1			
人数	Number of Persons	人	person						1			
次数	Number of Times	人次	person-times						1			
体育运动比赛记录	**Records Broken the Provincial Records**											
项目	Number of Events	项	item									
人数	Number of Persons	人	person									
次数	Number of Times	人次	person-times						15			

19-2 主要年份卫生事业基本情况
MAJOR YEAR'S BASIC STATISTICS ON PUBLIC HEALTH

年份 Year	卫生机构数（个）Health Institutions (unit)	#医院 of which: Hospitals	医疗床位数（张）Beds in Health Institutions (bed)	#医院 of which: Hospitals	卫生技术人员（人）Medical and Technical Personnel (person)	#医生 of which: Doctors	每千人口拥有医生数（人）Number of Doctors per 1000 Population (person)	每千人口拥有床位数（张）Number of Hospital Beds per 1000 Population (bed)
1949	80	26	1079	970	2637	1292	0.32	0.27
1952	260	34	2943	1691	3748	1559	0.37	0.70
1957	624	45	5163	2656	6941	2578	0.53	1.07
1962	849	149	7167	4526	8279	2972	0.64	1.55
1965	912	162	8428	5003	9051	3586	0.73	1.72
1970	712	170	8613	6603	9591	3761	0.70	1.60
1975	959	181	10902	9078	13558	4566	0.80	1.90
1978	1192	212	13084	10709	16921	5893	1.01	2.24
1980	1253	212	14170	11345	19265	6781	1.14	2.38
1985	1517	219	18469	13214	23413	9694	1.55	2.95
1990	1563	235	23541	16586	27932	13761	2.08	3.56
1991	1579	235	23727	16796	27772	13227	1.98	3.54
1992	1562	236	24765	17269	28305	13157	1.95	3.67
1993	1540	237	24885	17469	28705	13312	1.97	3.68
1994	1335	242	24732	17882	28938	13535	1.99	3.64
1995	1347	228	25282	18126	29816	13840	2.02	3.69
1996	2216	228	24334	18344	30048	13790	2.00	3.53
1997	2193	239	25201	19046	31121	14400	2.07	3.62
1998	2190	237	24887	19083	31623	14327	2.05	3.56
1999	2185	235	25481	19798	31965	14453	2.06	3.62
2000	2911	231	24392	20057	32160	14860	2.10	3.45
2001	3199	217	24755	20313	32765	15772	2.22	3.48
2002	3050	213	21370	20662	31469	13371	1.87	2.99
2003	3111	213	23980	21605	32337	13452	1.87	3.33
2004	2923	219	25432	23465	32937	13953	1.91	3.48
2005	2609	235	30627	28564	33942	15008	2.03	4.13
2006	2834	232	28724	26653	34360	15451	2.06	3.83
2007	2006	251	30062	28107	33807	15018	1.98	3.97
2008	1985	249	32350	29874	36574	16260	2.14	4.25
2009	2017	252	32803	30527	40217	16734	2.19	4.30
2010	2147	254	36066	33383	43285	17696	2.32	4.72
2011	2549	280	39980	35600	47347	18310	2.39	5.22
2012	2607	288	47254	41186	54488	21593	2.81	6.14
2013	2936	285	44876	39725	59961	24113	3.12	5.80
2014	3126	297	47081	42961	62738	24946	3.20	6.03
2015	3146	308	48601	45066	65264	26270	3.35	6.20
2016	7564	322	50649	47309	87733	27675	3.49	6.39
2017	7927	410	55798	46282	76146	30867	3.84	6.94
2018	8027	421	53154	50842	83975	34578	4.23	6.82
2019	8317	427	60519	58492	90361	37813	4.55	7.28
2020	8531	460	64423	62450	94854	39708	4.74	7.70
2021	8574	449	67748	65041	97048	39969	3.90	6.61

注：自2016年起，卫生机构及人员包含村卫生室。
Note: Health agency and personnel includes village clinic as of 2016.

19-3 各类卫生机构、床位、人员数(2021 年底)

NUMBER OF HEALTH INSTITUTIONS，BEDS AND EMPLOYED PERSONS（END OF 2021）

项　目	Item	机构数（个）Health Institutions（unit）	床位数（张）Beds in Health Institutions（bed）	人员数（人）Personnel（person）
总　计	**Total**	**8574**	**67748**	**115885**
一、医院合计	**Sub-total of Hospitals**	**449**	**65041**	**79676**
1. 医院	Hospitals	346	57911	71021
#综合医院	General Hospitals	175	32914	45381
中医医院	Hospitals Specialized in Traditional Chinese Medicine	43	7341	9004
中西医结合医院	Hospitals of Combination of Chinese and Western Medicine	4	501	714
专科医院	Specialized Hospitals	116	15834	15637
#口腔医院	Stomatological Hospitals	9	90	743
眼科医院	Ophthalmology Hospitals	13	800	1134
肿瘤医院	Tumor Hospitals	2	60	79
心血管病医院	Cardiovascular Diseases Hospitals	3	1105	1210
精神病医院	Mental Hospitals	29	6865	3407
传染病医院	Infectious Disease Hospitals	2	656	577
皮肤病医院	The Skin Disease Hospital	2	100	114
骨科医院	Orthopaedics Hospitals	6	347	344
2. 卫生院	Sanitation Stations	103	7130	8655
二、社区卫生服务中心	**Neighborhood Service Centers**	**95**	**639**	**4483**
三、门诊部	**Outpatient Service Stations**	**404**	**143**	**6833**
四、诊所	**Clinics**	**2957**	**10**	**9805**
五、卫生所、医务室、护理站	**Medical Houses Nursing Station**	**342**	**126**	**1056**
六、社区卫生服务站	**Neigborhood Service Stations**	**206**	**310**	**2879**
七、急救中心	**First Aid Centers**	**7**		**247**
八、采供血机构	**Institutions of Blood Collection and Supply**	**1**		**251**
九、妇幼保健院(所、站)	**Maternity and Child Care Centers**	**12**	**398**	**1534**
十、专科疾病防治院(所、站)	**Specialized Disease Prevention & Treatment Institutions**	**6**	**224**	**271**
十一、疾病预防控制中心(防疫站)	**Centers for Disease Control and Prevention (Epidemic Prevention Stations)**	**41**		**1398**
十二、卫生监督所	**Sanitation Control Stations**	**12**		**441**
十三、卫生监督检验所(站)	**Sanitation Control and Test Stations**			
十四、计划生育技术服务机构	**Family Planning Service Institutions**	**16**		**87**
十五、健康教育所(站、中心)	**Health Education Stations**			
十六、其他卫生机构	**Other Health Institutions**	**38**	**857**	**1567**
十七、村卫生室	**Village clinic**	**3988**		**5357**

注：床位数指实有床位数

Note：The number of beds refers to the number of beds actually available.

#卫生技术人员 Medical and Technical Personnel	#医生 Doctors	注册护士 Registered Nurses	药剂人员 Pharmacists	技师人员 Technician staff
97048	**39969**	**44078**	**4675**	**5077**
68448	**24516**	**34072**	**3048**	**4007**
61012	21473	31278	3048	3483
39619	14216	20192	1842	2157
7755	2906	3593	540	470
594	218	259	68	36
12880	4096	7120	589	816
614	290	287	11	17
780	269	436	31	32
65	32	26	3	4
1012	356	517	43	79
3088	613	2273	113	64
498	167	261	26	37
89	29	45	7	8
274	103	121	17	29
7436	3043	2794		524
3712	**1628**	**1433**	**336**	**211**
5636	**2753**	**2416**	**207**	**193**
9668	**5905**	**3599**	**124**	**23**
1001	**578**	**393**		**7**
2449	**1184**	**920**	**231**	**70**
167	**63**	**97**	**1**	**5**
186	**49**	**80**	**1**	**56**
1249	**479**	**532**	**64**	**70**
210	**90**	**73**	**15**	**16**
967	**501**	**56**	**14**	**126**
354				
29	**12**	**7**		**1**
847	**211**	**284**	**22**	**246**
2125	**2000**	**116**	**9**	

19-4 分市、区各类卫生机构数(2021年底)

NUMBER OF HEALTH INSTITUTIONS IN VARIOUS TYPES OF CITIES AND DISTRICTS (END OF 2021)

市、区名称	Region	机构数(个) Number of Institutions (unit)	医院小计 Sub-total of Hospitals	#医院 Hospitals	#卫生院 Sanitation Stations
全　市	**Whole Municipality**	**8574**	**449**	**346**	**103**
市南区	Shinan District	453	31	31	
市北区	Shibei District	833	66	66	
李沧区	Licang District	422	27	27	
崂山区	Laoshan District	496	28	26	2
黄岛区(西海岸新区)	Huangdao District (West Coast New Area)	1399	63	47	16
城阳区(含高新区)	Chengyang District (Including High tech District)	867	37	32	5
即墨区	Jimo District	1138	57	36	21
胶州市	Jiaozhou	999	37	23	14
平度市	Pingdu	1154	59	30	29
莱西市	Laixi	813	44	28	16

19-4 续表

Continued

市、区名称	Region	采供血机构 Institutions of Blood Collection and Supply	妇幼保健院(所、站) Maternity and Child Care Centers	专科疾病防治院(所、站) Specialized Disease Prevention & Treatment Institutions
全　市	**Whole Municipality**	**1**	**12**	**6**
市南区	Shinan District	1	1	1
市北区	Shibei District		2	
李沧区	Licang District		1	
崂山区	Laoshan District		1	
黄岛区(西海岸新区)	Huangdao District (West Coast New Area)		2	2
城阳区(含高新区)	Chengyang District (Including High tech District)		1	
即墨区	Jimo District		1	1
胶州市	Jiaozhou		1	
平度市	Pingdu		1	2
莱西市	Laixi		1	

社区卫生服务中心 Neighborhood Service Centers	社区卫生服务站 Neighborhood Service Stations	门诊部 Outpatient Service Stations	诊所、卫生所、医务室、护理站 Clinics Medical Houses	急救中心 First Aid Centers
95	**206**	**404**	**3299**	**7**
12	26	52	322	
26	58	70	604	1
15	45	35	295	
3	32	29	264	
17	14	76	547	1
12	6	70	326	1
2	19	24	360	1
4	0	18	242	1
2	0	24	250	1
2	6	6	89	1

疾病预防控制中心（防疫站） Centers for Disease Control and Prevention (Epidemic Prevention Stations)	卫生监督所 Sanitation Control Stations	村卫生室 Village health room	计划生育技术服务机构 Family Planning Service Institutions	其他卫生机构 Other Health Institutions
41	**12**	**3988**	**16**	**38**
1	1			5
2	2			2
1	1			2
1	1	130		7
1	1	668		7
9	1	395		9
23	1	630	16	3
1	1	693		1
1	1	812		1
1	2	660		1

19-5 分市、区各类卫生床位数(2021 年底)

NUMBER OF SANITARY BEDS IN VARIOUS TYPES OF CITIES AND DISTRICTS (END OF 2021)

市、区名称	Region	床位数(张) Beds in Health Institutions(bed)	#医院小计 Sub-total of Hospitals
全　市	**Whole Municipality**	**67748**	**65041**
市南区	Shinan District	8684	7634
市北区	Shibei District	16375	16156
李沧区	Licang District	4007	3957
崂山区	Laoshan District	1442	1372
黄岛区(西海岸新区)	Huangdao District (West Coast New Area)	10247	9564
城阳区(含高新区)	Chengyang District (Including High tech District)	3979	3978
即墨区	Jimo District	5466	5357
胶州市	Jiaozhou	5568	5373
平度市	Pingdu	7368	7138
莱西市	Laixi	4612	4512

19-6 分市、区各类卫生人员数(2021 年底)

NUMBER OF HEALTH PERSONNEL BY CITY AND DISTRICT (END OF 2021)

市、区名称	Region	人员数(人) Personnel(person)	#卫生技术人员 #Medical and Technical Personnel
全　市	**Whole Municipality**	**115885**	**97048**
市南区	Shinan District	15629	13279
市北区	Shibei District	26932	23553
李沧区	Licang District	8147	6961
崂山区	Laoshan District	5297	4220
黄岛区(西海岸新区)	Huangdao District (West Coast New Area)	17060	13912
城阳区(含高新区)	Chengyang District (Including High tech District)	9465	7560
即墨区	Jimo District	9307	7747
胶州市	Jiaozhou	8134	6737
平度市	Pingdu	9492	7827
莱西市	Laixi	6422	5252

医院 Hospitals	卫生院 Sanitation Stations	门诊部 Outpatient Service Stations	妇幼保健院（所、站） Maternity and Child Care Centers	专科疾病防治院（所、站） Specialized Disease Centers
57911	**7130**	**143**	**398**	**224**
7634		36		
16156		17		
3957		16		
1345	27	0		
7865	1699	28	100	114
3730	248			
4415	942	20	40	
4290	1083	6	98	
4978	2160	20	100	110
3541	971		60	

#医生 #Doctors	注册护士 Registered Nurses	药剂人员 Pharmacists	技师人员 Technician staff	其他人员 Other Personnel
39969	**44078**	**4675**	**5077**	**18837**
5118	6502	584	631	2350
9638	11021	1101	1307	3379
2883	3263	379	356	1186
2040	1624	218	229	1077
5741	6258	684	739	3148
3076	3230	393	402	1905
3339	3267	416	377	1560
2842	3064	287	315	1397
3128	3600	342	444	1665
2164	2249	271	277	1170

19-7 提供住宿的社会服务机构单位情况(2021年)

SITUATION OF SOCIAL SERVICE INSTITUTIONS PROVIDING ACCOMMODATION (2021)

市、区名称	Region	单位数(个) Number of Institutions (unit)	年末职工人数(人) Number of Staff and Workers at Year-end (person)	年末床位数(张) Number of Beds at Year-end (bed)
全 市	**Whole Municipality**	**301**	**6628**	**44145**
市本级	Municipal Level	4	173	1257
市南区	Shinan District	33	1429	3931
市北区	Shibei District	66	1402	9739
李沧区	Licang District	38	1014	4410
崂山区	Laoshan District	14	351	2355
黄岛区(西海岸新区)	Huangdao District (West Coast New Area)	32	585	4958
城阳区(含高新区)	Chengyang District (Including High tech District)	24	356	4932
即墨区	Jimo District	18	295	2311
胶州市	Jiaozhou	21	356	3843
平度市	Pingdu	34	273	3015
莱西市	Laixi	17	394	3394

19-8 社会救济情况(2021年)

BASIC STATISTICS ON SOCLAL RELIEF (2021)

市、区名称	Region	城镇居民最低生活保障人数(人) Number of Persons Receiving Minimun Living Allowance in Urban Area (Person)	城镇居民最低生活保障家庭数(户) Number of Households Receiving Minimum Living Allowance in Urban Area (household)	城镇低保资金支出(万元) Urban low-security capital expenditure (10 000 yuan)
全 市	**Whole Municipality**	**17557**	**12367**	**19257.6**
市南区	Shinan District	2901	2123	3269.8
市北区	Shibei District	10579	7323	11902.7
李沧区	Licang District	1704	1164	1779
崂山区	Laoshan District	109	58	96.3
黄岛区(西海岸新区)	Huangdao District (West Coast New Area)	672	521	546.4
城阳区(含高新区)	Chengyang District (Including High tech District)	201	141	205.8
即墨区	Jimo District	475	343	488.7
胶州市	Jiaozhou	474	359	507
平度市	Pingdu	284	209	303.5
莱西市	Laixi	158	126	158.4

年末在院人数（人） Residences at Year-end （person）	老年人 Senior Citizens	青壮年 Young and middle-aged	少年儿童 Youth
21877	**21380**	**284**	**170**
536	85	252	169
1937	1937		
6576	6576		
2561	2561		
680	669	11	
2156	2156		
2026	2026		
1064	1042	21	1
1509	1509		
1591	1582		
1241	1237		

农村居民最低生活保障人数（人） Number of Persons Receiving Minimum living Allowance in Rural Area（person）	农村居民最低生活保障家庭数（户） Number of Households Receiving Minimum Living Allowance in Rural Area（household）	农村低保资金支出 （万元） Rural low-security capital expenditure （10 000 yuan）
65062	**44107**	**49657.6**
1664	871	1369.7
11723	8248	8446.1
3213	2088	2851.8
16098	11464	15325.1
9700	6528	6717.3
17264	11233	11564.4
5400	3675	3383.2

19-9 分市、区婚姻登记情况(2021 年)

BASIC STATISTICS ON MARRIAGE REGISTRATION BY REGION（2021）

市、区名称	Region	准予登记结婚 Registered Marriages		
		合计（对） Total（couple）	初婚（人） First Marriages（person）	恢复结婚（对） Resumed Marriages（couple）
全　市	**Whole Municipality**	**48553**	**67375**	**99**
市本级	Municipal Level	27	42	
市南区	Shinan District	3895	5482	1
市北区	Shibei District	5126	6501	2
李沧区	Licang District	3060	4044	5
崂山区	Laoshan District	2902	4742	
黄岛区（西海岸新区）	Huangdao District（West Coast New Area）	9407	12781	13
城阳区（含高新区）	Chengyang District（Including High tech District）	4763	6781	1
即墨区	Jimo District	5826	9040	8
胶州市	Jiaozhou	4682	6265	
平度市	Pingdu	5682	7651	69
莱西市	Laixi	3183	4046	

再婚（人）Remarriages（person）		准予登记离婚（对）Registered Divorces（couple）	涉外婚姻登记（对）Registered Marriages with Foreigner（couple）
男 Male	女 Female		
14544	**15187**	**16188**	**10**
5	7	3	1
1196	1112	1372	1
1916	1835	2516	2
1037	1039	1262	1
555	507	675	
2959	3074	3013	1
1369	1376	1625	3
1227	1385	1524	
1488	1611	1475	
1699	2014	1774	
1093	1227	949	1

19-10 律师、公证、调解、社会治安基本情况(2000—2021年)
BASIC STATISTICS ON LAWYERS, NOTARIZATION, MEDIATION AND SOCIAL ORDER (2000—2021)

项 目	Item	单位	Unit	2000年	2005年	2009年	2010年	2011年
一、律师工作	**Lawyers**							
律师事务所	Law Offices	个	Unit	76	116	203	222	247
律师工作者	Lawyers	人	person	1439	1941	3144	2487	2801
专职	Full-time Lawyers	人	person	971	1542	1934	2377	2643
兼职(含特邀)	Part-time Lawyers	人	person	150	73	86	94	105
请常年法律顾问单位	Units with Permanent Legal Advisors	个	Unit	2508	3564	4457	4779	5180
全年办理民事代理	Agent of Civil Gases	件	case	5571	11104	29025	26935	27702
刑事辩护	Defender of Criminal Cases	件	case	1755	3003	3758	3964	4535
非诉讼事件	Agent of Non-litigious Legal Affairs	件	case	5251	6501	5897	4274	3576
解答法律询问	Agent of Legal Advisory Services	件	case	58385	27880	30123	21102	42428
代写法律事务文书	Agent of Legal Documents Written on Behalf of Clients	件	case	9335	8595	6015	6210	6762
二、公证工作	**Notarization**							
公证处	Notary Offices	个	Unit	15	15	13	13	13
公证人员	Notarial Personnel	人	person	152	196	214	214	221
公证员	Notaries	人	person	106	112	118	117	119
办理公证文书	Notarized Documents	件	case	120849	105787	97019	94077	88506
三、人民调解	**People' s Mediation**							
人民调解委员会	People' s Mediation Committees	个	Unit	9750	11480	9643	8014	8486
调解人员	Mediators	人	person	34714	46735	32675	27820	28094
调解民间纠纷	Civil Disputes Mediated	件	case	18501	13658	14660	20550	22882
四、社会治安	**Social Order**							
交通事故发生次数	Traffic Accidents	次	time	15601	7051	2570	2313	2164
#死亡人数	Deaths	人	person	1371	776	402	393	374
#受伤人数	Injuries	人	person	8620	6639	2943	2504	2240
#经济损失	Losses	万元	10000 yuan	4815.70	2208.20	854.80	811.27	861.05
火灾发生次数	Fire Accidents	次	time	3088	1948	773	683	369
#死亡人数	Deaths	人	person	10	3	5	9	1
#受伤人数	Injuries	人	person	43	3		4	2
#经济损失	Losses	万元	10000 yuan	1531.06	550.40	865.50	5566.11	598.20

注：1. 自2020年起，火灾发生次数改为全口径统计，含轻微火灾发生次数。

2. 2020年火灾发生死亡人数含刑事死亡人数；火灾发生受伤人数含刑事受伤人数。

Notes：1. Since 2020, the number of fire occurrences has been changed to full-caliber statistics, including the number of minor fires occurrences.

2. The death toll in 2020 includes criminal deaths; the number of fire injuries includes the number of criminal injuries.

2012年	2013年	2014年	2015年	2016年	2017年	2018年	2019年	2020年	2021年
266	285	322	337	355	371	394	427	458	501
3130	3143	3637	3896	4260	4839	5451	5960	6470	7187
2944	2980	3443	3728	4134	4578	5179		5911	6581
107	93	110	112	123	127	129		146	147
5228	5374	5647	6101	6294	6952			7702	11133
30586	31147	36317	39640	42216	47679	63277	75116	78940	96377
4935	4858	5370	5107	4560	4936	7490	8372	6205	8952
4251	4133	4833	4900	4624	5386	8486	9795	14569	12068
45388	53775	33717	34003	40884	55320				
6388	7376	5961	6272	7326	7112				
13	13	13	12	12	12	12	12	14	13
225	244	249	242	250	264	265	256	294	318
118	113	119	129	125	127	125	121	129	124
87703	99852	100553	96085	104423	105200	88619	88370	71102	84466
8426	8448	8027	7708	7861	7413	7366	7098	6416	2518
27421	27035	25646	25222	26318	23918	24761	24366	23396	17407
23999	19525	23737	23552	30084		29989	26880	31960	34095
1951	1896	1857	1814	1759	1847	1825	1787	1751	1734
343	333	321	313	308	324	319	315	311	307
1913	1840	1796	1785	1770	1828	1814	1782	1750	1721
652.10	609.80	561.80	509.1	506.6	528.7	573.8	545.7	533.6	520.4
366	742	1170	1001	1654	1458	1269	704	6925	7276
6	7	12	10	8	13	2	8	11	20
2	11	9	3	10	9	6	7	34	17
601.90	2348.10	1725.50	1491.0	1433.2	2739.7	3023.2	1208.2	2563.3	5704.8

19-11　分区、市殡葬服务情况(2021年)

BASIC STATISTICS ON FUNERAL SERVICES（2021）

区、市名称	Region	单位数（个）Number of Institutions (unit)	年末职工人数（人）Number of Staff and Workers at Year-end (person)	火化炉数（台）Number of Cremations (unit)	处理遗体数（具）Number of Remains Cremated (body)
全　市	**Whole Municipality**	**10**	**208**	**51**	**68626**
市本级	Municipal Level	1	43	10	14053
市南区	Shinan District				
市北区	Shibei District				
李沧区	Licang District				
崂山区	Laoshan District				
黄岛区（西海岸新区）	Huangdao District (West Coast New Area)	2	56	11	10428
城阳区（含高新区）	Chengyang District (Including High tech District)	1	15	5	7582
即墨区	Jimo District	1	10	7	10226
胶州市	Jiaozhou	1	8	5	7384
平度市	Pingdu	2	35	7	12249
莱西市	Laixi	2	41	6	6704

19-11 续表
Continued

区、市名称	Region	穴位数（个）Number of Graves (unit)	本年销售穴位数 Number of Graves Sold in the Year	安葬数（具）Number of Remains Buried (body)	本年安葬数 Number of Remains Buried in the Year
全　市	**Whole Municipality**	**100936**	**1203**	**50157**	**12061**
市本级	Municipal Level	22289	139	19813	1484
市南区	Shinan District				
市北区	Shibei District				
李沧区	Licang District				
崂山区	Laoshan District				
黄岛区（西海岸新区）	Huangdao District (West Coast New Area)	70623	640	26567	10412
城阳区（含高新区）	Chengyang District (Including High tech District)				
即墨区	Jimo District				
胶州市	Jiaozhou				
平度市	Pingdu	2165	255	2053	109
莱西市	Laixi	5859	169	1724	56

主要统计指标解释

卫生机构　按类别分为医院、社区卫生服务中心（站）、卫生院、门诊部（诊所、医务室、村卫生室）、急救中心（站）、采供血机构、妇幼保健院（所、站）、专科疾病防治院（所、站）、疾病预防控制中心（防疫站）、卫生监督所、卫生监督检验（监测、检测）所（站）、医学科学研究机构、医学教育机构、健康教育所（站）、其他卫生机构和社会团体 16 大类。

医疗卫生机构　包括医院、基层医疗卫生机构、专业公共卫生机构、其他医疗卫生机构。

（1）医院包括综合医院、中医医院、中西医结合医院、民族医院、各类专科医院和护理院，不包括专科疾病防治院、妇幼保健院和疗养院，包括医学院校附属医院。

（2）基层医疗卫生机构包括社区卫生服务中心（站）、乡镇（街道）卫生院、村卫生室、门诊部、诊所（医务室）。

（3）专业公共卫生机构包括疾病预防控制中心、专科疾病防治机构、妇幼保健机构（含妇幼保健计划生育服务中心）、健康教育机构、急救中心（站）、采供血机构、卫生监督机构、取得《医疗机构执业许可证》或《计划生育技术服务许可证》的计划生育技术服务机构。

（4）其他医疗卫生机构包括疗养院、临床检验中心、医学科研机构、医学在职教育机构、卫生监督（监测、检测）机构、医学考试中心、农村改水中心、人才交流中心、统计信息中心等卫生事业单位。

医院　包括综合医院、中医医院、中西医结合医院、民族医院、各类专科医院和护理院，不包括专科疾病防治院、妇幼保健院和疗养院，包括医学院校附属医院。

执业（助理）医师　指在医疗卫生机构中取得医师执业证书且实际从事医疗、妇幼保健、疾病防治等工作的执业医师和执业助理医师。

卫生技术人员　包括医疗卫生机构中执业医师、执业助理医师、注册护士、药师（士）、检验及影像技师（士）、卫生监督员和见习医（药、护、技）等卫生专业人员。

社会福利事业单位　指集中收养社会孤老、残、幼的机构，包括由民政部门管理的社会福利院、儿童福利院、精神病人福利院和城镇集体举办的福利院及农村集体举办的敬老院和具有收养能力的社区服务中心等。

Explanatory Notes on Main Statistical Indicators

Health Agency　according to categories，it is divided into hospitals，community health service centers（stations），health centers，outpatient departments（clinics，infirmaries，village clinics），emergency centers（stations），blood collection and supply institutions，maternal and child health care centers（stations，stations），and specialties Disease prevention and control institutes（stations，stations），disease prevention and control centers（epidemic prevention stations），sanitary supervision institutes，sanitary supervision and inspection（monitoring，testing）institutes（stations），medical scientific research institutes，medical education institutes，health education institutes（stations），16 categories of other health institutions and social organizations.

Medical and Health Institutions　including hospitals，primary medical and health institutions，professional public health institutions，and other medical and health institutions.

（1）Hospitals include general hospitals，hospitals of traditional Chinese medicine，hospitals of integrated traditional Chinese and western medicine，ethnic hospitals，various specialized hospitals and nursing homes，excluding specialized disease prevention and treatment hospitals，maternal and child health care hospitals，and nursing homes，including hospitals affiliated to medical schools.

（2）Primary medical and health institutions include community health service centers（stations），township（street）health centers，village clinics，outpatient departments，and clinics（medical offices）.

（3）Professional public health institutions include disease prevention and control centers，specialized disease prevention institutions，maternal and child health institutions（including maternal and child health and family planning service centers），health education institutions，emergency centers（stations），blood collection and supply institutions，health supervision institutions，and Family planning technical service organizations with "Medical Institution Practicing License" or "Family Planning Technical Service License".

（4）Other medical and health institutions include nursing homes，clinical testing centers，medical research institutions，medical on-the-job education institutions，health supervision（monitoring，testing）institutions，medical examination centers，rural water reform centers，talent exchange centers，statistical information centers，etc. Institutions.

Hospitals including general hospitals，traditional Chinese medicine hospitals，integrated traditional Chinese and western medicine hospitals，ethnic hospitals，various specialized hospitals and nursing homes，excluding specialized disease prevention and treatment hospitals，maternal and child health care hospitals，and nursing homes，including hospitals affiliated to medical schools.

Practicing (Assistant) Physician refers to the practicing doctors and assistant practicing doctors who have obtained the doctor's practice certificate in medical and health institutions and are actually engaged in medical treatment，maternal and child health care，disease prevention and treatment，etc.

Health Technician including health professionals such as practicing physicians，practicing assistant physicians，registered nurses，pharmacists（persons），laboratory and imaging technologists（persons），health supervisors，and trainee doctors（medicine，nursing，technology）in medical and health institutions.

Social Welfare Institutions refers to institutions that collectively adopt social orphans，the disabled，and children，including social welfare homes，children's welfare homes，mentally ill welfare homes managed by the civil affairs department，welfare homes organized by urban collectives，nursing homes organized by rural collectives，and community services capable of adopting Central，etc.

附　录

APPENDIX

2021 年省内各市主要经济指标情况

MAJOR ECONOMIC INDICATORS ON CTTIES OF THE PROVINCE (2021)

指　标 Indicator	单位 Unit	全省 Whole province	青岛市 Qingdao	济南市 Jinan	淄博市 Zibo	枣庄市 Zaozhuang	东营市 Dongying
生产总值（GDP）	累计(亿元) Total(100 million Yuan)	83095.9	14136.5	11432.2	4200.6	1951.6	3441.7
	增长(%) Growth(%)	8.3	8.3	7.2	9.4	8.3	8.5
规上工业增加值 YOY Growth of Industrial Added Value above Designated Size	增长(%) Growth(%)	9.6	8.1	5.9	14.1	10.8	13.4
固定资产投资 Investment in Fixed Assets	增长(%) Growth(%)	6.0	4.1	11.5	22.1	6.5	12.5
货物进出口总额 Imports and Exports	累计(亿元) Total(100 million Yuan)	29304.1	8498.4	1944.2	1192.4	315.1	2011.9
	增长(%) Growth(%)	32.4	32.4	40.1	33.6	20.0	44.6
# 货物出口 Exports	累计(亿元) Total(100 million Yuan)	17582.7	4921.3	1174.1	725.1	292.0	555.0
	增长(%) Growth(%)	34.8	27.0	55.6	48.3	16.9	22.8
货物进口 Imports	累计(亿元) Total(100 million Yuan)	11721.4	3577.2	770.1	467.3	23.1	1456.8
	增长(%) Growth(%)	29.0	40.7	21.5	15.8	80.1	55.0
社会消费品零售总额 Total Retail Sales of Consumer Goods	增长(%) Growth(%)	15.3	14.8	14.7	15.4	16.0	15.8
一般公共预算收入 General Public Budget Revenue	累计(亿元) Total(100 million Yuan)	7284.5	1368.3	1007.6	369.0	158.9	261.8
	增长(%) Growth(%)	11.0	9.1	11.2	14.8	12.9	5.0
全体居民人均可支配收入 Disposable income per capita of all residents	累计(元) Total(Yuan)	35705	51223	46725	42265	29772	45808
	增长(%) Growth(%)	8.6	8.6	8.5	8.6	8.7	8.5
城镇居民人均可支配收入 Per Capita Disposable Income of Urban Residents	累计(元) Total(Yuan)	47066	60239	57449	50096	37843	56625
	增长(%) Growth(%)	7.6	7.8	7.7	7.9	7.8	7.5
农村居民人均可支配收入 Per Capita Disposable Income of Rural Residents	累计(元) Total(Yuan)	20794	26125	22580	23010	19553	22255
	增长(%) Growth(%)	10.9	10.4	10.5	10.1	10.5	11.3

注：本表为快报数据。

Note：This table is for bulletin.

烟台市 Yantai	潍坊市 Weifang	济宁市 Jining	泰安市 Taian	威海市 Weihai	日照市 Rizhao	临沂市 Linyi	德州市 Dezhou	聊城市 Liaocheng	滨州市 Binzhou	菏泽市 Heze
8711.8	7010.6	5070.0	2996.7	3463.9	2212.0	5465.5	3488.7	2642.5	2872.1	3976.7
8.0	9.7	8.5	6.1	7.5	6.8	8.7	8.3	8.4	8.3	8.8
10.8	12.5	13.1	8.3	12.1	0.2	13.1	12.6	11.7	9.3	14.2
0.2	16.0	12.4	-29.4	6.0	3.0	11.4	-19.6	12.9	15.3	15.8
4115.0	2657.0	678.7	291.1	2032.5	1165.7	1766.8	513.6	530.4	1023.1	568.2
27.8	39.4	24.6	37.2	25.8	11.0	51.4	30.8	29.4	24.4	30.1
2448.6	1861.7	485.5	193.2	1494.0	403.0	1584.8	333.6	366.4	462.2	282.3
24.7	53.2	25.8	32.4	28.2	17.4	59.8	35.0	61.1	41.2	31.8
1666.5	795.3	193.3	97.9	538.5	762.7	182.0	180.0	164.0	561.0	285.9
32.6	15.2	21.6	47.6	19.3	8.0	3.8	23.8	-10.1	13.3	28.5
15.4	16.4	15.6	13.6	15.5	12.0	15.9	14.8	14.5	14.7	17.0
646.6	656.9	440.5	230.5	266.9	187.5	409.5	234.1	230.3	287.3	283.9
6.0	14.5	7.0	0.6	5.7	6.3	17.0	12.2	14.0	13.7	19.3
42629	37103	31845	33505	44612	31059	31528	25826	24512	32374	23854
8.5	9.4	8.8	8.3	8.4	8.2	9.1	9.3	9.0	8.9	9.7
53169	46616	41256	41741	54264	39380	42606	31927	32262	41566	31872
7.6	8.2	7.5	7.3	7.6	7.2	8.0	7.9	7.4	7.7	8.5
24574	24007	20747	21769	25692	20154	17783	19020	17512	20539	16872
10.2	10.9	11.2	10.6	10.0	10.3	11.7	11.9	11.4	11.0	11.7

2021 年十五个副省级城市主要经济指标情况

MAJOR ECONOMIC INDICATORS ON CTTIES UNDER PROVINCIAL LEVELS（2021）

指 标 Indicator	单位 Unit	青岛 Qingdao	沈阳 Shenyang	大连 Dalian	长春 Changchun	哈尔滨 Haerbin
全市生产总值（GDP）	累计（亿元） Total（100 million Yuan）	14136.5	7249.7	7825.9	7103.1	5351.7
	增长（%） Growth（%）	8.3	7.0	8.2	6.2	5.5
第一产业 Primary Industry	累计（亿元） Total（100 million Yuan）	470.1	326.3	513.3	523.7	628.2
	增长（%） Growth（%）	6.7	4.2	5.8	5.5	6.6
第二产业 Secondary Industry	累计（亿元） Total（100 million Yuan）	5070.3	2570.3	3301.6	2960.5	1239.2
	增长（%） Growth（%）	6.9	7.8	9.4	3.9	3.2
第三产业 Tertiary Industry	累计（亿元） Total（100 million Yuan）	8596.1	4353.0	4011.0	3618.9	3484.3
	增长（%） Growth（%）	9.2	6.7	7.5	8.1	6.1
三产占比 Three-yield ratio	占比（%） Ratio（%）	60.8	60.0	51.3	50.9	65.1
规上工业增加值 YOY Growth of Industrial Added Value above Designated Size	增长（%） Growth（%）	8.1	9.7	15.0	3.2	4.1
固定资产投资 Investment in Fixed Assets	增长（%） Growth（%）	4.1	4.1	1.2	11.6	4.2
社会消费品零售总额 Total Retail Sales of Consumer Goods	累计（亿元） Total（100 million Yuan）	5975.4	3985.1	1909.7	–	2380.3
	增长（%） Growth（%）	14.8	9.6	4.5	10.8	7.0
货物进出口总额 Imports and Exports	累计（亿元） Total（100 million Yuan）	8498.4	1416.0	4248.5	1179.8	344.6
	增长（%） Growth（%）	32.4	37.7	10.3	14.8	35.0
#货物出口 Exports	累计（亿元） Total（100 million Yuan）	4921.3	484.9	1931.7	165.9	171.3
	增长（%） Growth（%）	27.0	76.8	15.5	22.4	25.2
货物进口 Imports	累计（亿元） Total（100 million Yuan）	3577.2	931.1	2316.8	1013.8	173.3
	增长（%） Growth（%）	40.7	23.5	6.2	13.6	46.3
一般公共预算收入 General Public Budget Revenue	累计（亿元） Total（100 million Yuan）	1368.3	773.0	737.6	617.1	365.8
	增长（%） Growth（%）	9.1	5.0	5.0	5.9	7.7
城镇居民人均可支配收入 Per Capita Disposable Income of Urban Residents	累计（元） Total（Yuan）	60239	50566	50531	43281	42745
	增长（%） Growth（%）	7.8	6.6	6.7	8.2	7.4
农村居民人均可支配收入 Per Capita Disposable Income of Rural Residents	累计（元） Total（Yuan）	26125	21662	23763	–	21512
	增长（%） Growth（%）	10.4	10.5	10.2		9.6
居民消费价格指数 Consumer Price Index	上年同期 =100 （Preceding Year=100）	101.5	101.3	101.4	100.5	100.6

注：本表为快报数据。

Note：This table is for bulletin.

南京 Nanjing	杭州 Hangzhou	宁波 Ningbo	厦门 Xiamen	济南 Jinan	武汉 Wuhan	广州 Guangzhou	深圳 Shenzhen	成都 Chengdu	西安 Xian
16355.3	18109.0	14594.9	7033.9	11432.2	17716.8	28232.0	30664.9	19917.0	10688.3
7.5	8.5	8.2	8.1	7.2	12.2	8.1	6.7	8.6	4.1
303.9	333.0	356.1	29.1	408.8	444.2	306.4	26.6	582.8	308.8
0.8	1.8	2.8	5.3	7.1	8.7	5.5	5.1	4.8	6.1
5902.7	5489.0	6997.2	2882.9	3964.1	6208.3	7722.7	11338.6	6114.3	3585.2
7.6	8.6	9.8	6.7	3.6	12.1	8.5	4.9	8.2	0.9
10148.7	12287.0	7241.6	4121.9	7059.4	11064.2	20202.9	19299.7	13219.9	6794.3
7.6	8.7	7.1	9.0	9.2	12.3	8.0	7.8	9.0	5.7
62.1	67.9	49.6	58.6	61.8	62.5	71.6	62.9	66.4	63.6
10.0	10.6	11.9	11.9	5.9	14.2	7.8	4.7	11.4	5.7
6.2	9.0	11.0	11.3	11.5	12.9	11.7	3.7	10.0	–11.6
7899.4	6744.0	4649.1	2584.1	5126.1	6795.0	10122.6	9498.1	9251.8	4963.4
9.7	11.4	9.7	12.7	14.7	10.5	9.8	9.6	14.0	0.8
6366.8	7369.0	11926.1	8876.5	1944.2	3359.4	10825.9	35435.6	8222.0	4400.0
19.2	23.7	21.6	27.7	40.1	24.0	13.5	16.2	14.8	26.5
3989.9	4647.0	7624.3	4307.3	1174.1	1929.0	6312.2	19263.4	4841.2	2361.9
17.4	25.9	19.0	20.6	55.6	35.7	16.4	13.5	17.9	33.0
2376.9	2722.0	4301.8	4569.2	770.1	1430.4	4513.7	16172.2	3380.8	2038.0
22.3	20.0	26.3	35.3	21.5	11.2	9.6	19.5	10.7	19.8
1729.5	2387.0	1723.1	881.0	1007.6	1578.7	1883.2	4257.8	1697.9	856.0
5.6	14.0	14.1	12.4	11.2	28.3	9.4	10.4	11.7	18.2
73593	74700	73869	67197	57449	55297	74416	70847	52633	46931
8.9	8.8	8.6	9.6	7.7	9.8	8.9	9.2	8.3	7.4
32701	42692	42946	29894	22580	27209	34533	–	29126	17389
10.4	10.3	9.7	12.3	10.5	13.1	10.4	–	10.2	10.4
101.5	101.3	102.1	101.2	101.5	100.6	101.1	100.9	100.5	101.7

2021 年副省级城市之外部分城市主要经济指标情况
THE MAIN ECONOMIC INDICATORS OF SOME OTHER CITIES THAN THE SUB-PROVINCIAL CITY FOR（2021）

指　标 Indicator	单位 Unit	北京 Beijing	天津 Tianjin	上海 Shanghai	重庆 Chongqing	苏州 Suzhou	无锡 Wuxi
全市生产总值（GDP）	亿元 （100 million yuan）	40269.6	15695.1	43214.9	27894.0	22718.3	14003.2
同比增长 Year-on-year growth	%	8.5	6.6	8.1	8.3	8.7	8.8
#第一产业 Primary Industry	亿元 （100 million yuan）	111.3	225.4	100.0	1922.0	189.7	130.3
同比增长 Year-on-year growth	%	2.7	2.7	-6.5	7.8	-0.8	1.3
第二产业 Secondary Industry	亿元 （100 million yuan）	7268.6	5854.3	11449.3	11184.9	10872.8	6710.5
同比增长 Year-on-year growth	%	23.2	6.5	9.4	7.3	9.5	9.9
第三产业 Tertiary Industry	亿元 （100 million yuan）	32889.6	9615.4	31665.6	14787.1	11655.8	7162.4
同比增长 Year-on-year growth	%	5.7	6.7	7.6	9.0	8.1	7.9
第三产业增加值占 GDP 比重 Proportion taken by the added value in GDP for the Tertiary Industry	%	81.7	61.3	73.3	53.0	51.3	51.2
规模以上工业增加值同比增长 YOY Growth of Industrial Added Value above Designated Size	%	31.0	8.2	11.0	10.7	12.8	12.9
固定资产投资同比增长 YOY Growth of Investment in Fixed Assets	%	4.9	4.8	8.1	6.1	8.3	4.5
社会消费品零售总额 Total Retail Sales of Consumer Goods	亿元 （100 million yuan）	14867.7	0.0	18079.3	13967.7	9031.3	3306.1
同比增长 Year-on-year growth	%	8.4	5.2	13.5	18.5	17.3	10.4
货物进出口总额 Imports and Exports	亿元 （100 million yuan）	30438.4	8567.4	40610.4	8000.6	25332.0	6829.4
同比增长 Year-on-year growth	%	30.6	16.3	16.5	22.8	13.5	12.4
#货物出口总额 Exports	亿元 （100 million yuan）	6118.5	3875.6	15718.7	5168.3	14875.8	4221.8
同比增长 Year-on-year growth	%	31.2	26.1	14.6	23.4	15.0	19.0
一般公共预算收入 General Public Budget Revenue	亿元 （100 million yuan）	5932.3	2141.0	7771.8	2285.4	2510.0	1200.5
同比增长 Year-on-year growth	%	8.1	11.3	10.3	9.1	9.0	11.6
城镇居民人均可支配收入 Per Capita Disposable Income of Urban Households	元 （yuan）	81518	51486	82429	43502	76888	70483
同比增长 Year-on-year growth	%	7.8	8.0	7.8	8.7	8.3	8.9
农村居民人均可支配收入 Per Capita Disposable Income of Rural Residents	元 （yuan）	33303	27955	38521	18100	41487	39623
同比增长 Year-on-year growth	%	10.5	8.8	10.3	10.6	10.4	10.8
居民消费价格指数 Consumer Price Index	%	101.1	101.3	101.2	100.3	102.1	101.7